An Ontological Study of Death

An Ontological Study of Death

From Hegel to Heidegger

Sean Ireton

DUQUESNE UNIVERSITY PRESS
Pittsburgh, Pennsylvania

〜

Published in the United States of America by
DUQUESNE UNIVERSITY PRESS
600 Forbes Avenue
Pittsburgh, Pennsylvania 15282

Library of Congress Cataloging-in-Publication Data

Ireton, Sean Moore.
    An ontological study of death: from Hegel to Heidegger / Sean Ireton.
    p. cm.
    Summary: "Examines conceptions of death in German literature and philosophy
arguing that the dialectical thinking of Hegel and Hölderin erases the metaphysical
paradigm of death and sets the stage for the existential interpretations advanced by
Nietzsche, Rilke, and Heidegger. Identifies and describes common ground in the way
death is viewed—as the promise of possibility, freedom, and wholeness"—Provided
by publisher.
    Includes bibliographical references and index.
    ISBN-13: 978-0-8207-0396-1 (cloth : alk. paper)
    ISBN-13: 978-0-8207-0397-8 (pbk. : alk. paper)
    1. Death. 2. Philosophy, Modern. I. Title.
    BD444.I74 2007
    128'.5—dc22

                                                                    2006039040

∞ Printed on acid-free paper.

Contents

Acknowledgments

I would like to thank the University of Missouri Research Board and the University of Missouri-Columbia Research Council for supporting me in the completion of this book. I am also deeply grateful to Hellmut Ammerlahn and Jane K. Brown, both of whom gave me valuable feedback on earlier phases of this project. Here in Missouri, Roger Cook and Carsten Strathausen have offered much practical advice and provided me with ideal working conditions. Finally, I owe a special debt to Megan and Aidan for putting up with my strange habits and morbid preoccupations.

Abbreviations of Frequently Used Works and Editions

As a general practice, I will provide references to both German and English (when available) editions of works by Hegel, Hölderlin, Nietzsche, Rilke, and Heidegger. A major exception in this regard concerns the English version of *Being and Time,* which already features in its margins the page numbers of the German original. I will also occasionally modify existing English translations in order to convey important nuances and their implications for my argument. I have employed the following abbreviations for frequently cited texts:

Hegel

ETW *Early Theological Writings.* Translated by T. M. Knox. Chicago: University of Chicago Press, 1948.

PhS *Phenomenology of Spirit.* Translated by A. V. Miller. Oxford: Oxford University Press, 1977.

TE *Three Essays, 1793–1795: The Tübingen Essay, Berne Fragments, The Life of Jesus.* Edited and translated by Peter Fuss and John Dobbins. Notre Dame, Ind.: University of Notre Dame Press, 1984.

W *Werke.* Edited by Eva Moldenhauer and Karl Markus Michel. 4th ed. 20 vols. Frankfurt am Main: Suhrkamp, 1986.

Heidegger

BT *Being and Time: A Translation of Sein und Zeit.* Translated by Joan Stambaugh. Albany: State University of New York Press, 1996.

GA   *Gesamtausgabe: Ausgabe letzter Hand.* Frankfurt am Main: Vittorio Klostermann, 1975–.

OBT   *Off the Beaten Track.* Edited and translated by Julian Young and Kenneth Haynes. Cambridge: Cambridge University Press, 2002.

PM   *Pathmarks.* Edited by William McNeill. Cambridge: Cambridge University Press, 1998.

SZ   *Sein und Zeit.* 18th ed. Tübingen: Niemeyer, 2001.

Hölderlin

ELT   *Essays and Letters on Theory.* Translated and edited by Thomas Pfau. Albany: State University of New York Press, 1988.

H   *Hyperion and Selected Poems.* Edited by Eric L. Santner. The German Library 22. New York: Continuum, 1990.

PF   *Poems and Fragments.* Translated by Michael Hamburger. Cambridge: Cambridge University Press, 1980.

SWB   *Sämtliche Werke und Briefe.* Edited by Jochen Schmidt. 3 vols. Frankfurt am Main: Deutsche Klassiker Verlag, 1992–94.

Nietzsche

BoT   *The Birth of Tragedy.* In *Basic Writings of Nietzsche.* Edited and translated by Walter Kaufmann. New York: Modern Library, 2000.

BGE   *Beyond Good and Evil.* In *Basic Writings of Nietzsche.* Edited and translated by Walter Kaufmann. New York: Modern Library, 2000.

EH   *Ecce Homo.* In *Basic Writings of Nietzsche.* Edited and translated by Walter Kaufmann. New York: Modern Library, 2000.

GS   *The Gay Science.* Translated by Walter Kaufmann. New York: Vintage, 1974.

KSA   *Sämtliche Werke: Kritische Studienausgabe.* Edited by Giorgio Colli and Mazzino Montinari. 2nd ed. 15 vols. Berlin: de Gruyter, 1988.

KSB   *Sämtliche Briefe: Kritische Studienausgabe.* Edited by Giorgio Colli and Mazzino Montinari. 2nd ed. 8 vols. Berlin: de Gruyter, 2003.

PTA   *Philosophy in the Tragic Age of the Greeks.* Translated by Marianne Cowan. Chicago: Henry Regnery, 1962.

TI   *Twilight of the Idols.* In *The Portable Nietzsche.* Edited and translated by Walter Kaufmann. New York: Viking Penguin, 1982.

Z   *Thus Spoke Zarathustra*. In *The Portable Nietzsche*. Edited and translated by Walter Kaufmann. New York: Viking Penguin, 1982.

Rilke

Br   *Briefe*. Edited by the Rilke-Archiv. Wiesbaden: Insel, 1950.

DE   *Duino Elegies*. Translated by J. B. Leishman and Stephen Spender. New York: W. W. Norton, 1939. (Bilingual edition.)

MLB   *The Notebooks of Malte Laurids Brigge*. Translated by Stephen Mitchell. New York: Vintage, 1990.

SL   *Selected Letters of Rainer Maria Rilke, 1902–1926*. Translated by R. F. C. Hull. London: Macmillan & Co., 1946.

SO   *Sonnets to Orpheus*. Translated by M. D. Herter Norton. New York: W. W. Norton, 1942. (Bilingual edition.)

SW   *Sämtliche Werke*. Edited by Ruth Sieber-Rilke and Ernst Zinn. Frankfurt: Insel, 1987.

Others

BC   Michel Foucault, *The Birth of the Clinic: An Archeology of Medical Perception*. Translated by A. M. Sheridan Smith. New York: Vintage, 1994.

BN   Jean-Paul Sartre, *Being and Nothingness*. Translated by Hazel E. Barnes. New York: Washington Square Press, 1992.

HOD   Philippe Ariès, *The Hour of Our Death*. Translated by Helen Weaver. New York: Vintage, 1982.

IDH   Alexandre Kojève, "The Idea of Death in the Philosophy of Hegel." Translated by Joseph J. Carpino. *Interpretation* 3 (1973): 114–56.

IRH   Alexandre Kojève, *Introduction to the Reading of Hegel*. Assembled by Raymond Queneau. Edited by Allan Bloom. Translated by James H. Nichols. Ithaca, N.Y.: Cornell University Press, 1980.

SEP   *The Stoic and Epicurean Philosophers: The Complete Extant Writings of Epicurus, Epictetus, Lucretius, Marcus Aurelius*. Edited by Whitney J. Oates. New York: Modern Library, 1940.

Introduction

Philosophical, Historical, and Pathological Models of Death

> The decision to be without being is possibility itself: the possibility of death. Three systems of thought—Hegel's, Nietzsche's, Heidegger's—which attempt to account for this decision and which therefore seem, however much they may oppose each other, to shed the greatest light on the destiny of modern man, are all attempts at making death possible.
>
> —Maurice Blanchot, *The Space of Literature*

> Hölderlin's Empedocles, reaching, by voluntary steps, the very edge of Etna, is the death of the last mediator between mortals and Olympus, the end of the infinite on earth, the flame returning to its native fire, leaving as its sole remaining trace that which had precisely to be abolished by his death: the beautiful, enclosed form of individuality.
>
> —Michel Foucault, *The Birth of the Clinic*

> The idealist attempt to *recover* death was not originally the feat of philosophers but that of poets like Rilke.
>
> —Jean-Paul Sartre, *Being and Nothingness*

In his major philosophical work from 1943, *Being and Nothingness*, Jean-Paul Sartre outlines two paradigms of death based on the image of a borderline. As Sartre points out, every boundary is a *Janus bifrons:* it simultaneously looks in both directions, not only dividing space into two separate domains but also forming part of that which it demarcates. Whereas metaphysics and realist theories have long regarded death as a deferred reality "on the other side of 'the wall,'" the ontological or existential outlook interprets death as "an event of human life" (*BN* 680). This difference in perception—and ultimately of conception—is summed up as follows: "Whether it [death/boundary] is thought of as adhering to the nothingness of being which limits the process considered or whether on the contrary it is revealed as adhesive to the series which it terminates, in either case it is a being which belongs to an existent process and which in a certain way constitutes the meaning of the process" (*BN* 680).

Death can thus be understood in one of two ways: either as a constituent aspect of nonbeing or as an integral phenomenon of life. The former standpoint posits death as the transition to a nonhuman form of reality, whether physical corruption or metaphysical transcendence. In either case, our finality remains an experience that eludes our cognitive and empirical grasp and that furthermore turns us into another kind of existent, something utterly different from what we have been all along. According to the contrasting ontological view, death forms an inseparable part of our being and "influences [our] entire life by a reverse flow" (*BN* 681). As a result of this inverted perspective, death becomes interiorized, humanized, and individualized. Sartre states that the first attempts to "recover" death, that is to incorporate it into existence, stem from literary figures like Rainer Maria Rilke and André Malraux, while it was only later that Heidegger put his philosophical stamp on this humanization of mortality (see *BN* 681–82). Sartre's ensuing critique of Heidegger in *Being and Nothingness* is not of central concern here; nor do I intend to dispute his claim about the progenitors of what he conceives as a modern recovery of death. More important than the issue of his judgment about individual authors and their specific viewpoints is his overall dualistic model, which draws a visual distinction between two main concepts of human finitude. As we will see throughout the course of this study, an inherent tension exists between metaphysical attitudes toward death and the ontological holism adopted by a host of German poets and philosophers that include but also predate Rilke and Heidegger. To Sartre's list of key players in this ontologization of death one would have to add, following the example of Blanchot and Foucault in the opening quotations above: Hegel, Hölderlin, and Nietzsche.

This study examines the ontological turn in conceptions of death as manifested in German literature and philosophy from the late eighteenth to early twentieth century. In more precise terms, I argue that the dialectical thinking of Hegel and Hölderlin erases the metaphysical paradigm of death and sets the stage for the existential interpretations advanced by Nietzsche, Rilke, and Heidegger. All five of these philosophers and poets seek to integrate the traditional realm of nonbeing into the heart of existence. Moreover, throughout this development from the dialectical to the existential, death increasingly acquires an individualizing function. Whereas dialectics negates categories of individuality and raises them to a more comprehensive realm, existentialist thinking—and I use this term loosely—remains focused on the self-realization of the individual. The bookends of my study are formed by Hegel, who deems that death has little personal relevance but is all the more vital for the life of Spirit, and Heidegger, who converts death into *the* determining factor of selfhood. In between these two extremes, which are closer to one another than commonly believed, death is viewed in remarkably similar terms: as the promise of freedom, possibility, and totality. In fact, an entire complex of themes and motifs unites all of these authors, testifying to a shared intellectual discourse. Before describing the exact trajectory of my book, I will map out additional models of death in an effort to situate my argument within a broader theoretical framework of what thanatologists call "death systems." Such general patterns of dying and mourning prove relevant for the particular literary and philosophical diagnoses of death that constitute the main body of my analysis.

The most dominant model of death in the history of philosophy and theology is a metaphysical one.[1] Scholars often point to the Platonic doctrine of immortality as the origin or at least the epitome of metaphysical thinking about death. Plato's view, as expressed in such dialogues as the *Symposium, Phaedrus,* and especially the *Phaedo,* emphasizes the separation of body and soul upon our decease. Whereas the latter entity is indestructible and travels to the beyond, the former succumbs to the laws of nature. The fate of these two principal components of our being reflects the general dichotomy that underlies Platonic philosophy: the soul belongs to the ideal realm of immutable forms while the body remains part of the physical world, subject to its constant state of flux. Socrates' famous statement that "to practice philosophy in the proper manner is to practice for dying and death,"[2] says more about his (or Plato's) belief in spiritual transcendence than about cultivating the art of living. In the context of Platonism, the self-inflicted death of Socrates is not an affirmation of life but the ultimate step toward arriving at philosophical truth in the transcendent sphere of permanent ideas, which is precisely where the soul goes upon being released from its bodily prison. The body in fact only hinders the philosopher's pursuit of knowledge and consequently must be overcome. Death, according to Plato, thus functions as the gateway to a higher form of reality. In Sartre's terms, it leads us to "the other side of the wall" and hence comprises part of the nonhuman space that adjoins the outer boundary of our existence. This basic paradigm of the indestructibility of the soul and the transience of the body has, with minor modifications, held sway throughout the philosophical tradition all the way to Kant, who declares that immortality lies beyond our knowledge and can therefore only be believed but not definitively proved. Kant nevertheless perpetuates a bipartite worldview of the phenomenal versus noumenal and thereby reinforces the metaphysical schematic of Platonism. Christianity has of course its own version of Platonic metaphysics in its central notions of divine resurrection and the afterlife. The crucial difference here is that human beings die as a complete entity and are subsequently awakened with an eternal body and soul. But the essential dichotomous model still remains intact. These prevailing trends of Western culture have given rise to a number of seemingly insurmountable dualisms: immanence versus transcendence, matter versus mind, the here and now versus the beyond—and of course life versus death. Even in a patently materialistic philosophy such as Epicureanism, which espouses the perishability of both body and soul, death is divorced from life, indeed is reduced to an utter nonissue, as illustrated in Epicurus's famous letter to Menoeceus:

Become accustomed to the belief that death is nothing to us. For all good and evil consists in sensation, but death is deprivation of sensation. And therefore a right understanding that death is nothing to us makes the mortality of life enjoyable, not because it adds to it an infinite span of time, but because it takes away the craving for immortality. . . . So death, the most terrifying of ills, is nothing to us, since so long as we exist death is not with us; but when death comes, then we do not exist. It does not then concern either the living or the dead, since for the former it is not, and the latter are no more. (*SEP* 30–31)

Although these words were primarily written to assuage the common human fear of death and thus possess a certain rhetorical function, they nevertheless articulate the basic metaphysical view that life and death are altogether separate modes of being. At best these two realities conjoin such that life becomes a preparation for death, but at no point do they overlap and interpenetrate one another as in dialectical and existential ways of thinking.

One can also look at the problem of metaphysics versus ontology in terms of an opposition between universality and individuality. As James M. Demske has elaborated in his study of death in Heidegger, traditional metaphysics makes the sweeping claim that "'All men are essentially, i.e. according to their nature, mortal.'" In response to this generalized principle, modern philosophers of existence such as Kierkegaard state that "'*Each and every* man is mortal' or, even more accurately, '*I* am mortal.'"[3] Here one notes the following shift in emphasis: death in the abstract becomes reevaluated as a personally relevant experience. A perfect illustration of this difference between universal and individual validity can be found in Tolstoy's classic tale *The Death of Ivan Ilyich*. Here the terminally ill main character remains entrapped inside a metaphysically abstract mindset: "The example of a syllogism which he had learned in Kiezewetter's *Logic:* 'Caius is a man, men are mortal, therefore Caius is mortal,' had seemed to him all his life to be true as applied to Caius but certainly not as regards himself. That Caius—man in the abstract—was mortal, was perfectly correct; but he was not Caius, nor man in the abstract."[4] Ivan Ilyich thus considers himself exempt from, or at least not immediately affected by, death. But of course nothing could be further from the truth. By the end of the story he learns to embrace his final moment as his own personal and proper fate. This tendency toward an ontological individualization of mortality reaches its pinnacle in Heidegger, for whom death is not only one's most private possession but moreover a fundamental way of *being*. As Demske's Heideggerian interpolation of the above formulae goes: "'Each and every man *is* mortal,' i.e. 'I *am* mortal.'"[5] Man's entire existence thus becomes a continual reckoning with the inevitability and impendency of his end. In contrast to the metaphysical concept of death as a one-time event that lies in our future and strikes at some eventual point in time, the ontological perspective integrates this existentially remote finality into the very core of being. Again, to defer to Sartre's image of a boundary, death "is revealed as adhesive to the series which it terminates" (*BN* 680).

Both metaphysics and ontology can be said to have arisen in reaction to the natural decease of living beings. As a biological process that affects all organisms, death is a crude but necessary occurrence that humans are powerless to prevent but must somehow come to grips with. By allowing death to inform rather than simply terminate our lives, we are able to rise above our creaturely state and gain a certain measure of freedom, whether through metaphysical hope in the hereafter or a more immanent sense of existential fulfillment. We humans can conquer "our natural horror of death" (Hume)[6] by imbuing it with meaning. As a number of philosophers have stressed, man's ability to comprehend his inevitable extinction, and even actualize it if he so desires, sets him apart from animals and underscores all the more his unique quality of free will. Hume's apology of suicide, for instance, seeks "to restore men to their native liberty" and give them "power over their lives,"[7] things they have long been deprived of under the yoke of the Church. Hegel for his part often highlights the difference between humans and animals by pointing to the implicit freedom contained in the notion of suicide. To cite one of his many remarks to this effect: "I possess the members of my body, my life, only so long as I will to possess them. An animal cannot maim or destroy itself, but a man can. . . . [Animals] have no right to their life, because they do not will it" (*W* 7:110–11).[8] And as I will discuss at greater length in the corpus of this study, the Stoic idea of rational suicide serves, among other things, to preempt the tyranny of a natural and debilitating demise. This tendency to rationalize and in effect take control of death by ascribing a signification to it is a typically human endeavor and certainly one of the driving forces of philosophy, as Plato, Montaigne, Schopenhauer, and countless others have observed. Our valuation of death is at bottom an attempt, somewhere between desperate and noble, to make sense of our fleeting existence. As Herbert Marcuse has eloquently put it: "A brute biological fact, permeated with pain, horror, and despair, is transformed into an existential privilege."[9] The acceptance of death as a meaningful experience, whether as a future transcending event as in metaphysics or a continuous life-affirming presence as in ontology, thus insulates us from our animality. All other creatures *must* die, for they are products of a deterministic world. Man is the only being that *can* die: he is free to choose his own end. Death thus becomes our inalienable right; we have shed it from our natural selves and employed it for our own all-too-human needs.

Philosophical models of death are sometimes considered suspect, since they tend to conceal their deeper ideological roots. Marcuse has, for instance, suggested, "the traditional notion of death is a sociopolitical concept which transforms nasty empirical facts into an ideology."[10] For Marcuse, all philosophical and theological explanations of human finitude have arisen under certain historical conditions and function within relative systems of value. The voluntary end of Socrates as represented by Plato only reinforces blind obedience to the state, the sacrifice of Christ sanctions the urge to die in exchange for an eternal life, and the Heideggerian being-toward-death lays the ground for the reality of the holocaust.[11] This last point, which Marcuse casually drops on his readers and fails to pursue any further, is, to use his own famous term, somewhat "one-dimensional." While Heidegger's involvement with Nazism should certainly not be ignored or downplayed, his elaboration of death is a complex one that, as I will demonstrate, has deep philosophical, theological, as well as literary roots. As such, it resists reductionist interpretations, regardless of their intent or methodology—which is not to say that it does not open itself up to criticism on a number of fronts. Marcuse's basic point is nevertheless well taken: because humans have "appropriated" death from nature for their own anthropological ends, they are bound to assign it meaning according to the specific conditions of their historical self-understanding. There is, in other words, no such thing as death per se. It is a relative concept that we have shaped in order to justify to ourselves that sooner or later we all cease to be.

Jean Baudrillard's view of death as an ideological construct is, in its general intent, more radical and condemnatory than Marcuse's. In *Symbolic Exchange and Death* from 1976, he argues that the disjunction of life and death in contemporary Western society is the symptom of a larger cultural paradigm of social repression. Death is difference, delinquency, deviancy—and must therefore be abolished by the powers that be, whether the traditional Church or the modern State. This "exclusion of the dead and of death" by "the 'rationality' of our culture"[12] is caught up in his broader critique of the Enlightenment as an inhuman and authoritarian agency of omnicontrol. Death can be culturally eradicated in a variety of ways. Religion relies on man's hope for immortality in the afterlife, while the secular state appeals to our belief in the infinity of time, whereby we accrue life as a kind of capital. That is, our lives acquire value based on the economic-turned-existential principles of productivity and accumulation. Death then looms before us as "due payment,"[13] but we of course tend to ignore this final reality and, like good capitalists, insist on forever hoarding rather than opportunely exchanging our life assets. "Hence," remarks Baudrillard "the absolute impasse of political economy, which intends to eliminate death through accumulation: the time of accumulation is the time of death itself."[14] He stresses that this impasse—and therefore the entire opposition of life and death—is unique to modern Western culture. In primitive times and during the European Middle Ages, death functioned as an inseparable aspect of life and played an important role in the collective social consciousness. However, in the sixteenth century a major shift occurred: death began to lose its symbolic exchangeability and instead became a general equivalence before which everyone stood alone. Baudrillard's interpretation of death, a highly original one in its incorporation of semiotics and Marxism, fits in rather well with more conventional sociocultural theories that have been advanced over the last several decades.

Nobert Elias and Philippe Ariès, two of the more famous cultural historians of our era, have pointed precisely to the Renaissance as a defining moment in the formation of a new individualized consciousness of human mortality. In his short study *The Loneliness of the Dying,* which reads like a postscript compared to his colossal opus *The Civilizing Process,* Elias alleges that the growing trend of individualization from the sixteenth century onward has increasingly instilled in humans the sense that they die alone. This modern experience of isolation has a number of implications, ranging from the positive ideal of self-autonomy in the face of death to the negative feeling of utter abandonment during one's dying hour. At its most basic level, the phenomenon of dying alone corresponds to the modern individual's general situation of aloneness. That is to say, "the image of one's own death is closely connected to the image of oneself, of one's own life, and the nature of this life."[15] Once again, death proves to be a relative notion, its meaning fashioned according to the cultural circumstances of the time.

Philippe Ariès similarly states that there is a distinct "relationship between man's attitude toward death and his awareness of self, of his degree of existence, or simply of his individuality" (*HOD* 602). The sociohistorical model of death developed by Ariès has set a standard in thanatological studies. Although not everyone is in agreement with his overall scheme (Elias himself has some major objections),[16] it is often used as a point of departure for current discussions of death and dying. Ariès has explored the human relation to mortality from the Middle Ages to the twentieth century by scrutinizing a wide range of phenomena such as graveyards, testaments, and funerary practices. In his monumental study *The Hour of Our Death,* first published in 1977 as *L'homme devant la mort,* he pursues the mutations in our attitudes toward death based on four psychological themes: defense of society against untamed nature, belief in the existence of evil, belief in the afterlife, and the awareness of the individual. In the process, he postulates five historical models, each of which varies in its respective emphasis on the above four motifs.

The so-called "tame death" prevailed throughout the Middle Ages and persisted, with a number of significant variations, into the nineteenth century. In this model, the natural force of death was "tamed" through ritualization and human appropriation. It possessed a "familiar simplicity" and "public aspect" (*HOD* 18), which is to say that the dying person anticipated his decease with equanimity and through a communal network of support. Dying was an extended process whereby individuals prepared themselves for the final moment with the backing of family and friends. Bedside companionship, prayers of mourning, final goodbyes—all of these traditional rites helped alleviate the task of dying for both the individual and society, the latter of which is constantly deprived of its members and must therefore learn to absorb these losses. Some of the historical testimony that Ariès provides in defense of this theory includes the liberal burial practices of unmarked and even mass graves. These places of rest can be considered public insofar as bodies were indiscriminately grouped together with no concern for the individual identity of the dead. A posthumous egalitarianism thus ruled the day: all were equal in death. Furthermore, the cemetery gradually evolved into a communal gathering spot "for strolling, socializing, and merrymaking" (*HOD* 69). Over the course of time it became host to a wide variety of civic and illicit activities, ranging from sporting events and shopping to vagabondage and prostitution. In sum, it was a public site where life and death coexisted, where for instance an otherwise idyllic family picnic might be conducted in immediate proximity to decomposing corpses or the stacked bones of a charnel house.

The second model that Ariès presents is "the death of the self," which emerged during the late medieval era and continued into early modern times. He maintains that, from the fifteenth century onward, the awareness of individuality progressively began to outweigh the importance of community. He thus posits this transition a century earlier than Baudrillard and Elias do in their respective studies. For Ariès, furthermore, this transformation is not a definitive one and certainly does not signal the rise of the modern individual. Death was still tame; that is, people continued to acquiesce to it and brace for it all their lives, but the emphasis now lay on the destiny of the singular human being rather than on the welfare of the collective: "The individual insisted on assembling the molecules of his own biography, but only the spark of death enabled him to fuse them into a whole" (*HOD* 605). This is not to say, as we might assume from our contemporary vantage, that this surge in individuality necessarily equates with an ego-driven orientation toward the world and its pleasures. For the individual of the time, it was not so much a matter of leading a good life as of dying a good— that is, repentant—death. The individual hoped to gain immortality on the very basis of his individuality; the soul was not only immortal but also distinctly personal. The last will and testament is the most revealing document in this thanatological modulation: it *attested* to the *will* of the individual for gaining immortality by virtue of his accomplishments and conduct in life. The will thus functioned as a kind of "investment in heaven" (*HOD* 606) and a safeguard against eternal damnation in the hereafter. Another important testimony to this development is the increase in personalized tombstones. Whereas gravesites were previously overcrowded and anonymous (except in the case of the clerical elite), a growing segment of the nobility and middle class began to secure their own hallowed space for the erection of monuments that commemorated an individualized existence. Death, it would seem, ceased to be the grand equalizer.

The "remote and imminent death" is an attitude that grew out of the sixteenth century and lasted into the early nineteenth. Here the art of living (*ars vitae*) supplanted the art of dying (*ars moriendi*): the focal point changed from the final moment of death to the greater arc of one's existence. In more concrete terms, the traditional deathbed scene yielded to a life-long reckoning with one's impending end. In the representative words of Calvin: "'Even in the best of health we should have death always before our eyes'" (*HOD* 302). This reorientation toward life made death on the one hand more remote, but its perpetual imminence did not, on the other hand, go ignored. One was still fully prepared for the proverbial dying hour, but this preparation consisted in learning how to live well rather than in perfecting the final exit. Life thus became permeated by death, which served as a constant reminder of man's finite and ephemeral existence. This permeability manifested itself culturally in a variety of ways. The dead for instance formed a vital source of knowledge: the seventeenth and eighteenth centuries saw a dramatic rise in anatomical studies, which provided a previously unimaginable wealth of information about the human body. Even the living became affected by the seemingly indistinct boundary between life and death, as evidenced in the widespread fear of premature burial. Ariès in fact discerns a development beginning in the mid-1600s whereby the educated elite stipulated in their testaments a variety of precautions to be taken in order to ensure that they were verifiably dead. These measures ranged from predetermined intervals of rest before burial (usually one to three days) to scarification (whether in the form of a minor incision in the extremities to revive consciousness or a life-ending perforation of the heart), and even decapitation.

Ariès calls his next model "the death of the other." The Industrial Revolution and its resulting urbanization loosened if not destroyed the bonds of the traditional community in Northern Europe. Bereavement thus found its niche in the family, which at the time was the largest unit that could effectively mourn the loss of individual life. Within this nuclear realm, the death of the self became transferred to the other, who was either a close relation or an intimate loved one. Drawing on family documents (the journals and correspondence of the La Ferronays family) and Victorian literature (mainly the Brontë sisters), Ariès notes a pronounced sentimentalization of death. The corpse became depicted as an object of almost ethereal beauty and the requisite deathbed scene was replete with bathos. Although there was an obvious fascination with death during the early to mid-1800s, one can sense beneath this aestheticized veneer an uneasiness that is indicative of a turning point in historical attitudes toward human mortality. The natural ferocity of death had previously been tamed through a variety of cultural strategies: communal solidarity, hope in the afterlife, the art of living, and familial devotion. In the latter half of the nineteenth century an entirely new paradigm was formed, one that firmly established itself in the early 1900s and for the most part still influences us today.

In the second half of the nineteenth century, the beautiful death of romanticism and Victorianism disappeared from the literary scene and was replaced by depictions of the so-called "dirty death." In Flaubert's *Madame Bovary* (1857) and Tolstoy's *The Death of Ivan Ilyich* (1886), dying is presented as an ugly and indecent act: both eponymous protagonists suffer a physically agonizing and morally degrading end. Due to these gruesome torments, death is better left concealed from others. It is in fact hidden behind the closed doors of the bedroom, where the public and sometimes even the closest family members are denied access. The traditional gathering place for the community to pay its final respects has thus been sealed off to all but the doctor, the new confidant in matters concerning death and dying. For Ariès, Tolstoy's moral tale perfectly illustrates the transition from "the public death of the past" to "the hidden death of the future" (*HOD* 573). Ivan Ilyich dies at home but is utterly ignored by his kin. Only the pantry boy Gerasim cares for him, attending to all his physical and emotional needs. Ivan's terminal illness and eventual death are deemed a social impropriety. As a consequence of the all-around denial of his impending end, a denial that he himself perpetuates until his final hour, he exists in total isolation from his peers. He enters the vicious "medical cycle" (*HOD* 565) of repeated diagnoses and treatments. His life-threatening ailment subsequently takes on an existence all its own such that death is attributed to a malfunctioning organ rather to the fundamental condition of being human. In the words of Ariès, Ivan Ilyich "denies death by masking it with disease" (*HOD* 566). He continually hopes for a cure, but of course there is no remedy for this final state of being—at best it can only be delayed thanks to the advances of modern medicine. Tolstoy's story, according to Ariès, heralds the age of medicalized death.

Invisible death, hidden death, medicalized death—all of these labels designate the modern attitude toward what had been, in previous ages of our culture, a profoundly human and social experience rather than an object of science and bureaucracy. This new outlook arose as a result of a decisive change in the role of the community, whose historical function as a bulwark against nature faded into obsolescence during the early twentieth century. By this time most natural threats to human existence had been eliminated through scientific and technological progress. The community could thus abdicate its responsibility to provide for its members, who were free to become "an enormous mass of atomized individuals" (*HOD* 613). The general trend toward secularization further succeeded in diminishing the belief in evil and the afterlife. All of these factors contributed to the formation of an unfamiliar and untamed death, the precise opposite of the long-reigning model that dominated the Middle Ages and remained in place, with certain crucial variations discussed above, well beyond that distant epoch. Because death no longer needed to be domesticated, it became disregarded or outright denied. Paradoxically, these sociological currents only made it all the more antihuman and horrific. People are more afraid of death than ever before, since their habitual defense mechanisms against this inevitable reality of nonbeing have been dismantled. As Ariès concretely observes: "The death of the patient in the hospital, covered with tubes, is becoming a popular image, more terrifying than the *transi* or skeleton of macabre rhetoric" (*HOD* 614).

This modern version of *memento mori* is indicative of the twentieth century convention of removing death from society and rendering it invisible behind hospital walls, where it is turned into a private if not solitary affair. In the wake of modernity, humans began to die alone like never before, their deaths managed by the institution of the hospital, which gradually acquired "a local monopoly on death" (*HOD* 584). It is estimated that in 1949 nearly 50 percent of the US population died outside the home;[17] by the end of the century this figure rose to 75 percent.[18] Given these statistics there can be no denying that death has undergone an enormous degree of technologization and bureaucratization within a brief period of human history. Even the recent developments of hospices and nursing homes, which strive to humanize death, reflect a growing web of management that has taken over the physical care and emotional consolation traditionally provided by the family and community. The contrast to the tame death of earlier times, which was characterized by familiar simplicity and communal participation, could not be greater. As Ariès reminds us, "Death was always public. Hence the profound significance of Pascal's remark that one dies alone, for at that time one was never physically alone at the moment of death. Today his statement has lost its impact, for one has a very good chance of literally dying alone, in a hospital room" (*HOD* 19). Our present death system is, in other words, a completely depersonalized and desocialized one. Whether we realize it or not, we are alienated from our dying more than ever before, and it is the task of writers, philosophers, and general thanatologists to alert us to this fact and help restore us to our humanity.

A final model of death that proves of relevance for my study is found in Michel Foucault's *The Birth of the Clinic: An Archaeology of Medical Perception*. As Foucault states in the opening sentence: "This book is about space, about language, and about death" (*BC* ix). Not unlike Ariès in his methodology, Foucault draws on a surfeit of historical data and minutiae to support his arguments about shifting paradigms, specifically about the mutations that occurred in medical knowledge from the eighteenth to nineteenth century. In the transformation of medicine from a nosological to a pathological science, a number of important developments took shape with respect to the perception of death. Nosology, the branch of medicine that deals with the classification of diseases, fixed its gaze on the exterior of the body and attempted to specify disorders from the outside looking in. It deciphered diseases based on the bodily symptoms that presented themselves to the eye, but did not penetrate beneath this spatialized visibility of signs. As a result of this semiotic approach, whereby physical symptoms function as the equivalent of visible and readable signs, death remained outside the purview of the medical gaze. Death, rather, marked the end of disease and its diverse configurations; it formed the limit of nosography, since the ailment in question had run its course and could no longer be analyzed. In the synoptic words of Foucault: "Death was that absolute beyond which there was neither life nor disease, but its disorganizations were like all morbid phenomena. In its original form, clinical experience did not call into question this ambiguous concept of death" (*BC* 141). Yet in the early nineteenth century a new approach was adopted, one that Ariès also discusses from his own sociohistorical angle. Medical science turned to the cadaver as an object of investigation, and by literally opening up corpses in the deeper pursuit of disease, one in effect opened up a whole new field of knowledge.

Pathological anatomy replaced nosology as the regnant epistemic paradigm of medicine. By concentrating on the human cadaver and its previously concealed organs, the anatomo-clinical method made life, disease, and death into "a technical and conceptual trinity" (*BC* 144). The analysis of disease could now in fact only be conducted from the standpoint of death, for the corpse had become the source of all scientific information. In pathology a whole functional network of causes and effects was revealed to the eye: sequences, dependencies, and inter-actions—all of which attested to "the permeability of life by death" (*BC* 142). There could no longer be a strict separation between these two states of being, as death was shown to occur by gradation within and throughout the body. Like disease, death could be divided and repeatedly subdivided in terms of both time and space. For instance, the deaths of the heart, lungs, and brain do not occur simultaneously, nor do they necessarily involve one another. This recognition of mul-tiple organismic deaths is today a commonplace; even in everyday par-lance we distinguish between heart dead and brain dead. The latter category can be further broken down into the death of the whole brain versus higher brain functions, and of course there is the final condi-tion of cellular death. But 200 years ago such discoveries were revo-lutionary. Scientists like Xavier Bichat, the chief representative of this new direction in medicine and author of the book that gave it its name, *Anatomie pathologique* (1825), first determined that numerous incre-mental deaths transpire such that the precise status of the organism becomes ambiguous. Is it alive or dead? For a significant period of time, it is both. As Foucault declares: "Bichat relativized the concept of death, bringing it down from that absolute in which it appeared as an indivisible, decisive, irrecoverable event: he volatilized it, distrib-uted it throughout life in the form of separate, partial, progressive deaths, deaths that are so slow in occurring that they extend even beyond death itself" (*BC* 144). Disease and the decease that it causes thus both became functionally integrated into the life processes. Pathological anatomy effected a reversal of the eighteenth century nosological model. Whereas the latter viewed disease as an external phenomenon that endangers life, the former considered it a vital part of the living body. To the anatomo-pathological eye, death and illness indeed became *em-bodied* in the life of the individual. To illustrate this inversion in alternative terms: "It is not because he falls ill that man dies; fundamentally, it is because he may die that man may fall ill" (*BC* 155). One cannot fail to discern in this epistemological split between nosology and pathology the basic difference that defines the philosophical conflict of metaphysics versus ontology.

Disease had long been interpreted as an alien force that attacked life and ushered in the irreversible state of death. The nosological essences, which "hovered over the order of life and threatened it" (*BC* 154), even resemble Platonic forms in their function: they are not embedded in reality but serve as a higher frame of reference for the phenomenal analysis of physical disorders. But in the wake of Bichat, disease found its "ontological support" (*BC* 154) in the pathological life; it fully participated in the inner workings of the body. As Foucault puts it: "Disease breaks away from the metaphysic of evil, to which it had been related for centuries; and it finds in the visibility of death the full form in which its content appears in positive terms" (*BC* 196). According to this nonmetaphysical view, death and its vehicle of disease are thus not events that simply befall an organism and terminate its existence. Life, death, and disease instead form part of a greater ontological unity. Through their method of dissecting corpses, Bichat and his contemporaries turned death, paradoxically, into the source of disease and the a priori of knowledge about life. This inverse approach corresponds to Sartre's earlier point that the humanization of death "influences the entire life by a reverse flow" (*BN* 681). More important for Foucault is the fact that during the nineteenth century death became linked with the awareness of individuality. Because the anatomo-pathological gaze concretely localized illness in the cadaver, death/disease yielded knowledge of the individual. This new orientation is symptomatic of the broader shift in conceptions of finitude from the classical age (roughly 1650–1750) to the late eighteenth century. Whereas finitude was conceived as the categorical negation of the infinite in classical thought, it acquired a positive anthropological significance throughout the course of the nineteenth century. That is, finitude became reinterpreted as both the limit and origin of human beings, who during the nineteenth century began to understand themselves in terms of their limited existence. Medical pathology revealed to humans that they are the subject as well as the object of their own knowledge; more precisely, it drove home their primordial relation to mortality. According to Foucault, medicine thus plays a paradigmatic role in the human sciences and is arguably the most important discipline for illuminating "the philosophical status of man" (*BC* 198). The example of Freud stands out most in this regard, but Foucault also refers to two nonphysicians: Hölderlin and Nietzsche. To be more exact, he invokes their characters of Empedocles and Zarathustra to back his claim that "the experience of individuality in modern culture is bound up with that of death" (*BC* 197). He further mentions Rilke (see *BC* 198) as part of this trend that began toward the end of the eighteenth century, a trend that ontologized and individualized death, wresting it from "its old tragic heaven" of metaphysics and introducing it into "the lyrical core of man" (*BC* 172).

My argument about the ontological grounding of death in German literature and philosophy intersects at various points with the three models—philosophical, historical, and pathological—outlined above. The common thread that runs through these conceptions of human finitude concerns a basic antagonism between metaphysics and ontology. Although Heidegger has his own notion of what constitutes these two categories, his thinking is rooted in an ontological totalism that shares an essential goal with the early dialectics of Hegel and Hölderlin. Philosophies of both fundamental ontology and dialectical unification aim to replace the rigid structures of the metaphysical-positivistic worldview with a more dynamic and holistic experience of being. Nietzsche and Rilke take a similar totalistic approach, but are more trenchant in their critiques of metaphysical transcendence, especially in its religious form. According to all five authors, death holds the key to obtaining a complete and meaningful existence. As an ontological phenomenon, death rounds off and puts the signature touch on our lives. It thus functions within the compass of our being—or, as medical pathology would have it, within our very anatomy. This pivotal turn in medicine toward the end of the eighteenth century coincides with a similar paradigm shift in the thanatological discourse of certain poets and philosophers. In each case a decisive transformation takes place: death becomes interiorized and individualized. Foucault even states that Hölderlin's Empedocles manifests this transition to "the beautiful, enclosed form of individuality" (*BC* 198) that gained ascendancy throughout the 1800s.

The growing prominence of the individual during this period as hypothesized by Foucault goes hand in hand with the evolution of the dialectical and existential models of death pursued in this study. The sociohistorical theories of Philippe Ariès also inform my argument. This is most evident in the cases of Nietzsche, Rilke, and Heidegger, who after all directly bore witness to the rise of "invisible death" during the late nineteenth and early twentieth century. It is clear that all three are on some level reacting to the modern alienation from death that Ariès and others (Elias, Baudrillard) have detected at the heart of our society. Even Heidegger, who tends to insulate himself from social currents through a kind of ontological buffer, can be read as a commentator on certain cultural phenomena that became rampant in his time, most notably the denial of death. I will occasionally point to such broader sociological and medical perspectives in order to contextualize as well as reinforce the main focus of this book, whose structure I will now sketch out.[19]

The writings of Hegel and Hölderlin from the turn of the eighteenth to nineteenth century reveal a common tendency toward dialectical thinking, which is no doubt due to their close personal contact in Frankfurt between 1797–1800. During these years they developed a dynamic theoretical model that was designed to overcome the metaphysical dualisms of the day (mainly Kantianism) as well as to inject some much-needed lifeblood into the mechanical formalism of the Fichtean dialectic. Nevertheless, the precise nature of this intellectual collaboration remains difficult to determine, as there exists little to no documentary evidence about the details of this period. The consensus among scholars is that Hegel profited more from Hölderlin than vice versa.[20] Robert Solomon even goes so far as to claim that "the single most powerful influence on Hegel's vision in the *Phenomenology* [is] Friedrich Hölderlin."[21] Hegel, it is true, was somewhat of a late bloomer in comparison with his friends from seminary school, Hölderlin and Schelling, who were both published authors by the mid-1790s. Hegel's first publication, *The Difference between Fichte's and Schelling's System of Philosophy,* did not in fact come until 1801 and is mainly a defense of his former classmate, who was five years his junior and had already attained the rank of professor at the University of Jena. By the time Hegel's first full-length book, *System of Science* (later known by the title of its first and only completed part: *Phenomenology of Spirit*), appeared in April of 1807, Hölderlin had gone definitively insane and Schelling had since produced his most original body of work. Thus one can easily jump to the conclusion that Hegel was more on the receiving end in the transmission of ideas among his contemporaries, but this assumption does little justice to the profound eclectic nature of his thought. Hegel's genius is not that of an enthused poet like Hölderlin or a mercurial system-builder like Schelling; his mind works in a far more synthetic manner, seeking to assimilate as much knowledge as possible for the long-term development of his philosophical vision.

The more fruitful approach in tracing the evolution of the dialectic is to start with theory and then show its application to literature, which means that my discussion of Hölderlin will follow my opening chapter on Hegel. This further means that my interpretations of Hölderlin's literary texts will reflect many of the ideas presented in the theoretical context of Hegel's writings. However, this sequence has nothing to do with causality. The reader should continually bear in mind—and I will give ample reminders to this effect—that the dialectic cannot have been the sole brainchild of either Hegel or Hölderlin, but that it arose out of a rich philosophical dialogue between them both

I will begin with a discussion of Hegel's early manuscripts from the 1790s and then turn to the *Phenomenology of Spirit* from 1806–07. In these texts, Hegel equates negativity, the propelling motor of the dialectic, with death as a "negative" experience. Death, for Hegel, does not constitute an absolute negation and hence termination of life, but possesses a dialectical energy that spurs life onward, increasing its possibility. Hegel thus maintains that life and death share an intimate relation as two reciprocal forces; they are dialectically polarized rather than diametrically opposed. Hegel's goal is to transform the common idea of death as a fixed point of finality into a more fluid state of being. Like the anatomo-clinical inversion of perspective posited by Foucault and the "reverse flow" that Sartre speaks of with respect to the humanistic recovery of death, a similar reversal occurs in Hegelian philosophy through the inward turn of consciousness. His model of dialectics succeeds in overcoming the dualistic metaphysical scheme by integrating the boundary formed by death into the immanent realm of life. Consciousness in a sense rebounds off this terminal wall and pursues its journey *within* the phenomenal world rather than *beyond* it. Hence, there is no transcendent reality in Hegel, but rather an innerworldly movement toward new forms of knowledge. As a result of this original turn of consciousness, death becomes functionally engaged in the dialectic, playing a key role in the formation of Spirit: from the fight for survival between lord and bondsman to the sacrifice of Christ atop the Mound of Skulls, the throne of absolute knowledge.

In Hölderlin's dramatic project from the late 1790s, *The Death of Empedocles,* this dialectical view of death is exemplified in the hero of the tragedy. Hölderlin's fictionalized Empedocles, based on the historical pre-Socratic who allegedly committed suicide by leaping into the crater of Mount Etna, refuses to divorce life from its traditionally accepted opposite. By freely electing to die in the Sicilian volcano, Empedocles seeks to capitalize on the existential potential of his own mortality, thereby heightening his overall sense of being. This objective propels him forward through the course of the drama, much as negativity drives Hegelian Spirit onward in its odyssey toward complete comprehension of itself. In both cases, the negative equally acts as a positive force that succeeds in energizing the metaphysical apprehension of death as a static point of transition between two separate realms. Empedocles displays little tolerance for those who perpetuate such a divided worldview and especially for those who try to circumvent their death. He condemns the high priests along with the crowds that mindlessly obey them for holding fast to life and waiting for biology to dictate their end. Like the divided consciousness during the early phases of Hegelian Spirit, these rivals of Empedocles lead a divisive existence, which stems in part from their failure to recognize the dialectical importance of death.

My discussion of death in Hölderlin's tragedy unavoidably converges with another major theme. Empedocles's motivation to die is grounded in an existential guilt that he believes can only be expiated through an act of supreme sacrifice. The guilt that weighs on Empedocles is a primordial fact of his existence, a kind of ontological being-guilty (*Schuldigsein*) in a Heideggerian sense. In both cases, the fundamental condition of guiltiness forms the ground for one's possibilities and decisions, whether of Empedocles's resolve to end his life in the flames of Etna or of Dasein's anticipatory resoluteness in the face of death. Hölderlin's drama thus not only picks up on themes from the dialectical philosophy of Hegel but also points straight ahead to Heidegger's existential analytic in *Being and Time.*

I will preface my analysis of *Empedocles* with a consideration of Hölderlin's quest for holism as expressed in his letters, theoretical writings, and epistolary novel *Hyperion,* all of which were composed either before or during his work on the drama. Hölderlin's view of death cannot be separated from his more general concern with the problem of unification. The central question raised in *Hyperion* is: how to achieve classical harmony and cosmic unity in our modern fragmented world? The novel, however, is also pervaded by the theme of death and hence complements the analysis of *Empedocles.* Due to Hölderlin's distinctly organic way of thinking, it is often impossible to segregate his texts from one another or to isolate individual strands of his thought. His pantheistic vision of the world makes specialized topical studies difficult if not untenable. Moreover, one runs the risk of becoming precisely the compartmentalized *Fachmensch* that he denounces in the penultimate letter of *Hyperion.* My focus on death in *Empedocles* will thus be expanded to include additional works and themes. This procedure should be understood as an amplification of, rather than a deviation from, the immediate subject at hand.

For different reasons than those mentioned above, my Nietzsche chapter also considers a number of works beyond the primary text *Thus Spoke Zarathustra.* First of all, Nietzsche expressed his views on death in piecemeal fashion, which is largely due to his preference for the aphoristic form over the more traditional philosophical treatise. Hence, while Zarathustra's speech "On Free Death" contains Nietzsche's most distilled thoughts with regard to human mortality, one cannot over-look the various other pronouncements strewn throughout his works. Another reason for the inclusion of additional material has to do with the fact that Nietzsche intended to write his own *Empedocles* tragedy in the spirit of Hölderlin's. Sketches can be found in posthumously published notebooks from his early days as a professor of classical philology in Basel. Although this plan was never carried through to completion, the extant fragments reveal a number of similarities to Hölderlin's drama with regard to plot, characterization, and ideas. I will examine these drafts in order to reinforce the connection to Hölderlin and thereby better situate Nietzsche within the line of thought delineated in this book. But more important is the fact that some ten years later Nietzsche took up his abandoned *Empedocles* project under a different guise. *Thus Spoke Zarathustra,* written in four parts between 1883–85, can be considered an extension of *Empedocles*—his own project and Hölderlin's—insofar as it retains and expands on several of the original themes, including death. In *Zarathustra,* however, death takes on a deeper existential and ethical function. Contra the modern Christian devaluation of earthly existence and the resultant deflation of a life-affirming death, Nietzsche advocates the classical ethic of *ars moriendi,* urging us to "die at the right time." That is, rather than clinging to life at all costs, we should cultivate a free relation to death as the necessary egress from a stagnant and depleted existence. This notion of freedom, already an essential component of the dialectical models elaborated by Hegel and Hölderlin, plays an even greater role in Nietzsche's ideal of self-overcoming, which in its most extreme form calls for the individual to *will* his death as the ultimate yea-saying to life.

Like Hölderlin and Nietzsche, Rilke distinguishes between different modes of death. Although he does not use the precise term freedom, he still believes in death as the ultimate individualizing experience and as one's crowning achievement in life. In his early poetry as well as his novel *The Notebooks of Malte Laurids Brigge,* Rilke gives voice to his conviction that people should die with dignity and in their own signature way. But this individualized brand of death is threatened by the rise of mass society. As Rilke directly observes in fin-de-siècle Paris, the modern hospital now manages this once personal affair. Whereas in the not-too-distant past people died at home, in their own beds and among family members, city-dwellers of the new era perish anonymously—"invisibly" as Ariès would say—behind hospital walls. Indeed, Rilke's reflections on death in the age of modernity correspond in large part to the sociocultural analyses conducted by Ariès. Rilke even draws inspiration from *The Death of Ivan Ilyich* for many of the ideas expressed in his *Malte* novel, which, like Tolstoy's tale from 1886, stands at the threshold of a new historical attitude toward human mortality. The times when death was an authentic experience have faded; it has become monopolized, medicalized, and dehumanized by the institution of the hospital. With these two contrasting modes of finitude, Rilke thus follows in the footsteps of Hölderlin and Nietzsche, who elaborated analogous models of death as existential fulfillment on the one hand and biological decrepitude on the other. But a third brand of death becomes noticeable in the course of Rilke's writings, particularly in the *Duino Elegies* from 1912–22. Here he presents a more totalized and quasi-mystical view which can be put in the following formulistic terms: life + death = human existence. Rilke, that is, insists that we must learn to incorporate death into our lives, become intimate with our basic mortal predicament and thereby attain a more complete sense of being.

Heidegger's well-known analysis of death in *Being and Time* (1927) forms the culmination of the ontological thanatology that began with the dialectics of Hegel and Hölderlin only to pass through the existentialist views of Nietzsche and Rilke. His interpretation of human finitude as a supreme possibility that both intimates freedom and determines selfhood has obvious precedents in the ideas of his forebears. While I am not ultimately concerned with the question of influence, I do wish to explore the factical implications of his death analytic. Heidegger of course has his own special definition of many traditional philosophical terms, including metaphysics and ontology. I will deal with these notions more thoroughly at the appropriate time, but for now it suffices to note that, according to Heidegger, ontology must be founded in onticity. That is, his analysis of the formal structures of being (Sein) must be shown to have its roots in the being of particular entities (*Seiendes*) such as Dasein. Similarly, existential analyses need to find existentiell or practice-oriented corroboration if they are to be more than just arbitrary constructs. Heidegger's search for existentiell attestation leads him, in the case of his existential-ontological exposition of death, to the factical ideal of forward-running resoluteness. I will take his method one step further by suggesting that such attestation can in turn be concretized by examples from literature and even philosophy. In more direct terms, I am interested in determining whether the writings of Hegel, Hölderlin, Nietzsche, and Rilke provide reasonable testimony of an authentic and inauthentic being-toward-death. Heidegger himself finds such "pre-ontological evidence" (*BT* 405) in another context of his investigation: Dasein's basic structure as care is substantiated by the ancient *cura* fable, which survives in a Latin collection by Hyginus and was later reworked by Herder and Goethe (see *BT* 184–85, 405). Heidegger thus implicitly invites additional attempts to validate his philosophical postulations based on external sources, and I will take him up on this offer.

I emphasize that my focus lies on the early Heidegger, the philosopher—and, as some would maintain, theologian—whose philosophical classic *Being and Time* evolved from his university lectures at Freiburg (the first period between 1919–23) and Marburg (1923–28). Although both Hölderlin and Nietzsche figure prominently in this study, their role in Heidegger's later, so-called post-*Kehre* thinking is not of import here. Heidegger's engagement with Hölderlin's poetry and with Nietzsche's alleged metaphysics during the 1930s and 1940s has received more than its fair share of attention over the last several decades. Yet the impact of these two figures on the phenomenological analyses of *Being and Time* tends to go ignored. As I will lay out more thoroughly in the final chapter of this book, Heidegger has his own reasons for downplaying the influence of Hölderlin and Nietzsche at this beginning stage of his career. But ultimately, as indicated above, his fundamental ontology calls for existentiell testimony, whether in philosophy, literature, or life itself. In pursuit of such outside "authentication," I will try to show that Hölderlin's Empedocles and Nietzsche's Zarathustra served Heidegger as concrete exemplars for his deliberations on death in *Being and Time* and that they therefore provide yet a deeper ground for Dasein's internally apprehended "authentic" mode of being.

These literary and philosophical illustrations find even further support in the contemporary thanatological discourse about the dignity of death and the right to die. By way of conclusion, I will briefly address such medico-ethical issues based on the ideas raised in this sampling of German literature and philosophy from the late eighteenth to early twentieth century. Already in the 1950s, a number of psychologists, sociologists, and physicians began to search for solutions to the modern practice of institutional death management. Thus, even the medical community finally started to recognize what writers and philosophers had been proclaiming all along: we have become alienated from our mortal condition. A popularized debate gradually arose about the ethical treatment of the dying and the overall meaning of death for human existence. The most famous spokesperson in this movement was Elisabeth Kübler-Ross, who advocated a renewed humanization of death in the face of the depersonalized approach that was—and to a large extent still is—the standard. My concluding remarks thus serve to show that the ontological interpretations of death covered in this study are more than just intellectual musings from a select group of canonical German authors. This practical application of theories articulated by long-dead poets and thinkers shows, rather, the relevance of literature and philosophy for our everyday existence today.

As can be discerned from the above outline, my study is cross-disciplinary in nature. It combines not only literature and philosophy, but further integrates medical, sociohistorical, theological, and thanatological fields of discourse in a totalized effort to grapple with the issue of death. I prefer to think of my approach as *polyphonic* and hope that these multiple yet intersecting voices will speak to readers from a wide range of academic disciplines. In this sense, I seek to do justice to the holistic views espoused by the diverse host of authors covered in these pages, from Hegel, the quintessential abstruse German philosopher, to the more popular and readable Kübler-Ross. As will become apparent in the course of this investigation, there is no greater anathema to any of these figures than one-dimensionality. Indeed, their interpretations of human finitude largely aim to overcome this attitude, which they generally attribute to a modernized way of life that has grown out of sync with the deeper rhythm of human existence. Death, in its ontological reevaluation, thus becomes a kind of antidote to the ills of modernity. It offers the hope of a complete and fulfilled state of being, whether in the dialectics of Hegel and Hölderlin, the revived *ars moriendi* of Nietzsche, the mystical holism of Rilke, or the fundamental ontology of Heidegger.

1

Hegel
The Dialectic of Death

> This negative absolute, or pure freedom, manifests itself as
> death, and through the faculty of death the subject shows itself
> to be free and raised above all constraint.
>
> —Hegel, 1803

Hegel and Hölderlin were born in the same year, 1770, and in the same region of Germany, namely Swabia. Moreover, they became classmates at the Protestant seminary in Tübingen known as the *Stift*, where they even roomed together for a time (along with Schelling, the younger philosophical prodigy). Students of the seminary were given a theological training as preparation for their future careers in the state-run churches and schools of Württemberg, the duchy in which most of Swabia lay. Hegel and Hölderlin, however, displayed far more enthusiasm for ancient Greek culture and the ongoing French Revolution than for the religious dogmatism promoted by the university curriculum. This is not to say that religion played no formative role in their respective intellectual developments. As we will see, Hegel's early writings mainly revolve around issues of Judeo-Christian theology, whereas Hölderlin tends toward a more pantheistic fusion of Christianity, Greek polytheism, and elemental nature. Two mottos mark their thought and solidify the bond of their friendship from the Tübingen period onward: "*das Reich Gottes*" (the kingdom of God) and "*hen kai pan*" (the one and all). While the first phrase functions as the watchword for an inward, enlightened, and nonsectarian faith (Hegel equates this kingdom with an "invisible church"),[1] the second underscores the dynamic interaction of the particular and universal that is the hallmark of dialectics.

This dialectical pattern of thinking came to fruition during their years together in Frankfurt am Main, where they both held positions as household tutors or *Hofmeister,* a not uncommon job for young academics. (Kant and Fichte, for example, also served in such a capacity in their early careers.) Hölderlin, who had been employed in Frankfurt with the Gontard family since January of 1796, secured Hegel a position in the home of Johann Noë Gogel, a wealthy wine merchant with two youths in need of instruction. Hegel's enthusiasm for a reunion with Hölderlin is apparent in a poem from August 1796 that he dedicated to his friend. Although this piece, entitled "Eleusis," will never pass for fine lyrical poetry, it remains one of the few extant documents that help illuminate the intellectual connection between the two former classmates.[2] In the poem, whose title alludes to an ancient Greek town associated with Demeter and Dionysus, Hegel expresses his joy at the prospect of seeing Hölderlin again and of resuming their philosophical dialogue from their student days in Tübingen. Hegel, who for the last three years had been employed as a tutor in provincially conservative Berne, was isolated from his ties in Germany and hence eager for a change. When the terms of the offer in Frankfurt finally came through, Hölderlin gave voice to his own feelings of intellectual kinship in a letter that concludes with the lines: "I still have plenty to tell you, but your coming here will be the preface to a long, long, interesting, *unscholarly* book by you and me."[3] These words are open to interpretation, but it seems unlikely that Hölderlin had a concrete book project in mind. The repetition of "long" and emphasis of "unscholarly" suggest, rather, an enduring philosophical partnership and more general creative enterprise that was intended to rise above the uninspired academicism that was all too familiar to them from seminary school.[4] When Hegel finally reached Frankfurt in January of 1797, a critical phase of his development was launched. For the next three years, he and Hölderlin saw one another on a regular basis,[5] resulting in a decisive and sustained meeting of minds from which both would profit immensely.

In the following, I will trace Hegel's evolution from a Kantian dualist upon his arrival in Frankfurt to a dialectician by the time of his departure in January 1801. The texts that I will draw on have traditionally been labeled *Theologische Jugendschriften* (*Early Theological Writings*) after the title given to them by their editor Herman Nohl in 1907. But as is often pointed out, these manuscripts are fundamentally "anti-theological" insofar as they prove highly critical of established religion, whether Judaism, Catholicism, or the Reformed Church to which Hegel officially belonged.[6] For this reason, I will avoid Nohl's misleading term and refer to them according to the more philologically accurate categorizations of "Bernese" and "Frankfurt" manuscripts, based on the cities in which he composed them and in keeping with modern editorial practices. After elucidating the increased dialectical current of these early writings, with special attention devoted to the question of death, I will turn to Hegel's better-known *Phenomenology of Spirit* of 1806–07 and its more famous pronouncements on the dialectical function of death as negativity, possibility, and freedom. I will then explore the reception of Hegel by certain French existentialists whose readings shed a revealing light on the so-called existential element in a philosophy that is often considered to be overly abstract and systematized. More importantly, the insights of commentators like Jean Hyppolite, Maurice Merleau-Ponty, and Alexandre Kojève focus on such anthropological themes as death and furthermore point straight ahead to Heidegger, whose existential analytic in *Being and Time* considerably influenced these French interpretations of Hegel. Hence, this opening chapter on Hegel anticipates the concluding discussion of Heidegger as the final and most extreme figure involved in the ontologization of death.

FROM DUALISM TO UNIFICATION: THE BERNESE AND FRANKFURT MANUSCRIPTS (1793–1800)

It is commonly known that Kierkegaard disparages the Hegelian system, which fails to account for the subjective life of the individual before God. Had Kierkegaard, however, been familiar with the posthumously published writings of the younger Hegel, he would likely have retracted or at the very least amended his condemning words. Hegel's elaboration on such Christian notions as love and faith, his distinction between the message of Jesus as opposed to Church dogma, and the general sense of spiritual inwardness that pervades the early manuscripts— all of these features are essential to Kierkegaard's own religiosity. Furthermore, they challenge the traditional and by now clichéd image of Hegel as an ultrarationalist devoid of insight into the more subtle, human aspects of existence.

The Bernese Manuscripts (1793–96)

In the earliest Bernese fragment (see *W* 1:9–44/*TE* 30–58), which was actually composed during his final months in Tübingen, Hegel contrasts objective with subjective religion. The former category is characterized by reason and knowledge, the latter by faith. At this incipient point in this thought, Hegel does not yet distinguish between reason and understanding; he tends rather to use the all-inclusive *Verstand* for any form of rational thinking. Objective religion is, in a word, theology, which Hegel defines as a system of established tenets that aim at a metaphysical knowledge of God. Faith, on the contrary, comes from the heart and stems from individual rather than institutional needs. It is a kind of existential notion in Kierkegaard's sense, for it lies within the realm of the purely subjective and does not derive from official Church doctrine. Hegel in fact presents us with a near perfect correlation of his staunchest critic's dichotomy between Christianity and Christendom. Beyond the connection to Kierkegaard, whom I mention here only to demystify some of Hegel's reputed rationalism and to align him with the more existentialist company to come, this conflict between subjective and objective religion corresponds to the basic philosophical problem of faith versus knowledge. By placing all stock in the primacy of faith, the 23-year-old Hegel is still far removed from the mature thinker that envisions and indeed represents the state of absolute knowledge. More significant in light of the question of dialectics is the fact that the fledgling philosopher remains caught up in dualisms and utterly ignores the importance of mediation. He will not take the major step toward dialectical inquiry until his association with Hölderlin in Frankfurt.

The fourth fragment on religion contains a section that bears the heading "Concerning Variations in the Way Death Is Depicted" (*W* 1:67–69/*TE* 76–78). Once again Hegel differentiates between two principal views, this time between the values of ancient Greece and those of modern Christianity. Not surprisingly, he asserts the superiority of the former culture over the latter. He begins this subsection with the claim: "The entire life of the Christian is supposed to prepare him for this transformation" (*W* 1:67/*TE* 76). The Christian life is, in other words, a *meditatio mortis* and a *memento mori* (*W* 1:68/*TE* 76, 77). Yet Hegel remains critical of the metaphysics of death promulgated by the Church, since it shifts all focus to the eternal afterlife, thereby depleting our terrestrial existence of its pleasures. With more than a hint of sarcasm, he describes the typical Christian deathbed scene, where clerics and close friends typically gather while "groaning forth the printed and prescribed sighs over the anxiety-ridden soul of the dying one" (*W* 1:68/*TE* 77). This hollow and craven attitude toward death leads Hegel to pose the question: "how is it that a people whose religion makes preparation for death into a cardinal point, a cornerstone of the entire edifice, tend to die in so unmanly a fashion—while people of other nations calmly await the arrival of this moment?" (*W* 1:69/*TE* 77). While Hegel here offers no answer, he does elaborate on who these other nations might be: the Greeks. No doubt inspired by Lessing's treatise "How the Ancients Depicted Death" (1769) and Schiller's poem "The Gods of Greece" (1788), Hegel opposes the ancient ideal of death as "a beautiful spirit, the brother of Sleep" (*W* 1:69/*TE* 77) with its modern personification as *der Knochenmann,* a grim skeletal figure that entered the popular imagination in the late Middle Ages. And whereas death in antiquity reminds us of the sweetness of life, its recast image of morbidity functions as a scare tactic to keep us from enjoying earthly delights. The irony here lies in the fact that Christians are taught to fear both life *and* death—and therefore, unlike the Greeks, can truly embrace neither.

Hegel's critique of Christianity continues in a near 100-page text from 1795–96 that has become known as *The Positivity of the Christian Religion*.[7] Positive at this point in Hegel's development means authoritarian. Judaism is the protopositive religion insofar as it arose from laws that posit moral precepts and commandments. Jesus, of course, spoke out against the rigid statutes enforced by the priesthood, insisting on more fundamental virtues that do not depend on any state-sanctioned religion. Thus, in principle, he undermined the positivity or authoritarianism of Judaism but at the same time unwittingly laid the ground for the foundation of the Christian church that still dominates modern life. Hegel even points out a number of positive/authoritarian tendencies that reside in the character of Jesus himself. These include: the reliance on miracles, the assumed role of Messiah, the constant references to his own person (which gives rise to the epithets teacher and master), and the oracular nature of the Gospel. Following the death of Jesus, the positivity of the religion founded in his name only increases, from the universal Church of Catholicism to the all-powerful apparatus of the modern Protestant State, which mixes religious authority with political hegemony. Except for a brief aside, in which Socrates receives praise as a nondoctrinaire promoter of virtue, there is little sign of anything positive—here in the everyday sense of the word—about religion in Hegel's view. Until, that is, the very end of the text, where Hegel utilizes the Kantian concepts of reason and freedom to suggest what constitutes true religious experience. From this point onward, reason (*Vernunft*) takes on constructive and synthetic connotations, while understanding (*Verstand*) denotes a faculty that is one sided and thus limited in its perspective. As for the role of death in this essay, Hegel employs a central metaphor that will reappear in his writings all the way to the *Phenomenology:* he describes any type of rigid or dogmatic point of view as dead. Judaism, for instance, consists of "dead [*toten*] formulas," the Jewish nation of "lifeless [*toten*] machines" that blindly obey the laws laid down by their God (*W* 1:105–06/*ETW* 68–69). The imagery here is suggestive and harshly logical: rigidity, stiffness, ossification (from the Latin *os,* meaning "bone") are all qualities that one associates with corpses or skeletons. In his later Frankfurt years, Hegel will begin to juxtapose this figurative notion of death as extreme objectivity with a more dialectical concept that relates death to life and universality. For now, however, his conception of death is restricted to fixed categories of one-sidedness that result from religious positivism.

The Frankfurt Manuscripts (1797–1800)

In contrast to Hegel's Bernese writings, which display a penchant for binary oppositions (subjective versus objective religion, Christianity versus antiquity, positivity versus reason), his Frankfurt manuscripts reveal a synthetic style of thought. Instead of envisaging the world in terms of dualisms, a practice that undoubtedly stems from his immersion in Kantian philosophy while in Berne, Hegel learns to reconcile rather than reinforce extremes during his time in Frankfurt. Together with Hölderlin, he gravitates toward a philosophy of unification (*Vereinigungsphilosophie*), which eventually yields to a more fluid and dynamic approach generally considered to be dialectical—although this term does not make its appearance in any of the Frankfurt texts. Some key dialectical notions that do occur, however, include reconciliation, spirit, and the multiconnotative *aufheben*. What is more, the rhetoric of death as both a positivistic-metaphysical schematic and a contrasting dialectical-ontological phenomenon increases throughout the fragments of this period.

Hegel arrived in Frankfurt in the middle of January 1797. Whether or not Hölderlin met him partway in Darmstadt cannot be ascertained.[8] The first testament of potential coactivity between the two is a document that has generated much discussion and even controversy since its first publication in 1917, after mysteriously surfacing at an auction four years earlier. Opinions differ as to the authorship and dating of this fragment, which has come to be known as "The Oldest System-Program of German Idealism." Scholars have not only argued that it derives from Hölderlin and/or Hegel, but that Schelling played a major role in its making as well.[9] Furthermore, it remains open to debate whether the piece was written during Hegel's first months in Frankfurt or whether it dates back to the summer of 1796, when he felt the time had come to leave Berne. The facts are that the text has been preserved in Hegel's handwriting and that it landed in the estate of one of his later students. More significantly, it falls into a transitional period of his life and contains many essential ingredients of his later thinking.

Due to its fragmented and compendious character, the sketch lends itself to a wide range of interpretations. On its most basic level, "The Oldest System-Program" adumbrates the construction of a system founded on reason and encompassing diverse fields of human endeavor such as ethics, philosophy, poetry, and history. The ultimate goal of this system-program is to create a new mythology that will unite humanity both politically and aesthetically, restoring to modern life the lost ideals of freedom, harmony, and reason. The central unifying concept in this process is beauty, "taking this word in a higher, Platonic sense" (*W* 1:235).[10] Scholars tend to agree that Hölderlin deserves credit for articulating the superlative role of beauty that lies at the core of this project, but he of course only took it from Plato. Like the Platonic ideal of *to kalon,* the notion of beauty (*Schönheit*) here has a wide application, ranging from physical appearance to moral virtue to absolute truth. For Hölderlin and Hegel, however, beauty does not reside in a transcendent realm of forms beyond physical reality but acts rather as a force of unification in the very phenomenal world that we inhabit. In this sense, neither Hegel nor Hölderlin is a genuine Platonist. As Ernst Cassirer has pointed out, this brand of Platonism is "directed strictly toward the appearance of life and toward the appearance of the beautiful."[11] As we will see in subsequent texts by Hegel and, in the next chapter, by Hölderlin, this unifying idea of "the beautiful" will fluctuate a great deal in name: Nature, Love, God, and eventually Spirit. But whatever they happen to be called, these notions all operate as synthetic principles that bring order to the manifold aspects and chaotic tendencies of modern reality. Here lies the beginning of what one might call Hegel's unification philosophy, a holistic view of the world that bears the seeds of the more kinetic and teleological dialectic.

After outright rejecting Christianity in Berne, Hegel "seeks a reconciliation with it in Frankfurt."[12] This shift is indicative of a nascent dialectical outlook that tends toward fusion rather than division. In a handful of rough drafts from 1797–98, Hegel discusses the synthesizing power of love, which unites such traditional dichotomies as subject and object, freedom and nature, reality and possibility. At the same time, he formulates an implicit critique of Kantianism, which he at one point equates with his revised definition of religious positivity (see *W* 1:254).[13] Positive here no longer solely denotes a religion founded on authority, but has been amplified to mean any phenomenon or view that is overly objective and produces permanent oppositions instead of harmonious totalities. As Hegel makes perfectly clear in these writings, opposition itself is not the real problem; it represents a necessary step in the overall process of unification, one however that must eventually be overcome. In place of a positive dualistic paradigm, Hegel offers a more fluid triadic model. He delineates a sequence consisting of three stages: original unity–separation–new unity, whereby the last two both "cancel" and "preserve" their respective predecessors. The all-important verb *aufheben* thus makes its first regular appearance here. Also of consequence in view of the coming dialectic is the fact that Hegel likens this unification to an "activity" (*Tätigkeit*) and further indicates that the first and second phases "progress" (*fortschreiten*) toward the final state of restored unity. However, he does not yet introduce the central concept of movement, which remains perhaps the most defining quality of the dialectic.

The trouble with unification philosophy is that it seems somewhat inert compared to the sheer dynamism of dialectical movement described in the *Phenomenology*. Progression and activity indeed suggest some degree of motion, but these qualities receive only brief mention and pale before the emphasis that Hegel will later place on the inherent mobilizing energy of the dialectic. Thus, despite the obvious structure of identity–difference–union in these fragments, it seems a bit premature to speak of dialectics in the strict Hegelian sense of the term. I prefer to view his philosophy of this period as protodialectical, since only some, but not all, of the defining aspects of what later goes by the actual name of the dialectic can be discerned. What we find here is a rudimentary triadic model whose parts inexorably supersede one another through a reconciliatory process of *Aufhebung*. Yet the crucial attributes of movement and negativity remain underemphasized, showing none of their future primacy. When Hegel finally settles on the term dialectic by the time of the *Phenomenology,* he will mainly use it as an adjective describing movement. In other words: *die dialektische Bewegung.* The notion of movement is thus inseparable, both conceptually and lexically, from the dialectic, which is by no means the case in the late 1790s, when the motor of the dialectic is, so to speak, only just warming up. Furthermore, the stage of opposition that mediates between original and final unity in his Frankfurt writings cannot possibly compare in transformative power to the vast potential of negativity that becomes the trademark of his Jena years. Another way of illustrating the difference between unification philosophy and dialectics is contained in the following claim made by Hegel himself in 1798: "Union and being are synonymous; in every proposition the copula 'is' expresses the union of subject and predicate—a being (*ein* Sein)" (*W* 1:251).[14] In his Frankfurt years, Hegel thus thinks principally in terms of being. When he relocates to Jena in 1801 and gradually conceives his first book, this conception of union as *being* will give way to a dialectical movement characterized by *becoming.*[15]

The notion of being ultimately remains diffuse and empty—which is precisely the implication of Hegel's famous words from the *Logic:* "*Pure being and pure nothing are, therefore, the same*" (*W* 5:83).[16] In an effort to ground this abstraction in human reality, Hegel postulates love as the more appropriate metaprinciple of unification. The philosophical blueprint sketched out in the fragment on "Love" consists of "unity, separated opposites, reunion" (*W* 1:249/*ETW* 308). This bareboned structure can be fleshed out as follows: An individual is a unit unto itself with an identity all its own, but when it confronts another individual, a situation involving two separate identities occurs. This difference is subsequently overcome through the unifying power of love, which, as the cliché goes, brings people together. But overcoming difference is not tantamount to eliminating it. The mediating act of *aufheben* does not discard what it negates, but hangs on to it and raises it to the next stage of development. Love, which appears to be both human emotion and cosmic force here in Hegel, simultaneously cancels and preserves difference, for it produces harmony between two heterogeneous beings, both of which—as yet another cliché goes—find themselves in the other while still maintaining their separate identities. One can easily observe in this dynamic of love the basic outline of what has widely become known as thesis–antithesis–synthesis. Hegel does not, however, use these terms together in his philosophy and will in fact come to criticize his idealist predecessors for relying on such a mechanical formula. (He was of course unable to prevent later philosophers like Marx from propagating this ostensibly Hegelian terminology.)[17] As a vitally human force, love rises above fixed taxonomies and hierarchies, exerting its influence on animate life rather than on dead objects of the positive world. Hegel for instance writes: "True union, or love proper, exists only between living beings who are equal in power and thus in one another's eyes living beings from every point of view; in no respect is either dead for the other" (*W* 1:245–46/*ETW* 304). The metaphor of death as static objectivity thus continues to exhibit its presence, but there are also indications that death takes on a more dialectical function.

In some lines of text that Alexandre Kojève has elaborated on insightfully (see *IRH* 242–46), Hegel draws a distinction between two forms of demise: the dying (*sterben*) of human beings and the decay (*verwesen*) of other organic life forms, here specifically a plant. Whereas most organisms are products of their environment, wholly dependent on external factors of nature (for example, weather, soil, food supply), humans transcend their creaturely condition by virtue of the fact that they possess such qualities as autonomy and individuality. As conscious individuals, we have an awareness of death as a "possibility of separation" (*W* 1:246/*ETW* 305) and thus continually reflect on this threat of nonbeing. Plants and animals, on the other hand, simply perish, presumably with no understanding of their finitude. Of course sooner or later the possibility of death becomes an actuality, and while love may have overcome the separation of individuals, it would seem to be powerless against the far more definitive state of separation resulting from death. (Hence, presumably, the adage: Till death do us part.) But it is here that, according to Hegel, love sets into motion a further chain of unification, both canceling and preserving death/separation by "making the mortal element . . . immortal"

(*W* 1:247/*ETW* 306). In concrete terms, this means that the union of love between two formerly separate individuals becomes torn apart by death, yet manages to survive in the child, which embodies a new unity. Kojève summarizes the fundamental difference between human and natural death as follows: "Now, all this means that the 'decomposition' or 'corruption' of a natural entity which puts an end to its 'empirical existence' is a pure and simple (or 'identical') annihilation, where as [*sic*] human death is a 'dialectical' (or 'total') 'overcoming,' which annuls while preserving and sublimating" (*IRH* 246). The numerous terms in quotes all stem from Hegel, but are often loosely translated from the German and transposed from other contexts by Kojève. Despite the fact that Hegel does not yet directly speak in terms of the dialectic, Kojève, who tends to interpret Hegel's early works from the vantage of the *Phenomenology,* does consistently employ this later concept. His point, as I will explain more fully later in this chapter, is that the dialectical character of death motivates Hegel's entire philosophy. For now, let it suffice to say that a more nuanced view of death begins to manifest itself in the Frankfurt manuscripts, one that does not simply restrict its focus to lifeless objects of the material world. Death, rather, will steadily gain in ontological and dialectical magnitude, from its role as a divider of unity to its more synthetic potential as raw negativity.

The complex of texts known as *The Spirit of Christianity and Its Fate,* composed between 1798 and 1800, remains Hegel's greatest accomplishment of the Frankfurt years. Wilhelm Dilthey even considers them the most beautiful piece of writing in Hegel's entire oeuvre.[18] In these texts, Hegel makes his anti-Kantianism more apparent than ever, which is another way of saying that he rejects the inherent positivity of practical reason. For Hegel, Kant's ethics result in an antagonism between our natural inclinations and the abstract laws that theoretically govern all human activity. This dualistic split also characterizes Judaism, which arose out of a primal opposition between an omnipotent God and his human subjects. Hegel's famous dialectic of master and slave (*Herr* and *Knecht*) has both its conceptual and terminological roots here: God the absolute master rules over his obsequious slaves. In *The Positivity of the Christian Religion* from a few years earlier, Hegel similarly refers to the slavelike obedience of the Jews toward their God, but his remarks are brief and rely on the word *Sklave* rather than *Knecht*. Kantianism and Judaism thus reflect an analogous dualism, one that Hegel tries to surmount through his philosophy of unification.

As we have seen, love functions as the prime force of reconciliation or *Aufhebung,* since it brings two separate beings together, both erasing and preserving their individual identities. In *The Spirit of Christianity,* love is embodied by the figure of Jesus and the community of early Christianity, both of which Hegel no longer regards as authoritarian in character. True morality, he says, must be founded on the unifying principle of love rather than on the abstract postulate of duty. But even love has its limits, for it can only unite so many people. As a higher, more organized manifestation of love, religion now becomes the absolute totalizing experience, the union of humanity with the divine. Hegel for instance writes: "The mountain and the eye which beholds it are subject and object, but between man and God, between spirit and spirit, there is no such cleft of objectivity" (*W* 1:381/*ETW* 265). Such statements and images smack of mysticism, and Hegel indeed invokes this very notion in his essay. Dilthey goes one step further, locating in the Frankfurt writings a "mystical pantheism" that seeks to harmonize *all* oppositions in the world.[19] The point here is that Hegel's unification philosophy has reached an extreme, resembling a curious blend of philosophical dialectics and religious mysticism in the tradition of Meister Eckhart. The fact that he draws on Arabic rather than the standard of Greek culture for his ideal of harmonious unity seems symptomatic of this pantheistic, all-inclusive perspective. Unlike Europeans, who lead a one-sided and divisive existence, Arabs tend toward the view that the "individual is not simply a part of the whole; the whole does not lie outside him; he himself is just the whole which the entire clan is" (*W* 1:376/*ETW* 260). This fluid relationship between the individual and the universal is also characteristic of original Christianity, but, as Hegel insists, not of the modern Church.

Hegel's well-known tendency toward totalization is already evident in this beginning stage of his career, when he was little more than a domestic servant in a bourgeois household and still years removed from his status as the regnant king of philosophy in Berlin. In *The Spirit of Christianity,* he describes the essence of religion as "the return to the Godhead whence man is born," a kind of spiritual homecoming that "closes the circle of man's development" (*W* 1:389/*ETW* 273). This circularity, an essential concept of his mature thought, implies that unification does not involve the synthesis of two completely disparate parts, but rather that difference is already a preprogrammed factor of the world's natural trend toward harmony. As Hegel states, "The relation of spirit to spirit is a feeling of harmony, is their unification; how could heterogeneous elements be unified? Faith in the divine is only possible if in the believer himself there is a divine element which rediscovers itself, its own nature, in that on which it believes, even if it be unconscious that what it has found *is* its own nature" (*W* 1:382/*ETW* 266). Hegel's increasing use of the word spirit (Geist) throughout the Frankfurt manuscripts, not to mention in the very title of his essay on Christianity, is worthy of note. Spirit carries the implication of transindividuality and togetherness, which are preconditions for the ultimate synthesis of subject and substance. To elaborate on the passage quoted above, individuals are better able to connect with one another on a spiritual level, where they discover a greater sense of community than, say, in the realm of the purely physical. Our faith in God as the highest Spirit remains at bottom an intimation of our own divine essence. We may not be cognizant of our divine potential, but this does not alter the primordial fact that we are enmeshed in the fabric of being, at one with God and therefore already deified in our own existence. Here Hegel has worked out in considerable complexity what he had only vaguely envisaged as his ideals a few years earlier in Tübingen: *das Reich Gottes* and *hen kai pan.*

While Hegel is well on his way toward overcoming dualisms at this point in his philosophy, he still distinguishes between two classes of death. However, the dichotomy of a positive versus ontological view of human finitude does not truly qualify as a strict conflict within Hegel's thinking itself. His goal is to transform the common idea of death as a fixed and final event into a more fluid reality that permeates, rather than simply terminates, life. The fact that positivity, whether in the form of Judaism or Kantianism, persists in a reified and hence deadening view of the world, remains a problem that Hegel desires to correct through dialectics. Although this greater goal of reconciling the two divergent functions of death may not seem obvious in his Frankfurt writings, it forms an integral part of the historical dialectic of the *Phenomenology,* which moves from the original rift between subject and object to the climactic "Calvary of absolute Spirit" (*W* 3:591/*PhS* 493). As we will soon see, the sacrifice of Christ synthesizes the one-sided phenomenon of natural death with the richer potential of negativity or nonbeing, thereby "immortalizing mortality." Nevertheless, traces of this mediating role played by Jesus can already be detected in Hegel's essay on Christianity.

In contrast to the "the rending apart [*Zerreißung*] of life" and the "dead connection between God and the world" (*W* 1:375/*ETW* 259) that prevails in Judaism, Christianity holds the key to unifying life and death. Hegel metaphorically expresses the unification of these two supposedly antithetical concepts as follows: "The single entity, the restricted entity, as something opposed [to life], something dead, is yet a branch of the infinite tree of life. Each part, to which the whole is external, is yet a whole, a life" (*W* 1:374/*ETW* 258). Death at its most primitive is a quality of unmediated alterity, of objects that do not become integrated into the larger whole. But of course difference cannot remain a permanent contradiction in Hegel's increasingly dialectical philosophy; it must undergo further assimilation toward a harmonious state of totality. And this is precisely the accomplishment of Jesus, a divine being who reconciles the oppositions of the world, including the supposedly insurmountable divide between life and death. Through his resurrection, Jesus embodies the union of these latter two realms: death is converted into life. Christianity thus offers special insight into the unification of extremes. As it exists today, however, the Christian church has lost sight of its origins and become firmly entrenched in a dualistic mode of being, not unlike the Judaism of old, which never considered Jesus a god in the first place and consequently "elevate[d] the intellect [*Verstand*], absolute division, the destruction of life [*das Töten*], to the pinnacle of spirit" (*W* 1:380/*ETW* 264). Death here in Hegel's scheme of religious history seems a kind of double-edged sword, one that kills (*töten*) through objectification and grants life through unification. Which is perhaps but another way of saying that an inborn dialectic governs Hegel's reflections on death from the start. What can be said for certain, at any rate, is that death has evolved into an idea that remains inextricably linked with the more general issue of holism.

Hegel's last Frankfurt composition, which dates from 1800, "shows a great advance in dialectical dexterity"[20] and abounds with references to the twofold function of death. Similar to the "System-Program" from 1796–97, it contains in concentrated—and inevitably fragmented—form his overall worldview and has hence been dubbed "Fragment of a System." The principle of *hen kai pan* practically breathes through the entire piece. Hegel consistently emphasizes the dynamic interaction between part and whole that underlies such diverse spheres as nature, spirit, religion—and death. If there was any doubt about the intimate relation between life and death in his previous writings, it soon becomes dispelled upon examination of this text. The most illuminating section of the manuscript runs as follows:

> Within the living whole there are posited at the same time death, opposition, and understanding, because there is posited a manifold that is alive and that, as alive, can posit itself as a whole. By so doing, it is at the same time a part, i.e. something for which there is something dead and which itself is something dead for other such parts. This partial character of the living being is transcended in religion; finite life rises to infinite life. It is only because the finite is itself life that it carries in itself the possibility of raising itself to infinite life. (*W* 1:422/*ETW* 312–13)

Several important points emerge from this passage, some of which Hegel has already touched on in the preceding texts. His general holistic perspective is readily apparent. As an organic and multifarious whole, life embraces countless phenomena, including its own alleged antithesis: death. Through this incorporation of death into the system of organized totality, the static nature of dead objects is both canceled and preserved. Although they still function within the flux of "the living whole," these individual parts no longer operate as separate entities within their narrow pockets of reality; like everything else, they become absorbed into the system. Nevertheless, death exerts its influence even in this more comprehensive realm, annulling life and thereby curbing the span of totalization. A further *Aufhebung,* however, solves this problem: life cedes to the higher sphere of religion, where death outstrips the limits of finitude and becomes the ultimate transcendence that is immortality. This fragment concludes Hegel's maturation in Frankfurt and offers a revealing glimpse into the more elaborate system of knowledge that he will construct in Jena from 1801 to 1806, five critical years of philosophical evolution that culminate in the *Phenomenology of Spirit.*

DEATH AS NEGATIVITY: THE *PHENOMENOLOGY OF SPIRIT* (1806–07)

In Hegel's classic opus, completed in October of 1806 and published in April of the following year, death becomes associated with the negative driving force of dialectical movement. The dialectic, now a permanent and patented feature of Hegel's thinking, should not be seen as a rhetorical device or philosophical method by means of which one gains access to truth. Rather, as Hegel argues, the world and our experience of it are fundamentally dialectical in nature. In order to set up my discussion of death's key role as negativity, I will briefly summarize the basic concept and trajectory of the dialectic within the *Phenomenology of Spirit.*

Dialectical Movement in the Phenomenology

In his introduction to the *Phenomenology,* Hegel problematizes the conventions of philosophical methodology, soon making it clear that he rejects all epistemological tools of the philosopher's trade. According to Hegel, we should not impose an outside standard on consciousness, since it examines itself "so that . . . all that is left for us to do is simply to look on" (*W* 3:77/*PhS* 54). The self-examination of consciousness proceeds roughly as follows: When confronted with an object of knowledge outside itself, consciousness finds a disparity between the independent existence of the object and its own knowledge of it. Consciousness then reevaluates this discrepancy, readjusting to the gap in its knowledge and forming a new awareness of the object in question. Out of this activity of (self-)correction emerges the experience of consciousness as well as the initial movement of the dialectic. Negativity, which as "the energy of thought" disposes over "tremendous power" (*W* 3:36/*PhS* 19), functions as the catalyst in this process. Yet there are two types of negation: absolute negation or skepticism, which categorically denies the validity of false recognitions, considering them useless for any further knowledge; and what Hegel calls "determinate negation," which not only accepts (its) errors, but works with them to create a new and synthesized understanding.

In this latter attitude, consciousness carries out three acts, all of which are conveyed by the single German word *aufheben*. Already a key ingredient of his thinking before Jena, the notion of *Aufhebung* now underlies the entire conception and itinerary of Hegel's book, which charts the journey of Spirit through the phenomenal world. The first action taken by consciousness when confronting external reality is to "cancel/annul" the truth of its original perception. But unlike the skeptical practice of discarding what it negates, consciousness "hangs on to/preserves" the negative to then "raise" it to the next level of knowledge. All of these conceptual procedures are rooted in the everyday connotations of the verb *aufheben,* which literally means "to lift up" and thus carries a number of spatial implications. What one lifts up is: (1) elevated; (2) right there in one's hand; and (3) no longer where it originally was. *Aufhebung* therefore also implies movement, change, and mediation. The canceled/preserved/raised object is no longer its original self; it has been altered, if only in thought. In more speculative terms, it has been reflected upon and mediated. The resulting product is a more self-realized form of consciousness, a stage—not a state—of gained knowledge that was only made possible through the very negation of previous knowledge; that is, through a sort of inward turning of knowledge upon itself. This cycle is synonymous with the dialectical movement, which continues to generate new truths by negating and reprocessing them. Its steady advance through the world is further synonymous with experience (*Erfahrung*), development

(*Entwicklung*), and history (*Geschichte*), all of which describe the path of Spirit as it moves through its evolutionary moments of consciousness, self-consciousness, reason, religion, and absolute knowing. The title of Hegel's book announces this very progression: the *Phenomenology of Spirit* describes the way in which Spirit appears in the diverse phenomena of the world, continually overcoming them in their difference and pressing on toward the final *Aufhebung* of knowing subject and known substance. Hegel's title should therefore be read as a *subjective* genitive, for Spirit remains the true *subject* of the book insofar as it actively phenomenologizes itself over the course of its teleological movement toward self-realization. Consequently, Hegel sees himself not as the author/creator of the dialectic, but as a neutral observer who "simply looks on," describing the self-progress of Spirit with both philosophical detachment and narrative transparency.

Two important characteristics of the dialectic thus become apparent here. First of all, it does not serve as an epistemological but rather as an ontological model, one that transcends philosophical categorizations and describes an overall paradigm of being. Dialectical movement is the basic way of the world; it underlies and inhabits all phenomena, irrespective of such long-established divisions as subject/object, mind/body, or man/nature. It is perhaps because of this universal and self-evident presence that Hegel seems reluctant to give a straightforward definition of the dialectic—at least in the *Phenomenology*. His most concise and illuminating explanation can be found in section 81 of the *Encyclopedia:* "According to its proper determinacy, however, the dialectic is the genuine nature that properly belongs to the determinations of understanding, to things, and to the finite in general" (*W* 8:172).[21] The dialectic hence works within the human mind as much as within inanimate objects. All aspects of finite reality are dialectical, for they can be *aufgehoben* into ever higher forms of Spirit. The dialectic and Spirit are indeed kindred if not identical forces that pervade the world on all levels. They instantiate and move through everything, refusing to recognize any of the borders or delimitations drawn by traditional philosophical categories. This notion of movement constitutes the second major attribute of the dialectic.

Hegel seldom employs the word *Dialektik* in the *Phenomenology*, preferring rather the more suggestive composite *dialektische Bewegung*. Oftentimes, he drops the modifier altogether and simply writes *Bewegung*. These variants are complemented by frequent metaphors of fluidity, which further underscore the living dynamic of the dialectic. Like the river of Heraclitus, Hegel's dialectic is always in flux. It liquefies and hence loosens the rigid partitions of philosophical positivity. Dialectical movement comes to rest only at the very end of the *Phenomenology*, when Spirit finally achieves consciousness of itself. There is of course a built-in telos to Hegel's *Phenomenology*, which was originally conceived as the first part to a *System of Science*, a project that he was forced to abandon (mainly due to external circumstances such as his flight from Jena during the Napoleonic invasion) but later took up in the *Logic* and *Encyclopedia*. Yet for many modern interpreters of Hegel, this outcome of attained being in World Spirit is incompatible with the intrinsic kinesis of the dialectic and the historical reality of the twentieth century. Sartre, Adorno, Ernst Bloch, and a number of French poststructuralists, for instance, all tend to interpret Hegel's dialectic as open-ended if not eternally restless. Despite their differing views and ideologies, these diverse figures have at least one thing in common: they read Hegel against the grain, hinting that the dialectic is so deeply programmed by motion that it can never truly reach an absolute synthesis and historical finale.

This primacy of movement is precisely what sets Hegel's dialectic apart from the tripartite models of his predecessors and contemporaries. In the preface of the *Phenomenology*, he takes issue with the static formalism of Kant, Schelling, and Fichte, in whose systems "the *triadic form* . . . is reduced to a lifeless schema, a mere shadow . . . a table of terms" (*W* 3:48/*PhS* 29). His more specific critique of Kant's table of categories as a "lifeless and uncomprehended" triad (*W* 3:48/*PhS* 29) reinforces his point, especially in the original German. Here he employs the word *tot*, which only accentuates the extreme rigidity of the Kantian schematic. What also gets lost in translation is the near isomorphic apposition of *Schema* and *Schemen* (schema and shadow) from the first citation. (The two words are actually identical in their vernacular plural.) *Schemen*, which better translates as "wraith" or "ghost," connotes the idea of death even more than "shadow." Metaphors of this kind run through the entire work, especially the preface. The most recurring modifiers include: dead (*tot*), lifeless (*leblos, unlebend*), and fixed (*fest, fix, fixiert*). Even the noun "corpse" (*Leichnam*) makes an appearance (*W* 3:13/*PhS* 3). As we have seen in his Frankfurt writings, these same words (excluding the latter) all describe nondialectical patterns of thinking. The difference here in the *Phenomenology* is that such metaphors of death become directly and consistently linked with the idea of nonmovement. The following quote illustrates the contrast between dialectical mobility and positivistic death: "For what is lifeless [*das Tote*], since it does not move of itself, does not get as far as the distinctions of essence, as far as essential opposition or inequality, and therefore does not make the transition of one opposite into its opposite, does not attain to qualitative, immanent motion or *self*-movement" (*W* 3:45/*PhS* 26). (In the original, the last two nouns are one word, *Selbstbewegung,* no part of which is emphasized.)

Death, Negativity, and Nonbeing

Spirit may be self-movement, but it gains its momentum from the dialectic, which has in turn a deeper motor of its own: negativity. As a raw mobilizing force that drives the dialectical process ever onward through supersession, negativity is the most elemental ingredient in Hegel's philosophy. Without it, the entire system would remain immobile, rigid, calcified—in a word: dead. Yet Hegel's concept of death contains its own inherent dialectic, for it can denote both stasis and transformation. Its connection with the former notion has been obvious since his early Frankfurt days; and the idea of death as an inseparable phenomenon of life increasingly manifests itself during his period of collaboration with Hölderlin. In the *Phenomenology,* however, death takes on the function of negativity, which is to say that it becomes a prime vehicle of transformation—a determinate negation full of promise rather than an outright denial of future possibilities. While he was working on his book, Hegel made the following note in the manuscript of one of his lectures at the University of Jena: "death, pure *negativity,* immediate *nonbeing*."[22] In the preface to the *Phenomenology,* which he composed in January of 1807 while the main body of the work was being set by the publisher, Hegel establishes the connection between death and negativity in a far more thorough and vivid fashion:

> Death, if that is what we want to call this non-actuality, is of all things the most dreadful, and to hold fast what is dead requires the greatest strength. . . . But the life of Spirit is not the life that shrinks from death and keeps itself untouched by devastation, but rather the life that endures it and maintains itself in it. It wins its truth only when, in utter dismemberment, it finds itself. It is this power, not as something positive, which closes its eyes to the negative, as when we say of something that it is nothing or is false, and then, having done with it, turn away and pass on to something else; on the contrary, Spirit is this power only by looking the negative in the face, and tarrying with it. This tarrying with the negative is the magical power that converts it into being. (*W* 3:36/*PhS* 19)

This passage contains a crucial idea concerning the "negative" function of death, one that reappears throughout the *Phenomenology*. Contra positivity and metaphysics, Hegel suggests that life and death are not irreconcilable opposites, but that they share an intimate relation as two antagonistic yet productive forces. In other words, they are dialectically, rather than diametrically, opposed. As dialectical beings ourselves, we should not divorce the harsh reality of death from our lives and thereby ignore its enriching potential. Only by squarely confronting our finitude and learning to accept it are we able to transform the nothingness of death into an experience of being. In Hegel's more descriptive prose, we need to overcome our natural urge of "shrinking" and "closing our eyes" before death and instead "look it in the face," even "tarry with it." This last phrase is a rather stale translation of *verweilen,* a verb that becomes a kind of leitmotif in the preface (see also *W* 3:13, 33/*PhS* 3, 17) and carries major implications for Hegel's dialectical view. *Verweilen* ties in with the notion of enduring the negative and maintaining oneself in it as stated by Hegel above. It thus approximates the connotation of *Aufhebung* as a "preserving," but better underscores our fundamental intimacy with death, in whose presence we should "linger" or "abide." All of these idioms are alternative ways of articulating what one might call a *cultivation* of death. To cultivate death means neither to deny it nor to embrace it completely, for while the former attitude is utterly nondialectical, the latter is equivalent to an absolute negation and hence results in a preemption of being, that is, suicide. Between rejection and annihilation there lies a middle course of action. This can perhaps best be described as a continual reckoning with the possibility of death. By maintaining ourselves in the presence of death, we dwell both on it and in it, which means that we remain aware of its perpetual imminence as our ultimate negation, a dialectical negation that inwardly enhances rather than outright destroys our lives.

The struggle between master and slave is arguably the most famous section of the *Phenomenology*. It has given rise to numerous and varied interpretations, ones that stress economics (Marx, Lukács, Marcuse), desire and fear of death (Kojève), even sadism and masochism (Sartre). Countless other interpreters have devoted less audacious but all the more balanced studies to Hegel's parablelike account of emerging self-consciousness.[23] My own discussion has to some extent been inspired by Kojève's observations on death and freedom in the master-slave relationship (see *IRH* 3–30), but it adheres more closely to the semantic and syntactic elements of Hegel's text. Like Marx, Sartre, and other celebrated (re)interpreters of Hegel, Kojève has a tendency toward creative interpolation and occasional exaggeration. A more tempered analysis is offered here. As for the specific terminology of Hegel's *Herr-Knecht* dialectic, I will chiefly rely on Miller's rendering of "lord-bondsman" rather than the more established combination of "master-slave." A number of good arguments exist for either option, but in the end these two German terms are not all that historically loaded or precise.[24] Since I will be quoting from Miller's standard translation, it makes sense to follow his example, though I will not, so to speak, slavishly adhere to it.

The key to Hegel's dialectic of self-consciousness lies in the maintained possibility rather than the final realization of death. In other words, the struggle for mutual recognition between two consciousnesses cannot result in actual death; otherwise, there would be no opponent left to recognize and thereby validate the existence of the victor. The confrontation hence resembles more a highly charged face-off, continually fraught with danger, than an out-and-out fight replete with violence.

As Hegel points out, a two-way action underlies this clash of identities: each seeks the death of the other while risking its own life in the process. Yet only by "putting one's life at stake" (the most literal translation of *sein Leben daransetzen*) can there be any hope of acknowledgment from the other and consequently any gain of self-awareness. The gist of Hegel's parable can be considered "proto-Heideggerian"[25] and is furthermore reminiscent of Nietzsche's famous injunction to "live dangerously" (see *The Gay Science,* no. 283). The *risk* of life leads to recognition and ultimately freedom; a *loss* of life only brings the entire dialectical process to a standstill. Here we have the familiar contrast between determinate and abstract negation: whereas the former preserves what it annuls, raising the prospect of death to a whole new level of being, the latter simply produces a lifeless *positum* that impedes dialectical movement. The negation of the other does not translate into a murderous action. The life-and-death struggle between two opposing consciousnesses is, rather, a "trial" through which they "prove themselves" (both notions are conveyed by *Bewährung/sich bewähren*) and test their mettle as autonomous beings. As Hegel has shown since his early Frankfurt writings, the idea of sustained interplay remains a crucial component of unification philosophy and dialectics. And as he has indicated in the preface of the *Phenomenology,* only the life that "endures and maintains itself" in death belongs to Spirit. Dialectical opposition thus characterizes the predicament of consciousness during this phase of Spirit's evolution. The antagonistic standoff does not bring about the one-time destruction of either combatant, but elicits the reactions and solicits the long-term recognition of the other, whose hostile presence is dialectically overcome through a kind of revolt on the part of the individual consciousness personified as a bondsman.

Hegel suggests that there is an inherent inequality to conflict. History indeed attests to an eternal interaction between oppressors and oppressed, perpetrators and victims, haves and have-nots. The list of these two clashing forces is endless, but concretized here by the independent lord and dependent bondsman. The rapport of lord and bondsman exists precisely because a one-sided recognition has taken place in the wake of their strife as oppositional entities. The bondsman acknowledges the superiority of his lord by serving him and granting his every wish. The lord in turn sits back and enjoys the fruits of his servant's labors, consuming them in his insatiable desire, but he completely ignores the existence of his provider as an individual possessing any kind of autonomous identity. For Hegel, identity does not constitute a predetermined and immutable category; it is formed, rather, through its dialectical relationship with otherness. The lord is lord because the bondsman views him as such and vice versa. Indeed, expressions such as provider and benefactor are utterly relative in this context, for who really provides or bestows favors in this scenario? The lord through his munificence? The bondsman through his service? Each is dependent on the other, though the degree of self-sufficiency seemingly varies. But this difference in autonomy is only an illusion or at least a temporarily fixed and tacit understanding that cannot prevail for long given the incessant movement of Spirit.

A reversal of roles eventually takes place, one that is precipitated by the bondsman's "fear of death, the absolute Lord" (*W* 3:153/*PhS* 117). The apposition of these two objects of fear is deliberately ambiguous. (As we will soon see, Hegel pairs lord and death twice more in the *Phenomenology*, which suggests a conscious stylistic recourse.) The bondsman's anxiety results from the threat that the lord constantly poses to his existence in their ongoing struggle for recognition. The lord thus functions as an embodiment of death, or put in slightly different terms: death for the bondsman bears the guise of the lord. Hegel's language throughout this section has a certain literary quality and his philosophical examples seem right out of an uncanny novel. (Kafka especially comes to mind.) At the very least, his entire account resembles a parable, with all the requisite elements of fictitiousness, exemplary characters, and reader edification. He describes the effect of the bondsman's mortal fear as follows: "In that experience it [this consciousness, i.e. the bondsman] has been quite unmanned, has trembled in every fibre of its being, and everything solid and stable has been shaken to its foundations" (*W* 3:153/*PhS* 117). In the original German, this "unmanned" state of the bondsman is described more precisely as an "internal loosening" or "disintegration" (*es ist darin innerlich aufgelöst worden*), which further illustrates the lack of fixity in his deeply troubled being. And here his long-accepted status, and hence practical stasis, as the inferior and servile one undergoes a complete transformation. Indeed, the entire status quo is upset through "this pure universal movement, the absolute liquefaction [Miller's "melting-away" is a misleading translation of *Flüssigwerden*] of everything stable" (*W* 3:153/*PhS* 117). Through his transformative fear of death, the bondsman is thus loosened from his total dependence on the lord and begins to gain a sense of autonomy or, in Hegel's language, being-for-self. More importantly within the broader scope of the *Phenomenology,* this emergent freedom marks the first appearance of Spirit as "the unity of the different independent self-consciousnesses" (*W* 3:145/*PhS* 110), all of which have similarly confronted death in the manner that Hegel has sketched out in his paradigmatic tale.

In this section Hegel also illustrates how fear/anxiety (unlike Heidegger he does not draw a distinction between these two concepts) shatters one's fixed state of being and intimates a whole new sense of existence in the face of death. For Hegel, freedom and self-consciousness emerge as a consequence of risking one's life and abiding in the possibility of death. But fear of death is just the first step on the path to freedom. Only through service and the more literal transformative power of work does the bondsman become independent from the lord, who persists in his endless desire, growing ever more lethargic, stagnant, and eventually subject to his former vassal. In the meantime, this once subjugated servant forms—better yet, *trans*forms—the objects of the world through labor, a more controlled and productive mode of desire. While the bondsman reshapes his identity and definitively comes into his own through work, his fear of death is what initiates this process of self-discovery, wrenching him from his fixation on the particular and casting him into the current of the universal. The bondsman effectively engages in a process of enlightenment, emancipation, and self-realization. Indeed, the formation of self-consciousness that Hegel demonstrates through his parable is but another way of expressing the idea of freedom that dominated Enlightenment thinking. Charles Taylor has described this aspiration for autonomy as "expressivist," a notion that entails the idea of "authentic self-expression."[26] Freedom, according to this view, is more than just liberation from constraint, whether material, political, or social. People must also be able to express themselves in the deeper sense of realizing their goals and fashioning their lives. This does not necessarily mean that each person dwells within his or her own personal solipsistic space; true and equitable interaction, rather, ensues once a state of bondage has been overcome and universal freedom has been achieved. According to Taylor, expressivist consciousness strives for "unity, freedom, and communion with man and nature."[27] These are the very goals that emerge out of the formation of self-consciousness in the *Phenomenology:* an interpersonal and universal Spirit comes into existence, becoming ever more inclusive and self-apprehending. Robert Solomon similarly views Hegel's notion of freedom as self-expression and self-realiza- tion. As he for instance notes: "freedom does not mean the freedom to do any particular sort of thing. . . . Freedom means independence, autonomy, a sense of one's self *as* a self."[28] Once consciousness has attained such a definition of itself, it begins to branch out and embrace wider realms of reality in the form of reason followed by Spirit proper. And here death continues to play a major transformative role, super- seding all obstacles that stand in the way of Spirit's journey from self- consciousness to absolute knowledge.

True Spirit manifests itself in the ethical order or *Sittlichkeit,* and here death proves indispensable for the preservation of both the fam- ily and the state. As Hegel demonstrates through the example of *Antigone,* conflicts inevitably arise between human and divine law, the former represented by Creon, the latter by Antigone herself. As archon of the state and thus a representative of human law, Creon issues a decree that the traitorous Polynices, Antigone's brother, be refused a proper burial. Antigone, driven by the nonpolitical divine law, defies Creon's edict and performs the sacred funerary rites, thereby saving her brother's corpse from the elements and bringing him back into the famil- ial order. In these densely written pages (see *W* 3:328–34/*PhS* 266–72), Hegel seems to suggest that Antigone converts the natural/biological death of man into the speculative death of Spirit. That is to say, rather than let her brother rot in nature or more likely be devoured by wild animals, she keeps him within the family and broader ethical commu- nity, both of which constitute important moments of Spirit. To quote one of the more lucid sentences in this section: "Through this it comes about that the *dead,* the universal *being,* becomes a being that has returned into itself, a being-for-self, or, the powerless, simply isolated individual has been raised to universal individuality" (*W* 3:333/*PhS* 271). The act of Antigone is therefore dialectical, for it preserves the annulled existence of her kin, raising this singular family member to the level of universal Spirit. In an anthropological context, Antigone embodies an historical tradition that, as Philippe Ariès argues, "tames" death. Her efforts to save her dead brother from exposure and neglect are at the same time an attempt to domesticate the forces of nature that continually threaten the welfare of the community. Ritualization, whether through bereavement, burial, or a host of other social customs, serves as a necessary human defense against natural death. In the words of J. N. Findlay: "Here . . . Hegel seems unique among philosophers in recognizing the importance of death and funerary practices in early ethical life."[29] Death thus exhibits a presence on numerous levels in the *Phenomenology,* ranging from the highly speculative concept of negativity to the commonplace conventions of funeral rites, all of which naturally lie within the greater purview of Spirit.

Hegel is far better known for his comments on the necessity, if not desirability, of war than for his views on funerary practices. His most notorious remarks can be found in the *Philosophy of Right* (secs. 324–26 and 334–39). But even as early as the *Phenomenology,* he contends that the menace of death through war keeps individualizing tendencies in check and the spirit of the community intact. His language is strikingly reminiscent of the lord and bondsman episode that demonstrated the origins of self-consciousness, freedom, and Spirit. Once again, here in a continuation of his *Antigone* analysis, he draws a connection between "death" and "lord" (*W* 3:335/*PhS* 273). (Miller embellishes *Herr* as both "lord and master.") While he does not further personify the power of death as a literal and absolute sovereign, the effect of this supreme force upon individuals remains the same: the threat of lethal warfare shakes things up in society, preventing its members from becoming too entrenched in their independence and isolation from the greater whole. As we have witnessed in the case of the bondsman, the mortal risk of combat dissolves the rigidity of fixed structures, making way for the universalizing flow of Spirit. This general liquefaction of all forms of positivity keeps the dialectic moving. Hegel continues to employ variants of *Auflösung,* twice previously and once here (*W* 3:153, 335), though such stylistic details are often lost on English readers due to some of the inconsistencies in Miller's translation. The richly nuanced *Auflösung* is, for instance, now rendered as "melting-pot" (*PhS* 273), which at least manages to convey some sense of dissolution. Regardless of such relatively minor discrepancies, the dialectical principle operative in Spirit becomes readily apparent at this stage of its history: the negation (read: death/sacrifice) of individuals is essential for the preservation and longevity of the community. As Solomon observes in this context: "Death, here in the discussion of *Antigone* and elsewhere too, plays a shockingly positive role in Hegel's philosophy, as the ultimate argument against the vanity of individualism."[30] Though it may be a hard truth to swallow, history, according to Hegel, has yet to prove that individuals count for much. If the case were any different, Spirit would act in other ways, but the fact is that devastation cannot be separated from progress any more than evil can be cleanly divorced from good. As a metaphor from the preface illustrates, all such time-honored opposites are only two sides of the same coin (see *W* 3:40/*PhS* 22). Death in the form of war is the "negative essence" of Spirit, but at the same time "the real *power* of the community and the *force* of its self-preservation" (*W* 3:335/*PhS* 273; emphases from the original German). Death, war, and destruction are thus dialectical necessities in the history of civilization; without such negativity, there can be no room for movement, progress, and—as Hegel makes clear—"freedom" (*W* 3:335/*PhS* 273). Despite the grim resonance of these ideas, Hegel should not be labeled a fatalist. Charles Taylor offers excellent insight into the problem of the individual versus universal with respect to the question of death:

> But in Hegel's view such instances of individual fate are beneath the sweep of necessity; they fall in the domain of that interstitial contingency whose existence is necessary, as we have seen. We can be reconciled with this as well as with world history if we identify with what we essentially are, universal reason. If we really come to see ourselves

as vehicles of universal reason, then death is no longer an "other"; for it is part of the plan. We are in that sense already beyond death; it is no longer a limit. It is incorporated in the life of reason which goes on beyond it.[31]

But death does not always have this dialectical purpose. In the moment of Spirit that historically corresponds to the French Revolution, death becomes pure negativity, which is to say that it acts as a wholly destructive force devoid of all higher meaning. During this phase of self-alienated Spirit, abstract self-consciousness does away with difference, erasing the individual distinctions and structures through which the universal is normally reflected. The plurality of individual consciousnesses and the organization of spiritual spheres that took shape in culture and the ethical world are now immersed in an absolute freedom that refuses to recognize or at least tolerate difference. Because of its monolithic rule and lack of differentiation, this new form of consciousness is a "vacuous *Être suprême*" (*W* 3:434/*PhS* 358), utterly self-coincidental and hence nondialectical. Death now also takes on a completely contrasting function compared to its previous appearances in the *Phenomenology*. In this abstract stage of Spirit, death looms as an absolute, rather than determinate, negation, a "*fury* of destruction" (*W* 3:436/*PhS* 359) and "cold, matter-of-fact annihilation" (*W* 3:437/*PhS* 360). Death in this instance preserves nothing, nor does it elevate the individual toward the universal. In an obvious allusion to the *Terreur* of the Jacobin government, Hegel alleges that the threat of death in absolute freedom instills sheer "terror" as opposed to the more determinate reaction of "fear." A further historical allusion, here to the guillotine, underscores his theory that death during the French Revolution has been reduced to utter meaninglessness: "The sole work and deed of universal [i.e., absolute] freedom is therefore *death,* a death too which has no inner significance or filling, for what is negated is the empty point of the absolutely free self. It is thus the coldest and meanest of all deaths, with no more significance than cutting off a head of cabbage or swallowing a mouthful of water" (*W* 3:436/*PhS* 360).

Death, in other words, functions as a force of liquidation rather than liquefaction. Instead of attaining freedom through work, the individual consciousness becomes obliterated by an already existent absolute freedom—a kind of uncontrolled chaos that runs amok due to a total absence of mediation. Freedom is thus not an automatic ideal in Hegel's philosophy. In fact, nothing for Hegel is by definition positive or negative; every truth has been mediated and must therefore be viewed in light of the particular station that Spirit happens to have reached in its historical odyssey. Absolute/abstract freedom operates so ruthlessly because it is not willing to reconcile with its opposites; it negates them entirely. But this autocratic period of history cannot last long, for the general difference of pure negation must eventually yield to actual difference or diversity. And here Hegel seems to say that the fear of death, "their absolute master" (*W* 3:438/*PhS* 361), reorients individuals toward the distinct spheres of instantiated Spirit. The good old-fashioned fear of death thus brings consciousness back into the fold of difference, something that naked mortal terror cannot possibly do. In some interesting figurative language, Hegel states that Spirit becomes "refreshed and rejuvenated by the fear of the lord and master [death]" (*W* 3:438/*PhS* 361) and soon moves on toward its next goal, namely Kantian morality.

This chapter of Spirit's epic journey has plainly shown that Hegel views death in a richly nuanced fashion. It can be both a productive and destructive force, as well as a rigid category of positivistic thinking. Death, in sum, functions both dialectically and nondialectically. In the grand scheme of Hegel's philosophy the truth of death lies of course in its dialectical capacity, as is most clearly evidenced at the conclusion of the *Phenomenology,* where the Crucifixion of Christ leads to the final *Aufhebung* of Spirit.

In contrast to Hegel's Bernese and Frankfurt writings, Jesus never once appears by name in the *Phenomenology*. Hegel's discussion of revealed religion features, rather, the epithets: divine Man, human God, and Mediator. All of these aliases point to the crucial role of Jesus as a synthesis of the human and divine, the particular and the universal, the finite and the infinite. In this phase of Spirit, the relationship between God and man consists in identity. Whereas preceding stages of Spirit (natural and art-religion) posited the divine in terms of representation, God now directly manifests himself in the human form of man. The human and divine are dialectically identical, which is to say that they exist as both selfsame and other. As the Incarnation, Christ is immediate universality, a concrete embodiment of the abstract concept of God, a dialectical externalization and instantiation of the divine subject. The death and resurrection of Christ, the supreme Redeemer/reconciler of differences, amount to no less than a universalization of his individualized substance. With the passing of Christ comes the end of particularity and the beginning of a universal consciousness of communal religion. The religious community that Jesus leaves behind and for whose sake he has after all died, gains a whole new sense of spirit/Spirit—here writ both small and large in order to highlight the ordinary sense of community spirit and the more dialectical presence of World Spirit. A key passage from this section of the *Phenomenology* associates the death of Christ with negativity and brings out its connection with the all-embracing breadth of Hegelian Spirit:

> The *death* of the divine Man, as *death,* is *abstract* negativity, the immediate result of the movement which ends only in *natural* universality. Death loses this natural meaning in spiritual self-consciousness, i.e. it comes to be its just stated Notion; death becomes transfigured from its immediate meaning, viz. the non-being of this *particular* individual, into the *universality* of the Spirit who dwells in His community, dies in it every day, and is daily resurrected. (*W* 3:570–71/*PhS* 475)

Even to Jesus, the reality of death appears to be an "abstract" negation; that is, a nondialectical event that leads to "natural" universality, a kind of brotherhood of man. But as Hegel plainly demonstrates, Jesus—and thus religion—has limitations within the overall scope of Spirit. In contrast to his Frankfurt writings, where religion constituted the absolute, speculative knowledge forms the ultimate totalizing reality in the *Phenomenology.* A major difference between Hegel as a young tutor in Frankfurt and a middle-aged professor in Jena lies in the fact that philosophy now supersedes religion. Given this major paradigm shift, Jesus remains a mere embodiment of World Spirit, not fully aware of the dialectical function of his grandiose death. But whether Jesus realizes it or not, death once again fulfills the purpose of canceling and preserving the individual in a higher universal realm, here of Spirit rather than religion. In light of his example, the Christian community is expected to confront death dialectically, as if it were a daily possibility for the individual and a necessity for the progression of Spirit. The death of the Christian human-God is fraught with all kinds of dialectical symbolism, which the religious community is expected to internalize and thereby better understand itself within the larger context of Spirit. The Crucifixion (cancellation), for instance, results in the Resurrection (preservation) and Ascension (elevation). Moreover, the triadic movement of dialectics is apparent in the implicit structure of the Trinity: God is identity, his Son is difference/other, and the Holy Ghost is the synthetic unity of the two. This grand-scale death of Christ would appear to be the ultimate *Aufhebung* of Spirit, the point at which it becomes self-knowing as both substance and subject. As Hegel elaborates on the non-Nietzschean utterance that *"God Himself is dead"*:

> This hard saying is the expression of innermost simple self-knowledge, the return of consciousness into the depths of the night in which "I = I," a night which no longer distinguishes or knows anything outside of it. . . . This Knowing is the inbreathing of the Spirit, whereby Substance becomes Subject, by which its abstraction and lifelessness have died, and Substance therefore has become *actual* and simple and universal Self-consciousness. (*W* 3:572/*PhS* 476)

Despite these promising words, we have only reached the threshold of absolute knowledge. Spirit here finds itself between the last manifestation of religion and the self-transparency of speculative thought.

For Hegel, the problem with the death of God is that the Christian community tends to view the Crucifixion as an historical occurrence and the Parousia or Second Coming as a future event. Moreover, a residue of representation remains in revealed religion, for we still tend to identify with Christ as a noninternalized other. (Compare for example the predominance of religious images and icons in Catholicism and even many strains of Protestantism). Thus a separation or noncorrespondence prevails between subjective certainty and objective truth. In Hegelian terms, an unhappy consciousness continues to exist, one that is divided in its knowledge, albeit not in its heart. Until we grasp the unity of God and the human in the present, there can be no totalized identity between the essence of the community as an in-itself and its realized existence as a for-itself, which is but another way of saying that there can be no absolute knowing. Hegel's critique of Christianity as a religion that fails to live in the moment can perhaps best be illuminated by a brief consideration of Heidegger's early theological thought, specifically of his ideas regarding kairological and chronological time.

According to Heidegger in a university lecture from the winter semester of 1920–21, entitled *Introduction to the Phenomenology of Religion* (see *GA* 60, esp. 98–105),[32] Saint Paul thinks in terms of a "kairological" time while Old Testament and medieval Christianity remain bound to the chronological thinking of Judaism and Aristotelianism. In his letters to the Thessalonians, Paul speaks of the Parousia as the *kairos,* which has been translated by Luther as *der Augenblick,* a literal "blink of the eye." The *kairos* is precisely such a brief moment in which the Second Coming of Christ can abruptly occur. The original Christians lived in constant anticipation of the *kairos* and structured their existence around it so as not to be caught off guard should Christ unexpectedly arrive. For Paul there simply was no predictable time of occurrence: "But as to the times and the seasons, brethren, you have no need to have anything written to you. For you yourselves know well that the day of the Lord will come like a thief in the night" (1 Thess. 5:1–2). Judeo-Christian prophecy and eschatology, on the other hand, have sought to calculate such momentous events on a religious calendar of sorts (to speak with Paul, according to "the times and the seasons"). That Scholasticism later adopted Aristotle's objective concept of time only reinforces the chronological mindset of established Christianity. When theorized on a time-scale, things become fixed and objectified, therefore stripped of possibility. But beneath the surface of Church dogma, which has adopted a scientific-metaphysical model in its interpretation of the Divine, Heidegger's ideal of primal Christianity (*Urchristentum*) strives for a more existential experience of God. Heidegger's Christian models here include Paul, Augustine, Luther, Pascal, and Kierkegaard. Although he does not explicitly make this connection, kairological time is at bottom intimately linked with the question of death. Because the Second Coming can occur at any conceivable moment, we must strive to perfect our existence and live each instant as if it were the last, for only in this manner are we guaranteed a passage to the Kingdom of God. The briefest lapse into complacency can result in a forfeiture of salvation should it happen to coincide with the *kairos*. This continuous anticipation of an uncertain end inevitably leads to a heightening of existence, and death gradually becomes an integral part of life due to its ever-present menace. Given these circumstances, we cannot but incorporate it into existence—assuming of course that we are willing, like good primal Christians, to abandon the encrusted doctrines of conventional religion and put our faith in the hidden God of the New Testament.

Hegel's analysis of Christianity evinces a similar nonmetaphysical view of death. Traditionally, the Crucifixion and Resurrection give ultimate attestation to the immortality of the soul. The example of Jesus tells us that we will find life after death, an eternal beyond where our mortal condition is no longer an issue. Through his notion of dialectical death, Hegel however undermines this comforting Christian attitude and in a sense takes back the commonly accepted view of Christ's act. There is no real immortality here, for the individual does not survive death in the manner typically propounded by Christianity. Furthermore, the doctrine of immortality implies a dualism consisting of the "here and now" (*Diesseits*) versus the "beyond" (*Jenseits*). As we have seen, such dichotomous views are anathema to Hegel's entire way of thinking. For Hegel, death constitutes an internal and determinate negation rather than a sudden disruptive event that strikes from without. Death is a necessary and inseparable aspect of Spirit, an analogue of the very negativity that drives the dialectic onward and leads to the culminating experience of absolute knowing at the conclusion of the *Phenomenology*.

The final chapter of the *Phenomenology* adds nothing new, but is a kind of recapitulation—in Hegel's words, a "recollection/interiorization" (*Er-innerung*)—of Spirit's long and winding path toward self-knowledge. Not unlike Heidegger's practice in the second division of *Being and Time,* where he revisits his earlier phenomenological analyses of Dasein from the standpoint of temporality, Hegel underlines the importance of time for the process of self-apprehension. "Time," he states, "appears as the destiny and necessity of Spirit that is not yet complete within itself" (*W* 3:584–85/*PhS* 487). Once

Spirit has gained total self-identity, it enters the rarefied and ahistorical realm of speculative thought, the domain of Hegel's next major project, the *Logic*. The last section of the *Phenomenology* forms in fact a transition to his System of Science, where the differentiated unities of concepts are dealt with on precisely such a speculative level. Hegel, in other words, leaves behind the *becoming* of Spirit as history for the *being* of the absolute Concept. The shifting stages of Spirit thus culminate in a permanent state of knowledge. The real question here concerns the particulars of this final goal of absolute knowing. What does it mean to have reached this plateau? Hegel certainly does not intend to imply that absolute knowledge is equivalent to a quantitative, incremental sum of wisdom that Spirit, so to speak, racks up along its journey. Nor does this last section of Hegel's book offer an aggregate chunk of experience for the further formation of Spirit and added edification of readers. Self-knowing denotes, rather, a qualitative and consummate procedure of dialectical thinking. For this reason, the progressive "knowing" conveys the processual implications of Hegel's aim better than does the substantive "knowledge" (a distinction analogous to the articular infinitive *das Wissen* versus the abstract noun *die Weisheit*). Hegel shows us here, by way of review, that a sensible coherence underlies our multifarious and variegated world. Through the dialectical insight that the *Phenomenology* affords, we are better able to grasp the inner dynamic of reality. By learning to recognize unity in diversity through the specific pattern of externalization—division—unification, we come to understand the workings of the world in a far more nuanced and refined fashion than has hitherto been provided by philosophy. Like the omnipresent Spirit that has progressed through all its forms over the course of time, we find ourselves, at the end of Hegel's book, in a more advantageous position to reflect on our experiences and comprehend our existence. As the concluding lines of the *Phenomenology* reveal, comprehension for Hegel means both conceptual understanding and existential self-apprehension. Here Spirit finally attains its own "comprehended History" (*W* 3:591/*PhS* 493), which means that it has become aware of itself through its evolution over time, all the while filling in the gaps of its identity. Self-awareness hence corresponds to completion, holism, and totality.

More important with regard to the question of death, this comprehended History forms "the Calvary of absolute Spirit" (*W* 3:591/*PhS* 493). This obvious reference to the Crucifixion reinforces the idea of death as fulfillment, as an *Aufhebung* of the individual in the universal. What is more, it further attests to the capital significance of Christ's ultimate reconciliation with difference. Through this symbolic dialectical death, Spirit avoids turning into a positivistic entity that is "lifeless and alone" (*W* 3:591/*PhS* 493). It dialectically overcomes all such dead-ends, steadily moving toward its goal of absolute comprehension and totalization. The words of Christ on the Mound of Skulls could thus just as well be those of Geist on its throne of knowledge: "It is accomplished."

HEGEL IN FRANCE: EXISTENTIALISM AND DEATH

Twentieth century French interpreters of Hegel have largely disregarded the systematic character of his philosophy, instead stressing the significance of such fundamental human elements as existence, freedom, anxiety, suffering, and death. They have, that is, made Hegel into a kind of protoexistentialist—or at the very least, into a phenomenological precursor of Husserl and Heidegger. This trend, described by one critic as "the anthropological turn"[33] in French Hegelianism, was initiated by Jean Wahl's influential study from 1929, *Le malheur de la conscience dans la philosophie de Hegel* (*The Misfortune of Consciousness in the Philosophy of Hegel*).[34] In this book, Wahl interprets the unhappy consciousness in the *Phenomenology* not as an isolated historical moment of Spirit, but as an underlying problem of existence, whereby the divided self continually seeks unity and reconciliation. As the true subject of Hegel's philosophical narrative, the unhappy consciousness undergoes humanlike suffering in its torn identity until it finally achieves a state of wholeness at the conclusion of the *Phenomenology*. The dialectic of Spirit, its ongoing oscillations between self and other, is thus portrayed in concrete human terms. Wahl in effect anthropomorphizes Hegel's conception of Spirit and thereby paves the way for a host of other exegetes who will adopt a similar anthropological approach throughout the 1930s and 1940s. These figures include Jean Hyppolite, Alexandre Kojève, Alexandre Koyré, Maurice Merleau-Ponty, and Jean-Paul Sartre, all of whom tend to privilege Hegel's early writings, especially the *Phenomenology,* over the later speculative works like the *Encyclopedia.* This orientation is directed more toward Hegel the young Romantic than toward the more famous logician who laid out a rigid and elaborate System that threatened to stifle the existence of the individual human being. My main purpose in discussing this French reception of Hegel is twofold. First of all, I believe that many of these readings offer insight into the deeper implications of death in Hegel's philosophy as well as in our own existence. Secondly, these analyses point straight ahead to, and indeed are often informed by, the views of death developed by such oft-dubbed existentialists as Nietzsche, Rilke, and Heidegger. Especially in the hands of Hyppolite and Kojève, Hegel functions as a crucial forerunner of modern philosophical and literary interpretations of death.

Jean Hyppolite

In France, Jean Hyppolite is known as much for his translation of the *Phenomenology,* carried out between 1939–42, as for his extensive commentary on it, published in 1946 as *Genèse et structure de la Phénoménologie de l'esprit de Hegel* (*Genesis and Structure of Hegel's Phenomenology of Spirit*). Hyppolite's understanding of Hegel was deeply affected by Wahl's aforementioned book on the divided consciousness as well as by Alexandre Koyré's 1934 article "Hegel à Iéna,"[35] an examination of the philosopher's development during the years leading up to the *Phenomenology.* In his capacity as translator and commentator, Hyppolite gives us interpretations of Hegel that adhere closely to the original text. While there is a definite anthropological slant to his observations, he does not selectively cull sections of the *Phenomenology* for points that conveniently support his arguments, but rather devotes himself to the entire corpus of Hegel's philosophical epic. (Kojève, on the other hand, has been taken to task precisely for his unbalanced and somewhat tendentious analyses, which assign undue weight to the master-slave dialectic and generally view Hegel through Marxian and Heideggerian lenses.) Although Hyppolite is by

no means completely free of philosophical—especially anthropological—prejudice, he at least has the conviction and fortitude to comment on the entire *Phenomenology*. Hyppolite's *Genesis and Structure*
is marked by an existential undertone that brings to mind the language
of Kierkegaard, Heidegger, and Sartre. (The latter's *Being and
Nothingness* had just been published three years earlier.) Hyppolite
for instance asserts "a primacy of existence over essence"[36] and insists
that the human being "'never is what it is and always is what it is not.'"[37]
He further declares in patently Kierkegaardian terms that "consciousness is the act of relating to oneself."[38] On a more general level, he
often emphasizes the existentialist subtext of the *Phenomenology*,
noting that: "For Hegel philosophic doctrines are not abstract doctrines,
they are ways of life."[39] In this vein, he points to the "existential
anguish" of human consciousness and especially considers Hegel's discussion of self-certain Spirit "close to what we would call today 'existential analyses.'"[40] With respect to the latter quote, Hyppolite is no
doubt thinking of the similarities between Hegel's and Heidegger's
elucidations of conscience in chapter 6/C/c of the *Phenomenology* and
sections 54–60 of *Being and Time*, respectively.

More consequential are Hyppolite's remarks about death. As early
as his first chapter on the "generalities" of Hegel's ideas, he discusses
the contrast between death in nature and death in Spirit. Whereas the
former variety involves an "external" negation, the latter is described
in the following terms: "spirit carries death within itself and gives it
positive meaning. The whole *Phenomenology* is a meditation on this
death which is carried by consciousness and which, far from being exclusively negative, an end point in an abstract nothingness, is, on the contrary, an *Aufhebung*, an ascent."[41] This statement may seem somewhat
of an exaggeration, but Hyppolite explores the role of death on various occasions, particularly in the context of the family (Antigone's)
and of the Crucifixion.[42] In both cases, as we have seen, death dialectically preserves individual consciousness in the universality of Spirit.
As Hyppolite puts it: "Death is the movement of the individual into
the universal."[43] The fact that death is called a "movement" makes its
association if not equivalence with the dialectic all the more obvious.
To expand on Hyppolite's point, death may be the propelling motor

of the dialectic, but it also forms part of dialectical motion itself. Death is what actively raises the individual to the universal, whether through the family in the ethical world or through the greater community of religion. Unlike natural death, its spiritual counterpart does not exist as a given phenomenon or even occur as a precise event; it transcends all such categories of objectivity. Like the dialectic with which it is intimately entwined, death is be understood as a fluid, metamorphic potential that promotes universal Spirit and enhances the finite existence of Spirit's many instantiations. Hyppolite's earlier claim that the "whole *Phenomenology* is a meditation on this death" gives testimony to the central presence of this radical form of negativity in Hegel's thought. Sometimes implicit and inchoate, sometimes graphic and manifest, death moves throughout the *Phenomenology,* motivating the many supersessions of Spirit along its path toward self-realization. As Hegel vividly illustrates, this journey ends on a throne where both knowledge and death reign supreme: the Calvary of absolute Spirit.

In 1946, the year that *Genesis and Structure* was published, Hyppolite gave a lecture that soon appeared in print under the title "L'existence dans la *Phénoménologie* de Hegel."[44] The primary goal of this piece is to show that certain contemporary (read: existentialist) ideas have their origins in Hegel's early philosophy. These themes include: the awareness of death, the negativity of the for-itself, and the condition of being-for-others. Due to its brevity and distillation of philosophical topics, Hyppolite's published lecture better attests to the impact of Heidegger and Sartre than does his far more voluminous study of Hegel's chef d'oeuvre. My discussion of this short text is less concerned with individual influences and concentrates more on the anthropological function of death that, according to Hyppolite, permeates the entire *Phenomenology.*

Hyppolite conflates Hegel's notion of self-consciousness with human existence. This questionable move parallels the common existentialist conception (found for example in Kojève and Sartre) of Heideggerian Dasein as *réalité humaine.* Following in rough outline the Hegelian dialectic of self-consciousness and life, Hyppolite maintains that human existence transcends its brute nature by becoming conscious of it. Since human beings lack the self-coincidence of immediately given objects, they are able to reflect and capitalize on this difference, using it to raise themselves all the more above the static natural world. An animal is what it is, hence an in-itself. Human existence, on the contrary, is dialectical, which means that it consists of both identity and difference. As a dialectically determined for-itself, human existence is fraught with negativity; it constantly negates its being and thereby transforms itself into what it is not. Herein lies its freedom: human existence is self-creating. An animal is a *created* being, hence a *creature;* humans are precisely the opposite: *creators*.

This dialectical self-understanding on the part of human beings extends to their relation with death, which is after all an inseparable aspect of life. Such, at any rate, is Hyppolite's logic: "To become conscious of life in its totality is to reflect upon death, to exist in the face of death, and that is how authentic self-consciousness is experienced by us."[45] The notion of authenticity in the face of death is utterly Heideggerian, but Hyppolite's point is well taken within a Hegelian context. Self-consciousness becomes most aware of itself *as* a self through its most radical negation: death. This is essentially the experience of the bondsman, as Hyppolite explains through a loose analysis of self-consciousness in the *Phenomenology*. The risk of death leads to the bondsman's emancipation from the lord, thus giving him a whole new sense of selfhood and freedom. As Hyppolite further elaborates along Hegelian lines, an animal has no such consciousness of death; it perishes in a completely natural and unreflective manner. If humans are to be anything more than mere products of nature, they must overcome this biological end and "internalize death."[46] This interiorized death consists of a negativity that haunts our being and keeps us from lapsing into the paralysis of self-identity. Through this negativity, we not only distinguish ourselves from self-coincidental animals, but are able to rise above all constraint. The following citation reveals the intimate connection between death and existence, two traditionally conceived polar opposites: "Man cannot exist except through the negativity of death which he takes upon himself in order to make of it an act of transcendence or supersession of every limited situation. His *existing* is this very act."[47] Death is thus the ultimate experience of transgression. As an act of self-negation, death has a liberating effect, for it frees the individual from the pure givenness of animal life. It is in this sense that Hyppolite refers to a "freedom toward death" (*liberté pour la mort*),[48] a term that Heidegger made famous as *Freiheit zum Tode*. Hyppolite observes that this association between death and freedom appears throughout the *Phenomenology*. It ties in with the idea of liquefaction, which results from the fear of death as the absolute master (for example, the lord, war) and brings about the transformation, rejuvenation, and freedom of self-consciousness—or, for Hyppolite, human existence.

Maurice Merleau-Ponty

In a response to Hyppolite's paper, Maurice Merleau-Ponty both recapitulates and expands on his predecessor's arguments. The title of his piece is revealing in itself: "L'existentialisme chez Hegel" (Hegel's Existentialism).[49] In this discussion of Hegel's purported existentialism, Merleau-Ponty aligns the long-perceived idealist with a brand of philosophy that, by most accounts, arose in the wake of Kierkegaard. The common contrast drawn between Hegel and Kierkegaard, a contrast that the latter himself never ceased to emphasize, is largely conceived in terms of idealism versus existentialism. But Merleau-Ponty distinguishes between a younger and older Hegel, or the existentialist of the *Phenomenology* and the absolute idealist of the Berlin years. The existential implications of the *Phenomenology* lie in its profound and detailed exploration of human experience. Merleau-Ponty's anthropological stance emerges plainly in the following characterization of Hegel and his early masterpiece: "To be more exact, Hegel's thought is existentialist in that it views man not as being from the start a consciousness in full possession of its own clear thoughts but as a life which is its own responsibility and which tries to understand itself. All of the *Phénoménologie de l'esprit* describes man's efforts to reappropriate himself."[50]

Death offers the perfect opportunity for the reappropriation of the self-negating human being. For the most part, Merleau-Ponty's treatment of death follows the arguments put forth by Hyppolite, but his language is far more reminiscent of Sartre and at times of Heidegger.

By interiorizing death, he says, we transform it into life. That is, we negate death as an external, annihilating event and incorporate it into our existence, where it functions as a kind of void against which we define ourselves. This internal nothingness is the space of difference that allows us to develop dialectically; without it, we would be pure identity and hence overly determined, fixed beings—all essence and no existence. Through the alterity of an internalized death, we are able to create our own identity and shape our own existence. For Hegel, however, the true purpose of death does not consist in enhancing individual existence, but in promoting the movement of World Spirit. And it is here that Hegel's existentialism reaches its limits according to Merleau-Ponty (who actually attributes this point to Hyppolite, but no such comment can be found in the published version of Hyppolite's lecture). Bringing Heidegger into the mix, Merleau-Ponty makes the following argument: Whereas for Heidegger the prospect of death remains a defining individual experience, Hegel ultimately believes that the particular being dies for the sake of Spirit. Death, in Hegel's view, is not only dialectical in its function as negativity; it also fulfills the task of raising individual consciousness to the level of universality. Through this conversion of finite existence into higher forms of Spirit, Hegel leaves existentialism behind and enters the realm of absolute knowledge. And here a new phase of Hegel's development begins, one that is marked by a notable shift in terminology. As Merleau-Ponty points out: "The young Hegel speaks more willingly of death; the older Hegel prefers to speak of negativity."[51] This seemingly minor terminological difference nevertheless proves symptomatic of a broader reorientation in Hegel's thinking: he abandons the anthropological notion of death for the more speculative concept of negativity. In genuine dialectical fashion, he supersedes his existence-based philosophy and moves one step further in the direction of universal Spirit.

Alexandre Kojève

Alexandre Kojève is said to have influenced a whole generation of French intellectuals through his courses on the *Phenomenology of Spirit,* held between 1933 and 1939 at the École des Hautes Études in Paris.

These lectures were published in 1947, one year after Hyppolite's commentary appeared, under the title *Introduction à la lecture de Hegel* (*Introduction to the Reading of Hegel*). Like the work of Hyppolite, Kojève's opus numbers nearly 600 pages and seems equally comprehensive. As Allan Bloom writes in his introduction to the English translation, an edition that only includes about two-thirds of the original text: "[Kojève's] teaching is but the distillation of more than six years devoted to nothing but reading a single book [the *Phenomenology*], line by line. *Introduction to the Reading of Hegel* constitutes the most authoritative interpretation of Hegel" (*IRH* ix). This claim is certainly open to debate, but the fact is, Kojève has earned a reputation as the most influential promulgator of Hegel in France.[52] He furthermore has become known for attempting "to constitute the intellectual and moral *ménage à trois* of Hegel, Marx and Heidegger."[53] His interpretations of Hegel are indeed clouded by Marxian and Heideggerian jargon, but they offer a remarkably bold reading of Hegel that stresses the importance of negativity, death, and freedom. The most relevant sections of Kojève's book that pertain to these themes go by their own titles, although they reproduce the complete content of his lectures, which are otherwise arranged chronologically. The two texts in question are "The Dialectic of the Real and the Phenomenological Method in Hegel" and "The Idea of Death in Hegel's Philosophy."

The very first sentence of Kojève's book reads: "Man is Self-Consciousness" (*IRH* 3). This conflation of Hegelian terminology and philosophical anthropology determines, right from the outset, the direction of Kojève's entire hermeneutical enterprise. For Kojève, the *Phenomenology* represents Hegel's anthropology, whereas the *Encyclopedia* comprises his ontology and metaphysics. Kojève restricts dialectics to human existence, claiming (contra Hegel) that nature is nondialectical in essence, since it consists of pure identity and thus lacks any potential for self-negation. Humans, on the other hand, are dialectally privileged beings, for they are imbued with negativity and therefore understand themselves in terms of their otherness. Kojève, in effect, completely anthropologizes Hegel's monistic philosophy. He instead advocates an ontological dualism that is analogous to what Sartre will later conceive as "being-for-itself" (that is, human) and "being-in-itself" (that is, nature).[54] For Kojève, nature remains a mute and brute reality, but can be revealed as dialectical through human consciousness and discourse. That is, nature can be transformed through humans, but does not possess any negating power of its own. In sum, Kojève rejects the universality of the Hegelian dialectic as a movement both of thought and being, replacing it with a "dialectical Anthropology" (*IRH* 223). According to this human-centered view, man is a nonidentical and self-creating being whose essence lies in his existence, as the most basic tenet of existentialism goes. As we will see, this dialectically configured existence becomes infused with negativity and freedom, both of which are intimately related to, if not synonymous with, death.

There can be no doubt that Kojève's understanding of Hegel was significantly affected by his exposure to Heidegger, whose work was slowly being read in France. (Koyré, the first to translate Heidegger into French, was an influential mediator in this regard.) Much of Kojève's language is colored by Heideggerianisms and many of the ideas that he attributes to Hegel's *Phenomenology* are more consistently found in *Being and Time*. A handful of marginal references to Heidegger and his 1927 opus directly testify to this connection, one that I only wish to address briefly as a way of outlining the larger trajectory of my study. Kojève for instance notes that the underlying anthropological foundation of the *Phenomenology* predates the "phenomenological anthropology" developed by Heidegger in *Being and Time* (see *IRH* 259n). The fact that Heidegger never ceased to stress that his philosophy is anything but anthropological in tendency—that Dasein does not directly correspond to the human—of course does nothing to sway Kojève, who after all turns Hegel, the reputed absolute idealist, into an arch-existentialist. Kojève even makes the bold claim that *Being and Time* "adds, fundamentally, nothing new to the anthropology of the *Phenomenology*" (*IRH* 259n), but that it does at least shed new light on Hegel as a philosophical humanist. Kojève further hints that Heidegger borrowed some of Hegel's ideas, particularly the notions of being-toward-death, self-transcendence, and freedom (see *IDH* 148n, 156n). His only critique in this regard is that Heidegger overlooks the Marxian themes of struggle and labor, thereby ulti-mately failing to give an adequate account of history. Kojève's attempt to fuse Marx with Hegel and Heidegger can be seen as a kind of philosophical corrective, one that results in a socially conscious and ontologically sound humanism. Taking his cue from dialectics, Kojève thus develops a synthetic worldview, whereby Hegel becomes medi-ated through key ideas of subsequent philosophers.

In "The Dialectic of the Real and the Phenomenological Method in Hegel," Kojève explores the philosophical problem of death from a Hegelian perspective, but provides plenty of his own Heideggerian interpretations and interpolations. A sample quote from this text illus-trates the entwinement of death, negativity, and freedom: "If Death is an 'appearance' of Negativity, Freedom is, as we know, another such 'appearance.' Therefore Death and Freedom are but two ('phenome-nological') aspects of one and the same thing, so that to say 'mortal' is to say 'free,' and inversely" (*IRH* 247). These three notions (Kojève tends to capitalize all major Hegelian concepts in his lectures) thus merge into a single complex, one that Kojève proceeds to disentan-gle less in terms of causality than pure phenomenology. That is, Kojève does not necessarily posit any kind of causal relation between freedom, death, and negativity such that any one is to be viewed as a consequence of the other. Death does not result *in* freedom, nor does freedom result *from* death. Similarly, death is not a subcategory or gra-dation of negativity. All three concepts are but manifestations of one another: negativity manifests itself in the human realm as death, which in turn reveals to human existence its possibility or freedom.

In an effort to sort out this thorny problem of the freedom of death, Kojève grapples with the question of suicide. Only human beings, he argues, have the capability of taking their own lives. Unlike animals and other creations of nature, humans can voluntarily, that is freely, put an end to their existence. As dialectical beings defined by nega-tivity, we are free to die, like Kirilov in Dostoyevsky's *The Devils* (see *IRH* 226, 248n).[55] Indeed, Kirilov sees in his planned act of suicide the most radical freedom possible for humans: liberation from God and the deification of the individual. As Kojève indicates, however, suicide may well be the only way of definitively proving that God does not exist, but in the end it is fruitless, for it only converts the possibility of dying into the actuality of death. The negatively charged human being becomes a lifeless object, a static in-itself rather than a dialectical for-itself. Such an effected end erases any sense of freedom that stands to be gained from our existential understanding of our own mortality. Kojève, who repeatedly refers to the "dialectical" character of human death, insists that suicide "'manifests' freedom, it does not *realize* freedom, for it ends in nothingness and not in a free *existence*" (*IRH* 248). This delicate balance between a sustained cultivation of death and an immediate fulfillment of it finds graphic expression in the lord-bondsman conflict. In their fight for mutual recognition, neither lord nor bondsman actually kills his respective opponent; both combatants engage in an extended *risk* of life rather than an outright homicidal, or for that matter suicidal, attack.[56] This notion of risk implies "the real possibility of dying" (*IRH* 248), and hence further carries implications of freedom. As in any duel, the lord and/or bondsman can, but need not, die. In fact, a duel only defeats its own purpose if it results in the death of either antagonist. Its true meaning lies, rather, in a forced recognition of one's honor through the exposure to danger.

From the standpoint of dialectics, the possibility of death far outweighs its actualization. As Kojève declares, human death is a "dialectical overcoming" (*IRH* 254, 255) of the natural way of the flesh; it is transcendence in a nonmetaphysical sense. That is, in contrast to the metaphysical notion of death as the gateway to a transcendent reality (for example, immortality of the soul, Christian afterlife, pagan immortalization), Kojève's anthropological view entails *self*-transcendence on the part of the individual. In the absence of theology or metaphysics, death becomes sheer immanence, belonging solely to the domain of the human. Death thus acquires an individuating function, for it is the unique possibility and indeed property of each existing human being. As Kojève states in terms that we will eventually encounter in Rilke and Heidegger: "The death of Man . . . is an *immanent* law, an *auto-overcoming:* it is truly *his* death—that is, something that is proper to him and belongs to him as his own" (*IRH* 245). Of course, this idea of death as an individual experience is an anthropological revision of

Hegel, who sees in human finitude a necessary supersession of Spirit. But Kojève does not totally ignore this larger picture; he, too, regards death as a central ingredient of history, but of *human* history. His exploration of this broader historical context comes up somewhat short in these particular lectures from 1934–35, no doubt because he had already pursued the relations between the mortality of the autonomous individual and of the socialized citizen in his courses from the previous academic year. These courses were significantly grouped under the title "The Idea of Death in Hegel's Philosophy" as they draw on a broad spectrum of Hegel's works, from the obscure Jena lectures and writings of 1801–07 to the well-known *Philosophy of Right,* published in 1821.

Kojève's basic thesis is that death plays a major role in the Hegelian System—indeed that "the 'dialectical' or anthropological philosophy of Hegel is in the final analysis *a philosophy of death*" (*IDH* 124). Kojève places Hegel within a sweeping arc of cultural history that extends back to the Judeo-Christian separation of the human from nature. Judeo-Christianity, he claims, is at root an anthropocentric worldview insofar as it considers the essence of man distinct from that of the natural world. The human being, according to this long-established tradition, is a free and individual creation, not the representative of one animal species among others, as asserted for instance by Hellenic science. The Judeo-Christian human stands outside the laws of nature, which is, after all, associated with sin. The problem that this otherwise useful anthropology poses for Hegel/Kojève lies in the further religious elevation of man, as nonnature, into a spiritual and even immortal being. Man, created in the image of God, is not only opposed to his natural environment, but transcends it such that the final reality he strives for lies far beyond his known existence. This theological-metaphysical concept of transcendence in the beyond runs counter to the existential-anthropological notion of self-transcendence in the here and now. According to Kojève, Hegel finds himself halfway between these two paradigms: he accepts the Judeo-Christian conception of the human but not the metaphysics of immortality that goes with it. This means that Hegel ultimately rejects God and embraces man; his philosophy is thus fundamentally atheistic. The human is a finite being, forever attached to existence, and Spirit is "the spatio-temporal totality of the natural World"—or, as Kojève puts it more radically: "Spirit is Man-in-the-World: the mortal Man who lives in a World without God and who speaks of all that exists in it and of all that he creates in it, including himself" (*IDH* 123). This absence of God and the resultant deification of the human seems a more fitting description of Nietzsche's philosophy than of Hegel's. Kojève effectively turns Hegel into a philosophical anthropologist par excellence, one that surpasses even Nietzsche in investing man with the power of self-creation. Hegelian man never ceases to transcend himself through negation and hence has no need of becoming a "'*Super*-man'" (*IDH* 136)—for he has been overcoming himself all along. As "*Negativity* incarnate" (*IDH* 131), man is the true creator and fashioner of his existence. Humans therefore have no use for an ideal *Übermensch* and can certainly dispense with God as well.

Given the equivalence of negativity and death, the human is also automatically "*death* incarnate" (*IDH* 151). Kojève often describes the essence of man in precisely such poetically vivid terms. He for instance defines the human being as "[a] death that lives a human life" (*IDH* 134) and further declares that: "To be a Man—is, for Hegel, to be able and to know how to die" (*IDH* 148). From an existential point of view, death is thus the very lifeblood of man; it determines his entire identity and potentiality. Without its continual presence and menace, man would be reduced to a brute being, with no capacity for change. As Kojève never tires to mention, humans set themselves apart from animals by virtue of the fact that they have the freedom to dispose over their fate. Granted, animals fight each other too, but only because they are forced to out of the sheer necessity of survival (for example, consumption, self-defense, and mating). Only humans voluntarily submit to a life-and-death struggle for the sole sake of prestige or recognition. Moreover, man is the only being "capable of committing suicide" (*IDH* 151). This notion of capability (*Fähigkeit* in Hegel's German) remains the most crucial factor in the self-definition of man. Hegel, in the eyes of Kojève, is all about possibility, potentiality, and freedom. The fact that humans possess the ability, rather than feel the necessity, to kill themselves is precisely what constitutes their existentiality. Human beings must be willing to risk their lives if they expect to gain autonomy and selfhood.

But Hegel's philosophy does not solely revolve around the individual, even for Kojève. Death has both personal-existential and universal-historical significance. The mortality of particular individuals points to the more general issues of temporality and historicity. As a finite being, man exists temporally and therefore historically. Indeed, history becomes a kind of anthropogenesis; historical change is but another word for human development in Kojève's view. As a singular form of self-consciousness, man is gradually taken up and integrated into ever more organized communal structures, the highest of which Hegel, in his later philosophy, regards as the State. Within the context of this more expansive realm, citizens risk their lives in war for political rather than personal recognition. The struggle between lord and bondsman thus symbolizes two levels of death: that of the individual and that of the collective. Whether in the form of a one-on-one duel or a grand-scale war, the possibility of death remains critical for the determination of temporality, both of human finitude and world history. Death, says Kojève, functions as "the ultimate basis and the first mover of History" (*IDH* 142). What is more, he suggests that *absolute* knowledge consists of man's complete comprehension of his death as *absolute* freedom—not, presumably, the abstract and unmediated kind that runs rampant in times of revolution, but the synthesized realization of a true dialectical progression.

This view of death as absolute freedom forms the pinnacle of Kojève's already extreme anthropological and indeed thanatological reading of Hegel, who is anything but a rational idealist in the eyes of his twentieth century French interpreters. Jean Wahl, the original anthropological revisionist of Hegel in France, cites the following anecdote: "During a lesson in which the master was illustrating the way that systems destroy and then succeed one another, one of his disciples . . . made the remark: 'Look, this man is death itself; no wonder why everything is supposed to perish.'"[57] This statement seems telling given the French existentialist tendency to dwell on the superlative of death in Hegel's dialectical philosophy. Indeed, here the philosopher himself becomes the very incarnation of death, or, to speak with

Kojève: *la mort incarnée*. Death thus comprises more than just a major theme in Hegel's writings. It is the prime mover of the dialectic, and as such the basis of the entire Hegelian system.

2

Hölderlin

Dialectical Death and Ontological Guilt

[W]ithout death there is no life.
—Hölderlin, *Hyperion*

By the time the *Phenomenology of Spirit* appeared in the spring of 1807, Hegel's erstwhile companion and collaborator had suffered a mental breakdown from which he would never recover. Hölderlin, who had lost contact with Hegel since the latter's move to Jena in 1801, and had experienced his share of bouts with nervous disorders throughout the early 1800s, became permanently incapacitated in the fall of 1806. His life thus became split exactly into two halves. From 1770 to 1806 he functioned for the most part as a relatively normal—albeit highly gifted and somewhat temperamental—human being, producing some of the greatest poetry of the German language. The second half of his life, 1807–43, was spent back in Tübingen in the care of a family not his own. For these latter 36 years, a period during which his reputation as a poet was gradually spreading throughout Germany, he remained unaware of his past identity and previous literary production. The most critical phase of Hölderlin's development with respect to the problem of death remains, however, his Frankfurt/Homburg years, particularly the time he spent together with Hegel.

79

During this stretch of creative partnership from early 1797 through 1800, he worked on the second volume of *Hyperion* as well as on his *Empedocles* project, both of which evince numerous parallels to the main ideas expressed in Hegel's Frankfurt manuscripts. Generally speaking, a pronounced dialectical or at least synthetic mode of thought operates throughout Hölderlin's writings, whether these be literary, epistolary, or theoretical in nature. As with Hegel, Hölderlin's entire way of thinking revolves around the reconciliation of opposites and the overcoming of dualisms. More specifically, death pervades the pages of his texts. My discussion of Hölderlin will pursue this theme of death within the broader pattern of dialectics. I will mainly focus on his unfinished drama *The Death of Empedocles,* but will also consider a variety of other works, including the novel *Hyperion* as well as a selection of essays, letters, and poems.

THE PROBLEM OF UNIFICATION AND DIALECTICS

Even before his collaboration with Hegel in Frankfurt, Hölderlin was striving for a solution to the metaphysical dualisms that haunted the Enlightenment thinking of his day. Thus, while Hegel was still deeply entrenched in dualistic paradigms during his Kantian phase in Berne, Hölderlin had already been taking major steps toward developing a unification philosophy and aesthetic. He articulates this goal in a number of letters and essays and, more obliquely, in his poetic works. As a prelude to my analysis of death and its dialectical function in *Hyperion* and *Empedocles,* I will discuss Hölderlin's general conception of dialectics, though it is important to note that he never uses this precise term, even in its adjectival form. Like the early Hegel, Hölderlin does not advocate a dialectical philosophy as such; his approach is far less methodical. He is simply—and, in the end, rather naively—trying to restore a sense of unity to a fragmented world that has become alienated from its classical roots. Like Goethe, Schiller, Hegel, and many other Grecophiles of the time, Hölderlin yearned for the holistic life of the ancient Greek citizen, who was both autonomous individual and participant in the universal. The ideal of *hen kai pan* that Hölderlin and Hegel pursued well beyond their seminary days expresses precisely this aim of finding an underlying unity in the midst of a chaotic plurality. The comparatively brief years of Hölderlin's literary activity are filled with concerted attempts to overcome the subject-object divide and instill a sense of harmony in the torn existence of the modern individual.

"Judgment and Being" (1795)

In a theoretical sketch from 1795 that goes by the title "Urteil und Sein" (Judgment and Being), Hölderlin makes a tentative attempt to find a dialectical solution to the division between subject and object, a division that he believes inevitably arises through conscious acts of judgment or reflection. His point is more effectively made in the original German: *Urteil* (judgment) corresponds etymologically or at least morphologically to *Ur-teilung,* an "original separation."[1] Consciousness is thus more than just intentional; it is literally divisive, for it produces a troublesome rift between human existence and a totalized experience of being. This latter state, being, "expresses the connection between subject and object" (*SWB* 2:502/*ELT* 37), but it remains an unattainable ideal for us moderns. The best we can do is to strive for a more complete sense of identity through the very separating power of consciousness. This attempt involves steps already familiar to us from Hegel's Frankfurt writings. Yet Hölderlin is a couple years ahead of his friend in the pursuit of this problem. Hölderlin replies to the question of "how is self-consciousness possible?" by saying: "In opposing myself to myself, separating myself from myself, yet in recognizing myself as the same in the opposed regardless of this separation" (*SWB* 2:503/*ELT* 38). Here we have the basic dialectical pattern of identity–difference–differentiated identity that Hegel never tired to locate at the heart of reality. Hölderlin goes on to emphasize that identity is "not a union of object and subject" and hence not equivalent to absolute being (*SWB* 2:503/*ELT* 38). Identity is rather the mediated and constructed result of a three-stage progression carried out by consciousness, which is more than just a cognitive faculty; it is an activity. Absolute being, on the other hand, simply *is*—a primordial state impervious to change and off-limits to human consciousness.

One cannot but notice here the Hegelian categories of for-itself and in-itself, but Hölderlin does not rely on this terminology. His language in this text seems far more reminiscent of Fichte, whose writings he studied throughout 1794 and whose lectures he regularly attended at the University of Jena in late 1794 to mid-1795. In fact, Hölderlin probably composed this sketch for his own clarification of Fichte's challenging philosophy. Letters from the same year also contain deliberations on the Fichtean problem of subject and object.[2] By 1796, Hölderlin developed concrete philosophical goals in the wake of his preoccupation with Fichte.[3] In a letter to Immanuel Niethammer, a professor at Jena and a colleague of the famous philosopher, he describes the aims of his latest project: "In the philosophical letters, I want to discover the principle which explains to me the divisions in which we think and exist, yet which is also capable of dispelling the conflict between subject and object, between our self and the world, yes, also between reason and revelation" (*SWB* 3:225/*ELT* 131–32). Hölderlin never carried through with this plan to issue a series of "philosophical letters" in the tradition of Schiller's *On the Aesthetic Education of Man*. But his next major undertaking, one that did eventually reach completion, would grapple with what he perceived to be the fundamental crisis of modern existence: our alienation from a holistic state of being.

The Theme of All-Unity in Hyperion

Hölderlin's novel *Hyperion* occupied him throughout most of the 1790s. Although the final version consists of two volumes, published consecutively in 1797 and 1799, the original germination of the project dates back to 1792. A number of preliminary drafts have survived, the most important of which for my present purposes are the *Thalia*-fragment from 1794 (so dubbed because it appeared in Schiller's journal *Neue Thalia*) and the penultimate version from 1795. Based on these manuscripts and the final work itself, I will discuss some of the main dialectical elements in *Hyperion* and then pursue the theme of death within the overall scope of the novel, devoting special attention to the second volume. This part was composed during the initial stages of the *Empedocles* project and thus anticipates several key aspects of the drama. One notes above all a correlation between the death of

Diotima and that of Empedocles, both of whom refuse, in perfect keeping with the inward turn of dialectics, to separate life from death. As a consequence of this dialectical internalization of death, they draw existential meaning from their resolve to die and indeed embrace their mortality as a supreme affirmation of life.

All the drafts of *Hyperion* are replete with the word Geist (Spirit) as well as its cognates *Begeisterung* and *begeistert*. In the final version of the novel, at least one of these three variants appear on practically every page. For Hölderlin as for Hegel, Geist is not some kind of abstract entity or force that hovers somewhere above the real world; rather, it participates in our lives and instantiates the phenomena that we encounter daily. Spirit needs the phenomenal world in order to manifest itself and exercise its unifying influence. Like the power of love in the early Hegel, Spirit can bring people together and, more importantly, unite them with Nature and the Divine, the two chief metaprinciples of Hölderlin's unification philosophy. Those that Geist lays hold of are *Begeisterte,* individuals so filled with Spirit that they learn to transcend their distinct sense of individuality and gain insight into the underlying unity of all things. The common German word for "enthusiasm" and "rapture," *Begeisterung,* thus implies trans-individuality and universality. Hölderlin's texts rely on these variants of Geist as vital unifying attitudes to which all humans can aspire. He also invokes the element of ether (*Äther*) as a further force of unification. We all breathe and are therefore imbued with this intangible yet life-giving substance, a more rarified and coalescent form of air. Both Spirit and ether, like the Greek *pneuma* and Latin *spiritus,* breathe life into an otherwise dead world. Individuals infused with spirit, the "bespirited," are better able to overcome the partitions that delimit the manifold data of reality, including the sharply defined contours of their own subjectivity.[4]

Throughout the *Thalia*-fragment, Hölderlin insists on the necessity of "unification" (*Vereinigung*), or better put, *re*unification, since he envisions a lost ideal to which we will one day return. In Hyperion's discussions with the ethereal Melite, a forerunner of Diotima in the later drafts, a clear dialectical model is presented: original union–separation–reunion. In more concrete terms, Hölderlin outlines three cycles of human history: an ancient state of universal harmony; our modern existence of discord; and the future promise of a restored whole. But the real question remains: how to reinstate such an ideal? Hegel of course believes in the built-in teleology of dialectical movement, which gradually absorbs the differences of the world, especially the grand disparity between subject and substance. Hölderlin similarly realizes that reunification cannot be brought about without some kind of action or mediation. But he offers a more varied and nuanced solution to the problem.

Hölderlin suggests that through the process of *Bildung,* a loaded word in the German tradition implying "education" through literal "formation," we can become reintegrated with the absolute. Hegel, too, often speaks of *Bildung* in connection with the formative moments of the dialectic. But whereas Hegel envisions a fluid dialectical movement of universal Spirit, Hölderlin thinks in terms of a more halting and human-driven progression. In both the *Thalia*-fragment and the preface to the penultimate draft of *Hyperion* (see SWB 2:177, 256), he speaks of an "eccentric path" that we all must travel, one that extends from our naïve state of childhood to a more self-conscious and perfected form of existence known as *Bildung.* This nonlinear progress or orbit (Hölderlin's image is most likely borrowed from astronomy) describes the somewhat erratic development of Hyperion, the latter-day Greek who seeks a reunion with the totalized world of his ancient homeland.[5] It also demarcates the poles of a less historical and more personalized fulfillment of unity. That is, in contrast to the grand-scale and somewhat clichéd triadic paradigm of harmonious antiquity–discordant modernity–reharmonized futurity, Hölderlin outlines a scheme that more closely conforms to the arc of human development. At one end of the ontological spectrum lies the existence of the child, who displays an original proximity to being; at the other, there dwells the prospect of regaining wholeness through self-formation. As Hölderlin makes especially clear in the first volume of the published novel, children are concordant beings that possess all the ideals of unification philosophy: beauty, divinity, freedom, and immortality. "The child is wholly what it is, and that is why it is so beautiful" (*SWB* 2:17/*H* 5), says Hyperion early on in volume one. Translated into more philosophical terms, this means that a child represents complete self-identity.

The innocence of childhood soon, however, yields to the conscious phase of adulthood, during which we become disconnected from being and grow out of tune with the natural rhythm of the world. Since it is physically impossible to recapture the purity of our experiences as children, we can only strive to perfect ourselves and thereby achieve a totalized form of existence. This cultivation of our inner potential requires a conscious effort, which further implies that the feeling of totality we stand to gain will not completely resemble our original unity with being. As in any dialectic, the result will be reflected upon, hence mediated and modified. In other words, we will become more self-conscious, which has both its advantages and disadvantages. On the one hand, we will have lost the childlike innocence of pure identity; on the other, we will have effected a change through our own actions, thereby proving all the more worthy of a new union. Hölderlin's formulates this overall problem of modern existence as follows:

> The blessed unity, Being, in the true sense of the word, is lost to us and we had to lose it if we are to strive for it and attain it. We tear ourselves loose from the peaceful *Hen kai Pan* of the world in order to create it through ourselves. We have fallen out with nature, and what once, as one might believe, was One now finds itself in conflict, and lordship and bondage change on both sides. We often feel as if the world were everything and we nothing; but often, too, as if we were everything and the world nothing. Hyperion also divided himself between these two extremes. (*SWB* 2:256)

Hölderlin further indicates that we have no chance of reaching either of these extremes, but that only an "infinite approximation" (*SWB* 2:256) is possible. Any hope for a return to original unity thus remains foreclosed from the start and we must learn to accept the next best thing. In a letter to Schiller (dated September 4, 1795) written around the same time as this penultimate draft of Hyperion, he uses similar language to express his conviction that we can only approach, but never fully realize, this ideal:

> I am seeking to develop the idea of an infinite progress of philosophy, to show that the unyielding demand which must be put to every system, namely the unity of subject and object in an absolute Ego or however one wishes to call it, is indeed possible aesthetically, in the

intellectual intuition, but theoretically only through an infinite approximation, like the approximation of a square to a circle. (*SWB* 3:203)

Hölderlin makes a crucial qualifying statement here, namely that the union of subject and object is only possible in the realm of aesthetics. This implies that art, in contrast to theoretical modes of inquiry like philosophy, can perhaps succeed in bridging the gap between human existence and overall being. Schiller, after all, ascribes a similar totalizing function to beauty in his *Aesthetic Letters,* which were published earlier that year. Hölderlin's own belief in the unifying potential of art finds its most condensed expression in the transcendent concept of Beauty (*Schönheit*), which he identifies with a unified state of being. As he writes toward the very end of the preface of the penultimate draft: "It [being] is present–as Beauty. As Hyperion says, a new kingdom awaits us, where Beauty is queen" (*SWB* 2:257). This newly formulated ideal dominates the discourse of unification in the final version of the novel.

Beauty remains the most consistent manifestation of unity in *Hyperion* and is invoked throughout its pages. It is the cosmic "one and all " and as such the absolute ideal that Hyperion has been seeking amidst the spiritual ruins of modern humanity. Much like Hegelian Spirit, Hölderlin's concept of Beauty encompasses art and religion, and furthermore reigns with God-like supremacy. Hölderlin is obviously working with a Platonic model, as we have witnessed in the sketch he conceived together with Hegel and perhaps Schelling, "The Oldest System-Program of German Idealism." In the context of the novel, this notion of Beauty manifests itself both on an aesthetic/literary and a theoretical/philosophical level. With respect to the former, it becomes embodied in the figure of Diotima, with whom Hyperion falls in love less for her personality (which is practically nonexistent) than for the idea of Beauty that she personifies. Diotima comes across as anything but a flesh-and-blood character with a defined personality. She is, rather, completely one-dimensional and fulfills the sole purpose of grounding the abstract idea of Beauty in the material world so that Hyperion can concretely experience his long-sought objective. Moreover, she brings "equipoise" (*Gleichgewicht*) into Hyperion's easily agitated soul (*SWB* 2:87/*H* 63) and thus helps him along the way toward attaining a more harmonious condition. The absolute concept of Beauty is further conveyed philosophically in the phrase *hen diapheron heautô,* an axiom attributed to Heraclitus but which Hölderlin probably found in Plato's *Symposium,* from where he also borrowed the name of Diotima.[6] This principle, which Hölderlin translates as *das Eine in sich selber unterschiedene* ("the one differentiated in itself"), articulates the "very being of Beauty" (*SWB* 2:92/*H* 67). It is a more dynamic version of *hen kai pan* and illustrates, according to its originator Heraclitus, the simultaneity of harmony and strife that is embedded in all things. Its more standard rendering in English runs something like: "though at variance with itself, it agrees with itself."[7] In *Hyperion,* this Hericlitean phrase functions as a fitting motto for dialectics, since it contains *in nuce* the notion of an interactive relation between identity and difference. The One is both identical and non-identical to itself. It is split into different phenomena, but these do not operate independently from the greater whole; nor can the whole exist without its many distinct and unique parts. This formula for Beauty transcends unification thinking, which tends to privilege the final result of synthesis over the gradual process of differentiation and identification. Activity and movement underlie Hyperion's newfound maxim of *hen diapheron heautô,* according to which the unified totality actively divides itself and dynamically intermingles with the diverse instantiations of its own ultimate being. The interaction here is ongoing and never reaches a particular goal or point of termination. Hyperion, in other words, sees in this law a fundamental ontological truth rather than a teleological explanation of the world. Indeed, there is no higher teleology at work here, just the sheer inner workings of being.

Hyperion elaborates on the dialectical ideal of *hen diapheron heautô* during a speech praising the ancient Athenians, who he claims were able to find the proper balance between individual autonomy and universal freedom. Unlike modern Europeans, the citizens of fifth century Athens had no need of education/formation, as they were perfectly adapted to their environment from the start. They capitalized on the dialectic of unity and plurality, modeling their entire existence on its laws. The fact that Hölderlin applies Heraclitus's principle to a past culture does not mean that it should be viewed as historically restrictive and hence outmoded in the modern age. It is, on the contrary, a dialectic that has always been present in the world, but that has seldom been perceived by the humans who are intimately involved in its movement. Hyperion himself sometimes fails to discern this long-obscured essence of reality, but he nonetheless persists in his pursuit "to be one with all that lives," as he repeatedly exclaims in the novel. Through his contact with Diotima, the incarnation of Beauty, Nature, and the Divine, he gradually comes to realize that he is part of the greater dialectic of being. This awareness fully sets in during the Athenian episode that concludes volume one, a section of the novel that contains the kernel of Hölderlin's dialectical thinking. Here Hyperion states for instance: "'Sacred Nature, thou art the same within me and without. It cannot be so hard to unite what is outside of me and the divine within me'" (*SWB* 2:100/*H* 73). But unification is not so easy either. As we have seen in the *Phenomenology,* it requires a great deal of work—including some 500 pages of arduous reading—to synthesize subject and object. In order to better determine whether Hyperion realizes his ambition of uniting his individual subjectivity with the substance of the world and thereby participate in the cosmic *hen kai pan,* we need to look beyond the content of the novel and examine more closely its structure.

Structural and Dialectical Unity in Hyperion

Hyperion can be considered a dialectical novel insofar as it progressively overcomes the differences between the subjectivity of the main character and the external reality of his surroundings. Hyperion is constantly confronted with separation and must somehow try to reconcile himself with the numerous noncorrespondences that stand in the way of his quest for universal harmony. As he will eventually come to realize, discord is inseparable from unity, but this insight does not occur until the very end of the novel: "'Like lovers' quarrels are the dissonances of the world. Reconciliation is there, even in the midst of strife, and all things that are parted find one another again'" (*SWB* 175/*H* 133). As we will soon see, the novel's conclusion merges with its beginning, forming a kind of dialectical circle of development whereby the final outcome is already programmed into the initial point of departure. Like the *Phenomenology,* Hölderlin's *Hyperion* traces the journey of a divided consciousness toward self-recognition and features all the oscillations and vicissitudes found in Hegel's philosophical *Bildungsroman:* desire, conflict, departure, death, alienation—and ultimately reunion. Hyperion's final state of contemplation even resembles that of the absolute-knowing Spirit, for both reflect on their progress from the higher seat of a self-apprehended existence.[8]

Hyperion encounters difference on all levels, ranging from his narrow personal experiences to his general perception of the cosmos. He becomes "separated" (the expressions *Trennung* and *sich trennen* occur throughout the novel) from his various friends and mentors (Adamas, Alabanda, and Diotima), yet learns that this parting has a deeper dialectical necessity: "'We part only to be more intimately one, more divinely at peace with all, with each other'" (*SWB* 2:162/*H* 123). A more persistent sense of estrangement exists between the contemporary state of Hyperion's native Greece and its past golden age, a problem that he will, according to Diotima's prophesy, one day rectify in his capacity as a "'teacher of our people'" (*SWB* 2:100/*H* 73). The ultimate separation, however, lies between the fragmented condition of modern life and the pantheistic whole of being. The theme of difference is further manifested in Hyperion himself, who functions as both narrating subject and narrated substance. Hyperion actively reconstructs his experiences through the process of writing. The letters that he composes to Bellarmin form the premise of the novel, yet Hölderlin weaves a far more complex narrative than it appears on the surface.[9] *Hyperion* is an unconventional epistolary novel not so much because of its predominately monologic form. Goethe's *The Sufferings of Young Werther* from 1774, which set the standard for the genre in Germany, also lacks the quality of a genuine correspondence, as the letters of Werther's interlocutor remain excluded from the text. But Werther's epistles at least exude an emotional immediacy not unlike that of a journal. Hyperion's communications, while equally effusive, seem less direct and are clearly mediated by a kind of meta-author who looks back on his previous experiences. The entire novel can be said to constitute an act of recollection by means of which Hyperion gains a completely new understanding of his past actions and emotions—and, by extension, of his own existence.

The approximation of recollecting narrator and recollected protagonist is borne out in the novel's structure. The Hyperion that relates the events from his self-imposed exile at the end of the book merges into the Hyperion who has just returned to Greece on the opening page. The endpoint of narration thus seems to lead full circle into the actual storyline of the novel, which definitively gets underway after the first two transitional letters in which Hyperion gives voice to the sordid state of affairs in his homeland and to his uncontained desire for all-unity. Hence, between the second letter, which represents the chronologically most advanced point of the novel, and the final reflective one, Hyperion recounts the events that led him to this very juncture. This notion of circularity often serves as an ideal of literary narrative. Coleridge, for instance, asserts that "The common end of all *narrative,* nay of *all,* Poems is to convert a *series* into a *Whole:* to make those events, which in real or imagined History move on in a *strait* Line, assume to our Understandings a *circular* motion—the snake with it's [*sic*] Tail in it's [*sic*] Mouth."[10] Yet the circle never fully closes in *Hyperion,* or in Coleridge's metaphor: the snake never gets hold of its tail. Hölderlin inserts a kind of loophole into the greater circular structure of his novel, creating an Archimedean point of reflection from which Hyperion surveys his past development as it unfolds throughout the plot of the novel. With the closing words, "So I thought. More soon" (*SWB* 2:175/*H* 133), Hölderlin breaks the circle of narration, injecting an incongruous sense of futurity into the seam of his near perfectly rounded novel. Although this final statement led some of his contemporaries to anticipate a third volume, Hölderlin never had any intention for a sequel. From a dialectical point of view, he had already accomplished a consummately structured and self-contained work of art by adding a speculative spiral to the near-closed narrative circularity. The last two sentences create a gap through which Hyperion noticeably rises to a higher perch of consciousness. As one critic has effectively put it: "The circle never closes, it folds upward into a spiral that ascends to an overview over its own progression."[11] The image of an ascending circle or spiral is essential to the Romantic imagination, for it "fuses the idea of the circular return with the idea of linear progress."[12] Hegel's famous image of philosophy as a "circle of circles," in which one circle "breaks through" (*durchbricht*) its limits and creates an even wider one (see *Encyclopaedia* no. 15, *W* 8:60),[13] further describes the structure of *Hyperion* with striking accuracy.

The story that Hyperion tells also resembles a dialectical process of remembrance in the Hegelian sense of *Er-innerung,* whereby the constant mediation of difference culminates in the unity of subject and object. Like the Calvary of absolute Spirit, Hyperion's ultimate perspective affords a broader vista of his progression and a firmer grasp of his identity. It remains difficult to say, however, whether Hyperion actually arrives at complete self-identity through a final *Aufhebung*— or, for that matter, what Hegel's philosophical notion of absolute synthesis realistically entails. The figure of Hyperion was certainly conceived by Hölderlin as a "resolution of dissonances in a particular character" (*SWB* 2:13/*H* 1). Moreover, there can be no doubt that Hyperion attains a greater self-awareness and a more totalized existence as a result of his reflections. But to claim that he becomes a self-coincidental subject-object in the mold of absolute-knowing Spirit would only place excessive theoretical demands on the novel and result in a confusion of literature and philosophy. Nevertheless, *Hyperion* achieves its own aesthetic form of totalization. As Hölderlin declares in the preface to the final version, his book is to be understood not as a lifeless *Compendium* or handbook but as an organic whole, a "plant" (*SWB* 2:13/*H* 1), which is itself a spiraling life form. Not unlike vegetation, literature is trop-ical (from the Greek *trepein,* "to turn"): it does not follow a strictly literal and linear course, but twists and contorts itself in its diverse modes of expression. This idea of the organic work of art, which dominated aesthetic discourse in the late eighteenth century, further implies totality and autonomy, both of which describe the status of Hölderlin's novel and the eventual state of Hyperion within it. *Hyperion* the novel becomes a concrete manifestation of the unity that Hyperion the main character has been seeking all along. It is an aesthetic organism—the imagery of plant life reappears throughout the novel—in which all the parts smoothly mesh with the whole.

As such, it fits the artistic ideal of German Classicism and early Romanticism. Thus, while Hölderlin has his doubts about the possibility of overcoming the rupture between subject and object, he seems to suggest that there is a way around this problem. If unity can never amount to more than an "infinite approximation" (*SWB* 2:256) in theory and philosophy, then one can at least construct a cohesive and self-reflective system in the realm of art.

DIALECTICAL DEATH IN *HYPERION*

Much like art, death takes on a totalizing and even unifying function in *Hyperion*. It offers the possibility of unification through the cosmic *hen kai pan*. This dialectical function of death becomes most apparent in the figure of Diotima, who, as the very incarnation of Beauty, dies in a fashion that underscores the fundamental theme of unity in the novel. Her parting may appear to be a separation and hence an interruption of life, but she does not view it as such. Her death, rather, is as harmonious as her entire existence and more importantly *completes* her life in the sense that it perfects and totalizes it. (The German verb *vollenden* plays an important role in this context.) As for Hyperion, he deliberates on death but does not carry out his intentions to follow Diotima into the realm of all-unity. Nor does he capitalize on the freedom of death after the example of his friend Alabanda. Hyperion certainly shows an awareness of death as freedom and existential completion, but in the end elects to pursue his calling as a poet and educator of his people. As we will see later in this chapter, Hölderlin will conceive another project whose hero resolutely seeks death as a summation of life. But as Hyperion himself realizes toward the end of the novel, he is no Empedocles; that is, he does not yet have the plenitude of being that would justify committing such a grand act of self-realization.

In each of its drafts, *Hyperion* contains a surprising number of references to death, a theme that strangely seems to elude most interpretations of the novel.[14] Even as early as the *Thalia*-fragment, death and its compounds — for example, *Todesangst* (fear of death), *Todesbote,* (messenger of death), *Todesurteil* (death sentence) — appear on nearly every page. Subsequent drafts also feature numerous invocations of death. These are reworked in the final version and take on even greater significance, particularly in the second volume, which was published in 1799 and will receive the most detailed treatment here.

Barbarism and cultural decay prevail from the very outset of the novel. Hyperion, who has returned to his homeland after a long period of absence, finds himself surrounded by emptiness and death. He hears a jackal singing its "wild threnody" (*SWB* 2:14/*H* 2), sees the skeletal ruins of classical architecture, and feels as if a "coffin lid were being nailed shut over me" (*SWB* 2:14/*H* 2). His entire country resembles a "vast graveyard" (*SWB* 2:15/*H* 3) and Hyperion half expects to join the dead soon after his disheartening return home. This general atmosphere of death and stagnation pervades the first book of volume one. The idealistic Hyperion, who passionately seeks to be unified with nature, is devastated whenever he confronts the fragmented reality of eighteenth century Greece. Hyperion finds some consolation in the fact that he is not alone in his disillusionment with the modern world. He encounters two other figures that transcend the present state of humanity, Alabanda and Diotima, and he comes to regard them as more than just kindred spirits. He in fact latches on to both as if they were his salvation from the modern barbarism that has invaded Greece and uprooted classical Athenian culture from its native soil. More importantly, he witnesses or at least hears secondhand of Alabanda's and Diotima's deaths, subsequently resolving upon a suicidal course of action out of which he, however, emerges unscathed.

As an epitome of the heroic type, Alabanda strives to recover the classical ideal by forceful means: he is a member of the Nemesis League, a clandestine patriotic if not terrorist organization. Although Hyperion will later be repulsed by the crassness of the group and thereby jeopardize his relationship with Alabanda, he remains for the present at the side of his comrade. This bond of friendship finds expression in the figures of Castor and Pollux, who, far from remaining a mere symbolic constellation in the heavens, become embodied in Hyperion and Alabanda themselves (see *SWB* 2:44/*H* 27). The fact that Hölderlin conceives of their relationship in these terms is significant in light of the theme of death. Hyperion's role as the undying twin Pollux will become apparent by the end of the novel, for he alone goes on living despite his overenthusiastic claim "that it is better to die because one has lived than to live because one never lived!" (*SWB* 2:48/*H* 30). Alabanda/Castor, on the other hand, will choose death at the hands of the Nemesis League for breaking his oath of brotherhood in favor of renewed friendship with his twin Hyperion/Pollux. It is here in the second book of the second volume that Alabanda once again plays a major role in the novel. He appears at Hyperion's bedside after the latter is wounded in battle and reveals to his friend the conditions under which he entered the league. His decision to part from the secret fraternity amounts to no less than a death sentence, which he freely accepts. Alabanda even rejects Hyperion's suggestion to join him and Diotima in their future life together, instead opting for his ideal of "freedom," a word that he repeatedly utters in the novel. Alabanda's notion of freedom is wide-ranging; it transcends political goals and embraces the entirety of human existence. Which is to say that it extends to death, a prospect that Alabanda acknowledges and indeed welcomes. Hyperion's response to Alabanda's resolution underscores the notion of death as existential fulfillment and perfection: "'Yes! die,' I cried, 'die! Your heart is glorious enough, your life is ripe, like grapes in autumn. Go, perfected one [*Vollendeter*]! I would go with you, if there were no Diotima'" (*SWB* 2:154/*H* 116).

Hyperion does not yet realize that in the meantime Diotima also finds herself resolutely facing death. However, in contrast to Alabanda, she does not seek to die as a result of conscious deliberation. Her death, rather, occurs out of an inner necessity, as if her existence, even more so than that of Hyperion and Alabanda, were so irreconcilable with the modern world that the only possible recourse called for her to vanish from its face. There can be no doubt that her death is of central importance for any proper understanding of the novel and its central theme of unification. Bertaux ascribes, with some exaggeration, an even greater significance to Diotima's end, claiming that *Hyperion* could just as well be called *The Death of Diotima,* since her demise forms the cornerstone of Hölderlin's book.[15]

The exact cause of Diotima's death remains indeterminable. Her words to Hyperion also seem directed at the reader: "'seek not to explain this death to yourself!'" (*SWB* 2:160/*H* 121). Diotima does not commit suicide or otherwise appear directly responsible for her end. Her invocation of Portia, who swallowed burning coals upon her husband Brutus's military defeat, remains a comparison that has to do not with the precise manner of death but with the conduct unto it: "'I have used many words, yet the great Roman heroine died silent when her Brutus and her country were struggling in the throes of death. What better could I do in the best of my last days of life?—Yet still I feel an urgency to say many things. My life was silent; my death is loquacious'" (*SWB* 2:161/*H* 122). Indeed, Diotima speaks eloquently and extensively of her death, yet fails to shed much light on its cause. Again, she does not actively end her life, nor does she succumb to any ascertainable affliction. She simply loses all desire to go on living when she hears that Hyperion has perished in battle, and even the belated news of his survival cannot halt the course of her dying. This decline set in as early as Hyperion's departure from Calaurea and has now reached an irreversible stage. The remaining spark of life that she feels proves insufficient to rekindle her desire to remain among the living; in fact, it only leads her to reflect further on death. And here she reveals that death, far from being a sudden wish prompted by the separation from Hyperion, has actually been with(in) her for some time: "'Am I to tell you that grief for you has killed me? oh no! oh no! it was welcome to me, that grief, it gave the death that I carried within me form and grace'" (*SWB* 2:160/*H* 121). This is as plausible a cause for Diotima's end that the reader will glean from the plot of the novel.

However, on a more conceptual level Diotima's death has a definite logic and necessity. Realizing that she cannot change the world, let alone secure an adequate niche in it, she has no recourse but to die. From an existential point of view, Diotima has exhausted her potentiality and can only overcome this impasse through the possibility of death. Notara meditates on Diotima's end as follows: "'But a beautiful death is always better, Hyperion! than such a somnolent life as ours now is. . . . To grow old among young peoples seems to me a delight, but to grow old where all is old seems to me worse than anything'" (*SWB* 2:164/*H* 124). This idea of a "beautiful death" is subsequently taken up by Hyperion: "'My Diotima died a beautiful death'" (*SWB*

2:165/*H* 125). Diotima's death is thus both "necessary" and "beautiful." What this latter term is precisely supposed to mean leaves room for speculation. In a historico-anthropological context, one could interpret her death along the lines of the classical *ars moriendi,* according to which one was expected to die a good death, just as one cultivated a good life. Diotima's end in this sense is peaceful, even harmonious, much like the entire course of her existence. Like Alabanda, she has perfected herself and is thus dubbed a "[p]erfect one" (*Vollendete*) (*SWB* 2:115/*H* 83). Having brought her existence to completion, she has no choice but to fade from the scene, fully reconciled with her death as if it were a logical and natural step in her development.

Diotima's composure in the face of finitude perhaps also results from her anticipation of an afterlife. She expresses her belief in a higher sphere of unity that lies beyond the here and now. Death thus takes on metaphysical significance as a threshold to eternal life. This understanding differs, however, from the traditional Christian view, for Diotima never speaks in strict theological terms. Her death does not lead her to heaven or to God per se. In accordance with Hölderlin's own pantheistic tendencies, she invokes a plurality of gods with whom she seeks to be reunited in the ethereal spheres of the greater cosmos. This form of life-after-death corresponds to the ideal that Hyperion, Diotima, and Alabanda seek throughout the novel. Hence, rather than constituting a singular tragic event, death signals a liberation—Diotima speaks of "'the divine freedom that death gives us'" (*SWB* 2:162/*H* 123)—from the spiritually impoverished life that all three major figures are forced to endure in the modern world. Compare for instance the following words of Diotima, both a summation of her life and an assertion of her death, with the general ideal of universal harmony that recurs throughout the novel: "I shall be. How should I be lost from the sphere of life, in which eternal love, common to all, holds all natures together? how should I escape from the union that binds all beings together? . . . We part only to be more intimately one, more divinely at peace with all, with each other. We die that we may live" (*SWB* 2:162/*H* 123). Despite his constant yearning for divine union, Hyperion proves unable to follow Diotima into the world that she describes above. Nevertheless, he does have two near brushes with death. His suicidal rush into battle against the Turks is guided by self-probing questions involving freedom: "why, then, should I be afraid to seek so-called death? have I not freed myself a thousand times in thought? why should I hesitate to do it *once* in reality?" (*SWB* 2:135/*H* 101). Failing to find death in battle, he is equally unable to end his life after the loss of Diotima. In earlier drafts, Hyperion sought solace and perhaps courage in the heroic suicide of Ajax, but in each case he opted against carrying out the final act. In the published version of the novel, he contemplates his fate after the example of another classical figure, namely Empedocles. As legend would have it, the Sicilian Empedocles threw himself into the crater of Mount Etna, and Hölderlin refers here in part to Horace's account from *Ars Poetica:*

> And now tell me, what refuge remains?— Yesterday I went to the summit of Aetna. There I remembered the great Sicilian who, weary of counting the hours, knowing the soul of the World, in his bold joy in life there flung himself down into the glorious flames, for "the cold poet had to warm himself at the fire," said someone [Horace] later, to mock him.
>
> O how gladly would I have taken such mockery upon myself! but one must think more highly of oneself than I do before, thus unbidden, one can flee to Nature's heart. (*SWB* 2:166/*H* 126)

It is apparent from the above passage that Empedocles's act did not occur out of weakness or despair, but out of a sheer plenitude of being. Hyperion fails to follow suit because he does not deem himself worthy of such an assertive act in his present state of misery. Mount Etna offers him foremost a place of solitude, where he hopes to find refuge from his haunting memories of Diotima. It is not until he reaches the summit that Hyperion recalls the example of Empedocles and entertains the notion of a grand suicide. Again, in contrast to his predecessor, Hyperion has no "bold joy in life" that would, from an existential point of view, justify committing such an act. The fate of Empedocles remains an ideal, like that of Demosthenes, whose "self-sought death" and resultant "freedom" are invoked earlier in the novel (see *SWB* 2:87/*H* 62). Due to his current frame of mind, or perhaps to the more fundamental fact that he remains a modern, Hyperion is unable to assert his death in the classical manner. Although he is aware of the potential freedom that death holds, he can only look up—but not actively live up—to the precedents set by Ajax, Empedocles, and Demosthenes. One might say that he is not yet far enough along in existence to convert the prospect of death into possibility.

THE DEATH OF EMPEDOCLES: GENESIS AND DRAFTS

Of the many aspects pertaining to Empedocles's life and work, his legendary death by flame seems to have held the most fascination for Hölderlin. As I will show in this section, Hölderlin integrates into his play a number of biographical and philosophical details concerning Empedocles, demonstrating a remarkable knowledge of pre-Socratic thought at a time when their fragments had yet to be widely collected and interpreted. Still, true to the title of the unfinished drama, *The Death of Empedocles,* it is the hero's death that forms the cornerstone of Hölderlin's project, which occupied him for nearly as many years as his shaping of *Hyperion.* Due to the truncation of the work, the death of Empedocles announced in the title is never actually depicted in any of the three extant drafts. Nevertheless, this climactic moment was fixed from the start, and the fact that Hölderlin never completed the drama does not in the least diminish Empedocles's determination to die in the flames of Mount Etna. Indeed, as will later become apparent, this missing detail aligns the tragedy all the more with Heidegger's analysis of human finitude, which stresses not the moment of death but the life-long conduct unto it. In this sense, the play is perhaps best left unfinished, since Empedocles's being-toward-death remains a given from the initial scenes of all three versions.

The other major theme of the drama is the hero's tragic guilt, which motivates his determination to die in such a grandiose fashion. Although an analysis of guilt may at first glance appear to be a deviation from my main focus on death, this proves to be anything but the case upon closer scrutiny of the text. The guilt that weighs on Empedocles is a primordial fact of his existence, a kind of ontological being-guilty (*Schuldigsein*) in Heidegger's sense of the term. In both cases, the fundamental condition of guiltiness forms the ground for existential possibilities and decisions, whether of Empedocles's resolve to end his life in the crater of Etna or of Dasein's anticipatory resoluteness in the face of its own extinction. We will also see that Nietzsche takes up this theme of guilt in his early philosophy, particularly in his reflections on the tragic sense of existence.

There is no getting around the problem of fragmentation in *The Death of Empedocles,* and any attempt to analyze Hölderlin's tragedy must to some extent deal with this issue. For reasons that only allow for speculation, Hölderlin never completed the drama despite fairly detailed planning and a lengthy period of composition.[16] One may choose to note a certain irony in the fact that Hölderlin's effort to create a drama around the life and fragments of Empedocles itself ended in fragmentation. The philological tradition has striven to reconstruct the extant texts of both authors, ancient and modern, with varying results. Hermann Diels and Walther Kranz have produced what is now considered the standard edition of pre-Socratic fragments. In the last two centuries of Hölderlin scholarship, a number of editors have tried to establish a similar definitive text of the *Empedocles* drafts. Every edition of the play since its original publication in 1826 has presented the manuscripts in three distinct arrangements.[17] These often differ within themselves from one edition to the next, and in some cases discrepancies between the drafts occur so that lines from one version are transplanted to another. In the end no conclusive order exists, although Friedrich Beißner's *Stuttgarter Ausgabe,* a labor of painstaking philology that provides textual variants and a wealth of commentary on the genesis of the project, has widely been accepted as the standard edition. Dietrich F. Sattler's even more meticulous *Frankfurter Ausgabe,* a facsimile of the manuscripts, remains the culmination of textual fidelity but is not exactly what one would call reader friendly. The most recent editing job by Jochen Schmidt, which forms the basis of my analysis, claims to have improved on both of its immediate predecessors.[18] Generations of readers have of course approached the drama less critically than its editors and, on a certain level, have had to make sense of the fragments as a single work of literature, albeit an unfinished one. Yet despite its incompleteness, *The Death of Empedocles* can still be read in completion. In all of the editions, the entire text is basically there; readers from the mid-nineteenth to the early twenty-first century have merely been presented with its different configurations. What Nietzsche had read in one of the Schwab volumes from the 1800s, Heidegger for the most part encountered in the Zinkernagel and/or Pigenot editions of 1915 and 1922, and these in turn largely correspond to the versions that most readers rely on today. Thus, the basic whole of the drama has remained intact throughout its many published forms, while internally its parts have been subjected to varying degrees of alteration.

The Death of Empedocles thus presents an intriguing example of the hermeneutic problem. The relation between parts and whole is complicated by the formal aspect of the drama's threefold curtailment, which would seem to make it a text that defies the complete understanding and interpretability that hermeneutics strives to achieve. Although Hölderlin's drama may lack the self-contained wholeness that aesthetic theories since Kant have posited for the ideal work of art, it nevertheless exists in its factual entirety and hence constitutes an aesthetic corpus of its own. One can bemoan its fragmentation or appreciate it for the artistic torso that it is. Rilke's focus on the truncated statue in the poem "Archaic Torso of Apollo" parallels the latter approach. Rilke finds that the overwhelming presence of the torso more than compensates for the absence of those parts (head and limbs) that would, formally speaking, make the statue complete.[19] One must take a similar interpretive stance with *The Death of Empedocles,* whose missing acts and scenes need not detract from the aesthetic experience as a whole. In fact, as in Rilke's description of the fragmented statue, the sheer presence of the text overrides all concerns about its so-called incompletion. The circular movement of hermeneutic understanding will never reach total closure when dealing with a text like *The Death of Empedocles.* Yet only traditional hermeneutics insists on a closed circle of absolute comprehension. Modern hermeneutically inclined philosophers like Heidegger (whose own *Being and Time* remains not even half-finished) and Gadamer do not think in terms of final results. They stress, rather, the fundamental *experience* of interpretation, a potentially endless process that does not reduce the work of art to an aesthetic object of methodological inquiry. Interpreting Hölderlin's drama thus remains a hermeneutic endeavor that not only requires the reader to relate individual parts to the greater whole, but that further-more demands a processual and participatory engagement with the text much like Rilke's confrontation with the torso of Apollo. To take a cue from Gadamer: "all encounter with the language of art is an encounter with an unfinished event and is itself part of this event."[20]

Despite its splintered form, there is, after all, a unifying concep-tion behind *The Death of Empedocles,* even if Hölderlin reconceived certain themes, characters, and plot structures throughout the three drafts. Hölderlin based important elements of his tragedy on the historical figure of Empedocles, particularly the biographical detail of death by flame and the philosophical tenet of primordial guilt. A discussion of Empedocles's life and thought is thus necessary for a proper under-standing of the major ideas in the drama. This requires at least a brief examination of the original fragments attributed to Empedocles as well as of the various testimonia documenting his fate.[21]

Empedocles: Pre-Socratic and Literary Creation

Critics agree that the primary source Hölderlin consulted for the par-ticulars of his gestating play was the then standard *Lives and Opinions of Eminent Philosophers* by Diogenes Laertius. This work, written in the third century AD, is a curious compendium of material concern-ing philosophers from Thales to post-Socratic figures such as Plato and Aristotle. It indiscriminately mixes biography with philosophical teachings, and much of the information is unreliable, often apoc-ryphal. Nevertheless, the collection was the most widespread author-ity on pre-Socratic thinkers available in Germany during the eighteenth century. Hölderlin did not fail to read it in preparation for his project, as he indicates in a letter to his friend Isaak von Sinclair from December 24, 1798 (*SWB* 3:327). In his reading of Diogenes, Hölderlin would have encountered summaries of Empedocles's cosmogony as well as testimonies of his death, especially of his leap into the crater of Mount Etna. This is by no means the only version of Empedocles's death cited by Diogenes. Other sources claim that he died after falling from a char-iot at the age of 77; that he hanged himself; that he plunged not into volcanic fire but into the sea; and that he was not killed at all but exiled to the Peloponnesus.[22] Yet Empedocles's reputed suicide in the flames of Etna appears to have captivated Hölderlin more than any of the other testimonies, and tradition does in fact adhere to the version favored by Hölderlin for his play.[23] Despite his absorption in the circumstances surrounding Empedocles's death, Hölderlin does not lose sight of deeper philosophical issues. Empedocles developed the most advanced cosmogony of any pre-Socratic, one in which fire plays a fundamental part, as do the other prime elements earth, air, and water. In view of Hölderlin's own tendency to invoke such elemental forces, there would appear to be more that draws him to the ancient philosopher than mere biographical detail.

In his philosophical poem *On Nature* (*Peri physeôs*), written sometime in the mid-fifth century BC, Empedocles conceives of four pure substances that are both eternal and immutable: earth, air, fire, and water. These elements (Empedocles actually uses the term "roots" [*rizômata*], but tradition has favored the more scientific term "elements") have existed from the beginning of time and they cannot be destroyed or otherwise undergo change. They do not exist separate from reality, but inhabit all living matter in varying degrees. In addition to these four prime substances, Empedocles posits two agents that are responsible for their constant mixture and flux: Love and Strife (*Philotês* and *Neikos*). Love unites the elements and the matter that they form, while Strife or Hate separates them and causes universal dissension. Throughout the history of the cosmos, one force has tended to dominate the other. When Love prevails, the elements are uniformly mixed and the universe exists in a state of harmony, forming a single sphere as in the cosmology of Parmenides, Empedocles's philosophical predecessor. During the reign of Strife, the elements are unable to mix and thus amass separately so that each substance becomes one homogenous bulk. Empedocles maintains that his own era finds itself in a period of transition, during which both forces are active but none holds absolute sway.

The above details of Empedocles's philosophy play only a relatively minor role in Hölderlin's drama.[24] While references to the prime elements and their principal movers Love and Hate can be found in all of the drafts, they hardly occur with enough frequency to constitute a major theme. Nevertheless, Hölderlin does pick up on the dialectical undercurrent of the Empedoclean cosmogony, in which the forces of Love and Hate dynamically interact and fundamentally shape the universe. As we will soon see, the dialectics of unity and difference plays a decisive role in his literary re-creation of Empedocles, whose motivation to die in the crater of Etna stems in part from a desire to become reunited with the primal elements and thereby help equalize the dialectical imbalance of the world. But Hölderlin was also attracted to another facet of Empedocles's thought, one that the pre-Socratic expressed in his other major work, *Purifications (Katharmoi)*. Although scholars have recently tended toward the view that *On Nature* and *Purifications* actually constitute the same poem but became known under two different titles, this was not the case in Hölderlin's day, nor need it be of concern for the present analysis.[25] More important is the major shift in thematic.

The fragments that make up the *Purifications* have come to be categorized as Empedocles's religious teachings. In contrast to the physical philosophy of *On Nature, Purifications* deals with a more spiritual realm and tells a tale vaguely reminiscent of Milton, complete with such Judeo-Christian elements as Original Sin, fall from grace, and the hope for Paradise regained. Based on what one can best piece together from the fragments, Empedocles recounts the fate of the Daimones, who are transcendent entities that temporarily inhabit human bodies much like transmigrating souls. Daimones can be passed on and reincarnated without losing their essential identity. Like the Pythagoreans, who were also centered in the Greek colonies of southern Italy, Empedocles believed in palingenesis and vegetarianism. For someone like Empedocles, who claims to have been a boy, girl, bush, bird, and fish in previous lives,[26] the consumption of meat would amount to potential cannibalism. (His life as a bush, however, raises an interesting problem with regard to his prescribed vegetarian diet.) The blissful state of the Daimones, in which Love reigned supreme— here the connection to *On Nature*—and all creatures lived harmoniously, gradually gave way to the rise of Strife. For the first time, there was bloodshed, and the Daimones, soiled with this originary guilt, were exiled from their home and forced to enter the bodies of mortal creatures. "Wrapping [themselves] in an alien garb of flesh,"[27] they remain immortal but must be continually born into new living beings until their original state of Love is restored. The vegetarian imperative is thus a measure of survival according to fragment 136: "Will you not cease from harsh-sounding murder? Do you not see / that you are devouring each other in the carelessness of your thought?"[28] The consumption of meat not only leads to cannibalism, but on a more basic level repeats the same act of killing that brought about their fall. Although Empedocles never mentions the word, guilt is what characterizes the exiled state of the Daimones. It is questionable whether the Greeks, especially the pre-Socratics, had a conception of guilt or sin that approximates our own. The most common word for guilt in Attic tragedy is *aitia,* which derives from the verb *aitein,* "to ask for," "demand," often in the sense of demanding satisfaction or retribution for a crime. Hence the foremost definition of *aitia* as a "charge" or "accusation."[29] The word for sin in the New Testament is *hamartia,* which comes from a verb (*hamartanein*) that literally means "to miss the mark" (as in archery), hence "to err." At the time of Empedocles, it probably had limited moral overtones. In *Purifications* one finds, rather, the verb *amplakein* (fragment 115, v. 3), which means: "to come short of," "to lose, be bereft of," or "to sin." This latter definition is what McKirahan chooses in his translation of the crucial fragment 115, cited here in its entirety so as to give a better idea of the poem's content:

> There is an oracle of Necessity, an ancient decree of the gods,
> eternal and sealed with broad oaths,
> that whenever anyone pollutes his own dear limbs with the **sin** [my
>   emphasis] of murder,
> . . . commits offense and swears a false oath—
> divinities (DAIMONES) who possess immensely long life—
> he wanders away from the blessed ones for thrice ten thousand
>   seasons,
> growing to be through time all different kinds of mortals
> taking the difficult paths of life one after another.
> For the force of AITHER pursues them to the sea
> and the sea spits them out onto the surface of the earth, and the earth
>   into the rays

of the shining sun, and he [the sun] casts them into the vortices of
AITHER.
One receives them after another, but all hate them.
Of them I am now one, a fugitive from the gods and a wanderer,
putting my reliance on raving Strife.[30]

As becomes apparent in these final verses, Empedocles believes he
is possessed by a Daimon and consequently considers himself a sin-
ner. Indeed, his current profession as prophet, bard, and physician places
him at the upper end of the reincarnation scale.[31] Empedocles's claim
at the beginning of *Purifications* that he is a god ("I go about among
you, an immortal god, no longer mortal")[32] is probably an anticipation of his next stage in the cycle rather than an act of hubris as interpreted by Hölderlin and discussed later in this chapter. With this hint
at imminent divinity, Empedocles may be implying that the exile of
"thrice ten thousand seasons" is coming to a close. This, at least, is
the implication of the poem's title: through a series of purifications,
mainly by abstaining from the slaughter of animals, the Daimones can
cleanse themselves of sin and eventually regain paradise, in which case
the 30,000 seasons mentioned by Empedocles is not to be taken literally. Dietary and spiritual cleansing will thus hasten the purgation of
guilt and the return to an ideal state of being.

Due to the fragmentary nature of Empedocles's surviving body of
work, it remains difficult to make any definitive statements let alone
reach any final conclusions. One is utterly dependent on traditional
interpretations or accounts such as those collected in Diogenes. These
all tend to emphasize the aspects of Empedocles's philosophy discussed above: his elemental theory and religious notion of guilt.
While the former figures only marginally in Hölderlin's drama, the latter takes on all the greater importance, at least in certain phases of the
Empedocles project, a project that by no means consists solely of the
three dramatic drafts that make up the work entitled *The Death of
Empedocles*. Between 1797 and 1800 Hölderlin experimented with various literary forms (drama, poetry, essay), all in an attempt to come
to terms with the legendary death and guilt-based cosmogony of the
pre-Socratic philosopher. Since Hölderlin's project is fraught with
displacements, discontinuities, and ultimately failure, a chronologi-

cal discussion of its various stages seems the wisest approach.[33] Hölderlin continually reconceived plot, characters, and ideas throughout the genesis of *Empedocles* such that even the two most consistent themes of death and guilt undergo significant shifts in emphasis and function. A genetic analysis of these and related aspects will thus more effectively bring out the many connections to Heidegger and Nietzsche, who were both undoubtedly familiar with the various details as well as the broader scope of the tragedy.

The germ of Hölderlin's *Empedocles* enterprise can be situated as early as 1794, when he envisioned a drama revolving around the death of a more famous Greek philosopher: Socrates. At this point he was working on *Hyperion,* the first five letters of which had just appeared in Schiller's *Neue Thalia.* Hölderlin, unaware that the novel would occupy him for several more years, is barely able to contain his enthusiasm for another project, which he conveys in a letter to Neuffer from October 10, 1794: "I look forward to the day when I will be done with the whole thing, since I don't want to lose any time getting to another plan, one that lies almost closer to my heart; namely, to try to rework the death of Socrates in accordance with the ideals of Greek drama" (*SWB* 3:157). Hölderlin gives no further information about this proposed dramatization, yet two points mentioned above prove relevant for his later *Empedocles* undertaking. The first concerns death. As is the case with his later plans involving Empedocles, whose teachings are not the main impetus behind the play, Hölderlin's focus lies not on the *philosophy* but on the *death* of Socrates. His second point about the ideals of Greek drama follows from this emphasis on death. These ideals imply tragedy, and the exemplary tragic hero is hardly Socrates the elicitor of latent truth and gadfly of Athens. What makes for a good tragedy is, rather, the condemned man of the *Apology, Crito,* and *Phaedo,* who chose death over exile and calmly drank from the cup of hemlock, thereby sealing his fate in the classical manner that Hölderlin (and later Nietzsche) never ceased to admire.

Sometime between 1797 and 1800 Hölderlin composed the ode "Empedokles." A more precise dating is not possible (see *SWB* 1:667), but it suffices to note that the poem falls into the period of collaboration with Hegel in Frankfurt. In its entirety it reads:

Das Leben suchst du, suchst, und es quillt und glänzt
Ein göttlich Feuer tief aus der Erde dir,
Und du in schauderndem Verlangen
Wirfst dich hinab, in des Ätna Flammen.
So schmelzt' im Weine Perlen der Übermut
Der Königin; und mochte sie doch! hättst du
Nur deinen Reichtum nicht, o Dichter
Hin in den gärenden Kelch geopfert!
Doch heilig bist du mir, wie der Erde Macht,
Die dich hinwegnahm, kühner Getöteter!
Und folgen möcht' ich in die Tiefe,
Hielte die Liebe mich nicht, dem Helden.   (*SWB* 1:241)

You look for life, you look and from deeps of Earth
A fire, divinely gleaming wells up for you,
And quick, aquiver with desire, you
Hurl yourself down into Etna's furnace.
So did the Queen's exuberance once dissolve
Rare pearls in wine, and why should she not? But you,
If only you, O poet, had not
Offered your wealth to the seething chalice!
Yet you are holy to me as is the power
Of Earth that took you from us, the boldly killed!
And gladly, did not love restrain me,
Deep as the hero plunged down I'd follow.   (*PF* 31)

Several important points emerge from this poem. The initial words in the original, "Das Leben" (life), are perhaps most crucial, for they reveal an existential affirmation of death on the part of the title figure and presumably the author himself. Empedocles, in other words, is not attracted to death per se; his "schaudernde[s] Verlangen" (literally, quivering desire) remains anything but a morbid fascination with the phenomenon of death or even a resignation toward it. Nor does the metaphysical view of finitude as transcendence have any place in the poem. Empedocles's leap into certain doom results, rather, from his passion for life and its plenitude. Hölderlin seems to speak here with Goethe in the poem "Selige Sehnsucht" (Blessed Yearning): "Das Lebend'ge will ich preisen / Das nach Flammentod sich sehnet" (I wish to praise what is full of life / What yearns for a fiery death). Indeed,

Empedocles's suicidal act of self-realization lives up to Goethe's famous imperative from the same poem: "Stirb und werde!" (Die and become!)[34] Suicide is perhaps a misleading term, for Empedocles remains "kühn[-]" (bold-), not world-weary and weak. He is a "hero" whose actions inspire emulation, not sympathy. Death here does not offer an escape from hardship and woe, but forms the inevitable consequence of a fulfilled existence, one that is as intense as the fires of Etna. The metaphor of pearls dissolving in wine, an allusion to Cleopatra's ruse of consuming ten million sestercia, conveys both Empedocles's superabundance, "Reichtum" (wealth), and the raging intensity of the volcano to which he surrenders himself.

The wealth that Empedocles sacrifices may be that of a "poet," but it is important to recall that the historical Empedocles was foremost a bard who sang of creation, the cosmos, and human existence. In short, he was a poet of being. Indeed, the distinction between poet, philosopher, and scientist does not apply to the pre-Socratics, especially not to Empedocles, who was of all these professions and more: rhetorician, statesman, prophet, and healer—in sum, a *Universalgeist*. It is nevertheless interesting that Hölderlin chooses to call his hero "poet" rather than, say, thinker or philosopher. But "poet" remains the most fitting epithet for a number of reasons. First of all, Empedocles viewed himself as such in the already cited fragment 146, in which he suggests that his Daimon has attained the second-highest stage of reincarnation occupied by prophets, bards, and physicians. Furthermore, he is generally considered the most poetic pre-Socratic. He composed *On Nature* and *Purifications* in epic verse, dactylic hexameter, and even his nonsurviving works were essentially literary. He is said to have written tragedies (in verse), a historical poem dealing with the Persian War, and lyrics dedicated to Apollo. In this sense, he remains an ideal figure for Hölderlin, who also devoted himself to lyric poetry far more than to other literary genres. The exclamation "O poet" points then in two directions: at Empedocles, the object of the ode and bearer of its title; and at Hölderlin, who implicitly addresses himself through his protagonist.

Hölderlin thus identifies with Empedocles on two levels. Beyond his fellowship with the latter as poet, he is drawn to the self-affirming death of the pre-Socratic. However much Hölderlin seeks to follow in Empedocles's footsteps ("And gladly . . . I'd follow"), he is held back by his attachment to Susette Gontard, the mother of his pupil in Frankfurt and the biographical basis of Diotima. One may wonder about the earnestness of Hölderlin's claim to emulate his hero to such an extreme, as it smacks of overenthusiasm or Hyperion-like *Schwärmerei*. However, a glance at a poem composed immediately after "Empedocles" reveals his serious existential preoccupation with death during this period of his life. In his ode "An die Parzen" or "To the Fates," Hölderlin *anticipates* death in the sense that Heidegger will later advocate; that is, he does not *expect* it to occur as a concrete event, but opens himself up for its possibility. Hölderlin's poem reads as follows:

> Nur Einen Sommer gönnt, ihr Gewaltigen!
> Und einen Herbst zu reifem Gesange mir,
>   Daß williger mein Herz, vom süßen
>   Spiele gesättiget, dann mir sterbe.
> Die Seele, der im Leben ihr göttlich Recht
>   Nicht ward, sie ruht auch drunten im Orkus nicht;
>   Doch ist mir einst das Heil'ge, das am
>   Herzen mir liegt, das Gedicht gelungen,
> Willkommen dann, o Stille der Schattenwelt!
>   Zufrieden bin ich, wenn auch mein Saitenspiel
>   Mich nicht hinab geleitet; Einmal
>   Lebt ich, wie Götter, und mehr bedarfs nicht.   (*SWB* 1:197)

> One summer only grant me, you powerful Fates,
>   And one more autumn only for mellow song,
>   So that more willingly, replete with
>   Music's late sweetness, my heart may die then.
> The soul in life denied its god-given right
>   Down there in Orcus also will find no peace;
>   But when what's holy, dear to me, the
>   Poem's accomplished, my art perfected,
> Then welcome, silence, welcome cold world of shades!
>   I'll be content, though here I must leave my lyre
>   And songless travel down; for *once* I
>   Lived like the gods, and no more is needed.   (*PF* 33)

Death here forms a horizon against which Hölderlin projects his poetic endeavors. The poem that he mentions and regards as sacred may stand collectively for his lyric production, but it seems to refer to a single, more ambitious undertaking. Given the period in which "To the Fates" was written, a time when Hölderlin began to devote himself fully to his *Empedocles* drama, there is legitimate reason to believe that "the poem" refers to his nascent tragedy. The fact that he desires to complete it before the mythical Fates cut his life thread implies a lengthy and substantial enterprise, one that would surely exceed the figurative time frame of summer and fall stated in the ode. Empedocles and death thus merge in a strange nexus of personal biography and literary activity. Seventeen ninety-seven marks a year in which various projects were deliberated, sketched out, and gradually began to materialize. The odes "Empedocles" and "To the Fates" indirectly manifest Hölderlin's involvement in this conceptual process, yet the so-called "Frankfurt Plan," also from 1797, constitutes the most immediate step toward the final but never finalized drama. This detailed sketch, which was not published during Hölderlin's lifetime, remains today the most crucial document for any attempt to interpret the fragments that comprise *The Death of Empedocles*.

In the summer of 1797, Hölderlin drew up an outline that has since become known as the "Frankfurt Plan," after its place of origin. It sketches out all five acts, in some cases even individual scenes, of what at that point bore the title: *Empedocles: A Tragedy in Five Acts*. Although certain modifications were to occur in the future three drafts, this sketch offers the best overall insight into the *Empedocles* project and its emerging tragic hero. Moreover, it appeared in early editions of Hölderlin's complete works and therefore could not have been ignored by either Nietzsche or Heidegger.

The first point that Hölderlin makes in the "Frankfurt Plan" (see *SWB* 2:421–24) forms the basis of his protagonist's fate. Empedocles is opposed to any limiting factor that hinders the cultivation of a totalized existence. He is described as "a mortal enemy of all one-sided existence" and suffers from "particular conditions"; that is, any kind of particularization (*SWB* 2:421). His wish to be "like a god" (*SWB* 2:421) is not an act of hubris (as in later drafts), but a yearning for freedom from the fettered, one-dimensional lives of his contemporaries. He thus bears a resemblance to Hyperion, who allowed his feelings for the Germans to get the better of him in the penultimate letter of the novel. While the latter-day Greek takes offense at the disjointed existence of modern Germans, the ancient philosopher becomes irritated with the no less specialized mentality of his fellow citizens.[35] The first scene of the second act opens with the caption: "Empedocles upon Etna" (*SWB* 2:423). Here he meets with his disciples and more frequently with his "lover," Pausanias of the later drafts. Empedocles's contempt for the discordant state of humanity drives him to the heights of Etna, and it is here that he decides upon death as a means to become one with the elements and thereby (re)gain a sense of cosmic totality. His "devotion" to nature is emphasized in the first two acts, and by the fourth this attachment has developed into a firm and fatal determination: "His resolution, which had long been dawning in him, to become united with infinite nature through voluntary [*freiwillig-*] death now comes to fruition" (*SWB* 2:423–24). Empedocles worships the elemental forces so fervently that he surrenders himself to them in the prime of his life. Far from an act of suicide committed out of weakness and despair, his death is freely willed, the literal meaning of *freiwillig*. By the fifth act, this resoluteness yields to an inner necessity, and death now becomes unavoidable, indeed logical: "Empedocles prepares himself for his death. The accidental motives of his resolution fade completely from his mind and he views it [death] as a necessity that ensues from his innermost being [*Wesen*]" (*SWB* 2:424). After a final encounter with his lover, Empedocles "plunges . . . into the blazing Etna" (*SWB* 2:424), a crowning event that none of the later drafts depicts. The "Frankfurt Plan" concludes with an observance by his family and followers, who all gather on Etna "in order to mourn and to celebrate the death of the great man" (*SWB* 2:424).

While themes like death and resoluteness play a major role in the "Frankfurt Plan," another fundamental aspect of the tragedy goes unmentioned in the sketch: guilt. What is here "a necessity that ensues from his innermost being" will subsequently become an outward act of atonement for the guilt that he has incurred through hubris. With the introduction of guilt into later stages of the project, Empedocles's self-sacrifice acquires a more tragic motivation and sets yet another precedent for the ideas of Nietzsche and Heidegger.

The First Draft

Because he still had the second volume of *Hyperion* to finish, Hölderlin probably did not start writing his *Empedocles* tragedy until the latter months of 1798, a full year after he had conceived the "Frankfurt Plan." A number of critics consider this version of the play an essentially finished work, in large part due to its length and thematic scope.[36] The acts are long and cover much ground with respect to the plot and ideas that Hölderlin outlined in his original plan. Nevertheless, the crucial fact remains that by the end of this draft Empedocles's climactic plunge into the crater of Etna has yet to take place. Although he has meditated on death a number of times, the supreme act of sacrifice represented in the poem and dramatic plan is preempted in this so-called tragedy, which is not only reduced to two acts (as opposed to the standard five) but furthermore lacks such requisite elements of the genre as recognition, reversal, and climax. That *The Death of Empedocles* fails to meet these generic criteria at a time when Aristotelian tragedies flourished in Germany would seem to speak all the more for the drama's incompleteness.

Hölderlin strikes up the theme of death from the very beginning of the first draft. Following Diogenes Laertius, he includes a figure, Panthea, whom the historical Empedocles reportedly resurrected from the dead. Panthea serves to introduce the theme of death into the play as well as to foreshadow Empedocles's own impending end. Other characters that contribute to the problematic of death include Hermocrates, the high priest, and Critias, the archon of Agrigentum and father of Panthea. Whereas Critias remains somewhat reserved in his persecution of Empedocles, thanks to whom he has after all regained a daughter, Hermocrates is intent upon ruining the self-proclaimed god who refuses to abide by established religious laws. The first clear sign of Empedocles's suicidal intent occurs during a dispute with Hermocrates, Critias, and other citizens, who all obstruct the hero's "sacred quiet path of death" (*SWB* 2:300).

Empedocles distinguishes himself from his adversaries precisely with respect to the question of death. His contemptuous words to the crowd, "Die a slow death, and may you be accompanied / By the raven cries of priests!" (*SWB* 2:307), define his increasing determination to meet his end expediently, in contrast to the prolonged demise that he wishes upon the multitude that hounds him. This split between two diverse modes of death is most pronounced during a final confrontation with Hermocrates in the second act. Here the distinction is not temporal but qualitative: "It is in vain; we have different paths, / You shall die a base death, as is only fitting, / With the soulless emotion of a slave, to me / Has fallen another lot" (*SWB* 2:333). Hermocrates's relation toward death remains that of a slave, since it lacks the freedom of choice that Empedocles comes to recognize with regard to his own finitude. Like the crowd to which he preaches, Hermocrates will die a protracted and commonplace death, seeking to squeeze out as many years of life as biologically possible. The following remark by Empedocles further illustrates the difference between his attitude toward mortality and that of the everyday throng: "You may live / As long as you draw breath; not I" (*SWB* 2:347). His subsequent speech to the citizens of Agrigentum contrasts two fundamentally distinct modes of relating to death, his own ideal of departing at the proper moment and the predominant trend of growing old while clinging to existence at all costs. Empedocles here speaks in the plural, grouping himself among other mortals graced by the gods:

> Let these fortunate ones die, before they
> Fade away in overbearance, trumpery, and disgrace,
> Let the free lovingly sacrifice themselves
> At the appropriate time to the gods, to whom
> All first born of the time is sacred. This is my fate.
> And I am well aware of my lot; long ago
> On my youngest day I foretold it
> To myself. Honor it for my sake! And if you
> Do not find me tomorrow, say: he should not
> Grow old and count his days, not serve
> Care and sickness.   (*SWB* 2:347)

Empedocles, one of "the free," has the good sense to give up his existence "at the appropriate time" (*bei guter Zeit*) rather than live on in
a stagnant state of being and wait for disease to dictate his end.

A timely death, one that comes neither too early nor too late, is crucial for Empedocles's entire determination. He repeatedly expresses
the wish to die at the opportune moment, once as quoted above and
again in similar formulations: "at the right time" (*zu rechter Zeit*) and
"in good hour" (*bei guter Stund'*) (see *SWB* 2:339, 340, 345). He also
conveys this idea of a timely death in metaphorical language. One of
the more common images he invokes concerns that of a ripe fruit which
knows when to fall on its own (see *SWB* 2:339). Empedocles, in other
words, is aware that he has reached his prime, and unlike his adversaries he will not desperately hold fast to life. The right time to die
seems to hit Empedocles with full force toward the end of the first act,
when he realizes that he has skirted the issue long enough. It is no coincidence that he grants his personal slaves freedom now that he himself begins to sense a growing liberation within his own being. This
emancipating function of death is primarily portrayed as a form of
catharsis. Empedocles speaks of a "purifying death" (*SWB* 2:340) as
well as of a "time of purging" (*SWB* 2:345). As if to make up for the
lost time spent in a confined existence, he feels the need to accelerate
his fatal course, and the following metaphor describes this path as a
race toward death:

> Where to now, mortal paths? You
> Are many, where is mine, the shortest? Where?
> The quickest? For it is disgraceful to falter.
> Ha! My gods! I once steered my chariot
> Without concern upon a smoking wheel, and soon
> I wish to return to you, regardless of danger.   (*SWB* 2:316)

This chariot race may be metaphorical in the above context, but it
remains an activity in which Empedocles, according to Hölderlin at
least, actually engaged. At the opening of the play, Delia comments
to the recently resurrected Panthea that she once witnessed Empedocles
"upon a chariot / at the games of Olympia" (*SWB* 2:279).[37] This seemingly minor detail serves to convey Empedocles's resolve upon a

rapid course of death: he races toward this ultimate goal like a professional charioteer. In his final monologue, he looks back on existence and comes to regard his imminent end as a supreme summation of life:

> How do I feel? I am amazed, as if I were
> Just beginning to live, for everything has changed,
> And only now do I truly exist, exist—and was
> This why, idle one, a yearning so often
> Befell you in your devout rest?
> O, is this why life came to you so easily
> So that you would find the joys of the overcomer
> All in one final and complete act?
> I am coming. To die? Into the darkness it's only
> A step, and yet you should like to see, my eye!
> You have served me well, served me readily!
> Now it is time for the night to descend
> Upon me for a while. Yet joyfully, boldly
> The flame burns in my breast. Shuddering
> Desire! What? In the hour of my death
> Life at last blazes up before me?   (*SWB* 2:354)

At this indeterminable point before his plunge into volcanic fire, Empedocles's confrontation with death becomes a reckoning with life. This is precisely his realization in the above monologue, which occurs near the end of the first draft, but perhaps only midway through the projected course of the drama. The fact that he never fully carries out his resolution in the fragment is irrelevant, for from a dialectical standpoint the transformative process outweighs the transformed result. Or formulated more existentially: the anticipation of death counts for everything, while its actualization results in nothingness. It would seem that Empedocles has reckoned with his fate long before this final monologue, indeed that his path unto death has been determined from the very moment of his birth: "long ago / On my youngest day I foretold it" (*SWB* 2:347). His death is thus existentially grounded from the start and requires no further portrayal. The reader knows, through the tragic hero's own anticipatory words and accelerated actions, that it will come swiftly and "at the right time."

Empedocles's death is rooted in life, existence, being. Yet it has an even deeper ground: guilt. According to Hermocrates, Empedocles is being punished by the gods for having aspired to join their ranks (see *SWB* 2:286). As we have learned earlier, this aspect of self-deification comes from the *Purifications*. In these original fragments, however, the offense is not one of blasphemy or hubris, nor does the ensuing guilt apply solely to Empedocles as an individual. The entire race of Daimones has fallen from grace through an act of bloodshed and must henceforth refrain from further killing in their series of reincarnations from plants to humans. As exiled divinities forced to take on mortal form, they cannot be guilty of presumption; on the contrary, they have lowered their level of existence rather than sought to raise it. Whereas Hölderlin's Empedocles remains a mortal who strives for the divine, the Empedocles of the *Purifications* can consider himself a god because he was originally a Daimon and now hopes to attain this last stage of palingenesis in order to terminate his period of exile. This shift from a universal to a personal guilt and from a divine to a human perspective forms a major departure from the original pre-Socratic text. Hölderlin's Empedocles equates himself with the most notorious transgressor of the Greek world, or at least with the one whose actions had the most tragic consequences for posterity: "you have / Brought guilt upon yourself, poor Tantalus / You have desecrated all that's sacred / Severed the bond with insolent pride" (*SWB* 2:291). This identification with Tantalus, the father of the House of Atreus, contains the only form of the word *Schuld* in the first draft. (The original text reads: "du hast / Es selbst verschuldet, armer Tantalus.") In his next admission of blame, this time not to himself but to Pausanias, Empedocles again speaks of his insolent pride and, like Oedipus, voices the most existential lament, that of his very birth: "The gods became / Subservient to me, I alone / Was God, and declared it in insolent pride— / O believe me, would that I had never been / Born!" (*SWB* 2:296).[38]

The subsequent reaction of Pausanias to his master's confession has led some critics to speak of a *Wortschuld* ("guilt based on words") and consequently to underestimate the gravity of Empedocles's culpability:[39] "What? Because of a word? / How can you so despair, bold master" (*SWB* 2:297). Empedocles's response: "Because of a word? Yes"

(*SWB* 2:297), only seems to reinforce the fact that his guiltiness arises from blasphemous statements rather than actual deeds. Two revealing notes that Hölderlin wrote in the margins of the manuscript suggest, however, that the guilt of Empedocles results from more than just a verbal transgression. In the first of these marginalia Hölderlin insists on the deeply criminal nature of such blasphemy in the Greek world, even if the sacrilege only resides in words (see *SWB* 2:286). The second note, which accompanies a deleted passage pertaining to Empedocles's admission of guilt to Pausanias, draws a revealing Christian parallel: "His sin is the Original Sin, hence nothing less than an abstraction, just as the highest joy is an abstraction, only it must be represented in a genetically vivid manner" (*SWB* 2:1147).

One way of depicting Empedocles's guilt or sin in a "genetically vivid manner" is to fashion a plot that retells the Passion story.[40] Readers would naturally be far more familiar with the events leading to the death of Jesus than with the circumstances surrounding the demise of a relatively obscure philosopher from the fifth century BC. By creating parallels with the Passion, Hölderlin can better bring his tragedy to life and show more clearly the complex motives, developments, and twists of the dramatic action. In the course of the three drafts, Empedocles increasingly functions as a Christ-like redeemer who reconciles the realms of the human and divine. His healing of Panthea points to Christ's resurrection of Lazarus, while Hermocrates and Critias bring to mind Caiaphas and Pontius Pilate, who exercised similar roles as high priest and governmental ruler. Pausanias's part in the drama is both that of Greek pupil and lover (*erômenos*) as well as that of a disciple. He is even told by his master near the end of the draft to prepare a meal resembling the Last Supper (see *SWB* 2:353). Empedocles's subsequent departure from the world remains perhaps the most crucial similarity between his fate and Christ's. Despite their vastly different modes of death, both figures redeem guilt or sin not through outward punishment per se, but through an internally motivated self-sacrifice. While Christ accepts crucifixion in order to expiate the Original Sin of mankind, Empedocles overcomes his more personal guilt by embracing death in a volcanic crater. Empedocles's guilt is thus a fundamental component of his existence, just as Original

Sin, according to Christian dogma, belongs to the essence of mankind. Both forms of transgression are in a sense primordial, for their roots run deep into being. The pronouncement "I alone / Was God" is an ontological one: Empedocles once *was* a god, and his words, far from being an empty claim of divinity, describe this previous state of existence.

The Second Draft

The second draft is the only one of the three to bear a definite title in the manuscripts: *The Death of Empedocles / A Tragedy in Five Acts*. Despite the projected number of acts, only the first and end of the second are preserved. Because the second draft is far more fragmented than the first, it poses difficulties for any attempt at a comprehensive interpretation. The reader is thus forced to second-guess Hölderlin's intentions more so than in any previous stage of the project. But there is no need for overspeculation, since Empedocles's fate remains predetermined, his anticipation of death already a requisite element of the tragedy. A crucial aspect of this new version, however, concerns the motivation behind his resolute course of action. While still *driven* toward death by guilt (and metaphorically by his chariot), Empedocles commits a slightly different crime: rather than seeking to become a god out of sheer hubris, he takes on the role of a mediator between the human and divine—not for personal gain but for love of his fellow human being.

In the first draft, Empedocles joins the gods only to fall from their favor, consequently becoming guilty of a Tantalus-like insolence. Now his arrogance is modeled after the example of Prometheus, who out of his love for mortals fashioned them after the gods and gave them fire for protection. A certain degree of irony pertains to this motif: whereas Prometheus's *crime* lies in stealing this "fire of life" (*SWB* 2:363/*PF* 269), Empedocles's *atonement* is caught up in this very element. Nevertheless, they share a common guilt for having interceded in divine affairs. This is precisely what gives rise to the conflict between Empedocles and Hermocrates, who as high priest considers himself the official intermediary between man and the gods. In this version of the play, Hermocrates and the archon of Agrigentum, who is now called Mecades, conspire even more than in the first draft to bring about Empedocles's downfall. In fact, Hermocrates intends to take the first step in eliminating Empedocles from the politically tense scene. Mecades, like his predecessor Critias, opts for a less aggressive approach: "Leave him alone! Give him no cause to act! / If he, the arrogant, himself finds none / For insolent deeds, and only in words can sin, / He dies a fool and does us little harm" (*SWB* 2:366/*PF* 277). Again, the notion of sinning through words makes its appearance. Johannes Hoffmeister stresses the dialectical dimension that underlies this idea of verbality, theorizing that the theme of guilt was supposed to unfold throughout this second version of the play.[41] This development was to occur both dynamically through dramatic dialogue, the principal spokesman being not Empedocles but Hermocrates, and thematically through the broader concept of mediation. In both cases, guilt becomes dialectic; that is, dialogic and synthetic. Given the minimal length of the draft, it is impossible to trace any such dialectical progression of guilt and indeed difficult enough to discern its presence. However, the following situation seems clear: Empedocles is guilty of playing the arbitrator between humankind and the gods, yet in contrast to the first draft he himself has little to say about his crime or, for that matter, about his death. It is principally Hermocrates and Mecades that discuss his guilt, while Delia and Panthea are left to contemplate his self-destructive bent. Hölderlin even casts specifically named characters to represent the people of Agrigentum, whereas he previously had anonymous citizens do the talking. Although the text breaks off before these figures can be introduced, it is apparent that Hölderlin intends to create yet another perspective through which Empedocles, the grand mediator between the human and the divine, himself becomes mediated through the overall literary dynamic of dramatic action and poetic dialogue.

The second draft contains far fewer references to death than the first. As already mentioned, these references seldom come immediately— that is, without mediation—from Empedocles himself, but from his followers. This time, for instance, it is Panthea who describes his path of death as a reckless chariot race:

did you think
The goad [*Stachel*] would check him. The pain makes faster
His flight, and like the charioteer
When wheels begin to smoke on the track,
All the more swiftly
He, the endangered, rushes towards his garland [*Kranz*].

(SWB 2:385/PF 317)

The closer Empedocles comes to death, the more he picks up the pace. His metaphorical chariot hurtles along toward victory, symbolized by the garland. However, in the classical world this decoration served another important purpose. As Lessing demonstrated in his treatise "How the Ancients Depicted Death," garlands were also used to decorate corpses, urns, tombs, and funeral pyres.[42] Hölderlin in effect combines these two symbols, thereby underscoring Empedocles's view of death as a personal victory. *Siegerkranz* and *Totenkranz* thus merge into one inclusive emblem: the wreath toward which Empedocles races so swiftly will soon crown him in death. Pausanias and Panthea indeed remark that Empedocles "Festively . . . goes down" (*SWB* 2:386/*PF* 319) into the crater of Etna. This idea of death as a festival will later figure in Nietzsche's *Thus Spoke Zarathustra*. For now, in anticipation of this link between Hölderlin and Nietzsche, it is important to note that Empedocles affirms his death in the prime of life or in his *Blüte*, as Pausanias, Delia, and Panthea all agree (*SWB* 2:383, 384, 385/*PF* 311–13, 315, 317). In other words, Empedocles becomes ripe for death at the very height of existence. Within the framework of the second draft, the maturation of his resolve manifests itself in the very structure of the tragedy, for Empedocles is already given up for dead at the end of act two. Although he has not yet taken the fatal plunge, his intentions are clear from early on in the drama and only await finalization. His course of death appears to have accelerated at such a rate that the final three acts become, if not superfluous, then at least impossible to fill with further dramatic action. Once again, Hölderlin must call a halt to this breakneck pace and rethink the trajectory of his project.

The Third Draft

His drama now interrupted for the second time, Hölderlin engaged in a period of philosophical reflection, from which emerged an essay that is best known under the title "Grund zum Empedokles" or "The Ground for Empedokles."[43] This abstruse theoretical piece (which Hölderlin wrote not with an audience in mind, but for his own conceptual clarification) gives an entirely new foundation to the project. Here Hölderlin discusses the opposition of nature and art in terms of the principles *aorgisch* and *organisch*. The former notion encompasses such extremes as "the incomprehensible, the nonsensuous, the unlimited" (*SWB* 2:429/*ELT* 53), whereas the latter concept designates finite and mediated phenomena such as art and human existence. These two principles conflict with one another dialectically, much like the antagonistic forces of Love and Hate in the philosophy of the historical Empedocles. Hölderlin's Empedocles stands between pantheistic nature and rationalistic mankind, and must somehow reconcile these two seemingly incompatible worlds. As Hölderlin states in his essay, neither "song" nor "action" suffices to set things straight, since they do not possess enough reconciliatory power to overcome the deep divide between the aorgic and the organic. In other words, nothing that Empedocles does in his capacity as poet can rectify matters; nor will the more direct action of a revolutionary be of any avail. What is called for, rather, is a sacrifice by a "man within whom those oppositions are united *so* intimately that they become one within him, that they discard and reverse their originally differentiating form" (*SWB* 2:431/*ELT* 54–55). This dialectical function of Empedocles forms the basis of his death, which is still envisioned as a sacrifice, but one over which he no longer has any control. Of course there was always some degree of necessity to Empedocles's end, which, beyond its individualistic purpose of self-realization, had the further goal of attaining a more holistic and primordial state of being. Still, the determination to die always stemmed from Empedocles himself. But in Hölderlin's essay, Empedocles is deprived of all volition and becomes the product of a greater cosmic destiny. He is "the result of his time" (*SWB* 2:432/*ELT* 55), and has no say in the matter of his fate. His death can therefore no longer be considered freely willed or existentially imperative; its necessity instead remains that of a greater external force. It is not entirely clear how Empedocles's act of sacrifice can realistically bring about change, but Hölderlin is no doubt thinking in archetypal or mythological terms. Like the martyrdom of Christ, the immolation of Empedocles serves as an extreme example of reconciliation between the increasingly divergent realms of the human and divine. The fact that Hölderlin completely reconceives the motivation behind Empedocles's death and makes no mention of guilt throughout the essay has led a number of critics to ignore any further development of this motive/motif in the third draft of the play,[44] a draft that is even more incomplete than the previous two.

The third draft of the drama became known as *Empedocles upon Etna* through the editions of Zinkernagel and Pigenot in the early twentieth century. Arguing on the basis of the original manuscripts, Beißner however maintains that this title applies to certain scenes rather than to the drama as a whole. He also observes that Hölderlin, in a letter to Schiller written sometime in September 1799, refers to this version of the tragedy as "the Death of Empedocles"[45] (see also *SWB* 3:394). The title of the play hence remains unchanged since at least the second draft, and Empedocles's death also remains the focus of this final dramatic effort. Yet a crucial difference lies in the acceleration of his resolve. Whereas the first two versions do not introduce the character of Empedocles, let alone his decision to die, until well after the first scene, the third draft opens with his monologue on nature and death. Once again, Hölderlin seems to become caught in the very pitfall that plagued his earlier ventures: how to compose a full five-act tragedy when the tragic hero is ready to die right from the start? Empedocles's anticipation of death thus appears to work to the disadvantage of the play, for it outstrips the momentum of the plot and thereby undermines the entire structure of the work.

A further noteworthy shift concerns the cast of characters or at least their relations to one another. Pausanias remains Empedocles's follower, yet here in the more literal sense, as he is prepared to follow his master even into death. Empedocles repeatedly discourages Pausanias from emulating his actions, in one instance pointing to the basic difference between them: "No, you are not to blame" (*SWB* 2:403/*PF* 335), which is a misleading translation of a line containing the key word *Schuld:* "Nein! du bist ohne Schuld." A new figure, the Egyptian prophet Manes, reveals to Empedocles his destiny as a redeemer of humankind. Two characters listed in the *dramatis personae* that never actually appear in the first and only act of the play are Strato and Panthea, the latter now Empedocles's sister, the former his brother and principal adversary as ruler of Agrigentum. (Strato is apparently a composite of Hermocrates and Critias/Mecades.) By creating this fraternal link between Empedocles and his enemy, Hölderlin is better able to illustrate the inner polarity and dialectical opposition at the heart of his drama. The urgency of Empedocles's death, in other words, is not only due to abstract cosmic forces (as suggested in the essay) but also to the primal fact of his birth.

Yet the important question in light of the theoretical "Ground for Empedocles" concerns the precise motivation behind the hero's death. Given the limited progress that Hölderlin made on this stage of the project, it is difficult if not impossible to trace the roots of Empedocles's resolution and establish a definitive motive for his act—certainly not to the extent that Hölderlin justifies his figure's sacrifice in the essay. At right around 500 verses, this draft remains the shortest of the three, which leaves interpreters with little text, and virtually no *con*text, upon which to base any claims. Nevertheless there are enough references to guilt and sin to indicate that Hölderlin did not utterly abandon this central impetus behind the death of his Empedocles.

This version of the drama opens with a lengthy monologue in which Empedocles expresses both his guilt and desire to die. As mentioned above, he has been exiled from Agrigentum and now roams the slopes of Etna, reflecting on the banishment that his brother decreed and the citizens applauded:

> By Hades! amply I deserved it all.
> And it was good for me; poison heals the sick,
> And we are purged of one sin by another.
> For sinned I have, and greatly, from my youth,
> Never have loved men humanly, but served
> Only as fire or water blindly serves them.   (*SWB* 2:399/*PF* 327)

The source of Empedocles's guilt thus lies in the life-long neglect of his fellow man. There is no indication here of hubris, whether that of an arrogant mortal who fancies himself a god, as was the case in the first draft, or that of a Promethean mediator, as in the second. Empedocles's "black sin" (*SWB* 2:411/*PF* 353) results, rather, from a communal breach. In the course of Hölderlin's project, the ideal bond between Empedocles and his people becomes stronger, if not in execution then at least in conception. In the first draft, Empedocles feels little attachment to mankind; expelled from Olympus, he is forced to dwell among mortals, with whom he has an antagonistic relationship, particularly when it comes to the question of death. The second draft aligns him more closely with history and humanity; here his original self-promoting act of hubris yields to a crime committed out of altruism. In the final version of the play, Empedocles's guilt seems to have become secularized. His feeling of kinship is no longer with the gods above, but with the elements around him and—as Hölderlin meant to develop in the never completed acts of the drama—with the countrymen that he has hitherto ignored. "The Ground for Empedocles" clarifies this point: "However, as intrinsic a relation as he bears to the life of the elements, he also bears to his people" (*SWB* 2:437/*ELT* 60). Manes awakens Empedocles's latent calling as "the new saviour" (*GWB* 2:412/*PF* 355), who, again in the function of mediator, reconciles humanity with divinity. The crucial difference between the role of Empedocles as redeemer in the third draft and his intermediary function in the second resides in the basis of his guilt. Whereas in the second version he forsook the gods for the benefit of humans, he has now deserted his people for the sake of elemental nature. By refusing to join the greater body of humanity, Empedocles not only incurs guilt, but also ultimately prepares the way for his own death. As Hölderlin puts it in more theoretical language: "Thus his time is individualized in Empedocles, and the more it is individualized in him . . . the more necessary becomes his ruin" (*SWB* 2:434/*ELT* 57).

Empedocles's death may be necessary from a broader theoretical standpoint; within the context of the drama, however, it appears to be freely willed—at least in part. In the opening scene upon Etna he announces: "For death is what I seek. It is my right" (*SWB* 2:399/*PF*

327). But by the end of the first act, a hint of divine necessity becomes apparent:

> You rather, heavenly spirits,
> Who when I started were near to me,
> You far-designing ones, to you I owe it
> That here I may cut off and put an end
> To the long chain of suffering, liberated
> From other duties, in self-chosen death
> And in accordance with god-given laws!   (*SWB* 2:415/*PF* 361)

The fact that Empedocles's self-chosen death (*freier Tod*) meshes with god-given laws speaks all the more for his representative dialectical character. As Hölderlin argues in his companion essay, Empedocles reconciles the oppositions of the world. But his death can also be considered dialectical in another sense. Similar to its function in Hegel, death here becomes associated with life and with freedom. Through his free relation to death, his *freiwilliger Tod* in the "Frankfurt Plan" and *freier Tod* in the third draft, Empedocles is better able to steer the course of his own fate. In contrast to his harassers, for whom death remains a biological endpoint, Empedocles dialectically overcomes his finitude by incorporating it into his mode of being. Put plainly: Empedocles *can* die whenever he chooses; his detractors *have to* die when their final moment comes. Thus, whereas death remains an alien and outside force in the case of the others, it becomes internalized in Empedocles, functioning as a crucial component of his identity.

But in the true spirit of dialectics, death also raises Empedocles beyond a state of mere individuality. Through his leap into the volcanic inferno, he becomes reunited with the elements and thus with a more universal realm of nature: literally through dissolution in the fires of Etna and figuratively through a kind of mystical transcendence. His death thus fulfills more than just a personal-existential function; his sacrifice will also bring about a new era of cultural renewal. At various points throughout the three versions of the play, Empedocles espouses the (Hegelian) doctrine that the greater welfare of the community is predicated on death and destruction—in this case his own. The most revealing statement to this effect occurs in the first draft:

and by dying
All things return to the elements, so that,
As if by a bath, they may be refreshed and find
New youth. Humans have been given
The great urge to rejuvenate themselves on their own.
And out of the purifying death that
They choose for themselves at the right time
Nations arise, like Achilles from the river Styx.   (*SWB* 2:340)

Empedocles's timely and cathartic death hence serves a higher historical purpose, much like in Hegel's philosophy the demise of individual consciousnesses furthers the progression of world Spirit. The metaphor of a bath in the above passage points to a more specific parallel between Hölderlin and Hegel with respect to the dialectics of unity that underlies their common way of thinking. In *The Spirit of Christianity,* Hegel discusses the unifying effect of water, here in the Christian context of baptism. The following translation by Knox renders *Wasserfülle* as "sea," but this word stands for any "abundance of water," as the more proper translation should read in this excerpt:

> No feeling is so homogeneous with the desire for the infinite, the longing to merge into the infinite, as the desire to immerse one's self in the sea. . . . In the sea there is no gap, no restriction, no multiplicity, nothing specific. The feeling of it is the simplest, the least broken up. After immersion a man comes up into the air again, separates himself from the water, is at once free from it and yet it still drips from him everywhere. So soon as the water leaves him, the world around him takes on specific characteristics again, and he comes back strengthened to the consciousness of multiplicity. (*W* 1:391/*ETW* 275).

This passage vividly illustrates the power of liquefaction that occurs in the course of dialectical movement. As I have pointed out in the previous chapter, Hegel tends to employ variants of the term *Auflösung* to describe this process of unification. Empedocles will suffer precisely such a "disintegration" and "diffusion" of his being in the molten lava of Etna. While the particular element is different in each case, the ultimate effect remains the same: immersion in an all-encompassing whole and a resultant breakdown of individuality.

A number of further parallels exist between Hölderlin's various *Empedocles* drafts and Hegel's *Spirit of Christianity* essay, both of which were after all composed during the same time frame in Frankfurt and Homburg.[46] Empedocles resembles Hegel's Christ on a number of levels. Generally speaking, they are redeemer figures that seek to overcome the antagonisms of their respective worlds by sacrificing their own individualities. Moreover, they both come into conflict with their fellow people, the Agrigentians and the Jews. These, granted, accuse them of blasphemy, but the deeper parallel that Hölderlin and Hegel draw concerns the fundamental contrast between dialectics and positivity. Jesus and Empedocles are misunderstood precisely because they do not lead the particularized and discordant existence of their contemporaries. Their totalized, dialectical mode of being clashes with the dualistic mentalities of their respective times, and the ultimate solution to this basic rift would seem to lie in an all-unifying act of sacrifice. As we will see in the next chapter, Nietzsche creates a similar character whose ideas challenge established codes and who recognizes, indeed preaches, the importance of a self-affirmed death. Zarathustra, as he will come to be called, serves as both a counter-model of Christ and a re-embodiment of Empedocles.

3

Nietzsche

The Deaths of Empedocles and Zarathustra

> Let us guard against saying that death is opposed to life.
> —Nietzsche, *The Gay Science*, no. 109

The figure of Empedocles is as present in the work of Nietzsche as in that of Hölderlin. However, this presence is not readily apparent to the casual reader and must often be sought in Nietzsche's lesser-known writings. Like Hölderlin, he, too, struggled to compose an *Empedocles* tragedy but never progressed beyond preliminary notes and outlines. While neither dramatic project was carried through to completion, the extant fragments and drafts contain a number of similarities with regard to plot, characterization, and ideas. Nietzsche later took up his aborted drama under a different guise. His famous work *Thus Spoke Zarathustra,* written in four parts between 1883 and 1885, retains and expands on several of the themes from his original *Empedocles* plan, including death. As his posthumously published notebooks reveal, Nietzsche also intended to write parts of *Zarathustra* in dramatic form, which further speaks for a connection to the *Empedocles* project, both his own and that of his predecessor Hölderlin. On a more general level, Nietzsche and Hölderlin shared unique if not radical insights into Hellenistic culture and both identified deeply with certain pre-Socratic philosophers. As a professor of classical philology whose career at the University of Basel spanned exactly a decade (1869–79), Nietzsche had a far better opportunity to lecture and publish on this common area of interest than did Hölderlin, who essentially remained an itinerant tutor for the ten years of his literary activity (1794–1804). Nevertheless, Nietzsche's lectures and academic publications reveal a surprisingly limited preoccupation with Empedocles the philosopher. It would appear that he consciously sought to create a distance between himself and this particular pre-Socratic, in effect "postponing"[1] a serious encounter with the tragic figure that had made such an early impression on him through Hölderlin's drama.

This chapter on Nietzsche is divided into two main parts. The first discusses his reception of Hölderlin and traces his plans for creating a drama in the mold of *The Death of Empedocles*. Here his ideas about death, guilt, and tragedy not only serve to establish a firm connection to his literary forerunner but also point ahead to crucial themes that will resurface in *Thus Spoke Zarathustra*. This unique work—a blend of poetry, philosophy, and biblical parody—remains the focus of the second part of the chapter. Here I will examine the transformation of Empedocles into Zarathustra, two near-mythic characters that come to regard death as a summation of life and that more specifically seek to seal their fate in the mouth of a volcano (at least according to alternative endings that Nietzsche sketched out in his manuscripts). Zarathustra's speech "On Free Death" contains the kernel of Nietzsche's ideas about human finitude; I will elaborate on these ideas by scrutinizing other texts in which Nietzsche articulates his position on dying. Nietzsche's basic conception of death as freedom corresponds in a number of ways to the views that Hegel and Hölderlin developed in Frankfurt. Ultimately, however, Nietzsche displays a total disregard for the higher moments of synthesis and transcendence that distinguish dialectics. For Nietzsche, God is definitively dead, not *aufgehoben* into the speculative dominion of absolute Spirit. Thus he urges us to turn our backs on all "hinter-worlds" and remain "true to the earth." As a result of this reorientation toward more immanent and vitalistic values, death takes on a purely existential function, indeed becomes an integral part of what one might call an ethics of existence. Drawing on assorted moral philosophers of antiquity who sought to construct an ethical life around the issue of mortality, I will suggest that Nietzsche similarly creates an ethos that tells us how to live in the face of death. To what extent Nietzsche himself carried through with his ideal of a free and timely end is a question reserved for the conclusion of this chapter.

EMPEDOCLES AND THE PROBLEM OF TRAGEDY

At the age of 17, Nietzsche wrote a school essay under the title: "A Letter to my Friend, in Which I Recommend That He Read My Favorite Poet." This poet turns out to be none other than Hölderlin, who at the time (the piece is dated October 19, 1861) was not widely known in Germany. As Nietzsche in fact remarks at the end of the text, the purpose of his (fictional) letter is to spread the word about a literary figure "whom the majority of his own people hardly know by name."[2] If the German public had read anything by Hölderlin in the nineteenth century, it was most likely his poems, many of which met with only moderate success during his lifetime. Yet Nietzsche, typically the exception to any rule, expresses the most enthusiasm not for Hölderlin's poetry but for his *Empedocles* drama:

> You generally seem to be of the belief that he only wrote poetry. You are not, then, familiar with Empedocles, this ever so important dramatic fragment, in whose melancholy notes resounds the future of the ill-fated poet, the grave of his prolonged insanity—resounding not, as you may think, in garbled speech, but in the purest Sophoclean language and in an endless profusion of profound thoughts.[3]

Nietzsche goes on to extol the musical prose of *Hyperion* as well as the lyric quality of several poems, especially "Abendphantasie" (Evening Fantasy), three stanzas of which he quotes. But he soon comes back to *Empedocles,* highlighting the various motives behind the hero's death: "In the unfinished tragedy 'Empedocles' the poet shows us his own nature. Empedocles's death is a death out of godly pride, out of contempt for man, out of pantheism and satiety with the world. I have always been tremendously moved by the entire work; this Empedocles is filled with a divine sublimity."[4] The untimeliness of

Nietzsche's interest in Hölderlin is evident in the teacher's commentary to the essay: "I would like to offer the author some friendly advice: stick to a healthier, more lucid, and more German poet."[5] In a similar vein, Cosima Wagner noted in her diaries from 1873 that both she and her husband "recognize, with some alarm, the great influence that this writer [Hölderlin] has exerted upon Professor Nietzsche: rhetorical bombast, improper images piled one upon another . . . , but also a fine, noble disposition" (*KSA* 15:53). This early, indeed formative, impact of Hölderlin will become all the more apparent in my discussion of Nietzsche's own preoccupation with Empedocles and the later resurrection of this tragic figure in Zarathustra. For now it seems clear that Hölderlin exhibits a strong presence in Nietzsche's intellectual development, from his teenage days at boarding school in Pforta to his professorial years in Basel.

In 1869, at the mere age of 24, Nietzsche was appointed professor of classical philology at the University of Basel. To use current academic terminology, he was hired as an ABD, yet he had no real need to start let alone complete a dissertation, as he had already assembled a formidable publication record. His most important article at the time was "De Laertii Diogenis fontibus" (On the Sources of Diogenes Laertius), which his mentor Friedrich Ritschl originally encouraged him to write and submit to an annual essay contest at the University of Leipzig. Nietzsche's composition took first prize and soon appeared in the professional journal edited by Ritschl, *Rheinisches Museum für Philologie*.[6] His study of Diogenes Laertius, specifically of the sources Diogenes drew upon, thus parallels Hölderlin's (granted, less scholarly) preoccupation with the classic *Lives and Opinions of Eminent Philosophers*.

This incidental parallel takes on greater significance in view of the motto that Nietzsche gave to his manuscript on Diogenes: "*enoi enoi hoios essi*" (Be, be who you are!).[7] These slightly modified words from Pindar's second Pythian Ode—the original reads "*Genoi hoios essi*" (Become who you are!)[8]—will later function for Nietzsche as a kind of existential slogan or code of self-fashioning (see for example aphorisms 270 and 335 of *The Gay Science*). Zarathustra, the very model of self-overcoming, similarly invokes this credo (see *KSA* 4:297/*Z* 351), as does Nietzsche himself in his final and most personal work, *Ecce Homo,* whose subtitle reads "How One Becomes What One Is." This exhortation of Pindar also takes on significance in the work Hölderlin, who employs the dictum in the third draft of *The Death of Empedocles,* though with some modification. Pausanias's words to Empedocles "Think of yourself, / Be what you are " (*PF* 337)[9] feature the verb "to be" rather than "to become," but given the degree of overlap between these two verbs in Greek, Hölderlin's formulation can hardly be criticized.[10] In his translations of Pindar's odes, which he probably worked on while composing the final draft of *Empedocles,* Hölderlin adheres more closely to the original Greek. Here he properly translates *gignesthai* and includes the requisite participle *mathôn:* "Werde welcher du bist erfahren" (*SWB* 2:723).[11] It would of course be unreasonable to suggest any direct influence of Hölderlin upon Nietzsche with regard to Pindar's phrase. Even Nietzsche's advice to his close friend Erwin Rohde, "*genoi hoios essi,*"[12] which echoes Pausanias's words to his equally trusted companion Empedocles, cannot seriously be considered a conscious appropriation from Hölderlin's tragedy. Nevertheless, the fact that Empedocles, Diogenes Laertius, and Pindar all join to form a common link between Hölderlin and Nietzsche seems the result of more than just coincidence. Indeed, an element of necessity enters this constellation with Heidegger, who may have had both of his predecessors in mind when he too quoted from Pindar, here in the context of Dasein's self-understanding: "only because it [Dasein] *is* what it becomes or does not become, can it say understandingly to itself: 'become what you are!'" (*BT* 136). Heidegger, who gives no precise source for this quoted motto of Dasein, could be citing Pindar, Hölderlin, or Nietzsche—or better yet, all three.

In 1871, Nietzsche made plans for a drama around the figure of Empedocles. Yet it is not so much the pre-Socratic philosopher that spurred Nietzsche's imagination in this dramatic endeavor; the main impulse stems, rather, from his "favorite poet" Hölderlin, whose *Empedocles* still appears to occupy him some ten years after his school essay from 1861. Nietzsche was more than an enthusiastic reader of Hölderlin; his educational background and later professorship in classical philology made him an authority on numerous aspects of Greek and Roman culture, including pre-Socratic philosophy. Given, however, his ten years of teaching and scholarship at the University of Basel, one finds an astonishingly limited treatment of Empedocles in his academic writings. It is almost as though Nietzsche felt that the figure of Empedocles was a force to be reckoned with outside of the academy, that scholarly publications and pontifications could not possibly do justice to the romanticized hero of his youth.

At Basel Nietzsche repeatedly held a lecture course entitled "The pre-Platonic Philosophers."[13] Here he summarized the thought of the main pre-Socratics—or as he refers to them, the "pre-Platonics"[14]—from Thales to Socrates, after first devoting some attention to their precursors Homer and Hesiod. His discussion of Empedocles begins with the Sicilian's genealogy and then touches on the *Purifications,* whose central theme of guilt Nietzsche briefly addresses: "With difficulty he [Empedocles] walks in this world of pain, of opposition; he can only explain his presence in this world through a transgression; at some point in time he must have committed a crime, a murder, perjury. In such a world, guilt is caught up with existence."[15] Following some observations about Empedocles's political role in Agrigentum, Nietzsche enters into the diverse accounts of the philosopher's death. Here he no doubt draws on the testimonies found in Diogenes, as this remains the best source for such biographical information even today, and Nietzsche was of course already quite familiar with this text. He mentions the conflicting stories of Empedocles's exile and eventual disappearance in the Peloponnesus; his fatal fall from a chariot; and his leap into the crater of Mount Etna. Nietzsche's final assessment of the anecdotes surrounding Empedocles's death remains impartial and synoptic: "The religious legend has him disappear, the ironic one throws him into Etna, the pragmatic one has him break a rib and be buried at Megara."[16] As will soon be seen, this noncommittal summary on the part of Nietzsche the scholar does not hold for Nietzsche the aspiring dramatist, who opts for the more spectacular death by volcanic flame, both in his *Empedocles* sketches and in his notes for a sequel to *Zarathustra.*

The Tragic Sense of Existence

Nietzsche tends to associate Empedocles with tragedy. In his lecture on the pre-Platonic philosophers, he makes the claim: "He is the *tragic philosopher*, the contemporary of Aeschylus."[17] Several notes from the mid-1870s similarly state this connection in the broadest of terms (cf. *KSA* 8:100, 105, 119), but in none of these does Nietzsche give a proper definition of tragedy or otherwise elaborate on Empedocles's potential role as a tragic hero. Even a previous remark from the early 1870s offers little more than a motivation for the protagonist's death: "Empedocles is the pure tragic man. His plunge into Etna—the thirst for knowledge! He yearned for art and found only knowledge. But knowledge is what makes Faust" (*KSA* 7:118). Again, Nietzsche does not adequately explain why Empedocles, more than any other ancient philosopher, should be considered a representative of the tragic. Indeed, the parallel that he draws between Empedocles and Faust, often considered *the* representative figure of German tragedy, only confuses the issue.[18] Is the fate of the tragic hero necessarily caught up with his yearning for art or knowledge? And what do these two pursuits have to do with tragedy in the first place? Nietzsche's notion of what constitutes tragedy is difficult to ascertain, as he has expressed his opinion on the matter in a number of different contexts. One source that may shed light on the role of Empedocles as an embodiment of the tragic is the early treatise from 1872, *The Birth of Tragedy Out of the Spirit of Music*.

In this first major work Nietzsche traces the development of tragedy from the choruses of early satyr plays to the "enlightened" dramas of Euripides, all under the rubrics of the Apollinian and Dionysian. Nietzsche's book on tragedy remains less a rigorous philological study of the genre than a poetic rapture on its roots and rebirth in the philosophy of Schopenhauer and the music of Wagner. It hence departs radically from the aesthetic tradition that began with Aristotle's *Poetics* and that still dominated literary discourse in nineteenth century Germany. Unlike the endeavors of, for instance, Lessing and Schiller to define tragedy according to technical and generic criteria, Nietzsche takes a more philosophical approach, interpreting tragedy not as a specific art form but as a comprehensive worldview and fundamental expression of existence. With *The Birth of Tragedy,* Nietzsche took the first step toward emancipating himself from the field of philology to which he was professionally bound but which threatened to stifle his artistic creativity and philosophic originality.

In *The Birth of Tragedy,* Nietzsche maintains that the ideal tragic drama arises from the conflict between the Apollinian principle of individuation and the integrative force of the Dionysian. Although these two concepts are introduced as aesthetic categories, their role is not restricted to the realm of art. Nietzsche views them, rather, as universal aesthetic principles that underlie all reality in accordance with the central tenet of his book that "it is only as an *aesthetic phenomenon* that existence and the world are eternally *justified*" (*KSA* 1:47/*BoT* 52). The Apollinian, like the sun god from whom it derives its name, is the principle of light, clarity, delineation; it governs the visual arts of sculpture, architecture, and painting as well as the narrative element of poetry and drama. The Dionysian, on the other hand, is primarily associated with music, the least corporeal art form not to mention the most emotive, passionate, and irrational. Its defining experience is intoxication, whereas the Apollinian creates the illusory perception of a dream. Beyond their narrower artistic domains, these two impulses dictate their laws to nature such that the Apollinian perpetuates the metaphysical illusion of individuation, while the destructive intensity of the Dionysian destroys this partition to reveal the brute reality of existence. The tragic view of life constantly confronts this harsh underlying reality as the true and original font of existence. The deeper meaning of tragedy consists in the hero's attempt to gain insight if not access to the original Dionysian condition in which "the spell of individuation is broken, and the way lies open to the Mothers of Being, to the innermost heart of things" (*KSA* 1:103/*BoT* 99–100). Representative tragic characters such as Prometheus and Oedipus "are mere masks of this original hero, Dionysus" (*KSA* 1:71/*BoT* 73), who suffers under the individuating tendency of human existence. Much like the mythical Dionysus succumbed to the laws of individuation in being rent asunder by the Titans, the tragic hero similarly finds the intactness of his being put into question due to the mere fact that he dwells in a world removed from its primordial state. This return to the well-springs of being again finds its mythical parallel in the fate of Dionysus, who becomes reborn through Demeter and thereby overcomes his Apollinian destruction. For Nietzsche, the hero of Greek tragedy is therefore not an individual in the modern sense; that is, one who defines himself against others and strives for self-realization. As direct descendents and indeed embodiments of Dionysus, figures such as Prometheus, Oedipus, and presumably Empedocles do not strive to develop their individual natures, but rather seek to regain the lost cosmic unity that lurks behind terrestrial existence. This process ultimately calls for them to surrender their individuality as the principal cause for their misfortune, suffering, and punishment by the gods.

This insight into the tragic sense of existence is not solely exemplified in Greek tragedy through the competing forces of the Apollinian and Dionysian. Nietzsche also grounds his theory in the Semitic myth of the Fall, which Western—or as he calls it here, Aryan—civilization has tended to interpret along Promethean lines. The following quote raises interesting parallels with regard to the concept of guilt in Hölderlin's *Empedocles* drafts:

> What distinguishes the Aryan notion is the sublime view of *active sin* as the characteristically Promethean virtue. With that, the ethical basis for pessimistic tragedy has been found: the justification of human evil, meaning both human guilt and the human suffering it entails.
>
> . . . In the heroic effort of the individual to attain universality, in the attempt to transcend the curse of individuation and to become the *one* world-being, he suffers in his own person the primordial contradiction that is concealed in things, which means that he commits sacrilege and suffers. (*KSA* 1:69–70/*BoT* 71)

Acts of hubris or sin thus cast human beings into a world of particularization, severing them from an original unity with the gods and subjecting them to constant suffering. One may note here traces of the Hegelian unhappy consciousness: the basis of suffering resides in the fundamental condition of nonidentity between the human and the divine. Nietzsche expresses a similar view in *Philosophy in the Tragic Age of the Greeks* (1873), an unfinished treatise that examines the problem of tragic existence from the standpoint of pre-Socratic philosophy. In connection with Heraclitus, for instance, he argues that an initial crime of hubris is responsible for individuation, cosmic pollution, and guilt. His words could just as well be a summary of Empedocles's *Purifications:*

> Is not the entire world process now an act of punishment for hybris? The many the result of evil-doing? The transformation of the pure into the impure the consequence of injustice? Is guilt not now transplanted into the very nucleus of materiality and the world of becoming and of individuals thereby unburdened of responsibility, to be sure, but simultaneously sentenced to carry the consequences of evil forever and anew? (*KSA* 1:830/*PTA* 61)

More important for Nietzsche's point is the philosophical doctrine of Anaximander, an early pre-Socratic whose only surviving fragment reads (in Nietzsche's own translation): "'Where the source of things is, to that place they must also pass away, according to necessity, for they must pay penance and be judged for their injustices, in accordance with the ordinance of time'" (*KSA* 1:818/*PTA* 45).[19] Nietzsche comments on this famous fragment as follows:

> It may not be logical, but it certainly is human, to view now, together with Anaximander, all coming-to-be as though it were an illegitimate emancipation from eternal being, a wrong for which destruction is the only penance. Everything that has ever come-to-be again passes away, whether we think of human life or of water or of hot and cold. Wherever definite qualities are perceivable, we can prophesy, upon the basis of enormously extensive experience, the passing away of these qualities. Never, in other words, can a being which possesses definite qualities or consists of such be the origin or first principle of things. (*KSA* 1:819/*PTA* 46–47)

Nietzsche, in other words, sees in certain pre-Socratic cosmogonies such as those of Heraclitus and Anaximander more than just a physical explanation of the world. He locates, rather, an underlying moral problem in which anthropomorphic notions of guilt and retribution become projected onto the cosmos. According to this more ethical point of view, there is a primal cosmic guilt for which all creation—things that have arisen or become rather than just *are*—must pay penalty. All creatures owe their existence to some source outside of themselves and thus bear a constant debt toward whatever power created them, a debt that revolves around the very question of being. One could call this an ontological debt. No human can be held accountable for his birth, nor is humankind as a whole responsible for its origin. In Heidegger's terms, we are "thrown" into the world and thereby delivered into the facticity of existence. Nietzsche views this problem as one involving the categories of being and becoming. Being is eternal and immutable, a pure and remote presence, whereas the world of becoming undergoes constant change. In this perpetual flux resides an inherent injustice, for all created things must eventually perish, whether they deserve to or not. Hence, not only is existence a debt that we owe to our creator; it is furthermore riddled with guilt and punishment. The notion of becoming, Nietzsche insists, carries with it a primordial sense of guilt, which must somehow be expiated. And it would seem that death functions as the ultimate form of atonement for the inherent injustice of existence:

> From this world of injustice, of insolent apostasy from the primeval one-ness of all things, Anaximander flees into a metaphysical fortress from which he leans out, letting his gaze sweep the horizon. At last, after long pensive silence, he puts a question to all creatures: "What is your existence worth? And if it is worthless, why are you here? Your guilt, I see, causes you to tarry in your existence. With your death, you have to expiate it." (*KSA* 1:820/*PTA* 48)

Although Nietzsche does not directly include Empedocles in his investigation of pre-Socratic guilt, he does not ignore the precedent set by Anaximander:

> We can easily credit the tradition that he [Anaximander] walked the earth clad in an especially dignified garment and displayed a truly tragic pride in his gestures and customs of daily living. He lived as he wrote; he spoke as solemnly as he dressed; he lifted his hands and placed his feet as though this existence were a tragic drama into which he had been born to play a hero. In all these things, he was the great model for Empedocles. (*KSA* 1:820–21/*PTA* 49)

All of Nietzsche's reflections on tragedy, whether from a Dionysian/ Apollinian, biblical, or pre-Socratic perspective, bring to mind the guilt of Hölderlin's Empedocles, who falls from grace with the gods to dwell in a world of one-sidedness and discord. The character description of Empedocles given in the "Frankfurt Plan" most clearly lays out the conflict between his holistic nature and the disruptive forces that surround him. His desire to exist in harmony with his environment is thwarted by the fact that he lives in an age of particularization and thus becomes bound to the positivistic laws of succession. Hölderlin's Empedocles can be considered a tragic figure in Nietzsche's sense; that is, one who has fallen from an original state of being and is forced to suffer in an Apollinian world of individuation or in a pre-Socratic world of becoming. His premeditated death forms the ultimate attempt to regain his lost condition of wholeness. The fact that Empedocles intends to carry out this act of atonement by leaping into the crater of Mount Etna only underscores his tragic "fall," here literalized in the image of a suicidal plunge. As we will see in the case of Nietzsche, this notion of both a literal and figurative "downfall" (*Untergang*) becomes a requisite element in his own plans for a tragedy, which he was not content to just theorize about. Undoubtedly inspired by Hölderlin, Nietzsche actively sought to create a dramatic work of art that would complement the theory behind his tragic view of existence.

The Empedocles Project (1870–72)

Sometime during the autumn of 1870 or the early winter of 1870–71, Nietzsche composed three dramatic sketches for an *Empedocles* tragedy. The first reads as follows:

> Act I. E[mpedocles] overthrows Pan, who refuses to answer him. He feels despised.
> The citizens of Agrigentum want to elect him king, unheard-of honors. He realizes the folly of religion, after a long struggle.
> The crown is brought to him by the most beautiful woman.
> II. Terrible plague, he prepares grand festivities, Dionysian Bacchanalia, art reveals itself as the prophetess of human woe. Woman as nature.

III. While at a funeral ceremony he resolves to annihilate his people, in order to free them from their misery. He finds the survivors of
the plague even more piteous [*bemitleidenswerter*].
At the temple of Pan. "Great Pan is dead." (*KSA* 7:125; 5[116])[20]

These last words, which Nietzsche quotes from Plutarch's *The Decline
of Oracles,* can also be found in *The Birth of Tragedy.* Here the context is clearly the death of tragedy and of literature as such: "But when
Greek tragedy died, there rose everywhere the deep sense of an
immense void. Just as Greek sailors in the time of Tiberius once heard
on a lonesome island the soul-shaking cry, 'Great Pan is dead,' so the
Hellenic world was now pierced by the grievous lament: 'Tragedy is
dead! Poetry itself has perished with her!'" (*KSA* 1:75/*BoT* 76). It thus
seems curious that Empedocles, the most tragic figure among the pre-
Socratics according to Nietzsche's notes, should put an end to the reign
of Pan, who can be considered the very representative of tragedy in
its raw Dionysian form as chorus; that is, without the Apollinian component of dialogue. As Nietzsche demonstrates in his book, the origin of tragedy lies in the early Hellenistic satyr plays, which consisted
of chorus, music, and dance. The satyr himself was "the Dionysian
chorist" (*KSA* 1:55/*BoT* 58) who embodied the brute force of nature
and gave expression to the primordial urges of human beings, shattering any illusion of culture that the civic-minded Greeks brought with
them to the theater. The chorus in these early stages of tragedy functioned as a kind of partition that sealed out all vestiges of civilization
and created its own aesthetic space, as in Schiller's claim from the preface of *The Bride of Messina.* However, Nietzsche tends toward a
more extreme view than Schiller, for whom the tragic performance
operates within an ideal and autonomous realm (see *KSA* 1:54/*BoT*
58). But tragedy in the eyes of Nietzsche cuts far deeper into the fabric of existence and ultimately has little to do with the aesthetic category of literature: "The sphere of poetry does not lie outside the world
as a fantastic impossibility spawned by a poet's brain: it desires to be
just the opposite, the unvarnished expression of the truth, and must
precisely for that reason discard the mendacious finery of that alleged
reality of the man of culture" (*KSA* 1:58/*BoT* 61).

The conflict between tragedy/poetry and culture is an ongoing one. The modern age has created the figure of the shepherd and the idyll of the pastoral as an antidote or civilized alternative to the untamed satyr and his Dionysian mode of articulation, the tragic chorus. Although Nietzsche never explicitly says as much, Pan can be viewed as a kind of supreme specimen among satyrs: whereas these are lesser deities, multitudinous and diverse, Pan takes on the role of a singular and representative god. The antagonism between the satyr and the man of culture as laid out in *The Birth of Tragedy* appears then to find a more concrete illustration in the rivalry of Empedocles with Pan. Unfortunately, due to the provisional nature of Nietzsche's notes, this conflict remains undeveloped. All that can safely be said based on the first outline of his *Empedocles* drama is that Nietzsche obviously conceived of some form of contest if not showdown between Empedocles and Pan, which was to result in the death of the latter—and perhaps by extension, in the death of tragedy. The line from Plutarch "Great Pan is dead" signifies here in the dramatic sketch, as in *The Birth of Tragedy,* the end of the Dionysian principle and thus of the tragic sense of life. The precise role of Empedocles in this process remains impossible to determine. Despite his seeming victory over Pan, a presumed spokesman for Dionysus or the satyr chorus, Empedocles nevertheless seems to embrace the Dionysian by preparing bacchanalian festivities.

A subsequent sketch from the same notebook depicts Empedocles as an individuated Apollinian man of culture rather than a tragic Dionysian figure:

> Empedocles, driven through all stages of religion, art, and science, dissolving the latter, turns against himself.
> Abandons religion, realizing that it is a deception.
> Now joy in artistic illusion, driven from it by recognizing world suffering. Woman as nature.
> Now he observes world suffering like an anatomist, becomes a tyrant, uses religion and art, grows ever more harsh. He decides to annihilate his people, because he recognizes their incurability. The people are gathered around the crater: he goes mad and proclaims the truth of rebirth before disappearing. A friend dies with him. (*KSA* 7:126; 5[118])

Here Empedocles displays anything but a penchant for the Dionysian. He is, rather, a man of art and science, one who prefers Apollinian deception (*Trug*) and illusion (*Schein*) to the crude reality of Dionysian existence. His "joy in artistic illusion" recalls the more detailed description from *The Birth of Tragedy:* "and we might call Apollo himself the glorious divine image of the *principium individuationis,* through whose gestures and eyes all the joy and wisdom of 'illusion,' together with its beauty, speak to us" (*KSA* 1:28/*BoT* 36). Empedocles's status as king of Agrigentum is also anti-Dionysian insofar as it implies individuation, specifically a separation from the people through sociopolitically defined roles. In Dionysian revelry, all differences in rank, character, and even subjectivity break down such that "one feels himself not only united, reconciled, and fused with his neighbor, but as one with him, as if the veil of *mâyâ* had been torn aside and were now merely fluttering in tatters before the mysterious primordial unity" (*KSA* 1:29–30/*BoT* 37). This is not the case with Empedocles, who is forced to destroy his people so as to spare them a slow and agonizing death from the plague. Here Nietzsche is clearly taking up an incident in Diogenes (cf. VII, sec. 70),[21] according to whom an epidemic caused by the vapors of a local river threatened to destroy the population not of Agrigentum but of another city, Selinuntia. Empedocles saved the populace by single-handedly diverting two nearby rivers into the problem one, thereby flushing it of its contamination. Why Nietzsche felt the need to depart from the account in Diogenes and have his Empedocles resort to the drastic measure of wholesale destruction is again a question that only allows for conjecture. Perhaps the answer has to do with the very issue of death. According to both fragments, Empedocles seeks to spare his people prolonged suffering from pestilence, yet for some reason he instead asserts his own death in the crater of Mount Etna while the crowd looks on and a friend, presumably Pausanias, follows in his footsteps. This sudden transition from genocidal to individual annihilation seems destined to remain a riddle, as Nietzsche provides no real motive nor indicates any higher justification for his hero's grand act of suicide. He only suggests that "the truth of rebirth" enters into the matter. This, at any rate, is the upshot of Empedocles's self-sacrifice in these particular notes written sometime between September 1870 and January 1871.

A quarto notebook that Nietzsche used from the winter of 1870–71 through the fall of 1872 contains eight further sketches of an *Empedocles* drama. Here one finds a greater exposition of the tragedy and hence more solid ground for interpretation. Nevertheless, it is important to bear in mind that these are only conceptual blueprints and, unlike for instance Hölderlin's "Frankfurt Plan," lack any further literary execution.

The first two notes share a number of common elements with the previous ones listed above. Pan, the plague, a nameless heroine, and the Apollinian principle all recur here:

Greek memorial festival. Signs of decline. Outbreak of the plague. The Homeric rhapsode. Empedocles appears as a god, in order to cure.

Infection through fear and pity. Antidote: tragedy. When a minor character dies, the heroine tries to reach him. Empedocles holds her back, enflamed. She burns for him. Empedocles shudders before nature.

The plague spreads.

Last day of the festival—sacrifice of Pan on Etna. Empedocles puts Pan to the test und demolishes him. The people flee. The heroine remains. In an excess of pity Empedocles wants to die. He goes into the cavity and calls out "Flee!"—She: Empedocles! and follows him. An animal rescues itself near them. Lava surrounds them.

An Apollinian god turns into a man obsessed with death.

The strength of his pessimistic knowledge causes him rage.

In a bursting excess of pity he can no longer bear existence.

He cannot cure the city, because it has fallen from its Greek way of being.

He wants to cure it radically, indeed annihilate it, but here it salvages its Greek way of being.

In his godliness he wants to help.

As a man full of pity, he wants to annihilate.

As a daimon, he annihilates himself.

Empedocles becomes ever more passionate. (*KSA* 7:233–34; 8[30–31])

The first point to be noted is that the contagion brought about by the plague consists of fear and pity, while the potential cure lies in tragedy. This rather strange twist on Aristotle, according to whom the tragic plot *incited* these two emotions rather than eliminated them (cf. *Poetics,* 49b), seems symptomatic of Nietzsche's unconventional view of tragedy, which is in turn typical of his unceasing effort to "reverse" (*umkehren*) the validity of whatever he opposes, be it Christian values, Platonism, even simple truisms and phrases. The fact that Empedocles wishes to die "in a bursting excess of pity" is perhaps a further critique of the Aristotelian notion, but again, there is too little text—both in Nietzsche and Aristotle—upon which to base anything more than a tentative thesis. Even the more explicit line from the last sketch of this series, "fear and pity prohibited" (*KSA* 7:236), fails to cast much light on this question of Aristotelian aesthetics. In fact, Nietzsche's general view on the function of tragedy is not at all apparent in the fragments. It only seems clear that he in some fashion seeks to overturn or at least rethink the tragic tradition, a task that he however carried out more effectively in *The Birth of Tragedy*.

Here one finds a more forward critique of the aesthetic tradition that followed in Aristotle's wake. According to Nietzsche, this tradition has overemphasized the functions of pity, fear, and catharsis. It may be helpful to recall in this context Aristotle's celebrated definition of tragedy "as the imitation of an action . . . with incidents arousing pity and fear, wherewith to accomplish, its catharsis of such emotions."[22] The notion of catharsis has been interpreted along vastly different lines over the last several centuries, yet two principal views hold sway. The most favored interpretation is a quasimedical one, in which catharsis functions as a purging of the very emotions, pity and fear, that the tragic incidents aroused in the first place. Pity and fear, according to this view, exert a homeopathic affect on the audience; that is, the very incitement of such emotions brings about their purgation. The second dominant interpretation, propounded by such tragedians as Corneille, Dacier, and Dryden, takes a moralistic or didactic stance: the audience learns through catharsis to steer clear of those passions that lead to the tragic hero's downfall. Catharsis in this sense curbs rather than cleanses emotions, and the process remains a spiritually uplifting rather than a physiological one. Nietzsche, however, insists that these tragic effects of moral edification and purgation do nothing to further our understanding of tragedy as a purely aesthetic phenomenon:

> Never since Aristotle has an explanation of the tragic effect been offered from which aesthetic states or an aesthetic activity of the listener could be inferred. Now the serious events are supposed to prompt pity and fear to discharge themselves in a way that relieves us; now we are supposed to feel elevated and inspired by the triumph of good and noble principles, at the sacrifice of the hero in the interest of a moral vision of the universe. I am sure that for countless men precisely this, and only this, is the effect of tragedy, but it plainly follows that all these men, together with their interpreting aestheticians, have had no experience of tragedy as a supreme *art*. (*KSA* 1:142/*BoT* 132)

Nietzsche therefore posits an Apollinian and Dionysian "excitement of the hearer" (*KSA* 1:141/*BoT* 132) against the prevailing medical and ethical theories of his day. In so doing, he brings to light yet another important aspect of Hellenistic culture that the philological method was hitherto unable to uncover. Not only does Nietzsche believe that he has discovered the true function of the tragic chorus; he furthermore claims to have ousted the modern critic from his sovereign throne and reinstated the aesthetic spectator in the latter's place. With this profound insight into the essence of tragedy and the role of its ideal viewer, Nietzsche proved once again that he was more than just a professor of classical philology. Here he shows his future potential as a philosopher and aesthetic theoretician, two capacities for which he is best known to posterity. The fact that he was also an aspiring tragedian lends further credence to his views regarding the tragic, even if his efforts in this more artistic realm have largely been ignored to this day.

In conceiving his *Empedocles* tragedy Nietzsche clearly appropriated elements from Hölderlin's dramatic project, although most of the critical literature has overlooked if not outright dismissed this connection. Curt Paul Janz, who otherwise unearths a wealth of source material that Nietzsche drew upon throughout his life, observes "surprisingly no connection at all"[23] between the two *Empedocles* projects. David Farrell Krell has attempted to rectify this deficit in Nietzsche scholarship. Krell's words serve to guide my following observations regarding both tragedies: "Why insist on the conjunction of Nietzsche and Hölderlin here? Because I am convinced that Curt Paul Janz and others have woefully underestimated the impact of Nietzsche's reading of Hölderlin's *Der Tod des Empedokles*."[24]

Nietzsche's sentence "Empedocles shudders [*schaudert*] before nature" (*KSA* 7:234) strikes the reader as a deliberate nod at Hölderlin's lines from both the ode and first draft of the play: "shuddering desire/*schauderndes Verlangen*" (see *SWB* 1:241 and *SWB* 2:354). The fact that in the second of the above two plans (8[31]) Empedocles originally appears as an Apollinian god only to become "a man obsessed with death" also parallels the development of Hölderlin's tragic figure. As discussed previously, the Empedocles of Hölderlin's project finds himself surrounded by a world of particularity. His longing for totality leads him to seek communion with nature, but even this ideal has been lost amidst the prevailing fragmentation of modern life. He must therefore take a more radical step and embrace death as the only means to attain cosmic unity. His dissolution in the molten lava of Etna is thus a literal and at the same time highly symbolic act of fusion with the elements. Hölderlin's Empedocles of course accomplishes this goal alone, while Nietzsche's figure perishes together with a companion—in this cluster of notes with a heroine, earlier with a male friend. (Even an animal is involved in the former case.) Although Empedocles's partners in death are not named here, subsequent sketches make their identities apparent: Corinna and Pausanias. The former carries on the role of Panthea, displaying both spiritual and amorous devotion toward Empedocles (see *KSA* 1:236–37; 8[37]). She, too, is an attested historical figure (though not in Diogenes), namely a poetess who was said to have instructed Pindar and even defeated him in a poetry contest.[25] As for Pausanias, he of course bears the name given to him by tradition, one to which Nietzsche and Hölderlin, in this respect at least, both adhered.

Another parallel, this one of both a conceptual and structural nature, between the two *Empedocles* dramas becomes apparent in the following two sketches:

1st act: scene of entry
2nd act: worship and arrangement of the festivals. King's crown turned
     down.
3rd act: the contests
4th act: the plague spreads. The death plan. Bacchic frenzy among the
     people.
5th act:
     Pan on Etna.

He is free of fear and pity, until the heroine's act.
In the fourth act an increase of pity. The death plan.
In the fifth he is happy, knowing that the people have been saved.
Contradiction: his plan fails, death appears as a greater calamity than
the plague.
The people honor him ever more highly, to the level of Pan. (*KSA*
7:234–35; 8[32–33])

Like Hölderlin's "Frankfurt Plan," these preliminary outlines call for
a five-act tragedy. The "death plan" mentioned above corresponds to
the resolution that Hölderlin's Empedocles eventually settles on, and
in both cases this decision to die occurs in the fourth act. Yet the respective motivation differs considerably. Hölderlin's character of course
longs to rejoin infinite nature, while the death wish of Nietzsche's re-
creation seems linked with the widespread pestilence and his growing pity for its victims. Indeed, one wonders whether his "death plan"
is not intended as some sort of sacrifice in exchange for the salvation
of his people, which might explain the so-called "contradiction" indicated in the fifth act: "his plan fails, death appears as a greater calamity
than the plague." Again, as is often the case when interpreting
Nietzsche's schematic notes, few definitive conclusions can be drawn.
One does, however, notice that the Empedocles of these fragments shows
a greater attachment to his people than does Hölderlin's hero in any
of the drafts except perhaps the third. In nearly all of the sketches,
Nietzsche's Empedocles participates in the activities of the *polis*, particularly in its tragic and poetic contests. He is after all the ruler of the
city, whereas Hölderlin's figure takes on the role of a social outcast
who has all but been forced into exile. In the "Frankfurt Plan," the only
stage of the project to depict the climactic death scene, only a handful of followers gather at the crater of Etna to commemorate his

grandiose act. Nietzsche's Empedocles on the other hand, perhaps because he is willing to die for his people rather than for lofty ideals, enjoys a more popular status, as the second of the above fragments illustrates.

In the final sketch from this notebook, Nietzsche fleshes out the five acts that he previously outlined in somewhat skeletal fashion. Of all the dramatic fragments, this is the only one to run over a page, which still makes it less than half the length of Hölderlin's "Frankfurt Plan." Due to this factor of length, it need not be cited here in its entirety. It offers only a limited number of fresh insights into Nietzsche's project, chiefly detailing what had been sketched out earlier in the most cursory and condensed form. Nevertheless, some important points emerge from this fragment.

In the third act, during the citywide tragic festivals, Empedocles again proclaims his doctrine of reincarnation (cf. the previous sketches above in *KSA* 7:126; 5[118]), yet this time long before he stands at the crater's rim. Following this pronouncement, the people honor him "as the god Dionysus" (*KSA* 7:236), which marks a complete transformation from his earlier status as an Apollinian deity in the second fragment of this cluster. Empedocles-Dionysus has now become a truly tragic figure who no longer shows any traces of an individuated Apollinian existence. He is, rather, filled with "the desire to destroy" (*KSA* 7:236), and this Dionysian bent toward (self-)destruction only increases by the fifth act, the outline of which is cited here:

> Empedocles among his pupils.
> Nocturnal celebration.
> Mystical speech on pity. Annihilation of the life-drive, death of Pan.
> The people flee.
> Two streams of lava, they cannot escape!
> Empedocles und Corinna. Empedocles feels like a murderer, deserving of endless punishment, he hopes for a rebirth of penitential death. This is what drives him into Etna. He wants to save Korinna. An animal approaches them. Korinna dies with him. "Does Dionysos flee in the face of Ariadne?"   (*KSA* 7:237; 8[37])

This is the first indication in the sketch of Empedocles's resolve to die. In contrast to the five-act schemes discussed above, both of which fix the "death plan" in the fourth act, this final sketch gives no hint of the protagonist's fate until the very end of the conceived drama. Here death takes on the function of penitence, a notion that evokes both Hölderlin's play and the cosmogony of the historical Empedocles. As in the original *Purifications,* this more modern Empedocles "feels like a murderer, deserving of endless punishment." Although Nietzsche does not specify that this feeling stems from a primal act of bloodshed, his curious and otherwise inexplicable inclusion of an animal at the end of this and previous fragments might be linked with the Empedoclean prohibition of consuming meat. All of these aspects directly pick up on the ideas presented in the *Purifications* and to some extent in Hölderlin's *The Death of Empedocles.* More importantly, however, Nietzsche finally provides a motive for his hero's sacrifice: "he hopes for a rebirth of penitential death. This is what drives him into Etna." This sketch is the only one that makes any mention of atonement, yet it is not entirely clear what precise crime Empedocles seeks to expiate. Again, it seems unlikely that the primordial transgression of murder, which figures so strongly in the *Purifications,* plays a significant role in the conception of Nietzsche's drama. His preoccupations up until this point have been with different themes, most of which relate to fundamental questions of tragedy. Moreover, he has shown little fidelity to the original doctrines of Empedocles, instead using the pre-Socratic as a means to communicate his own views. The Empedocles in these dramatic plans has little if anything to do with the historical figure who composed *On Nature* and *Purifications,* or for that matter with the reconstructed philosopher described by Diogenes Laertius. Empedocles will, in fact, only be further transformed, resurfacing some ten years later as Zarathustra, the main spokesman of Nietzsche's later philosophy. This transformation, first announced in *The Gay Science,* still occurs under the rubric of tragedy, as the title of aphorism 342 plainly reveals: "*Incipit tragoedia*" (*KSA* 3:571/*GS* 274). However, what Nietzsche fails to express here is that this incipient tragedy involving Zarathustra actually began as early as 1871, in a series of unpublished notes revolving around the figure of Empedocles.

THE EXISTENTIAL FUNCTION OF DEATH IN *THUS SPOKE ZARATHUSTRA* AND OTHER WRITINGS

The tragedy announced in *The Gay Science* is not meant to be that of Empedocles, but of Zarathustra, the titular hero of Nietzsche's conceptually and stylistically most unique work. Nevertheless, this book, which was written between 1883 and 1885, can be considered an extension of the *Empedocles* project from the early 1870s for several reasons. First of all, *Thus Spoke Zarathustra* remains a curious mixture of philosophy, poetry, and drama. Not only does Nietzsche pick up on the pre-Socratic tradition of philosophizing in a poetic and doctrinal manner, but he also creates a diverse cast of characters whose verbal and physical interactions lend a certain dramatic quality to the text. Moreover, posthumously published notes from this period reveal that Nietzsche still toyed with the idea of writing a play, this time around his newly conceived figure. Despite the fact that Zarathustra owes his name to the ancient Persian philosopher better known as Zoroaster, the two have little else in common. Nietzsche modeled his creation, rather, on Hölderlin's tragic hero, as the numerous similarities between *Thus Spoke Zarathustra* and *The Death of Empedocles* demonstrate. The most essential parallel between the two works concerns the notion of death, which both characters come to regard as a summation of life and which both furthermore carry out—at least according to working sketches—in the mouth of a volcano.

From Empedocles to Zarathustra

Countless interpreters have endeavored to answer the question, first formulated as such by Heidegger: "Who is Nietzsche's Zarathustra?"[26] If there is any consensus on the issue of Zarathustra's identity and function it is that he shares practically no kinship with his namesake Zoroaster, the founder of a pre-Islamic religion in which the conflicting principles of good and evil influence the course of the world. Nietzsche has effectively undermined any alliance between these two figures, who go by the same name in the following passage:

I have not been asked, as I should have been asked, what the name of Zarathustra means in my mouth, the mouth of the first immoralist: for what constitutes the tremendous historical uniqueness of that Persian is just the opposite of this. Zarathustra was the first to consider the fight of good and evil the very wheel in the machinery of things: the transposition of morality into the metaphysical realm, as a force, cause, and end in itself, is *his* work. But this question itself is at bottom its own answer. Zarathustra created this most calamitous error, morality; consequently, he must also be the first to recognize it. . . . The self-overcoming of morality, out of truthfulness; the self-overcoming of the moralist, into his opposite—into me—that is what the name of Zarathustra means in my mouth. (*KSA* 6:367/*EH* 783–84)

As has been observed in light of this statement, Nietzsche's Zarathustra is an anti-Zoroaster.[27] Nietzsche, in other words, deliberately uses Zoroaster as a foil, reversing his role as religious moralist into that of a heathen destroyer of values. Zarathustra thus takes on precisely the opposite function of his Persian predecessor. To what extent Nietzsche effects a similar transvaluation of Zarathustra's more influential forerunner Empedocles remains to be seen.

The very title of *Thus Spoke Zarathustra,* which derives from the closing refrain of the protagonist's speeches, points more to the pre-Socratics than to Zoroaster. As Curt Paul Janz has argued, the formula "Thus spoke . . ." can be regarded as a translation of *tade legei* or *hôde legei,* which are common opening lines to pre-Socratic writings.[28] According to an eminent authority on early Greek philosophy, Hermann Diels, the original sayings of Heraclitus probably followed this protocol, a fact that Nietzsche could not have ignored. Diels even goes so far as to claim that Nietzsche's *Thus Spoke Zarathustra* is directly descended from this tradition.[29] Beyond this common idiom, the labels attached to individual sections of Nietzsche's book also pick up on a pre-Socratic convention. Many of Zarathustra's discourses begin with *von* plus the appropriate definite article, for example "Von den Tugendhaften" (On the Virtuous). Such headings hark back to ancient treatises whose subject matter tended to be preceded by the preposition *peri* plus the genitive. This is, for instance, the case with the cosmological fragments of Heraclitus and Empedocles, which have been grouped under the title *peri Physeôs* or *On Nature.*

Nevertheless, Zarathustra bears a far greater resemblance to Empedocles the tragic hero than to the historical philosopher of cosmic creation and guilt. Like the fictionalized character of Hölderlin's drama, Zarathustra is a prophet whose teachings meet with the intolerance of resentful priests and mean-spirited villagers, which results in his self-imposed exile to heights above the common herd. The banished Empedocles and Zarathustra are each joined by a few loyal disciples with whom they discuss the present ills and future potential of humanity. Beyond this general scope of plot, Nietzsche took over numerous aspects from Hölderlin's drama.[30] The broader concept behind the figure of Zarathustra recalls the unifying role that Hölderlin ascribed to his character in the "Frankfurt Plan" and "The Ground for 'Empedocles.'" As Nietzsche states retrospectively in *Ecce homo:* "in him [Zarathustra] all opposites are blended into a new unity" (*KSA* 6:343/*EH* 761). In the work proper, Zarathustra's function as conciliator becomes especially apparent in the section entitled "On Redemption." Here one finds an obvious allusion to Hölderlin, not, however, to *The Death of Empedocles* but to *Hyperion.* Zarathustra's condemnation of his contemporaries echoes Hyperion's invective against German philistinism in the penultimate letter of the novel:

> "Verily, my friends, I walk among men as among the fragments and limbs of men. This is what is terrible for my eyes, that I find man in ruins and scattered as over a battlefield or a butcher-field. And when my eyes flee from the now to the past, they always find the same: fragments and limbs and dreadful accidents—but no human beings."[31] (*KSA* 4:178–79/*Z* 250)

One of Zarathustra's many goals is to overcome this human fragmentation and, like Empedocles (Hyperion's extreme idealism prevents him from effecting any change), reintroduce some sort of harmony into the world: "'And this is all my creating and striving, that I create and carry together into One what is fragment and riddle and dreadful accident'" (*KSA* 4:179/*Z* 251). There is even some indication that this reconciliation or redemption, both of which are recurring terms in this section, is motivated by a primordial guilt as in Hölderlin's drama: "'No deed can be annihilated: how could it be undone by punishment?

This, this is what is eternal in the punishment called existence, that existence must eternally become deed and guilt again'" (*KSA* 4:181/*Z* 252).

In contrast to Empedocles, Zarathustra finds no need to sacrifice himself in a volcano in order to reconcile the guilt and strife of existence—at least not in the version of *Thus Spoke Zarathustra* that one reads today. However, posthumously published notes from the summer of 1883 reveal that Nietzsche contemplated the same fate for Zarathustra as for Empedocles. At this point he had finished writing the first two parts of the book (part 1 appeared in April, part 2 in August) and now apparently considered adopting a dramatic form for the third, as the following three sketches demonstrate:

Act I. The temptations. He does not yet deem himself ripe.
(Selected people)
Loneliness out of self-shame.

Act II. Zarathustra attends the "great midday" incognito
Is recognized

Act III. Catastrophe: everyone turns away after *his* speech.
He dies of pain.

Act IV. Obsequies
"We killed him"

is convincing of the reasons

For Act I. He refuses. Finally in tears because of the children's choruses.
A *fool!*
2 kings lead the donkey.
For Act 2. When the procession does not know which way to turn, the emissaries arrive from the plague-ridden city. Decision. Like in the forest. Fire in the marketplace, symbol[ic] purification.
Annihilation of the *metropolis* the end.
I want to seduce the *pious.*

Zarathustra sitting upon the ruins of a church Act 4
The mildest one must become the hardest—and perish in the process.
Mild toward humanity, hard for the sake of the Übermensch[.]
Collision.
apparent *weakness.*
He prophesies to them: the doctrine of recurrence is the *sign.*

> He **forgets himself** and teaches recurrence **based on** the *Übermensch:* the Übermensch *withstands it* and *disciplines by means of it.* When returning from his vision he dies from it.
>
> (*KSA* 10:377–78; 10[45–47])

Given the fact that Zarathustra perishes in the third act of this plan and that his obsequies take place in the fourth, it would seem that Nietzsche had no intention of composing a full five-act tragedy as he did in the case of his *Empedocles* project. And the additional fact that Zarathustra dies from grief or heartbreak rather than through a more assertive act of sacrifice remains yet another departure from the earlier fragments. His death, ultimately caused by the people ("We killed him"), is characterized by passivity and thus forms the precise contrast to the self-destructive, Dionysian bent that Empedocles displays in the manuscripts from 1870 to 1872. Nor does one find any mention of Etna or volcanic flame in these sketches. Nevertheless, Nietzsche shares with Hölderlin the view of fire as a purifying and regenerative force; that is, as a form of catharsis in its original, non-Aristotelian sense. The outbreak of fire in the marketplace consumes and presumably cleanses the pest-ridden city, much as the fiery end of Empedocles symbolizes purgation and perhaps a phoenixlike rebirth in the context of Hölderlin's drama. This notion of renewal is implied in Zarathustra's doctrine of recurrence, which he prophesies while perched upon the ruins of a church, a scene symbolizing the death of religion. Nietzsche's concept of eternal recurrence, a central theme in the still unwritten part 3, appears as early as the *Empedocles* plan, where the hero proclaims "the truth of rebirth" (*KSA* 7:126) immediately before his plunge into the volcano. This doctrine of palingenesis has of course Pythagorean-Empedoclean roots and figures strongly in the *Purifications.* It even receives passing mention in Hölderlin's drama, where Empedocles's proclaims: "Everything recurs" (*SWB* 2:409/*PF* 349).

Another four-act sketch from the summer of 1883 proves more reminiscent of Nietzsche's own *Empedocles* plans from a decade earlier:

Act I.   Zarathustra among animals. The cave.
         The child with the mirror. (It is time!)

The various queries, mounting. Finally the children seduce him with song.

Act 2. The city, outbreak of the plague. Zarathustra's procession, healing of the woman. Springtime.

Act 3. Midday and Eternity.

Act 4. The sailors.
Scene on the volcano, Zarathustra *dying among children*.
The funeral.

Omens.

For Act 3: Zarathustra saw and heard nothing, he was transfixed.

Then gradually a return to the most frightful knowledge. The disciples indignant, his favorites leave, Zarathustra tries to stop them. The serpent darts its tongue at him. He recants, excess of pity, the eagle flees. Now the scene with the woman in whom the plague again breaks out. He kills out of pity. He embraces the corpse.

Then the ship and the appearance on the volcano. "Zarathustra is going to hell? Or does he now want to redeem the underworld?"—Thus the rumor spreads that he is also the Evil One.

Final scene on the volcano. Complete bliss. Oblivion. Vision of the woman (or of the child with the mirror) The disciples gaze into the deep grave. (Or *Zarathustra among* **children** at the temple ruins.)

The greatest of all funerals makes up the end. Golden coffin is plunged into the volcano. (*KSA* 10:444–45; 13[2])

With Zarathustra's death scene now moved to a volcano, Nietzsche falls back on the Empedocles tradition, although he does not completely follow all the details found in Hölderlin and Diogenes. Zarathustra dies not *in* the volcano itself, which here remains nameless, but upon its slopes or at the edge of its summit crater. In contrast to his both literal and figurative forerunners, he does not race forward into death, but instead succumbs to some fatal weakness (his cause of death is not entirely clear) only then to take the postmortem plunge into the volcano, his body encased in a golden casket. His end, while ceremonious and triumphant, lacks the resoluteness that his predecessors displayed in the face of extinction. Nevertheless, there can be no doubt that Nietzsche ascribed central importance to these final moments of Zarathustra, noting for instance in the superlative: "The greatest of all funerals makes up the end." Other sketches too numerous to cite (some dozen in all), show that he intended to entitle one of the chapters "The Funeral" (*Die Todtenfeier*), a heading that never made it into the completed work. Indeed, Zarathustra does not give in to the "temptation of suicide" (*KSA* 10:480) in the published version. After periods of despair at the plight of humanity, he instead experiences a revitalization of his powers and leaves the gloom of his cave for the bright midday sun, a recurring symbol of the future in which man as we know him will be "overcome" (*überwunden*) by the "overman" (*Übermensch*). The closing words of part 4 testify to his renewed vigor and passion: "Thus spoke Zarathustra, and he left his cave, glowing and strong as a morning sun that comes out of dark mountains" (*KSA* 4:408/*Z* 439).

It apparently took Nietzsche several years to arrive at this optimistic ending, for during the course of his project he pondered a number of different fates for his character, all of which entail distinct manners of death. As mentioned above, his notes from the summer of 1883 depict a mysterious and gentle end upon an equally mysterious and gentle volcano, one that bears no specific name nor shows any signs of dangerous activity such as flowing lava or spewing flames. In later sketches, the volcano disappears altogether and Zarathustra's death no longer occurs in connection with this Empedoclean landmark.[32]

In drafts from the autumn of 1883, Nietzsche attributes the cause of his figure's death to the fatal emotion of pity, thereby taking up a crucial idea from his earlier *Empedocles* plans. Zarathustra becomes overwhelmed by feelings of compassion for the principal female figure, Pana (a possible throwback to the Panthea of Hölderlin's drama or to the Pan of Nietzsche's own project), who for reasons not to be divined from the fragments has intentions of killing him:

> When he guesses Pana's identity, Zarathustra dies of pity for her pity.
>
> At first they all abandon Zarathustra (this *is to be portrayed gradually!*). Zarathustra transfixed, notices nothing. Pana intends to kill him. *At the moment she wields the knife, Zarathustra comprehends everything and dies of pain over this pity.* This is *to be made clear!* (*KSA* 10:512–13; 16[38,42])

Nietzsche's notion of pity here and elsewhere in *Thus Spoke Zarathustra* seems to have little to do with Aristotle's tragic effect of *eleos*. It is more closely related to the Christian virtue of commiseration, which Nietzsche criticized in his later thinking as one of the chief obstacles to be overcome in the transvaluation of all values. Pity only succeeds in lowering the pitying subject to the level of the pitied object: by sympathizing (like the Greek *sum-paschô,* the German *mit-leiden* literally means "to suffer with/together") with a less fortunate human being, one cannot help but identify with that person to some degree. Such an attitude is fatal for the vitality of a culture, as it reduces the "pathos of distance" that separates the handful of noble individuals, the true bearers of culture, from the afflicted masses, who can either inhibit cultural growth or serve it as raw material. This aristocratic view is necessarily a ruthless one, but then again the very act of creation is at bottom harsh and merciless. As Zarathustra affirms: "But all creators are hard" (*KSA* 4:116/*Z* 202) and must remain so if they expect to produce anything new rather than merely perpetuate the status quo. Perhaps this crisis in creativity is what contributed to the death of God, Who died from the very same ailment as Zarathustra in the above fragments: "'God is dead; God died of his pity for man'" (*KSA* 4:115/*Z* 202). Zarathustra must avoid falling into the same emotional snare if he hopes to overcome himself and eventually usher in a higher type of human being, the so-called *Übermensch*. The next time that Pana intends to kill him in the fragments, Zarathustra thus does not give in to pity, but exhibits precisely the opposite reaction: he breaks out into peels of laughter. And his subsequent death occurs not on a volcano, but nonetheless in a mountainous setting: "[Zarathustra] [c]limbs upward to the rocky outcrop, laughing; upon arrival he dies happily" (*KSA* 10:594).

Dying at the Right Time

In these notes from 1883, Nietzsche is following up on a central section from the already published part 1 of his book: Zarathustra's speech "On Free Death." This discourse contains *in nuce* Zarathustra's, and presumably Nietzsche's own, view of death as the ultimate possibility of self-overcoming. Zarathustra begins as follows: "Many die too late and a few die too early. The doctrine still sounds strange: 'Die at the right time!' [Stirb zur rechten Zeit!] Die at the right time—thus teaches Zarathustra" (*KSA* 4:93/*Z* 183). The formulation of this maxim recalls the exemplary death "at the right time" (*SWB* 2:339, 340) that Empedocles promulgates in the first draft of Hölderlin's play. For Nietzsche as for Hölderlin, the "right time" to die occurs at that point in existence when one is no longer able to push the limits of possibility. This is an idea related to Zarathustra's major doctrine of self-overcoming, according to which the ideal human—the future *Übermensch* anticipated throughout the work—engages in a continual process of becoming, forever surpassing his previous accomplishments. It is interesting to note that Empedocles also considers himself an "overcomer" precisely with regard to the question of death: "O, is this why life came to you so easily / So that you would find the joys of the overcomer / All in one final and complete act?" (*SWB* 2:354). With the imperative "Die at the right time!" Zarathustra, along with his distant forebear Empedocles, thus intends to say the following: rather than linger in a halting stage of development, one should instead carry out what may be the most supreme act of self-overcoming: an affirmation of death while still in one's prime. Yet most people are not capable of determining this moment on their own; for them there is no proper time to die, as they have never properly lived. One of Zarathustra's many condemnations of the masses in this vein runs as follows: "Of course, how could those who never live at the right time die at the right time? Would that they had never been born! Thus I counsel the superfluous" (*KSA* 4:93/*Z* 183). This negative perspective remains as present in Zarathustra's speech as the more creative, life-promoting one conveyed in the existential mandate: "Die at the right time!" Nietzsche thus outlines two contrasting attitudes toward mortality, the one a model for a perfectly configured existence, the other a forfeiture of self-autonomy.

Zarathustra's critique of the superfluous that outlive rather than overcome themselves is made manifest throughout his oration. A variety of rhetorical tropes appear in his speech on free death. The most significant of these in light of Hölderlin's *Empedocles* and an entire tradition of thanatological discourse emerge in the following passage, which is replete with organic metaphors:

> One must cease letting oneself be eaten when one tastes best: that is known to those who want to be loved long. There are sour apples, to be sure, whose lot requires that they wait till the last day of autumn: and they become ripe, yellow, and wrinkled all at once. . . .
>
> Some never become sweet, they rot already in the summer. It is cowardice that keeps them on their branch.
>
> All-too-many live and all-too-long they hang on their branches. Would that a storm came to shake all this worm-eaten rot from the tree!
>
> Would that there came preachers of a *quick* death! I would like them as the true storms and shakers of the trees of life! But I hear only slow death preached, and patience with everything "earthly." (*KSA* 4:94/*Z* 184–85)

Through this imagery of ripe and rotten fruit Nietzsche draws a dichotomy between two modes of conduct toward finitude. Here he takes up an important aspect of Hölderlin's drama, in the first draft of which Empedocles condemns the popular view of death sanctioned by Hermocrates the high priest. Empedocles, who in his haste to die finds himself harassed by Hermocrates and the populace of Agrigentum, even delivers to his adversaries the key words that Zarathustra unleashes at the end his invective: "Die a slow death" (*SWB* 2:307). Empedocles thus takes on the role of a "preacher of quick death" insofar as he attempts to shake the masses out of their complacent attitude. Like the metaphorical fruit that, according to Zarathustra, clings to the branch long past its time, the people of Agrigentum seek to extend their lease on life and postpone an encounter with their inevitable extinction. This is not the case with Empedocles, who relies on a remarkably similar image in describing his impending end: "Today is my autumn and the fruit falls / Of its own" (*SWB* 2:339). Another organic metaphor that Empedocles uses to convey his idea of the "right time" to die runs as follows: "Like a noble seed, the heart of mortals / Often sleeps in a dead shell [*Schale*], / Until their time is come" (*SWB* 2:342). This association of a ripened fruit with a timely death is not particular to Hölderlin and Nietzsche but is a topos that can be found in other works dealing with the problem of mortality. In *The Bohemian*

Ploughman, written in the early fifteenth century by Johannes von Saaz (a.k.a. Tepl), the allegorical character of Death argues along similar lines with the Ploughman, who mourns the premature passing of his wife: "Over-ripe apples are prone to fall into slosh [*Kot*] and pears into the slough [*Pfütze*]."[33] Here, too, a conflict of viewpoints is presented. On the one hand, the Ploughman holds fast to existence and refuses to accept death, the personification of which he curses for all eternity. Death, on the other hand, repeatedly makes a case for its necessary presence in the midst of life. Like Zarathustra, he calls for mortals to die at the height of their powers, beyond which time it is too late to lead a plentiful existence: "'T'is best to die when it's best to live!' he hath no easy death who desireth death; he hath lived too long who calls on Us for the sake of dying."[34] Also relevant in this context are the following words of Pierre Charron, a close friend of the renowned meditator on death, Montaigne: "Every man hath his time and season to die: some prevent it, others prolong it: there is a weaknesse and valour in them both, but there is required discretion. . . . There is a time to gather fruit from the tree, which if it hang too long, it rotteth and growes worse and worse; and the losse is as great too, if it be gathered too soon."[35]

All of these authors, whether late medieval, Renaissance, or modern, distinguish between two opposing mentalities: one that fully acknowledges the imminence of death throughout existence and one that postpones or altogether evades the issue. And they furthermore illustrate this problem through the metaphor of fruit, which can either be plucked at its peak or left to go foul. In aphorism 185 from *The Wanderer and His Shadow* (1880), Nietzsche designates these two modes of death respectively as voluntary/rational and involuntary/natural. The latter manner of demise is one that ensues not through the individual's volition, but through the inexorable process of nature. Eventually, of course, everyone dies and most people die of natural causes that set in well beyond the prime of life. In describing this phenomenon of an involuntary death, Nietzsche does not altogether abandon the organic tropes that play a central role in *Zarathustra:* "Natural death is independent of all reason, indeed an *irrational* death, one in which the wretched condition of the shell [*Schale*] determines how long the seed shall continue to exist" (*KSA* 2:632–33). Instead of waiting for an outside force to decide upon our fate while our existence only becomes ever more stagnant and prolonged, we are expected to take the initiative and choose death over debility. Such a voluntary or freely willed—the original German relies on the word *freiwillig*—death is a rational one because it is willed counter to nature, resulting from human resolve rather than from the natural and inevitable order of things. Nietzsche sums up these two comportments toward finitude by posing the following rhetorical question, this time opting for a different metaphor, indeed a highly inorganic one that seems especially relevant today in view of the countless terminally ill patients wasting away on life-support: "What is more rational, to turn off the machine once it has performed the work demanded of it—or to let it run until it comes to a halt on its own; that is, until it is ruined?" (*KSA* 2:632).³⁶

The notion of *freiwilliger Tod* (free-willed death) resembles that of *freier Tod* (free death) in both name and concept. Death is free because it is willed by the individual, or in Zarathustra's words: "My death I praise to you, the free death which comes to me because *I* want it" (*KSA* 4:94/*Z* 184). Death is not something that will one day simply befall Zarathustra as an extraneous event beyond his control. Rather than let nature or the physical laws of the body determine one's final moment, Zarathustra insists that the decision instead be placed in the hands of the individual. As a self-overcomer, Zarathustra is the maker of his own existence, which means that he is also the artisan of his own death. The self-overcomer shapes his life such that he never regresses or stagnates but continually transcends himself toward whatever goal may loom before him, whether the consummate work of art, the stylization of character, or the perfection of existence. Eventually even self-transcendence has its limits and it is then that death, paradoxically, becomes the only existential possibility for further growth. This idea is borne out by the following statement from Zarathustra's address: "Free to die and free in death, able to say a holy No when the time for Yes has passed: thus he [the man] knows how to die and to live" (*KSA* 4:95/*Z* 185). In other words, one's affirmation of life inevitably turns into a negation, a negation necessitated by the aporia of a static existence. The only way to break out of such an existential stasis is to cultivate a free relation to death and embrace this freedom when life no longer offers the possibility of self-overcoming.

The Stoic Ideal of Voluntary Death

The practical implications of free death remain, however, difficult to imagine. Is one truly expected to die of one's own free will upon having lived to the fullest? And what precise or concrete actions does free death require such a determined individual to undertake? In aphorism 80 of *Human, All Too Human,* Nietzsche indicates that he does in fact advocate death at one's own hand as was practiced by "leaders of Greek philosophy and the bravest Roman patriots," though he appears to suggest this more in light of modern Christian efforts to keep a weak and dying person alive at all costs:

> In contrast, the mania of prolonging our lease on life from day to day, anxiously consulting doctors and leading an embarrassing existence, all the while deprived of the strength to come closer to life's real goal, is much less respectable. Religions are well versed in skirting the issue of suicide [*Selbsttötung*]; in this manner, they ingratiate themselves with those enamored of life. (*KSA* 2:85)

Nonetheless, given Nietzsche's life-long assertion of ancient ideals, particularly his later attempt at a transvaluation of Platonic-Christian values, it would seem likely that he did in part seek to reinstate the classical ideal of suicide. Karl Jaspers for one interprets the notion of voluntary/rational death as an outright act of suicide, and he links Nietzsche with a thanatological tradition that culminated in the Stoics. According to Jaspers, Nietzsche praised a voluntary death over a natural one throughout his writings and, like the Stoics, tended to view suicide as an expression of the greatness in man, as the mastery of reason and volition over the natural laws of the body.[37] A brief examination of the role of suicide in antiquity may help to illumine the implications of free death, especially as they relate to Zarathustra's programmatic speech.

Socrates, whose voluntary end Walter Kaufmann suspects underlies Nietzsche's notion of free death,[38] is the most famous figure of antiquity to die at his own hands. Of course the underlying freedom of Socrates' death is subject to debate, since he was condemned by a tribunal and forced to act as his own executioner. Yet it is important to recall that Socrates had the choice of exile or imprisonment but in the end elected death over the two. His advanced age may certainly have played a role in this decision, but the fact that his self-chosen death was highly celebrated in the classical world would appear to be symptomatic of the widespread practice of suicide in antiquity, a practice that, in the words of one renowned scholar on the subject, had its "golden age" in ancient Greece and Rome.[39] What Socrates says about his self-inflicted death in the *Apology* probably only echoes the views of Plato, who, though he tends to disapprove of suicide, allows for exceptions under certain circumstances. In the *Phaedo* (61b–62d) and the *Laws* (873cd) Plato maintains that it is wrong for us to take our own lives, since this remains an affair of the gods, who are responsible for our existence and therefore also for our deaths. This argument resembles of course that of Christianity, according to which the *ens creatum* has no right disposing over its own fate; life and death are matters deferred to the divine creator. For Plato, however, the prohibition of suicide is not an absolute. He holds that it is acceptable under three conditions: by order of the state (as in the case of Socrates); when suffering from incurable pain or illness; and when faced with unbearable shame, including poverty. Suicide on any of these grounds remains more a civic privilege or duty than an exercise of individual freedom. On the other hand, a suicide committed for reasons not sanctioned by the state constitutes a punishable offense, which is not as paradoxical as it may seem, for one's corpse could always be refused proper funeral rites. Here a striking similarity exists to the Christian custom of denying religious burial to those who have taken their own fate into their hands. Indeed, it would be facile to insist on a strict opposition between ancient and Christian attitudes toward death, Nietzsche's transvaluation of values notwithstanding. To defer to one of the authorities on the issue: "The essential difference between classical and medieval attitudes toward voluntary death lies in the plurality of opinions in ancient times versus the monolithic stance of Christianity."[40] In the following, I will explore some of these pluralistic views in an effort to uncover the deeper roots of Nietzsche's ideas about a self-willed death.

The Cynics and especially the Stoics display a less civic-minded view of suicide, which they tended to equate with individual freedom from external constraints, whether as imposed by the body, society, or politics. Suicide in this sense functions as an *eulogos exagôgê* or "rational exit" from the compulsions of life. Seneca, Epictetus, and Marcus Aurelius are the principal Stoics to have reflected on suicide, though it should be noted that their opinions do not entirely overlap on this issue. Moreover, they represent later Stoicism, which differs in various respects from the original Stoic school of thought founded by Zeno in the third century BC. Nevertheless, their names are the ones most often invoked in connection with the classical *meletê thanatou,* a praxis-oriented meditation or more literal "exercise" on death. Generally speaking, the Stoics philosophized about the art of living in a pragmatic rather than theoretical fashion, and this included asking fundamental questions about the role of death as the inevitable pre-emption of the ideal ethical existence. Death, especially in later Stoicism, is caught up with the question of one's virtue and moral stature. Morality and mortality thus become inextricably linked in Stoic philosophy.

In terms popularized by Foucault, *meletê thanatou* forms a crucial ingredient of the "care of the self" as practiced in ancient Greece and Rome. This cultivation of the self is directly related to the issue of individual freedom, which in turn ties in with the broader category of ethics. As Foucault comments in this regard: "The Greeks problematized their freedom, and the freedom of the individual, as an ethical problem. But ethical in the sense in which the Greeks understood it: *êthos* was a way of being and of behavior. It was a mode of being for the subject, along with a certain way of acting, a way visible to others."[41] Ethics according to this definition is nonreligious and nonjuridical, hence the complete reverse of what we find in our modern Judeo-Christian era. The classical notion of ethics implies a fundamental way of relating to oneself, a *rapport à soi,* a hermeneutic of the subject, an aesthetics of existence—all varying and basically synonymous formulations that Foucault uses to describe this ethical concern with the self from fifth century

Athens to second century Rome. Foucault's theory about the care of the self can be compared to Nietzsche's demand of "giving style to one's character" (see *KSA* 3:530/*GS* 232).[42] The perfection of this more personal brand of ethics requires a number of regular practices, and Foucault investigates a wide variety of these daily procedures, from dietary control to the keeping of personal notebooks. One such technique of self-cultivation was the *meletê thanatou,* which Foucault briefly discusses by invoking the example of Seneca's meditations on death. My own observations on Seneca expand on Foucault's thesis that *meletê thanatou* "is a way of making death actual in life" and of urging one to "live each day as if it were the last."[43] By teaching themselves to reckon with the daily possibility of death, the Stoics created an ethos by which to live. In Stoicism, the art of living (*ars vitae*) goes hand in hand with the art of dying (*ars moriendi*).

In a letter dated May 24, 1880 Nietzsche writes that the most recurrent idea in Seneca's philosophy is "suicide" (*KSB* 6:20). Although this statement seems somewhat extreme, Lucius Annaeus Seneca did in fact reflect on the meaning of voluntary death in several of his writings and even killed himself in accordance with his philosophical principle of the timely exit. Seneca's famous death scene has often been compared to that of Socrates. Both were condemned by the ruling powers of their respective cities (Socrates by the court of Athens, Seneca by the Roman Emperor Nero); both died from drinking hemlock (Seneca's initial method of severing his arteries was not effective); and both faced their end with equanimity, philosophizing right up to the final moment. Most of Seneca's reflections on human finitude can be found in his *Moral Letters to Lucilius,* in which he expresses the necessity to "meditate upon death" (*meditare mortem*) in preparation for the real event.[44] As suggested above, this meditation is not the detached activity of an idle thinker; it serves, rather, a more practical and life-oriented purpose. As Seneca for instance states: "If you will give ear to my advice, ponder [*meditare*] and practice [*exerce*] this,— how to welcome death, or even, if circumstances command that course, to invite it."[45] Seneca is thus not interested in the phenomenon of death per se or in questions of immortality. He instead examines our existential comportment in the face of finitude, attempting to determine its effect on our moral constitution. According to Seneca, we must learn to convert the natural laws of death into human possibility and freedom. The true Stoic continually anticipates the advent of death and does not hesitate to take this "path to freedom"[46] when the appropriate occasion presents itself. As in Plato, these occasions include physical or mental infirmity, poverty, and political persecution. The important thing for Seneca is not how long, but how well, one lives, and ideally one should entertain the notion of suicide long before it becomes an absolute necessity. When the moral good life is no longer possible, death becomes an honorable and rational option of conduct. The crucial word here is rational. Suicide committed in an emotional frame of mind, whether in passion or despair, defeats its own ethical purpose. Zarathustra's command "Die at the right time!" finds its equivalent in Seneca's claim that "the wise man will live as long as he ought, not as long as he can."[47] Moreover, such an opportune death functions as a crowning achievement of life, a sovereign act that sums up existence and makes it complete, as in Zarathustra's notion of "the death that consummates" (*der vollbringende Tod*) (*KSA/Z* 183 4:93). Seneca expresses this idea various times in his seventy-seventh letter, for instance as follows: "At whatever point you leave off living, provided you leave off nobly, your life is a whole."[48] The conclusion of this letter offers perhaps the best summation of his ideas on death, which he in turn regards as a summation of the good life: "It is with life as it is with a play,—it matters not how long the action is spun out, but how good the acting is. It makes no difference at what point you stop. Stop whenever you choose; only see to it that the closing period is well turned."[49] These lines, which draw a metaphorical connection between life and art, imply a characteristically Nietzschean aestheticization of existence. Like an artistic masterpiece, which is defined not by quantity but by quality, human existence constitutes its own aesthetic corpus and autonomous whole.

Epictetus is less concerned with the individual's assertion of death if only because he ascribes little importance to one's physical fate, emphasizing in its place the soul or intellect. Hence, he only appears to condone suicide in extreme cases of affliction. He instead advocates indifference and fortitude, true Stoic virtues, in the face of suffering. Epictetus is mainly opposed to the fear of death, which tends to tyrannize our lives, keeping us from enjoying a pleasurable existence. We should therefore learn, through the teachings of philosophy, to overcome this primal anxiety. For Epictetus, true freedom comes with an acceptance of death's inevitability and with the elimination of our ultimately useless fear of extinction: "Will you realize once for all that it is not death that is the source of all man's evils, and of a mean and cowardly spirit, but rather the fear of death? Against this fear then I would have you discipline yourself; to this let all your reasonings, your lectures, and your trainings be directed; and then you will know that only so do men achieve their freedom" (*SEP* 405).

To a certain degree, Epictetus's arguments about death resemble those of Epicurus, who insists that the issue of our mortality should not affect our daily lives. Unlike for instance Seneca, who never ignores the presence of death in the midst of life, Epictetus is more inclined to separate the two realities, in compliance with the famous Epicurean adage that "death, the most terrifying of ills, is nothing to us, since so long as we exist, death is not with us; but when death comes, then we do not exist" (*SEP* 31). Again, this tendency partly stems from his extreme Stoicism, which transforms the Epicurean ideal of *ataraxia* (imperturbability) into the Stoic qualities of *apatheia* (indifference) and *karteria* (endurance). Nevertheless, Epictetus offers some important insights that point ahead to Nietzsche. The latter for instance remarks that the profoundly moral teachings of Epictetus were originally perceived as immoral, much like those of Jesus, Buddha, and Zarathustra himself (see *KSA* 9:636). With respect to the narrower question of death, Epictetus reproaches those who hold fast to life well beyond their prime. The sarcastic edge of the following fragment brings to mind a typical aphorism by Nietzsche: "If a man dies young he accuses the gods, and an old man sometimes accuses them because he still is put to trouble when the time for rest has fully come, and yet, when death comes near, he is fain to live and sends to his doctor and bids him spare no pains or effort. Wondrous, he said, are men, for they are unwilling to live or to die" (*SEP* 465). More pertinent, however, is a passage in which

Epictetus contributes to the tradition of organic images that Nietzsche and others employ to illustrate the idea of a timely death. An excerpt of this extended metaphor reads as follows:

> For instance, why do ears of corn grow? Is it not that they may ripen in the sun? And if they are ripened is it not that they may be reaped, for they are not things apart? If they had feelings then, ought they to pray never to be reaped at any time? But this is a curse upon corn—to pray that it should never be reaped. In like manner know that you are cursing men when you pray for them not to die: it is like a prayer not to be ripened, not to be reaped. (*SEP* 291)

The curses mentioned here are far more subdued than the ones Zarathustra, or for that matter Empedocles, hurls at the multitude. Nonetheless, like Epictetus, both Nietzsche and Hölderlin reinforce their opinions about death through any number of rhetorical tropes, the most common of which concerns metaphors of ripened fruit and grain. Their language may be figurative, but the imagery lends itself to an easy enough interpretation, even by the masses that bear the brunt of these moralizing words. The fact that Epictetus, Zarathustra, and Empedocles are branded as immoralists only speaks for the untimeliness of their views regarding the timeliness of death.

The *Meditations* of Marcus Aurelius Antoninus offer the perfect example of the ethical concern with the self that Foucault examines in his later writings. Indeed, the Greek title of this celebrated work only reinforces Foucault's theories about the ethics of the subject in later antiquity: *Ta eis heauton* or "Matters Concerning the Self." Here the philosopher-turned-emperor reflects on countless aspects and details of existence in an attempt to come to a better understanding of his own self and its place in the world. The most recurring topic of reflection concerns the transitoriness of life; in other words, the constant presence, if not imminence, of death. Marcus Aurelius's meditations have a moral function insofar as they instruct us how to lead better lives in the face of our ineluctable extinction. Because our existence is ephemeral, we must learn to construct it such that every moment counts; for only in this manner does it become imbued with deeper meaning. Various aphorisms therefore urge us to conduct ourselves as if we were living our last day (see *SEP* 498, 499; *Meditations,*

2.5, 2.11), a practice that continually promotes the cultivation if not perfection of our character. This moral directive requires a delicate balance between embracing life on the one hand and relinquishing it on the other. That is, we must avoid becoming "tenaciously stuck to life" (*SEP* 516; *Meditations,* 4.50) yet at the same time strive to lead a full and meaningful existence. The solution to this quandary lies in knowing when the "proper time" has come. In an aphorism from book 12, Marcus Aurelius repeatedly mentions this key phrase "proper time" (*kairos* in the original Greek) and additionally speaks of a "seasonable" (*hôraios*) death (*SEP* 582; *Meditations,* 12.23), all of which recalls the terminology that Nietzsche and Hölderlin utilize in their own efforts to advocate an opportune exodus from life. (The term *kairos,* especially as used in the epistles of Paul, later becomes a crucial concept for Heidegger.) Although it would be an exaggeration to claim that he advocates suicide like Seneca, he nevertheless sees it as a necessity in adverse circumstances: "As thou intendest to live when thou art gone out, . . . so it is in thy power to live here. But if men do not permit thee, then get away out of life, yet so as if thou wert suffering no harm. The house is smoky, and I quit it" (*SEP* 523; *Meditations,* 5.29). This last sentence actually stems from Epictetus, with whom Marcus Aurelius agrees that suicide offers a way out of extreme hardship. Which does not necessarily mean that it results from a preceding state of weakness or inferiority. Suicide is, rather, characterized by the virtues of "simplicity and freedom and modesty" (*SEP* 564; *Meditations,* 10.8). Furthermore, it should not be carried out rashly, all at once interrupting the course of life—on the contrary, suicide ought to be a rational plan of action, one that forms the culmination of a well-lived existence. Ultimately, it is not the precise length of one's life that matters to Marcus Aurelius, but the overall sense of its completion. Like Seneca, he relies on a metaphor involving drama to emphasize that there is no pre-established duration of human existence:

> Man, thou hast been a citizen in this great state (the world): what difference does it make to thee whether for five years (or three)? For that which is conformable to the laws is just for all. Where is the hardship then, if no tyrant nor yet an unjust judge sends thee away from the state, but nature who brought thee into it? The same as if a praetor who has

employed an actor dismisses him from the stage.—"But I have not finished the five acts, but only three of them."—Thou sayest well, but in life the three acts are the whole drama; for what shall be a complete drama is determined by him who was once the cause of its composition, and now of its dissolution: but thou art the cause of neither. Depart then satisfied, for he also who releases thee is satisfied. (*SEP* 584–85; *Meditations,* 12.36)

Despite their similar comparisons between the analogous intensity of life and drama, a fundamental difference exists between Seneca's earlier metaphor and the one cited here by Marcus Aurelius. Whereas the former believes that we are the authors of our own existence and can therefore terminate the dramatic action whenever we choose, the latter insinuates that higher powers are responsible for our fate. Yet this deference to the superior logic of cosmic laws does not wholly discount the autonomy of mortals. As various aphorisms cited above attest, the individual must also take action and depart from this life at the right time—freely, calmly, and rationally. That is, one must learn to live as well as to die in accordance with the principles of nature, which themselves are rational though not always entirely fathomable.

Free Death: Theory and Practice

Despite the obvious similarities between the Stoic and Nietzschean concepts of death as a self-willed act of freedom, some important differences cannot be ignored. The Stoic notion of freedom implies liberation *from* constraint, whether from physical suffering or other severe forms of adversity. Yet it is important to distinguish between two modes of freedom: freedom *from* and freedom *to*. Whereas the Stoics stress the former, departing from one's deprivation of liberty as the impetus for suicide, Nietzsche adopts a view of death as a freedom *unto* or a possibility *toward* self-realization, regardless of one's degree of subjugation. These distinct conceptions of freedom do not go ignored by Zarathustra: "Free *from* what [*wovon*]? As if that mattered to Zarathustra! But your eyes should tell me brightly: free *for* what [*wozu*]?" (*KSA* 4:81/*Z* 175). In the end, the two perspectives differ perhaps only in emphasis. The Stoic and more common definition presupposes an object, whether concrete or abstract, from which one seeks to become liberated, for example a specific oppressor or a general state of oppression. Nietzsche, on the other hand, conceives of a more dynamic and open-ended freedom that transcends all given conditions of reality. Here we find the essential disagreement between what Robert Solomon, in his interpretations of Hegel's philosophy, calls "negative" and "positive" freedom.[50] The former assumes a previous condition of privation and becomes actualized with the elimination of this problem. The latter, in contrast, does not issue from any necessary set of outside circumstances, nor does it ever reach a clear and definitive goal. Freedom in this more existential sense is equivalent to self-overcoming. It thus implies an ongoing transformative process, one that continues to push the limits of possibility. The self-overcomer continually becomes free, even when confronted with the ultimate depriving force of death.

Another crucial difference between Nietzsche and tradition concerns precisely this relationship between freedom and death. The proximity between these two notions is not unfamiliar to speakers of German. *Freitod* is a common euphemism for *Selbstmord,* which, like the Latinate "suicide" (*sui caedere*), literally means a "killing of the self." No such linguistic connection between a voluntary death and freedom exists in English, though it is interesting to note that during the seventeenth and eighteenth centuries the foreign word "suicide" gradually replaced and undoubtedly softened the more graphic "self-murder."[51] An analogous euphemizing trend can thus be discerned in both languages, but the specifics of this parallelism diverge widely. *Freitod, freiwilliger Tod, den Tod frei wählen* (to choose death freely) are all fairly normal ways of expressing "suicide," a word that does not seem to possess any variations connoting freedom in English. Even more curious is the noncompound *freier Tod.* We have seen it in Hölderlin (*SWB* 2:415)—albeit translated by Michael Hamburger as "self-chosen death" (*PF* 361)—and now in Nietzsche, but the truth is that one almost never encounters this formulation in German prose. The unorthodox *freier Tod* can perhaps best be considered a somewhat literary or at any rate more inventive twist on the standard *Freitod.* Based on pure grammar, this construction underscores the aspect of freedom, for as an adjective *frei* modifies and in a fashion determines the noun *Tod*. (This, at any rate, is the general effect of adjectives on nouns when located in attributive position as opposed to their more normalized function when integrated into compounds.) Unlike the notion of *freiwilliger Tod,* the traditional German term used to describe Stoic suicide,[52] Zarathustra's insistence on *freier Tod* perhaps then ought to be understood not as an actual and definitive killing of the self but as a projected end meant to further the freedom of existence and increase the potential of life.[53] Free death results as a consequence of one's entire mode of existence and denotes more a life-long attitude than a singular act of suicide. As Maurice Blanchot has noted with respect to this question of freedom: "One doesn't kill oneself, but one can. This is a marvelous resource. Without this supply of oxygen close at hand we would smother, we could no longer live. Having death within reach, docile and reliable, makes life possible, for it is exactly what provides air, space, free and joyful movement: it is possibility."[54]

There are indeed indications of this view elsewhere in Nietzsche's work, particularly in the following excerpt from aphorism 88 in *Mixed Opinions and Maxims:* "*How one dies is of no consequence.*—The entire manner in which a man reflects on death in the course of his plentiful and vigorous life may speak volumes for what we call his character; but the hour of dying itself, the way he conducts himself on his deathbed, is practically of no consequence for this question of character" (*KSA* 2:411). Here Nietzsche treats death as a basic phenomenon of life, emphasizing not the final confrontation with one's final moment but the many years leading up to it. Nietzsche, in other words, is principally concerned with the effect of finitude on the greater arc of one's existence. In another aphorism (322) from the subsequent publication *The Wanderer and His Shadow,* he alludes to death as a potential enhancement of life but cannot contain his criticism of the prevailing modern attitude toward this elemental human experience: "*Death.*—Through the certain prospect of death every life could be mixed with a precious, sweet-smelling drop of levity—and now you ridiculous apothecary-souls have turned death into a foul-tasting drop of poison, one that makes all of life repugnant!" (*KSA* 2:695).

Perhaps Nietzsche's most revealing statement on death comes from *The Twilight of The Idols,* a work that he completed shortly before his mental breakdown in January of 1889. Here, in a lengthy aphorism that bears the heading "Morality for physicians," he once again contrasts two basic mentalities with respect to the problem of death and dying. As the title indicates, Nietzsche weighs in on this issue from an ethical perspective, one however that has more to do with a general ethos of existence than with the finer points of medical ethics. He takes as his point of departure the modern practice of keeping patients alive well beyond their years, describing, in remarkably contemporary language, how the terminally ill "go on vegetating" (*fortvegetieren*) and thereby forfeit their "right to live" (*KSA* 6:134/*TI* 536). Nietzsche observes in such cases "an unfree death, death *not* at the right time, a coward's death" (*KSA* 6:135/*TI* 537). Against this dominant societal trend he asserts: "From love of *life,* one should desire a different death: free, conscious, without accident, without ambush" (*KSA* 6:135/*TI* 537). In the following excerpt, he makes his opinion abundantly clear with respect to these two conflicting attitudes:

> To die proudly when it is no longer possible to live proudly. Death freely chosen, death at the right time, brightly and cheerfully accomplished amid children and witnesses: then a real farewell is still possible, as the one taking leave *is still there;* also a real estimation of what one has achieved and what one has wished, drawing the *sum* [*Summierung*] of one's life—all in opposition to the wretched and revolting comedy that Christianity has made of the hour of death. One should never forget that Christianity has exploited the weakness of the dying for a rape of their conscience, and the manner of death itself, for value judgments about man and the past. (*KSA* 6:134–35/*TI* 536–37)

This aphorism, Nietzsche's final published testimony concerning death, contains all the critical elements from his previous deliberations on the subject, including the questions of timeliness and freedom. To this mix he adds a number of points highlighted by Philippe Ariès, including the important bedside presence of family and friends. One also detects a greater polarization between classical and modern ethics. It is clear that Nietzsche vehemently privileges the former, yet one cannot help but wonder to what extent he was able to live up to his existential imperative of dying at the right time.

Throughout much of his life, Nietzsche was plagued by ill health and while none of his ailments seems to have been life threatening, he nevertheless grew accustomed to the "proximity of death"—a phrase that becomes a kind of leitmotif in his letters. For the most part, he proved remarkably resilient and was able to conquer, indeed sublimate, his physical afflictions by creating a vast body of highly original work. His correspondence, however, affords insight into some of the darker sides of his existence. Here, in language unfiltered by philosophy and aesthetics, he speaks more candidly of the various problems that wracked his being: his never-ending bouts with illness, his frequent spells of melancholy, his perennial loneliness, and his deep desire for death. The year of 1879 proved to be especially bad: Nietzsche counts 118 days of "attacks," which include migraines, fever, stomach cramps, and vomiting; in sum, "a general feeling of incapacitation from head to toe" (see *KSB* 5:475; *KSB* 6:6,7). Looking back on this period of his life from the late 1870s to the early 1880s, he even estimates that an average year consisted of "200 days of pain" (*KSB* 8:289). In view of this near unremitting torment,[55] he begins to wonder if there is any point to his habitual practice of self-overcoming, a technique that otherwise enabled him to deal with, and even capitalize on, his sufferings. He of course eventually turned this self-treatment into a core principle of his thought. As is often the case with Nietzsche, he forged some of his most important philosophical ideas out of his own existential predicament. Many of the doctrines presented in *Thus Spoke Zarathustra* can for instance be interpreted against the background of Nietzsche's life, which sank to a physiological low during the years in which he conceived the work. Yet as we have seen through an examination of the manuscripts, his *Zarathustra* project underwent numerous metamorphoses, especially with respect to the protagonist's tragic downfall. The fact that Nietzsche hovered between life and death during the early 1880s may help explain the numerous oscillations in the fate of Zarathustra, in whom many of the author's most personal experiences are projected. Indeed, Zarathustra's speech on free death takes on new meaning in light of such biographical facts as Nietzsche's chronic sickness and recurring thoughts of suicide.

Beginning in 1877, the watershed year of his health, Nietzsche occasionally toyed with the idea of killing himself, sometimes out of obvious despair, other times out of what passes for more Stoic motivations. Yet in view of his acute sufferings, it remains difficult to distinguish between mental depression and incurable illness. Nietzsche for example "thirsts for some freedom from pain" (*KSB* 6:92), which remains a perfectly acceptable reason for suicide from the standpoint of Stoicism, especially given the precarious state of his wellbeing. Seneca, too, was beleaguered by physical maladies throughout his life and in his *Moral Letters* he sometimes draws the connection between this biographical/biological fact and his more philosophical ruminations on suicide (see especially the seventy-eighth epistle). The severity of Nietzsche's own condition is evidenced by the claim that he often endured five times more pain than what it would take the average person to kill himself (see *KSB* 6:405, 407). The following remark from 1881 is even more revealing with respect to Stoic virtues: "Even if I had taken my life in Recoaro [a city outside of Venice], one of the most steadfast and reflective of individuals would have died, not one in despair" (*KSB* 6:103). A letter from 1879 proves of special interest, as the issue of Nietzsche's health becomes compounded with that of his age. Being at the end of his thirty-fifth year, Nietzsche finds himself at the traditional midpoint of life and contemplates this basic existential fact as countless others had before him:

> I'm at the end of my thirty-fifth year of life; the "middle of life," as has been said about this period for the last one-and-a-half millennia; Dante had his own notion and speaks of it in the first lines of his poem. Right now I'm so "surrounded by death" in the middle of life that I feel it can grab hold of me at any hour; given the nature of my suffering I have to imagine a *sudden* death, one caused by convulsions (although I would one hundred times prefer a slow clear-minded death, where one is still able to converse with friends, even if it costs more pain). (*KSB* 5:441)

This last parenthetical remark indicates that Nietzsche perhaps sensed his inability to follow through with the "quick" death that he preaches through his mouthpiece Zarathustra. Upon learning of Wagner's passing in 1883, he further hints at the difficulty of departing at the apex of life: "it is difficult to die at the right time" (*KSB* 6:335). There is no need to dwell on or overinterpret this discrepancy between biographical reality and philosophical paradigm. It seems clear that Nietzsche, while he may not have actually died at the proper moment, nevertheless spent countless hours on the verge of death. From a clinical standpoint, this may be overstated, for there is no evidence that Nietzsche's disorders were fatal. On a deeper level, however, he configured his existence as if death were an ever-present possibility. The fact that his father died at the age of 36 led him to believe that he, too, would meet a premature end, and he consequently "gave style to his character" in view of this limited horizon of opportunity. Moreover, he went through sufferings that intimated, on an almost daily basis, his mortality. He of course experienced anything but the well-timed death that Zarathustra urges upon the individual; nor was his end by any means the "clear-minded" one that he envisioned in the letter cited above. Like Hölderlin, he died after years of mental decrepitude, unaware of his true identity and previous philosophical activity—indeed, completely oblivious of the implications that his notion of free death carried.

More striking is the fact that even Zarathustra, Nietzsche's grand promoter of free death, fails to comply with his existential imperative: "Die at the right time!" By the end of part 4, Zarathustra is still alive, indeed revitalized after several spells of sickness and melancholy. This deferral of death constitutes a major problem in the overall conception of the *Zarathustra* project insofar as the main character now refuses to end his life in the timely manner of Empedocles, whether in that of Hölderlin's tragic figure or of Nietzsche's own re-creation.[56] In his *Zarathustra* sketches, Nietzsche intended his Empedoclean character to die by the end of the drama, either in the crater of a volcano or through some other form of *Untergang*. This word, which forms a central motif in *Thus Spoke Zarathustra*, never quite takes on the meaning of a literal "downgoing" into volcanic depths as it does in Hölderlin's play. In all three versions of *The Death of Empedocles*, an implicit connection is made between the hero's figurative downfall and his literal plunge into Etna. The words *untergehen* and *Untergang* appear throughout the drafts as do synonymous locutions such as *Fall* (fall), *fallen* (to fall), and *hinabgehen* (to descend). Zarathustra's *Untergang* consists, however, in the simple fact that he comes down from his refuge in the mountains in order to share his wisdom with humankind. Nietzsche also plays with the idea that every *Überwindung* (overcoming) or *Übergang* (crossing) necessitates an *Untergang,* as exemplified by the tightrope walker's symbolic fall in the preface of the work. Yet Zarathustra's downgoing does not lead to such a tragic end in the course of parts 1–4, despite his periodic yearnings for death and his impassioned speech on the subject. Still, Nietzsche was obviously torn between letting his character live on as a prophet of the *Übermensch* and having him suffer a fatal *Untergang* after all. A note for a planned fifth part of the work depicts a voluntary (*freiwillig-*) death, as had been Nietzsche's intent from the very beginning:

> Note.—he moved and again closed his lips and had the look of one who still has something to say and hesitates to say it. And it seemed to those looking on that he was blushing slightly. This lasted awhile; but then, all at once, he shook his head, voluntarily [*freiwillig*] closed his eyes— and died. Thus occurred Zarathustra's downfall. (*KSA* 11:468; 34[144])

Had Nietzsche carried through with this final installment of *Zarathustra,* he would have succeeded in closing the chapter on his long—and prolonged—engagement with the problem of tragedy. One of his letters even mentions an "inevitable fifth and sixth part" in which he would like to "help my son Zarathustra find a beautiful death" (*KSB* 6:557). As it stands, however, the connections between such requisite tragic elements as guilt, pity, and death are not clearly resolved in the complex of his *Empedocles* and *Zarathustra* manuscripts. Nevertheless, his debt to Hölderlin could not be more evident. We will soon see that Heidegger's efforts to elaborate an authentic being-toward-death are in turn indebted to both Hölderlin and Nietzsche. But first, another figure needs to enter the discussion, one that also interprets death from a holistic perspective. Although it remains difficult to determine to what extent the thanatological views of Rainer Maria Rilke were influenced by Hölderlin and Nietzsche, whose work he otherwise admired (it is doubtful that he ever seriously read Hegel), the impact of his ideas on Heidegger were nothing short of profound.

4

Rilke

The Holistic Recovery of Death

[L]ike the moon, life surely has a side continually turned away
from us, which is *not* its opposite, but rather its complement
toward perfection, toward completeness, toward the real, whole,
and full sphere and globe of *being*.
—Rilke, letter from January 6, 1923

In August of 1902 Rilke left the northern German idylls of Worpswede
and Haseldorf—the former an artists' colony, the latter an isolated estate
belonging to aristocratic acquaintances—to settle in Paris, the modern city par excellence. The clash between these two environments
exerted a profound impact on the young poet, bringing about a reorientation in his way of perceiving and poetically articulating the world.
Life in the bustling metropolis offered plenty of social ills to go along
with its cultural splendor, and while Rilke partook of both worlds, it
is the chaos of an urban landscape that exhibits the strongest presence
in the works under discussion here. As his letters attest and his creative endeavors illustrate, Rilke was overwhelmed by the filth, noise,
and stench of Paris. Here he came face-to-face with the underbelly of
existence: disease, indigence, and prostitution besieged him on the
streets; hospitals, poorhouses, and maternity wards seemed to emit cries
of suffering on every corner. Following the example of Baudelaire, Rilke

learned to confront these repellent aspects of modern city life and develop an aesthetic based purely on the power of visual perception, regardless of traditional criteria of beauty. By adjusting his sights to the special features of his new milieu ("learning to see" as he repeatedly describes this practice), Rilke was able to overcome the artistic crisis that beset him during his initial years in Paris.

Of greater consequence for my present purposes is the fact that Rilke's observations in the French metropolis radically shaped his ideas regarding death. As a result of his encounters with the diseased and dying on the backstreets of Paris, Rilke began to reflect more deeply on the problem of human finitude. Like Hölderlin and Nietzsche, the early Rilke distinguishes between different modes of death. Whereas in the not-too-distant past people tended to die in the familiar surroundings of their homes, modern city-dwellers perish anonymously in overcrowded infirmaries, alienated from death as much as from life. Death, for Rilke, has become increasingly depersonalized with the rise of mass society in the early twentieth century. People no longer accept their mortality and incorporate it into their existence, but passively undergo whatever end lies in store for them. Indeed, the institution of the hospital has largely taken over the once personal affair of death. A further connection to Hölderlin and Nietzsche becomes apparent in the imagery that Rilke employs in order to bolster and visually augment these two divergent conceptual attitudes. Like his predecessors, he also relies on organic metaphors but in the end presents a more sophisticated network of tropes around this central image. Another crucial departure concerns the fact that Rilke conceives a third mode of death, one that is more holistic than individualistic. He thus presents three models, which I will label as modern, authentic, and totalistic.

The two principal texts that reflect Rilke's outlook on death based on his Parisian years are part three of *Das Stunden-Buch* (*The Book of Hours*), composed in 1903, and his modernist novel *Die Aufzeichnungen des Malte Laurids Brigge* (*The Notebooks of Malte Laurids Brigge*), which he worked on intermittently between 1904 and 1910. The first half of this chapter will examine these two texts in view of the death-related motifs mentioned above. The second half is devoted to Rilke's later work, especially the *Duineser Elegien* (*Duino*

Elegies). Here Rilke presents a holistic view, one that fuses the phenomena of life and death into an ontological totality. Rilke insists that we must learn to integrate death into our lives, become intimate/familiar (*vertraut*) with our mortality and thereby achieve a more complete sense of being. Although I can hardly claim to make any significant scholarly advancements with respect to the already much written about *Elegies,* I hope that a discussion of their place within the larger framework of death from Hegel to Heidegger will afford new insights into Rilke's own position within this thanatological line of thought. At the very least, their inclusion will serve to set up my remarks on Heidegger's interpretation of human finitude as the essential component in the structural whole of Dasein.

MODES OF DEATH: MODERNITY, AUTHENTICITY, AND TOTALITY

With Rilke's arrival in Paris, death does not all at once make its first appearance in his writings. The numerous plays he wrote between 1894 and 1904 evoke this theme often enough, as do his *Geschichten vom lieben Gott (Stories of God),* a collection of prose pieces from the turn of the century. Indeed, death was a vogue topic that permeated the literary scene during this time, whether in the work of Maurice Maeterlinck, Gerhart Hauptmann, or Hugo von Hofmannsthal—all of whom Rilke read and admired. One can find an interesting testimony of this trend in a popular anthology of death scenes from Tolstoy's oeuvre that was published in Paris under the title *La mort.* Nevertheless, on a deeper personal level, the human misery that Rilke witnessed on an almost daily basis in the French capital opened his eyes to the everyday reality of dying and no doubt contributed to the early polarization of his views. In the following, I will trace the conceptual development from an initial dichotomy of attitudes toward death (modern versus authentic) to a later and more refined outlook that aims to capture the totalistic experience of mortality.

The Book of Poverty and Death *(1903)*

Rilke wrote the third and final part of his *The Book of Hours* over the course of eight nights in the spring of 1903. Whereas the first volume of this poetic cycle reflects his travels through Russia in 1899 and the second draws on his stay in Worpswede, the concluding installment arose out of the still raw experiences of his marginalized existence in Paris. The title of this last piece announces its two major themes: *Das Buch von der Armut und vom Tode (The Book of Poverty and Death)*. This latter theme dominates the first half of the text. The narrator, a monk who has been sent by God to the "immense" (*übergroß-*) (*SW* 1:343) cities, observes all kinds of modern ills, including anxiety, overcrowding, and alienation. He wishes to return to a more desolate environment—the steppes of Russia or the moors of northern Germany described in the previous two books—but remains trapped in the "cities" (he always speaks in the plural), where he bears witness to the harsh reality of urban life. And the problem that occupies him most, one that apparently typifies an entire paradigm shift in the age of modernity, is death.

In this third part of *The Book of Hours,* the contrast between two fundamental modes of human finitude is conceived in the following terms: *der kleine Tod* versus *der große Tod.* The former, the so-called "little death," prevails in the cities and would appear to be a degenerate version of the "great death" that Rilke describes in more elaborate detail. The few words that he says about *der kleine Tod* imply that it stands for the modern way of dying. It is associated with the hospitals into which "lonely" (*einsam*) urbanites "anxiously" (*angstvoll*) wait to be admitted (see *SW* 1:346). This kind of death is presumably described in diminutive terms because it "diminishes" the dignity of the individual, reducing him to an anonymous patient and stripping him of the most inalienable aspect of his being. Rilke soon makes it clear that our death is something that dwells within us from the very moment of our birth and thus belongs to us as a kind of personal possession. Furthermore, it must be cultivated throughout the course of our existence and eventually brought to fruition. This is the essential meaning of *der große Tod,* a more organic notion according to which death informs our lives regardless of age and health. This brand of death is a natural presence that accompanies us from childhood and need not be feared or shunned. In the following stanza Rilke juxtaposes the two styles of death while introducing the important imagery of fruit:

> Dort ist der Tod. Nicht jener, dessen Grüße
> sie in der Kindheit wundersam gestreift, —
> der kleine Tod, wie man ihn dort begreift;
> ihr eigener hängt grün und ohne Süße
> wie eine Frucht in ihnen, die nicht reift.   (*SW* 1:347)

> [Death is there. Not the one whose greetings touch them wondrously
> in childhood—the little death, as it is understood there; their own
> hangs green and without sweetness inside of them like a fruit that does
> not ripen.] (My translation.)

In view of the above metaphor, *der kleine Tod* can also be considered
"small" in the sense that it never grows beyond a certain point; it remains
a perennially immature fruit that offers no sweetness or abundance.
Rilke in a sense radicalizes the topos that we have observed in authors
such as Johannes von Saaz, Hölderlin, and Nietzsche, suggesting that
in modernized society the natural, life-enhancing progress of death has
become arrested in its development. The fruit, so to speak, never gets
the chance to grow sweet let alone overripe or rotten. To put it once
again in human terms: we completely repress or outright ignore the
existential relevance of death and thereby forfeit, right from the start,
the possibility of leading a full life. Hence Rilke's plea, which only
reinforces the organic symbolism:

> O Herr, gieb jedem seinen eignen Tod.
> Das Sterben, das aus jenem Leben geht,
> darin er Liebe hatte, Sinn und Not.

> Denn wir sind nur die Schale und das Blatt.
> Der große Tod, den jeder in sich hat,
> das ist die Frucht, um die sich alles dreht.   (*SW* 1:347)

> [Oh Lord, give to each his own death. The dying that issues from the
> life in which he had love, meaning, and need.
> For we are but the shell/rind/skin and the leaf. The great death that
> each has within, that is the fruit around which everything turns.]
> (My translation.)

The idiom *eig[e]ner Tod* carries the implication that death is a personal experience—and indeed property. It is an idea, or at least term,
that Rilke borrowed from the Danish author Jens Peter Jacobsen and

would later pass on to Heidegger. In his novels *Niels Lyhne* and *Marie Grubbe,* Jacobsen divests God of all power over human mortality and places the responsibility of dying squarely in the hands of the individual. Death thus becomes a strictly human affair as well as a determining factor of one's independence from otherworldly attachments. Rilke, who has his lyrical double directly implore God to grant us this individualized death, obviously differs from Jacobsen on the issue of divine influence, though his religiosity here is largely an artistic pose. Nevertheless, Rilke's notion of *eigener Tod* is a more internal one than Jacobsen's; it is rooted in the question of one's individuality and autonomy irrespective of the greater problem of God.[1] The above trope visibly conveys the interiority of death, which resides within us like a fruit inside its "skin" or "rind" (the crucial word *Schale* that Hölderlin and Nietzsche similarly invoked). As Rilke clearly states, we all bear this fruitlike potentiality deep inside and its successful cultivation will significantly enrich our lives. Death, in other words, constitutes the very core of our being. But again, most of us fail to realize that we are the fashioners of our own deaths. And because we do not actively foster this inner force, we end up passively suffering a fatal end that is not our own, one that strikes like the storm that Zarathustra wishes upon all the rotten fruit that desperately clings to the trees of life:

> Denn dieses macht das Sterben fremd und schwer,
> daß es nicht *unser* Tod ist; einer der
> uns endlich nimmt, nur weil wir keinen reifen.
> Drum geht ein Sturm, uns alle abzustreifen.   (*SW* 1:348)

> [For this makes dying strange and hard, that it is not our death; one that finally takes us because we ripen none. Thus a storm comes to peel us all.] (My translation.)

Rilke's also devises another metaphorical complex, one that radically departs from the figurative language of his predecessors. He amplifies the range of his organic imagery to include fruits of the womb, thereby illustrating that we must give birth to our death as if to a child. Rilke's array of metaphors in this context includes miscarriages, embryos, caesarians, and birthing tables. Combined with the earlier evocations of tenements, deathbeds, and hospitals, these images create a phantasmagorical landscape that reflects the bedlam of Paris in the throes of modernity. Furthermore, all of these elements function within the greater thematic web of death. Beginning with the eighth poem of the third cycle ("Herr: Wir sind ärmer denn die armen Tiere . . . / Lord, we are poorer than the poor creatures"), the modern problem of dying is conveyed in terms of human infertility. Here one finds depictions of barren women and unproductive pregnancies. Like his extended metaphors of unripe fruit, the diverse tropes of childbirth underscore the intimate connection between life and death. Of course the problem is that this holistic relationship is disrupted in "the cities" where there seems to be no fruitful production of any kind. The deaths that we are supposed to nurture within us, so that they will complement and complete our lives, turn out fallow and stillborn. Once again, the narrator calls upon God for aid. First, he wishes for the guidance "to tie up life in espaliers" (*SW* 1:348) in order to correct the problem of stagnant growth. His next appeal picks up on the motif of birth and adds a provocative twist to the Nativity: he seeks a divine "bearer of death" (*Tod-Gebärer*) in place of the God that was brought forth by the Virgin Mary (called here *die Gottgebärerin*). The role of this new Messiah is not to instruct us about the Christian virtues of love and charity, but to promote the all-important gospel of death. And through his mouthpiece of the praying monk, Rilke hints that he himself will serve as the herald of this future deity, thereby following in the footsteps of John the Baptist. In his own way Rilke has thus revaluated some of the key tenets and players of Christianity. God is not *dead,* as in Nietzsche; God, rather, is *death*—or at least extremely well versed in the art of dying. In the wake of this new religion, a different kind of Covenant has been established, one that stipulates an agreement between the basic forces of life and death. Throughout the rest of his literary career, from these early years of artistic struggle in fin-de-siècle Paris to his physical struggles with leukemia in 1926, Rilke never ceased to emphasize the inseparable connection between human existence and its finitude.

The Notebooks of Malte Laurids Brigge *(1904–10)*

Life and death become juxtaposed in the opening sentence of *The Notebooks of Malte Laurids Brigge,* a novel that grew out of the experiences of Rilke's first year in Paris: "So this is where people come to live; I would have thought it is a city to die in" (*SW* 6:709/*MLB* 3). All told, 17 deaths occur in the course of the book, each of which "serves Malte as an excuse to meditate on death, to approach its cold, black core from a different angle."[2] For the most part, this theme has been well explored in the near 100 years of the novel's reception. I will how-ever attempt, whenever possible, to touch on points that have been under-emphasized in previous scholarship. Moreover, I will contextualize the novel within philosophical, sociological, and medical discourses. My analysis will generally trace the three principal genres of death which in turn correspond to the major realms of Malte's existence: the institutionalized death that prevails in the modern city; the authentic death that literally grew within individuals before the arrival of moder-nity; and the holistic relation to death that would seem to be timeless. These divergent attitudes are exemplified by the people and places that have shaped Malte's own identity: Paris with its anonymous outcasts (*Fortgeworfene*); Ulsgaard, the landed estate of the Brigges; and Urnekloster, the ghostly domain of the Brahes, the maternal side of his family.[3] Malte finds himself torn by these three conflicting reali-ties. Throughout the novel he reminisces on his childhood in Denmark while struggling with his precarious existence in Paris, fearing that he will become one of the nameless specimens of humanity that have "come to live" in the city only to die *en masse* in its hospitals.

The novel opens with Malte walking the streets of Paris, taking in the sights, sounds, and smells of a city that teems with anxiety and death. Many of the same urban landmarks mentioned in Rilke's third *Book of Hours* make their reappearance in the beginning pages of the novel, for example: birthing clinics, homeless shelters, and hospitals. Malte seems especially focused on this last institution. After a cursory reference to the military sanatorium Val-de-grâce, he devotes greater attention to the Hôtel-Dieu, an infirmary located near Notre-Dame. His musings on this historic site raise a number of important points with respect to the problem of death in modernity:

> This excellent hotel is very ancient; already in the time of King Clovis people were dying here, in a few beds. Now there are 559 beds to die in. Like a factory, of course. With production so enormous, each individual

death is not made very carefully; but that isn't important. It's the quantity that counts. Who is there today who still cares about a well-finished death? No one. Even the rich, who could after all afford this luxury, are beginning to grow lazy and indifferent; the desire to have a death of one's own is becoming more and more rare. In a short time it will be as rare as a life of one's own. (*SW* 6:713–14/*MLB* 8–9)

Once the exclusive property of the individual human being, death is now a purely anonymous event. The individual has ceased to be the author of his own fate. In the original, Rilke even uses the passive voice to accentuate the depersonalized nature of this modern attitude toward human mortality. The sentence "Now there are 559 beds to die in" reads in German as "Jetzt wird in 559 Betten gestorben" (*SW* 6:713). People thus no longer actively assert their "own" deaths but passively undergo whatever end lies in store for them. Death has been transformed into a mass-produced commodity for general consumption. Rilke compares it to a "ready-made" article of clothing that the salesperson presents with the perfunctory phrase: "Voilà votre mort, monsieur" (*SW* 6:714/*MLB* 9). This garment is not hand-tailored, but comes right off the rack, from the factory (hospital) to the consumer (patient) via the intermediary of customer service (doctors). The worlds of medicine and economics thus converge in Rilke's vast catalogue of death metaphors. The economic paradigm demonstrates that the virtue of quality has ceded to the value of quantity. Rilke even calculates the hour of death at two francs, the going rate of horse-cabs hired to deliver the dying to the Hôtel-Dieu (see *SW* 6:713/*MLB* 8).

Rilke goes on to comment that death has become so externalized that it belongs less to the individual than to the specific ailment from which that person suffers. To understand Rilke's point, one need only consider some basic tendencies of modern medical pathology. Generally speaking, science transfers the phenomenon of death to an organ or other physical locality where it can pinpoint a fatal disease. In strict nosological terms, there is no such thing as death. Heart failure, cancer, and brain tumors are definite realities to the perceptive "medical gaze" (to borrow Foucault's expression from *The Birth of the Clinic*), but death as such remains an elusive object of knowledge. From a scientific standpoint, this procedure of specifying a disease is of course an internal one, as problems are tracked down *within* the human body. But from Rilke's holistic perspective, the drive to uncover a precise locus of death only deprives human existence of its innermost potentiality. Death is not a *positum* that can be explained away by the diagnoses of specialists; it is a lifelong process that must be cultivated, perfected, and ultimately given meaning by the individual himself. To translate this inner experience into a physical theory is tantamount to saying that *we* don't actually die, but that heart disease, cancer, and all kinds of other maladies kill *us*. An implicit passivity underlies this attitude: we become the objects of life-threatening processes of the body. Rilke thus indirectly critiques the methods of modern medical science whose narrow focus on particular diseases loses sight of the greater question of human existence. In Tolstoy's *The Death of Ivan Ilyich,* a work whose influence can be detected throughout *The Notebooks of Malte Laurids Brigge,*[4] a similar restrictive medical perception dominates the main character's thoughts about his terminal illness: "the real business was the assessing of probabilities to decide between a floating kidney, chronic catarrh or appendicitis. It was not a question of Ivan Ilyich's life or death but one between a floating kidney or appendicitis."[5] Eventually, Ivan Ilyich comes to regard his condition less in terms of physiological deficiencies and more as an all-invading presence that directly impacts his life. But Rilke's intellectual diagnosis of death in the hospitals of Paris leaves no such room for optimism. For Rilke, the fashionable methods of scientific analysis only alleviate patients of their existential burden:

> You die as best you can [Man stirbt, wie es gerade kommt]; you die the death that belongs to the sickness you have (for since all sicknesses are well known, it is also known that the various fatal endings belong to the sicknesses and not to the people; and the sick person has, so to speak, nothing more to do). (*SW 6:714/MLB 9*)

Disease has thus become the nature of our decease. Again, the notion of passivity is at work here: illness takes on the role of active culprit while we remain the passive sufferers. We have "nothing more to do" but wither away in hospital wards, which, as Philippe Ariès observes, have acquired "a local monopoly on death" (*HOD* 584).

The modern hospital and those in its employ have thus relieved us of the onus of dying. Rilke's remaining portrayal of this institution is a brief but masterful piece of prose, at least in the original German:

> In den Sanatorien, wo ja so gern und mit so viel Dankbarkeit gegen Ärzte und Schwestern gestorben wird, stirbt man einen von den an der Anstalt angestellten Toden; das wird gerne gesehen.
>
> [In the sanatoriums, where people die so willingly and with so much gratitude to the doctors and nurses, it is one of those deaths which are attached to the institution; that is looked on favorably.] (*SW 6:714/MLB 9*)

The apposition of *gestorben wird* and *stirbt man,* separated only by the requisite comma of clausal constructions, once again points to the lack of individuality that underlies this institutionalized genre of death. Rilke relies on both grammatical structures at various points during his reflections on the Hôtel-Dieu. Because they fail to come out in translation, it is worth dwelling on them here for a moment. Granted, the passive voice and impersonal pronoun *man* (one) appear far more frequently in German than their equivalents do in English, but Rilke consciously exploits this linguistic feature of his native language in an effort to lend more rhetorical force to his ideas about the depersonalization of death. The above lines convey absolutely no sense that an individual subject is dying. Rilke, rather, creates the impression that death befalls a faceless collective of humanity. Indeed, it is perhaps not even possible here to speak of death in strict terms, for it has been reduced to an utter nonevent, a brief blip in the uneventful flatline of modern life. As Rilke continually reminds us, the diminution of death brings about a devaluation of existence. The hospital, the home of *der kleine Tod,* goes to great lengths to accommodate the dying and erase the unpleasant reality of their waning health. The above-quoted sentence, with the jarring alliteration (repetition of the prefix *an-* and the phoneme -*st-*) and syntactical intricacy of the phrase *einen von den an der Anstalt angestellten Toden,* expresses the actual purpose of the sanatorium in all the density (*Dichte*) of genuine poetry (*Dichtung*). Behind hospital walls, invisible from the public eye, death is carried out in a discreet and agreeable fashion. Here languishing patients, far removed from home and kin, receive specialized care from total strangers, namely doctors and nurses. As numerous social historians have observed, the hospital has become a center for modern death management. In the representative words of Ariès:

> Death no longer belongs to the dying man, who is first irresponsible, later unconscious, nor to the family, who are convinced of their inadequacy. Death is regulated and organized by bureaucrats whose competence and humanity cannot prevent them from treating death as their "thing," a thing that must bother them as little as possible in the general interest. (*HOD 588*)

These comments only confirm Rilke's ideas about the anonymity of dying. Even in the case of death at home, an increasing rarity in these times of modernization, people die in a "polite, genteel" (*höflich*) (*SW* 6:714/*MLB* 9) manner and gloss over the event with fancy funerals—at least those with the financial means to do so. The poor have no such luxury; they die a "banal" death, content that it "more or less fits" (*SW* 6:714/*MLB* 9). All social classes of city-dwellers thus suffer an empty and alien death, one that they have failed to incorporate into their existence as the future promise of their individuality. This "anguish of anonymous death, the anguish of the 'They die' and the hope for an 'I die,'"[6] leads Rilke to construct one of the most individualistic cases of physical decease in Western literature.

After ruminating on the modern impersonal brand of death exemplified by the factorylike production of the Hôtel-Dieu, Malte thinks back to the time of his childhood, when people still knew how to die with "dignity" and "pride" (*SW* 6:715/*MLB* 10). He invokes a familiar organic image in this context: "Then, you knew (or perhaps you sensed it) that you had your death *inside* you as a fruit has its core" (*SW* 6:715/*MLB* 10). His paternal grandfather, Christoph Detlev Brigge, serves as an extreme example of this individual variety of death that grows within us throughout our lives. Chamberlain Brigge dies a personally distinctive death, one that typifies Rilke's ideal of *eigener Tod*. Over the course of several pages, Rilke describes Brigge's demise, which drags on for ten weeks and terrorizes the entire village of Ulsgaard. The manor-house becomes too small for Brigge's giant death throes: his body grows bigger, presumably due to his affliction of dropsy, and he must be dragged from room to room until he is finally brought to the chamber where his mother died 23 years earlier. Here he lies sprawled on the floor, too massive for the bed, and commences to die his "his own hard death" (*SW* 6:720/*MLB* 16). The notion of *eigener Tod* thus appears here in a radical, if not twisted, form: Brigge's interior death soon takes on an autonomous life of its own such that the Chamberlain now becomes *its* property. Rilke's organic metaphor now becomes more gruesome than wholesome; the death that grows inside Brigge and bloats him beyond recognition bursts forth to take complete possession of its host organism. As Rilke writes: "Christoph Detlev's death was alive now, had already been living at Ulsgaard for many, many days, talked with everyone, made demands" (*SW* 6:718/*MLB* 13). Paradoxically, it demands to die and begins to scream as if in protest that it is still alive. These screams can be heard throughout the district and have a drastic effect on the local populace: villagers are unable to sleep at night, pregnant women feel the cries issue from within their own bodies, calves refuse to be born, and the minister can no longer understand God. Even the church bell remains powerless against the bellowing of the estate owner, who has become possessed by death. In this episode, Rilke presents a grotesque case of *der große Tod;* the Chamberlain's death is "great" in all senses of the word: colossal, imperious, supreme. More important, it conforms to the character of the one that it has inhabited all along, which is ultimately what Rilke means by a "great death," namely that it should be authentically one's own. Brigge comes across as a larger-than-life feudal lord who is looked up to by his subjects, and his death is no less commanding. While this image seems anachronistic for the setting of nineteenth century Denmark, Rilke nevertheless suggests precisely such an historical analogy, one that proves reminiscent of Hegel's lord-bondsman parable. Rilke even applies the term *Herr* to both the Chamberlain and his masterly death (see *SW* 6:719, 720), an appellation that Hegel, with deliberate ambiguity, also attached to his two "absolute masters." The following passage makes the connection between these lords, the declining Brigge and his mounting death, all the more obvious:

> Christoph Detlev's death, which had moved in at Ulsgaard, refused to let itself be hurried. It had come for ten weeks, and for ten weeks it

stayed. And during that time it was master [*Herr*], more than Christoph Detlev Brigge had ever been; it was like a king who is called the Terrible, afterward and for all time.

This was not the death of just any old man with dropsy; this was the sinister, princely death which the Chamberlain had, all his life, carried inside him and nourished with his own experiences. Every excess of pride, will, and authority that he himself had not been able to use up during his peaceful days, had passed into his death, into the death that now sat squandering these things at Ulsgaard. (*SW 6:720/MLB 15*).

This death is even more sovereign than its original owner and therefore more than just his personal property or *Eigentum*. The Chamberlain's ghastly end, while definitely unique, would seem to contradict Rilke's notion of a natural and organic course of death. The prolonged sufferings of Malte's grandfather can hardly serve as a basis for emulation—even for us moderns who are supposedly alienated from our own deaths. The underlying problem with *eigener Tod* is that it remains an utterly relative concept and thus offers a wide range of exemplary cases. If each person is supposed to die his own distinctive death, then ultimately any attempt to arrive at an objective judgment or theoretical standard is futile. Rilke's earlier appeal "Oh Lord, give to each his own death" is as vague as it is precise. The question of ownership could not be clearer, but the exact nature of this death must forever remain nebulous. We cannot dispute the authenticity of Christoph Detlev Brigge's death, for he has laid claim to it all his life. Nevertheless, one cannot shake the suspicion that there is something wrong about this grandiose yet eerie demise. Rilke in fact appears to be paying homage to the literary tradition of the so-called dirty death. As Ariès points out (see *HOD* 568–70), a number of nineteenth century writers attempted to portray the hideousness and indecency of dying. Flaubert's Emma Bovary, for instance, perishes amid vomiting, screams, and convulsions as a result of her self-poisoning. Thomas Mann depicts an even more protracted deathbed scene in *Buddenbrooks,* a novel written between 1897–1900 and one that Rilke praised highly in a review (see *SW* 5:577–81). Here Elisabeth Buddenbrook, the matriarch of the family, slowly dies over the course of some three pages, and as in the case of Christoph Detlev Brigge, this struggle soon undergoes a reversal in its objective: "And then the struggle began anew. Was it a struggle with death? No, she was wrestling now with life to gain death."[7] But Rilke's most obvious influence is Tolstoy, who created one of the most convincing confrontations with death in all of literature—and therefore had to be surpassed.[8] The fact that Ivan Ilyich screams for three days and can be heard from three rooms away pales in comparison with Chamberlain Brigge's agony, which lasts for more than two months and resounds throughout the region with the many bizarre effects mentioned earlier. Rilke's stylized portrait of death clearly outdoes those of his literary predecessors in terms of the length and intensity of the represented *exitus*. Of course Flaubert, Mann, and Tolstoy all keep their scenes within the bounds of realism, whereas Rilke conjures up an over-the-top grotesquerie, one that would seem to be incongruous with his poetic sensibility and holistic worldview. The Chamberlain's end strikes the reader as far too monstrous and horrific to be a truly Rilkean ideal. Clearly, there is something not right about the Brigge family.

The death of Malte's father is far more subdued than that of the Chamberlain, but in its own way just as macabre. Moreover, this case of death proves to be a modern one: the Ulsgaard estate has since passed into foreign hands and his father dies in a Copenhagen apartment house that seems "utterly hostile and alien" (*SW* 6:851/*MLB* 155). Malte, who has already been living abroad, is summoned to his father's deathbed but arrives too late. He sees only the made-up body, which has been given a semblance of life by the art of morticians. These professionals have succeeded in erasing all signs of suffering from the dead man's features, described here as having "been tidied up like the furniture in a guest-room after a visitor has moved out" (*SW* 6:852/*MLB* 155). They have even dressed him in a stylish Master of the Hunt uniform. The illusion of life thus still persists about this corpse. But Malte sees right through these false appearances, noting that his father's crossed hands look "artificial and meaningless" (*SW* 6:852/*MLB* 155). Regardless, the illusion is soon to be shattered for good. Two doctors perform a postmortem operation that makes death a "certainty" (*SW* 6:853/*MLB* 157): they perforate the heart of the deceased. This technique, a not uncommon practice for the time, ensured that the victim was clinically dead and would not regain consciousness after burial.

Ariès points out that doctors of the time seemed particularly troubled by the thought that death might intermingle with life: "the debate over apparent death raised the possibility that death could be, at least for a time, an ambiguous condition. They [doctors of the late nineteenth century] did not accept the idea that there could be a state that partook of both life and death; it had to be one or the other" (*HOD* 403). Numerous accounts of such "ambiguous" cases exist, including one that deeply affected Hölderlin.[9] The measures that Malte's father has prearranged are thus by no means unrealistic or overly morbid given the historical context. Rilke's depiction of the surgical procedure is, however, a different matter: "[The doctor] carefully withdrew the instrument, and in that spot something like a mouth appeared, from which, twice in succession, blood spurted out, as if the mouth were uttering a two-syllable word. The young, blond doctor, with an elegant movement, quickly soaked it up in his piece of cotton. And now the wound stayed motionless, like a closed eye" (*SW* 6:855/*MLB* 158–59).

As the metaphorical imagery of the above passage suggests, there is a deeper symbolic level to this operation. The two syllables that the pierced heart utters most likely refer to the Danish word for death, *døden*. As Malte soon discovers, his father has recorded an anecdote about the famous king of Denmark, Christian IV, who finally managed to pronounce this word before dying (see *SW* 6:858/*MLB* 162). Malte realizes that with the literal death of his father the figurative "heart of our family" (*SW* 6:855/*MLB* 159) has been punctured and will forevermore cease to beat. He compares this clinical perforation with a past custom according to which a nobleman who had become the last of his family line would have his helmet shattered. The death of Malte's father thus signals the end of the Brigges. Malte himself does not even count in the sequence of patriarchs, for he has long since abandoned his past and sought to carve out an existence of his own as a poet. Having been homeless for years, Malte now becomes fatherless and thus finds himself one step closer to the modern condition of alienation. Another important symbolic dimension of this piercing has to do with the attitude that Malte's father exhibits toward death. Like the doctors of his era, he always sought a clear distinction between life and its opposite: he must either be irrefutably alive or definitively dead. And now that his heart has been officially punctured with the appropriate medical instruments, he has his guarantee. There can no longer be any doubt that he has departed from the realm of the living, a doubt that, however slight, still existed when Malte first saw him decked out for public display.

Malte's father always felt uneasy at Urnekloster, the home of his in-laws, who tend not to differentiate between the spheres of life and death. Count Brahe, Malte's maternal grandfather and the head of the household, does not even recognize the flow of time: past, present, and future all merge into one immediate and continuous reality. As a result of this perception, "death was a minor incident which he completely ignored; people whom he had once installed in his memory continued to exist, and the fact that they had died did not alter that in the least" (*SW* 6:735/*MLB* 31). Count Brahe's lack of concern about death thus differs radically from the indifference found in the modern city. The latter attitude has arisen due to the chaos of modernity; in the metropolis, all sense of a central and unified whole has been lost. The existence of the Brahes, however, is characterized by a more fluid state of being, one in which an eternal present rules the day and fixed metaphysical boundaries do not exist. Here the traditional separation between life and death does not apply. This view also diverges from the authentic internal death that Malte's other grandfather, Christoph Detlev Brigge, has cultivated all his life. While Brigge's *eigener Tod* is intimately linked if not organically grafted to his existence, it functions on a purely individual level. Death remains the Chamberlain's personal possession and his own possibility for existential self-realization. It thus becomes a paramount matter for Christoph Detlev and all those who strive for such an individualistically determined end. For Count Brahe, on the other hand, death is not such a blatant issue, since it forms part of a larger totality of being. It is a constant presence and therefore not really worth thinking about, especially since the living and the dead often interact in his home anyway.

The other characters that inhabit this fantastical realm have a similar tendency to blend life with its commonly accepted negation. Malte's uncle, in his own way just as eccentric as the count, occasionally performs secret operations on corpses, which he tries to embalm or otherwise preserve against the natural decay of the body. Like the morticians who exercised their skills on Malte's father, the hobbyist uncle blurs the lines between life and death, at least on the surface. Mathilde Brahe, a distant cousin of Malte's mother, is utterly devoted to an Austrian spiritualist. While she apparently does not dabble in this activity herself, Rilke nevertheless hints at her sympathy with a pseudoreligious movement that seeks communication with the dead. (Later in the novel Rilke introduces the character of Sten, Count Brahe's long-trusted valet, who does directly commune with spirits.) Erik, a youth approximately as old as Malte, is destined to die at a premature age and will leave behind only a portrait that the family commissioned as if they had long reckoned with his early departure. Other members of the Brahe household put in only occasional appearances— for they are dead. These figures include Ingeborg and Christine. Whereas the former turns up just once, as revealed in a story told by Malte's mother (see *SW* 6:790–92/*MLB* 88–90), the latter materializes more regularly and has become a kind of permanent fixture of Urnekloster. As the count responds to the query of Malte's terrified father: "'Who is that?' my father shouted, interrupting. 'Someone who has every right to be here. Not a stranger. Christine Brahe'" (*SW* 6:738/*MLB* 34). Malte's father, whose entire existence is predicated on the strict separation of life and death, eventually departs from Urnekloster after further sightings of Christine. Both he and Malte are never again to return to this mixed realm of the living and the dead.

Rilke's holistic view of death, which defines much of his later poetry, is already evident here in *The Notebooks of Malte Laurids Brigge,* where it functions as a contrast to the individualistic *eigener Tod* and the anonymous dying of The urban masses. Existence in the Brahe household is completely devoid of the anguish, severity, and toil that fill the rooms of the Hôtel-Dieu in Paris and the chambers of the Brigge manor in Ulsgaard. Indeed, the very name of Urnekloster implies a connection between religious mysticism and death: *Urne* (urn) and *Kloster* (cloister). On this Danish estate, which like Ulsgaard passes out of family hands with the arrival of modernity, the Brahes live in a self-contained monastic world that fully integrates the basic human experience of death. This world is strikingly reminiscent of the mystical states of being that Rilke describes in two sketches from 1913, which he grouped under the simple title "Erlebnis" or "Experience" (see *SW* 6:1036–42). In both instances, he not only succumbs to a general sense of oneness with nature but also feels as though he has gained access to a whole new mode of existence, one in which life and death blend into a single all-inclusive reality. His evocation of this near outer-body experience in the garden of Duino Castle, recorded in the first sketch, recalls the ethereal atmosphere of Urnekloster. Rilke, speaking in the third person as if he truly were outside of himself, was even "prepared to see Polyxène or Raimondine or some other departed member of the family emerging from the turn of the path" (*SW* 6:1039/*DE* 125). Here he is referring to the long-dead relations of Princess Marie von Thurn und Taxis-Hohenlohe, the owner of the castle, but he could just as well be expecting Ingeborg or Christine Brahe. The point is that Rilke truly believes in the totality of life and death—indeed profoundly experiences it on occasion.

This holistic recovery of death constitutes a central theme of the *Duino Elegies* and prefigures Heidegger's endeavor to determine the wholeness of Dasein through an ontological analysis of its finitude. But before entering into a discussion of the *Elegies,* it is important to address this issue of totality in *The Notebooks of Malte Laurids Brigge.* As we have seen in Hegel, Hölderlin, and Nietzsche (and will soon find to a greater extreme in Heidegger), death fulfills a totalizing function; it makes human existence both coherent and complete. In his *Malte* novel, Rilke similarly strives for a greater sense of holism. Although it does not appear that death holds the key to finding a totalized existence here in the novel, as it does later in Rilke's poetry, it is nonetheless worth exploring to what extent Rilke manages to construct a unified work of art as a reflection of his integrative worldview. Unlike philosophy, a discipline that places content over form, literature strikes a balance between both—and some of the best literary works strive for a perfect correspondence between substance and structure. Rilke was attentive to this problem throughout his thirty-some years of literary activity, and many of his poems ("The Panther," for instance) flawlessly mesh semantic and syntactic layers of meaning. Even a cursory reading of *Malte* reveals a noticeable departure from the formal conventions of the novel; whether or not its structural oddities are evidence of a more intimate connection to the issue of holism remains to be seen.

Artistic Totality in Malte

Like Hölderlin's *Hyperion*, Rilke's *Malte* relies on a formalistic device that problematizes the distance between the narrator and the reality he records. We have seen that Hölderlin exploits the genre of the epistolary novel for his own attempt at a dialectical mediation between knowing subject and known object. Rilke for his part draws on the form of the diary to create the impression of immediacy between Malte and his Parisian surroundings. But ultimately, this tactic is about as plausible as the stratagem of letters in *Hyperion*. Both narrative techniques are fraught with inconsistencies and improbabilities that call into question their purported level of verisimilitude. The logistical problem of Hyperion's correspondence with Bellarmin and Diotima has already been addressed. The titular notebooks into which Malte transcribes his experiences and that materially make up the novel evince a similar incongruity with the hard facts of realism. The notes that we read in the novel soon outstrip the realistic premise of journal entries, only the first of which is dated: "September 11th, rue Toullier" (*SW* 6:709/*MLB* 3). After 18 alleged entries, some of which do not even deal with his life in Paris, approximately half a year has elapsed (carnival is mentioned on *SW* 6:751/*MLB* 48).[10] It would thus seem that Malte is not dutifully chronicling his daily impressions. What is more, the fragments increasingly depart from the diary format and digress ever further into memories of his childhood and into meditations on his readings. Rilke is certainly aware of these various directions into which his novel is furcating. As he for instance states to his Polish translator in a letter from 1925, he consciously arranged this tripartite structure around his semiautobiographical character (see *Br* 890–91/*SL* 391). As I will demonstrate in the following, the novel becomes a kind of depository of recollections whose purpose is to help Malte, the mediated narrator, gain a more cohesive identity and a more totalistic grip on reality. Malte's notebooks thus resemble Hyperion's letters on both a narrative and metanarrative level: each set of documents functions as a concrete expression of the unity that the fictive narrator seeks in his own discordant world.

The Notebooks of Malte Laurids Brigge consists of 71 sections, which vary in length, tone, and subject matter, but are all supposedly composed by Malte during his period of residence in Paris. The arrangement of these fragmentary notes may first strike readers as random if not disjointed, but Rilke has put a definite, albeit somewhat loose, structure in place. The first third of the novel revolves around Malte's hardships in Paris; the second third features numerous recollections from his childhood in Denmark; and the final third reflects the fruits of his wide readings. Through the course of these narrative spheres one notes a shift from the immediate present to the distant past, from a state of acute subjectivity to a more tempered and objective point of view. Rilke's novel begins with a credible enough journal entry, including even the formalities of date and place. Although this pseudo-realistic device never reappears (Malte is, after all, writing notebooks, not diaries), the sections dealing with Paris attest to his initial perceptions of the urban disorder around him. They are grounded in the immediacy of his experiences and are for the most part composed in the present tense. These chunks of text are fragments in a revealing sense of the word: they mirror the splintered reality that Malte encounters on the streets of Paris. Malte tends to perceive his urban environment as a jumbled array of images. The fragmentation of his world becomes symbolized by a windowpane that shatters into pieces on the street (see *SW* 6:710/*MLB* 4) and by the disengaged human body parts that confront him at various points in the narrative, particularly in the Salpêtrière clinic (see *SW* 6:759–60/*MLB* 56–57).[11] Malte, in other words, sees parts of things but never their whole. He even comes to the realization that he himself has been reduced to a heap of fragments: "I have fallen and I can't pick myself up, because I am shattered to pieces" (*SW* 6:756/*MLB* 53). (This last crucial clause, "weil ich zerbrochen bin," is strangely missing from the English translation.) As Rilke more directly puts it in a letter recording his initial impressions of Paris: "O what a world is this! Bits, bits of people, parts of animals, remains of perished things, all of them still animate, still fluttering about in a mysterious wind" (*SL* 25). We have here the basic problem of modern existence raised by Hyperion and Zarathustra, who both walk among the fragments and limbs of their contemporary fellow beings.

Malte's own struggle to find any sign of harmony amidst the human rubble of his day finds expression in his fragmented and disconnected notebook entries, which constitute an attempt to make sense of his chaotic surroundings. These fragments furthermore testify to the impossibility of storytelling that characterizes modern literature. As Malte realizes: "The days when people knew, really knew, how to tell stories must have been before my time" (*SW* 6:844/*MLB* 146). However, the tentative and staccato notations of Malte's Parisian journals yield to a smoother narrative flow whenever he reflects on his childhood, a time when people—for instance his grandfather Brahe—still "knew how to tell stories." From the standpoint of pure style, these sections are unmatched in the novel and could not offer a greater contrast to the modernist prose of the big-city fragments. This disparity is especially evident in the episodes of Christoph Detlev Brigge's death and Christine Brahe's apparition, both of which occur in the early stretch of the novel dominated by Malte's troubles in Paris. (The fact that Rilke chose to read these two parts of the novel in public speaks all the more for their stylistic perfection.)[12] The reader increasingly senses that Malte is making significant advances in his storytelling abilities and has found a voice that conforms to the nineteenth century mode of narration. But Malte not only narrates his own past in a remarkably fluid fashion; he also relates the stories of various historical figures with whom he identifies on some private level. These personages include Grishka Otrepyov, the false "False Dmitri"; Charles the Bold, the Duke of Burgundy; Charles VI, the "Mad King" of France; and John XXII, the "anti-pope" of Avignon. The details of Malte's affinity with these diverse individuals need not occupy us here, though the problems of death, exclusion, and identity form major points of connection. The more important issue concerns his efforts to retell their lives in his own words and thereby further flesh out his personality.

The case of Grishka, a pretender to the Russian throne in the early 1600s, particularly illustrates Malte's improved storytelling abilities. Thinking back to "the little green book" (*SW* 6:880/*MLB* 187) that he owned as child and in which he first read of Grishka, Malte fills in the gaps of his memory by chronicling the rise and fall of the Russian imposter. He remains most fascinated by the demise of the false tsar, musing: "It is possible even now to imagine a storyteller who would devote a great deal of attention to these last moments" (*SW* 6:883/*MLB* 190). After portraying these final moments for an entire page, he still insists that "we need someone who knows how to tell a story" (*SW* 6:884/*MLB* 191). But this is exactly what Malte is doing: telling a story. In fact, he has been adeptly weaving tales—his own as well as those of his relatives and historical doubles—for some time now and will continue to do so for the remainder of the novel. His early writing ventures are not successful from the standpoint of conventional narrative, but they stand in their own right as masterful prose pieces. In these beginning fragments dealing with his Parisian experiences, one notes a deep divide between the narrating subject, Malte, and the objects of his narration, namely the dead, dying, and suffering outcasts who surround him on all sides yet whose ranks he refuses to join. This distance between subject and object is gradually overcome throughout the novel as Malte increasingly projects himself into his historical and metaphorical analogues, thereby giving a more oblique interpretation of his life. On a stylistic level, the initial first-person outpourings of the heart cede to third-person narrations that exhibit more restraint, fluency, and cohesiveness.

Rilke concludes his novel with a third-person narration that retells the legend of the prodigal son. This final section, which has all the trappings of a fictional narrative (plot, characters, and main idea) confirms Malte's consummate storytelling abilities and furthermore hints at his integration into a greater whole. The piece is also composed in a poetic style that somehow seems timeless or at least premodernist. As for its content, Malte paints a thinly veiled self-portrait by filtering his subjectivity through an archetypal figure whose stations of life parallel his own: sheltered childhood, exile, poverty, and homecoming. The fact that Malte reconfigures himself in a third-person narrative speaks all the more for his method of self-reflexivity. Indeed, a transcendental "I" appears at various points in the text, which only reinforces the metalevel of reflection. By the end of the tale it becomes clear that Malte has developed into an accomplished storyteller through the course of the 71 sketches that comprise his note-books. This maturation process leads him, like the prodigal son, back into the fold of his own family, which once excelled in the art of nar-ration. As already mentioned, Count Brahe is singled out as one such former spinner of tales. Like Malte and the prodigal son, he in fact also seeks to recapture his childhood. He dictates his memoirs to his daughter Abelone, who for her part lacks the ability to tell stories (see *SW* 6:844/*MLB* 146). Through this act of recollection, the count con-verts his long-lost past into a vivid present: "And it was quite natu-ral, according to him, that this very distant time had taken control of him now; that when he turned his gaze inward, it lay there as in a bril-liant northern summer night, intensified and unsleeping" (*SW* 6:846/*MLB* 149). Malte likewise mixes levels of time in his notebooks: his past childhood, present exile, and future life as intimated in the story of the prodigal son all merge in the greater flow of his self-nar-rative. As Rilke comments with respect to this connection: "Not for nothing is Malte the grandchild of old Count Brahe who regards everything, past and future, as quite simply 'present'" (*Br* 891/*SL* 391). Malte thus comes full circle in the arc of his family history, ultimately finding a way back into the holistic Brahe sphere from which he was completely cut off at the start of his notebooks. As a consequence of his storytelling efforts, he manages to construct a more complete iden-tity as well as a more totalized view of the world. As with Hyperion, his act of writing has a therapeutic and restorative effect: he recovers, at least partially, his own alienated self through reflection and mediation.

The unity of *Malte* principally resides in its structure, which is built around a central figure that seeks his own sense of harmony in the world. While death certainly plays a major role, it does not seem to have a significant unifying purpose within the overall scope of the novel. One could of course argue that its presence throughout the notebooks cre-ates a certain thematic continuity or that Malte's return to the Brahe realm of timelessness implicitly leads to a holistic acceptance of death. These may be perfectly valid points, but they pale in comparison to the unifying function of death in Rilke's post-*Malte* writings.

THE HOLISM OF LIFE AND DEATH

After the publication of *Malte* in 1910, Rilke's view of death under-goes a marked shift in emphasis. For the most part he abandons his trichotomous model and puts all of his artistic powers into conveying the message that death is neither anonymous nor individual, but part of the greater totality of being. The Brahe sphere, only one of three major components of Malte's identity, thus takes over Rilke's entire way of thinking and finds its most significant elaboration in the *Duino Elegies,* composed between 1912 and 1922. The fact that Rilke needed ten years to complete this cycle of only ten poems speaks for the supreme difficulty of articulating his vision of the holistic relation between life and death. Even this highly gifted poet apparently struggled with the limitations of language in his efforts to describe a mode of being that lies beyond everyday human experience. Although he eventually formed such concepts as *das Offene* and *Weltinnenraum,* these merely label the hidden reality that Rilke felt he had accessed but do not truly capture it in all its detail and depth. Attempts to interpret the *Elegies* can easily run into similar linguistic hurdles and stumble in inco-herencies as a result. Rather than plunge directly into an analysis of these poems, I will take a slightly more circuitous route and approach them gradually, first exploring some of the contexts out of which they arose and clarifying some of the ideas upon which they are based.

Holistic Spaces of Being: The Experience of Weltinnenraum

The original inspiration for the *Elegies* overtook Rilke like a storm—indeed, under stormy conditions—at Duino Castle on the Adriatic Coast of northern Italy. Here Rilke spent the winter of 1911–12 alone, his only company the servants and ghosts of the estate. In this atmosphere of otherworldliness, reminiscent of the Brahe way of life at Urnekloster, Rilke not only wrote the first two elegies of his future cycle but also had a kind of mystical revelation that significantly contributed to the formation of his views on death. This vision of all-unity, which I briefly touched on earlier, will recur in Rilke's life and work, but he offers the most detailed description of this near inexpressible state of being in the first of two sketches entitled "Erlebnis." Here Rilke describes his experience from both a temporal and narrative distance, which brings to mind Malte's technique in the latter parts of the novel: the depicted events occurred over one year in the past (Rilke actually composed the piece in 1913 while living in Ronda, Spain) and are narrated from a third-person perspective. This practice is consonant with the overall effect of Rilke's mood in the castle gardens: "In general, he was able to observe how all objects yielded themselves to him more distantly and, at the same time, somehow more truly; this was no doubt due to his vision, which was no longer directed forwards, and which out there, in the open, thinned away; he was looking, over his shoulder, as it were, backwards at things" (*SW* 6:1039/*DE* 125). This sense of distance may seem incompatible with the nearness that Rilke, here transformed into a narrative "he," feels to nature as he leans back in the branches of a tree and absorbs its vibrations. The sensation of oneness with the tree forms the basis of his sketch, but clearly there is more to his experience than just a corporeal fusion with external phenomena. What Rilke perceives, rather, is an interpenetration of proximity and remoteness, a realm in which traditional conceptions of time and space do not apply. Although this state of otherness cannot adequately be put into words, Rilke musters what for him is a fairly satisfactory description, "saying to himself, that he had got to the other side of Nature" (*SW* 6:1038/*DE* 125). From this vantage he is able to see things in an entirely different light, with a detachment and transparency that define a whole new level of perception. As previously mentioned, he senses the presence of the castle ghosts, Polyxène and Raimondine, who belong to a world that can best be described as "the other side."[13] But even ordinary objects show another facet of their existence. In a section of text not included in the English translation by Leishman and Spender, Rilke mentions a flower that he must have seen often enough on his walks but that never before fully caught his attention. In his present state of receptivity, this vinca or periwinkle "touched him now out of a more spiritual distance, but with such inexhaustible meaning, as if there were nothing more to be hidden" (*SW* 6:1039). Indeed, as Rilke further observes in a crucial statement already quoted above, "all objects yielded themselves to him more distantly and, at the same time, more truly." Rilke, however, does not divulge what true meaning these everyday entities reveal to him. Perhaps this deeper signification is too ineffable for words or too relative to individual perception. All that can be said with certainty is that Rilke has discovered an "extraordinary condition" (*SW* 6:1039/ *DE* 125) of intimacy and unity with the world around him—and in him.

Whereas Rilke's experience at Duino revolves around the faculty of sight, another sketch describes a related state of harmony based on the sense of hearing. "Erlebnis II," which takes place on the Italian island of Capri, evokes a sensation in which the call of a bird manifests itself "both outside and within him" (*SW* 6:1040/*DE* 126). This sound passes right through the walls of his body and "gathered inner and outer together into one uninterrupted space" (*SW* 6:1040/*DE* 126). Closing his eyes so as not to be distracted by his own physical presence, Rilke feels "the infinite" penetrating him from all sides and the stars from above filling his breast. In this same sketch, he also recalls peering at the starry sky through the branches of an olive tree and looking straight into the depths of the universe (see *SW* 6:1040). An infinite distance thus becomes reduced to an intimate nearness. The external and remote *Weltraum,* the German word that Rilke uses here for "universe," is interiorized into a space that he elsewhere calls *Weltinnenraum.* He introduces this important notion in an untitled poem from 1914, the fourth stanza of which reads:

> Durch alle Wesen reicht der *eine* Raum:
> Weltinnenraum. Die Vögel fliegen still
> durch uns hindurch. O, der ich wachsen will,
> ich seh hinaus, und in mir wächst der Baum.   (SW 2:93)
> [*One* space spreads through all creatures: world-inner-space. Birds quietly fly right through us. Oh, wanting to grow, I look outside and in me the tree grows.] (My translation.)

Another poem written ten years later depicts a similar scene of flying birds and growing trees, but calls upon the reader to actively create this space, which now goes by the shorter name of *Innenraum:*

> Durch den sich Vögel werfen, ist nicht der
> vertraute Raum, der die Gestalt dir steigert.

(Im Freien, dorten, bist du dir verweigert
und schwindest weiter ohne Wiederkehr.)
Raum greift aus uns und übersetzt die Dinge:
daß dir das Dasein eines Baums gelinge,
wirf Innenraum um ihn, aus jenem Raum,
der in dir west. Umgieb ihn mit Verhaltung.
Er grenzt sich nicht. Erst in der Eingestaltung
in dein Verzichten wird er wirklich Baum.   (*SW* 2:167–68)

[What birds plunge through is not the intimate space in which you feel
all forms intensified. (Out there in the open you are self-denied and vanish without return.) Space reaches out from us and translates things:
in order to feel the existence of a tree, cast inner-space around it, out
of the space that dwells within you. Surround it with retention. It
knows no bounds. Not until its re-formation in your renouncing is it
truly tree.] (My translation.)

   Rilke's notion of *Innenraum* can obviously not be interpreted
according to strict spatial criteria. What he essentially means by this
concept is an invisible space, an aperture in which the traditional perceptions of interiority and exteriority translucently overlap. In his
experience at Duino, he for instance compares his body to a window
through which he gazes "out and beyond" (SW 6:1039/*DE* 125) the
common limits of human perception. In his Capri sketch he speaks of
a "spatiality so humanly unarranged that they [other people] would
only call it 'the empty [*das Leere*]'" (*SW* 6:1042). The above poems
describe a similar ill-defined space. The *Weltinnenraum* referred to in
the first excerpt permeates all of creation and opens up an entire network of interrelations among the diverse inhabitants of the world. The
barriers between individual beings have been lifted such that humans,
birds, and trees intersect in their existence and activity. In the second
poem, *Innenraum* seems to be more internal. It not only lacks the component *Welt-*, but apparently exists within the individual, who is able
to cast it, like a net, around external phenomena and thereby better
grasp them in their being. It is difficult to say whether Rilke specifically
means that we must internalize the manifold objects of the world
in order to gain a proper understanding of their relevance to our own
existence. He certainly makes it clear that this interiorized space

paradoxically "knows no bounds." Again, Rilke does not envision the three-dimensional spatiality that we take for granted and upon which we base our dealings with the world. Maurice Blanchot has called this common perception of reality "a 'bad extension,' where one thing necessarily supplants another, can't be seen except hiding the other."[14] The human body, in other words, is not a *res extensa* that impedes the flight of birds, nor is the human mind a *res cogitans* that represents an exterior tree. Long before Heidegger began to explore the spatial implications of *vor-stellen,* Rilke had already been critiquing, in his own poetic way, Cartesian notions of space and consciousness. The diverse texts that I have commented on above give some idea of his conviction that interiority and exteriority form a continuous rather than contiguous space. And as for the problem of consciousness, which organizes the broader field of existence into the epistemological (and ostensibly ontological) categories of subject and object, he has a more theoretical paradigm that illustrates his belief in the wholeness of being.

If Cartesian spatiality is a "bad extension," then consciousness can only be described as a "bad interiority."[15] For Rilke, there is no internal cognitive faculty that processes external data, which is but another way of saying that he does not view the world in terms of a subject-object relation. In a letter from August 11, 1924, Rilke introduces his idea of a "pyramid of consciousness," which serves him as a counter-model to the traditional metaphysical explanation of reality. The connection to his notion of *Innenraum* becomes apparent in the following excerpt:

> However extensive the external world may be, with all its sidereal distances it hardly bears comparison with the dimensions, the *depth-dimensions,* of our inner being, which has no need even of the vastness of the universe to be itself all but illimitable. . . . It seems to me more and more as though our ordinary consciousness dwelt on the summit of a pyramid, whose base broadens out in us and beneath us so much that the more deeply we see ourselves able to penetrate into it the more boundlessly do we seem implicated in those factors of our earthly, and in the wildest sense, *worldly* being which are independent of space and time. Since my earliest youth I have entertained the idea (and have also, when I was adequate to it, lived accordingly), that if a cross-section

were made lower down through this pyramid of consciousness, Being, in its simplest form, would become "eventual" [*könnte zum Ereignis werden*] in us. (*Br* 871/*SL* 386)

Rilke thus does not deny the existence of consciousness, but merely claims that it cannot serve as the basis of our experiences since it is far too limited in scope. The rich interior world that he describes here may seem strikingly similar to the notorious *Innerlichkeit* that has dominated the intellectual tradition in Germany and, some have argued, played no small part in the fateful course of its history. But it must again be emphasized that Rilke thinks beyond such dichotomies as interiority/exteriority, subjectivity/objectivity, and human consciousness/raw being. He instead strives for a condition that is "independent of space and time" and in which being can occur as a Heideggerian "event." Count Brahe, as Rilke mentions in the same letter, exists in precisely such a realm of spacelessness and timelessness. Even though Rilke alludes to a fictional character that he himself contrived, he is still "convinced that this conception corresponds to a *real* state of things, even though it be repudiated by all the conventions of our ordinary life" (*Br* 872/*SL* 386). Rilke therefore seeks to gain a sphere of existence that he outlined years before and contrasted with other modalities of being. If the world of the Brigges is characterized by individuality and differentiation, modern life is defined by anonymity and alienation. Both of these modes can be overcome through the holistic ideal that Rilke approaches from diverse angles and articulates in a variety of ways. Whether he succumbs to a kind of *unio mystica* in the presence of nature, poeticizes a space of unification, or constructs a theoretical paradigm of being, Rilke is in each case attempting to express his view of ontological totality.

Rilke's conception of *Weltinnenraum* ultimately fulfills a key function in his ongoing attempt to arrive at a better comprehension of death. Of course any hope of gaining a true understanding of this phenomenon is paradoxical: one dies at the very moment of absolute insight. Herein lies the basic problem that Hegel tried to overcome through dialectics and Heidegger will confront through the existential ideal of anticipation, itself a form of understanding. Rilke approaches the epistemologically inaccessible realm of death by creating an ontological space in which it can better come to him. This meeting ground of life and death underlies concepts like *Innenraum* and the experiences of all-unity outlined above. The nonspatialized state of being that periodically invades Rilke enables him to abide in a realm where death, in the words of Hegel, can be "endured" and "maintained." In his "extraordinary conditions" of otherness, Rilke breaks through a kind of metaphysical boundary and reaches a side of existence that is characterized by a coalescence of subject and object, the particular and the universal, even life and death. He alludes to this last connection in a letter from January 14, 1919. Here he writes in reference to the first "Erlebnis" sketch: "The one leaning against the tree became so to speak nothing but an indicator between the two scales of life and death" (*Br* 570). In the same letter, he even suggests that this figure in the gardens of Duino, though living, stands on "the side of death" (*Br* 571), which is but another way of saying that he has broken through the false frontier built by metaphysics and found a zone in which life and its traditional negation can coexist. As Rilke states more directly in another letter, we must learn to "read the word 'death' *without* negation" (*Br* 806). Human existence is thus a space, like *Weltinnenraum,* that encompasses both realities, where there is no metaphysical barrier that separates being from nonbeing. When Rilke speaks of "the other side," he does not mean a transcendent domain that lies beyond our terrestrial existence. This other side merely designates a condition of alterity that allows for the entwinement of life and death. It is an alternative mode of being, one that we are both close to and distant from. Rilke's ultimate message is that we must strive to attain and continually maintain this holistic form of existence in which: "there is neither a This-side [*Diesseits*] nor a That-side [*Jenseits*], but a single great unity" (*Br* 896/*SL* 393). Rilke repeatedly emphasizes this point about the totality of life and death in his correspondence after the completion of the *Elegies* in 1922. He thus becomes a philosophical commentator of sorts on his own literary work. I do not wish to dwell on his many interpretive remarks about the role of death in the *Elegies,* as they are for the most part self-explanatory. For the present, I will merely focus on a letter in which Rilke lays out his basic antimetaphysical stance. His comments here not only provide a useful theoretical framework for the interpretation of his later poetry; they further serve to align him with the other figures of this study who counter the metaphysics of death with their own dialectical and existential models.

In a letter dated November 8, 1915 (see *Br* 510–16/*SL* 263–68),[16] Rilke outlines his ideas about the false metaphysical path that our relationship with death has taken over the course of human history. These reflections bring to mind the equally sweeping historical reassessment of finitude that Kojève gives in "The Idea of Death in Hegel's Philosophy." Like Kojève, Rilke situates his argument against the broader backdrop of theology and specifically addresses the tension between metaphysical transcendence and ontological immanence. He departs from the premise that we humans have fashioned gods in order to make sense of the destructive forces of life. These deities eventually become reservoirs into which all the unpleasant aspects of existence are diverted. Through this distancing effect we are better able to cope with factors that are too menacing to bear on our own. By projecting our negative experiences onto a more general being, one with whom we share a certain kinship but not a perfect identity, we create a kind of buffer to insulate ourselves from the dangers that we have conveniently attributed to an external source. (Although Rilke does not explicitly mention this example, the wrathful God of the Old Testa-ment can be seen as one such supernatural being that embodies many of these harsh realities.) Death, the most basic threat to our existence, is consequently deferred to a realm that is separate from the one we already inhabit. As a result, it has been "banished and excommunicated" (*Br* 512–13/*SL* 265) from the core of our being only to turn against us and become our own worst enemy. Rilke elaborates as follows:

> He [death/*der Tod*], who is probably so close to us that the distance between him and the inner centre of our hearts cannot be registered, he was made into something external, something to be held daily at a greater distance, something that lurks in the outer voids ready to pounce [on] this man or the next with his baneful choice. More and more the suspicion grew up against him that he was the antithesis [*der Widerspruch*], the opponent [*der Widersacher*], the invisible opposite [*der unsichtbare Gegensatz*] in the air. (*Br* 513/*SL* 265–66)

As Rilke then points out, we may have successfully repressed the issue of our mortality, but nature knows better and revels in the coexistence of life and death. He gives some examples in a passage that has been slightly mistranslated but that I have touched up as follows: "when a tree blossoms, death blossoms in it as well as life; every field is full of Death, which reaps a rich expression of life from its [the field's] prone countenance, and the animals pass patiently from one to the other [i.e. from life to death]" (*Br* 514/*SL* 266). Rilke further underscores the omnipresence of death with the claim that it "peers out at us from the cracks of things" and even affects the existence of a rusty nail "that sticks up out of a plank [and] does nothing but rejoice over him [death] day and night" (*Br* 514/*SL* 266). In view of the universal immanence of death, it seems ludicrous that we humans have turned this basic experience into a transcendent event and thereby deprived ourselves of its life-enhancing power. By postponing death to the beyond, we oust it from our inner space and lay upon it the shackles of time. But Rilke seeks the precise opposite: death should be both spaceless and timeless, an intimate and constant presence, as in the alternative modes of being occupied by the Brahes and, on occasion, Rilke himself.

The Poem "Death" (1915)

In a poem from 1915 that bears the simple title "Der Tod," Rilke contrasts the metaphysical attitude toward death with his own holistic view. Since my interpretation of this poem will address most of its verses, I include it here in its entirety, first in the German, then in the translation by William H. Gass, which succeeds as both a faithful and artistic rendering of the original:

> Da steht der Tod, ein bläulicher Absud
> in einer Tasse ohne Untersatz.
> Ein wunderlicher Platz für eine Tasse:
> steht auf dem Rücken einer Hand. Ganz gut
> erkennt man noch an dem glasierten Schwung
> den Bruch des Henkels. Staubig. Und: "*Hoff-nung*"
> an ihrem Bug in aufgebrauchter Schrift.
>
> Das hat der Trinker, den der Trank betrifft,
> bei einem fernen Frühstück ab-gelesen.

Was sind denn das für Wesen,
die man zuletzt wegschrecken muß mit Gift?

Blieben sie sonst? Sind sie denn hier vernarrt
in dieses Essen voller Hindernis?
Man muß ihnen die harte Gegenwart
ausnehmen, wie ein künstliches Gebiß.
Dann lallen sie. Gelall, Gelall . . . .

. . . .

O Sternenfall,
von einer Brücke einmal eingesehn—:
Dich nicht vergessen. Stehn!   (*SW* 2:103–04)

[There stands Death, a blue residue
in a cup without a saucer.
An odd spot for a cup:
balanced on the back of a hand.
One can clearly see along its glazed
curve a crack showing where the handle snapped.
Dusty. And HOPE on its side in washed-out letters.

The one who was to drink this drink
spelled it out at breakfast long ago.

What sort of specters are these, then,
who have to have a poison push them off?

Otherwise would they remain? Would they gnaw on
this food full of hindrance forever?

One must pull the harsh present
from them like a set of false teeth.
Only then they mumble. Mumble . . . umble . . .
umble . . . .

. . . .

O shooting star,
seen from a bridge once, a penetrating ray:
Never to forget you. Stay.][17]

This poem, which Rilke aptly labeled "grotesque" (*Br* 570), is framed by images that symbolize two contrasting genres of death. The first image, a cup mysteriously resting on the back of a hand, derives from a vision that Rilke had while walking through a park in Munich;

the second stems from a more physically credible scenario that he witnessed in Toledo, Spain. According to Princess Marie von Thurn und Taxis-Hohenlohe, this latter sight of a falling star represented in Rilke's mind "wonderful death" (*der wunderbare Tod*).[18] Although she does not expand on this point, the relevance of *Weltinnenraum* cannot be ignored. In a letter, Rilke himself refers to this connection, claiming that this star, like the ones that he observed in Capri, belonged to the space of both *Weltenraum* and *Innen-raum* (see *Br* 571). In other words, he once again experiences a sense of oneness whereby interiority and exteriority collapse within his being and life coalesces with death. The poem's last stanza sums up Rilke's totalistic worldview and, more specifically, his belief that death forms part of this greater totality. The image of a shooting star reminds the poet of death's constant presence, a presence that he hopes to preserve for the intensification of his own existence: "Never to forget you. Stay."

The major portion of this poem is concerned with a less wholesome attitude. In one of the strangest metaphors of Rilke's oeuvre, death appears as a blue residue in a broken cup that symbolizes the fragmentation of human existence. Not only is the cup missing its handle, but it also rests on an isolated hand, one of the key symbols of disjuncture in *Malte* (see especially the episode of the severed hand in *SW* 6:792–97/*MLB* 90–95). Even the inscription on the side of the cup is fragmented or in this case hyphenated (*Hoff-nung* in the original), as is the verb that reflects the act of reading this message (*abgelesen*). This lexical effect of disruption recalls Rilke's statement about the appropriate reception of *Malte:* "Dies Buch ist *hinzunehmen,* nicht im Einzelnen auf-zu-fassen" (*Br* 891). The juxtaposition of two separable prefix verbs, one of which is improperly riddled by hyphens, visually conveys the difference between holism and fragmentation. The published English translation of this sentence does its best to bring out the contrast that Rilke was more naturally able to communicate through the intricacies of the German language: "The book is to be accepted whole, not taken up in single details" (*SL* 392). But this opposition is precisely the problem in the first two stanzas of the poem: human existence does not form an intact whole but remains irreparably fractured. The cup is also incomplete insofar as it lacks a saucer and contains only the remains of a fluid, here an unpalatable deposit. This is Rilke's way of saying that our lives have no solid foundation in view of the fact that death has been reduced to a useless leftover. The broken and empty cup functions as the symbolic obverse of the various metaphors of plenitude that Rilke employs in other contexts. In a letter dated January 6, 1923, he for instance writes: "death is not *beyond* our power, it is the measuring mark on the brim of a vessel: we are *full* whenever we reach this mark" (*Br* 807). Here Rilke draws on a more common notion of spatiality to express the function of death as a gauge that determines the fullness of life. But there is no such mark on the broken cup in the poem, only discolored sediment at the very bottom. Death, in other words, is a bitter reality that people seek to avoid at all costs. Even though their lives have been depleted of all meaning, like the cup that has been drained of everything but its dregs, the dying must be forcibly removed from their place here on earth, as yet another metaphor suggests: "One must pull the harsh present / from them like a set of false teeth." Rambling incoherently, perhaps because they have grown feeble minded in their old age, they drift off into permanent sleep. Metaphysics thus reaches its nadir in this derisive poem: all Christian "hope" in the beyond has faded[19] and death acts as a "poison" that keeps people desperately clinging to what they call their lives.

The Duino Elegies *(1912–22)*

The *Duino Elegies* are widely considered to be Rilke's supreme artistic achievement. The amount of criticism devoted to the *Elegies* is immense, and the argument that life and death form a whole in this poetic cycle is by now practically a cliché. My own discussion of the *Elegies* does not aspire to advance far beyond the already existing scholarship,[20] nor can I possibly give all ten poems their due given the parameters of my study. My analysis has, rather, two principal aims. First of all, I will focus on the death-related motifs that I have been pursuing all along, from Hegel and Hölderlin to Nietzsche and the early Rilke himself. In this manner, I hope to show that the *Elegies* have their place in the larger continuity of literary and philosophical reflections on human finitude. Secondly, I will touch on aspects of the poems that anticipate my next chapter on Heidegger, who purportedly made the claim that his philosophy expresses the same ideas, only in different language, as the *Duino Elegies.*[21] Rilke's second major poetic work, the *Sonnets to Orpheus,* issued from his pen as a kind of "natural overflow" (*Br* 752) of the *Elegies.* During the month of February 1922, while in the grips of a feverish inspiration similar to that under which Nietzsche churned out his *Zarathustra,* Rilke composed all 55 of the *Sonnets to Orpheus* and over half of the *Duino Elegies.* In view of this simultaneity of composition, it comes as no surprise that both projects display a significant degree of overlap with regard to their major themes and motifs. Although I do not intend to devote a separate discussion to the *Sonnets,* I will refer to them in my analysis of the *Elegies* when the appropriate occasion presents itself.

In a famous letter to his Polish translator, Rilke contrasts Malte's crisis-ridden life with the holistic existence thematized in the *Duino Elegies:* "In the Elegies life . . . becomes possible once more, indeed it experiences here that ultimate affirmation towards which the young Malte, although on the right and difficult road '*des longues études,*' could not yet guide it. *Affirmation of life as well as of death prove themselves one in the Elegies*" (*Br* 896/*SL* 392). While the conflicting modes of death found in the novel do not play a major part in the poetic cycle, traces of their presence remain. A closer examination of their role will reveal that Rilke does not completely abandon his earlier conceptions of death as a mass-produced commodity and a fruitlike potentiality. But, in contrast to their prominence in *Malte,* these varieties of death pale before the overwhelming sense of wholeness that emerges from the *Elegies.*

The "Fifth Elegy," which Rilke actually composed last, invokes a metaphorical figure that personifies the anonymous death of the big city. Madame Lamort is a Parisian fashion designer who produces stylish hats and represents death à la mode. While she does not exactly turn out these articles in factorylike production, as the Hôtel-Dieu generates its daily quota of the dead in the novel, she nevertheless embodies a modern trend that goes against Rilke's timeless ideal of holism. Madame Lamort is an updated version of the Fates, to whom Hölderlin dedicated one of his poems about death, as I have discussed previously.[22] Like her ancient predecessors, she spins the threads of human destiny, only in her own modish way. As Rilke writes:

Plätze, o Platz in Paris, unendlicher Schauplatz,
wo die Modistin, Madame Lamort,
die ruhlosen Wege der Erde, endlose Bänder,
schlingt und windet und neue aus ihnen
Schleifen erfindet, Rüschen, Blumen, Kokarden, künstliche
Früchte—, alle
unwahr gefärbt,—für die billigen
Winterhüte des Schicksals.

[Squares, o square in Paris, infinite show-place,
where the modiste Madame Lamort
winds and binds the restless ways of the world,
those endless ribbons, to ever-new
creations of bow, frill, flower, cockade and fruit,
all falsely-coloured, to deck
the cheap winter-hats of Fate.] *(DE* 52/53)

The hats that Madame Lamort manufactures thus feature all kinds of decorative trappings, which symbolize the artificiality of contemporary human existence. She is in effect the complete opposite of the Parcae from whom Hölderlin requests a reprieve in order to complete his *Empedocles* drama. While these latter goddesses are called upon to grant a brief yet plentiful period to a poet who feels that his days may be numbered, their twentieth century counterpart elaborately spins "endless ribbons" signifying the protracted and superficial lives of city-dwellers who refuse to accept their mortal condition. Indeed, the detail of "künstliche Früchte" *(DE* 52), which is not literally translated by Leishman and Spender, reinforces another key motif from Rilke's previous works. These "artificial fruits" adorning Madame Lamort's hats bring to mind, negatively, the organic imagery that Rilke often relied on to illustrate the individualistic mode of finitude that predates modernity. While her winter-hats of death are decorated with a synthetic imitation, like the ornamental fruit found in many households today, Rilke explores the implications of a more natural ripening process in his next elegy.

In the opening lines of the "Sixth Elegy," Rilke praises the organic development of a fig tree in the context of what he calls *der gärtnernde Tod* or the "gardening Death" *(DE* 54/55). Metaphors of cultivation and growth dominate the first stanza. Whereas in his earlier writings

Rilke always spoke of fruit (*Frucht*) in general terms, only enumerating such generic details as skin/rind (*Schale*) and seed/pit (*Kern*), he tends to draw on concrete examples in the *Elegies* and *Sonnets*. Here in the "Sixth Elegy" we have a fig tree, in the Fourth an apple. In the thirteenth sonnet to Orpheus (part 1) several types of fruit are listed, all of which contain more than just taste: "Voller Apfel, Birne und Banane, / Stachelbeere . . . Alles dieses spricht / Tod und Leben in den Mund " ("Full round apple, pear and banana, / gooseberry . . . All this speaks / death and life into the mouth") (*SO* 40/41). These fruits are "full" in the sense of being whole, for they consist of both life and death; like all organic matter, they have come to be through a natural cycle of growth and decay. The deeper message of Rilke's sonnet is that such fruits intimate to us humans, who insist on divorcing life from death, the inseparability of both realities. Similarly, the "Sixth Elegy" seeks to impart a message about the fundamental relation of death to human existence. As the first sentence reads:

> Feigenbaum, seit wie lange schon ists mir bedeutend,
> wie du die Blüte beinah ganz überschlägst
> und hinein in die zeitig entschlossene Frucht,
> ungerühmt, drängst dein reines Geheimnis.

> [Fig tree, how long it's been full meaning for me,
> the way you almost entirely omit to flower
> and into the seasonably-resolute fruit
> uncelebratedly thrust your purest secret.]   (*DE* 54/55)

Rilke thus highlights the fig's accelerated rate of growth, describing how it all but bypasses its flowering in the urge to attain fruition. The symbolism here seems apparent enough: the fig tree (human existence) is so bent on producing its fruit (death) that it almost forgets to blossom (to live). The subject of the elegy reveals why this might be the case. Rilke is not describing the existence of the average mortal, who, as he makes clear, lingers too long in the blooming stage and reaches the fruit's core too late (DE, 54/55). The true focus lies on the hero, a higher form of being that lives so intensely and recklessly that it has no patience for the normal course of existence. Heroes rush through life and find fulfillment in a death that by most accounts is premature.[23]

As one scholar has argued, Rilke's choice of a fig tree (*Feigenbaum*) as a metaphor for the hero may also be motivated by another definition of *feige* in German. In its adjectival form this word (*veige* in Middle High German) signified "doomed to death," and not until the late fifteenth century did it take on the meaning of "afraid of death" or "cowardly."[24] Rilke thus manages to convey the idea of a heroic end by drawing both on an organic image—a patented practice in his oeuvre—and on the etymological resources of his own language.

Later in the poem Rilke employs another key metaphor to express the hero's brazen conduct toward death. Here a correlation to Hölderlin's Empedocles cannot be ignored:

> Diese [Helden] stürzen dahin: dem eigenen Lächeln
> sind sie voran, wie das Rossegespann in den milden
> muldigen Bildern von Karnak dem siegenden König.

> [These [heroes] go plunging ahead: preceding their own
> victorious smile, as the team of horse in the mildly-
> moulded reliefs of Karnak the conquering King.] (*DE* 54/55)

This brief passage, whose details Rilke based on reliefs that he had seen on a temple wall in Karnak during his travels through Egypt during the winter of 1910–11, perfectly describes Empedocles's comportment toward death. In his "Frankfurt Plan" Hölderlin uses the same verb *stürzen* in connection with his own hero's plunge into the flaming jaws of Etna (see *SWB* 2:424). We have also seen that the metaphor of chariot-racing underscores Empedocles's headlong course along his "path of death" (*SWB* 2:300). The swiftness of this forward trajectory is more apparent in the syntax of the original German. Rilke uses the *voran*-plus-dative construction in the following analogy: "dem eigenen Lächeln / sind sie voran, wie das Rossegespann . . . / . . . dem siegenden König." What Rilke in other words means is that these heroes hasten toward death at such a rate that they always keep one step ahead of themselves, just like the sprinting horses precede the royal chariot that they pull. In terms that Heidegger will later employ, these heroes are characterized by a *sich-vorweg-sein;* that is, by a "being-ahead-of-themselves." They live in a perpetual state of anticipation, even when it comes to death, which they react to with smiles of victory rather than grimaces of fear. As Rilke puts it in the thirteenth sonnet to Orpheus from part 2 of the cycle: "Sei allem Abschied voran, als wäre er hinter / dir, wie der Winter, der eben geht" ("Be in advance of all parting, as though it were / behind you like the winter that is just going") (*SO* 94/95). Once more, the key word is *voran* and the key concept anticipation. Here Rilke urges the reader—specifically in this context Orpheus—to live in such a manner that death (the metaphorical "parting"/"winter") does not limit and preempt existence. The individual is called upon to project himself forward into possibility rather than linger in stasis. As Rilke fully realizes, this conduct implies a continual risk. Heroes, he says, are exposed to a "constant danger," which is the literal translation of "stet[e] Gefahr" (*DE* 56):

> Wunderlich nah ist der Held doch den jugendlich Toten. Dauern
> ficht ihn nicht an. Sein Aufgang ist Dasein; beständig
> nimmt er sich fort und tritt ins veränderte Sternbild
> seiner steten Gefahr.
>
> [Yes, the Hero's strangely akin to the youthfully-dead. Continuance
> doesn't concern him. His rising's existence. Time and again
> he takes himself off and enters the changed constellation
> his changeless peril's assumed.]   (*DE* 54–56/55–57)

In the more straightforward terms of Nietzsche, the hero "lives dangerously." By refusing to remain in a fixed state of being and relentlessly seeking change, the hero puts himself to a position of continual imperilment. This is an idea that Hegel, Hölderlin, and Nietzsche have all addressed through their own particular examples. The bondsman risks his life in order to gain autonomy, Empedocles propels himself toward certain doom in his longing for cosmic unity, and Zarathustra preaches the transformative ideal of self-overcoming, even in its most extreme form of self-destruction. In all three cases, the prospect of death raises the individual to a higher plane of existence, a process that is summed up in the above-quoted words of the elegy: "Sein Aufgang ist Dasein" (His rising's existence). But we have seen, particularly in the motifs worked out by Hölderlin and Nietzsche, that *Aufgang* also implies *Untergang;* ascendancy is dialectically determined by downfall. These two notions also play out in the *Elegies*. The hero's *Aufgang* here in the "Sixth Elegy" finds its dialectical complement in the first, where Rilke writes: "es erhält sich der Held, selbst der Untergang war ihm / nur ein Vorwand, zu sein: seine letzte Geburt" ("the Hero continues, even his fall / was a pretext for further existence, an ultimate birth") (*DE* 22/23). Again, the parallel to Empedocles—and to a certain extent Zarathustra—cannot be ignored. The plunge of the former into volcanic flames entails an analogous heightening of being through a pantheistic immersion in the elements. His death is in a sense but a pretext for the more permanent and transcendent goal of all-unity. A further link to Hölderlin concerns the notion of resoluteness, which Rilke applies to his metaphor of fruit in the third verse of the "Sixth Elegy." Here he speaks of "die zeitig entschlossene Frucht" ("the seasonably-resolute fruit") (*DE* 54/55), thereby suggesting that death should be affirmed in both a timely and determined fashion. Hölderlin equally emphasizes Empedocles's "resolve" (*Entschluß*) for death, which he of course also expresses through organic imagery at various junctures in the dramatic fragments. This idea of determination in the face of finitude will take on even greater importance in my forthcoming discussion of Heidegger, who seems to have picked up on the themes of anticipation and resolution in both Hölderlin and Rilke for his own ideal comportment toward death, which he calls *vorlaufende Entschlossenheit* or "forward-running/anticipatory resoluteness." As Heidegger never tired to point out, *Entschlossenheit* also connotes openness and exposure, which makes even better sense in the context of Rilke's image of the fig. According to this logic, the fruit has come out into the open and actualized its potentiality. Of course, in the end, both meanings merge into one, just as the hero and the fig tree converge to express the idea of an opportune death.

The hero that Rilke eventually singles out in the "Sixth Elegy" is Samson, who finds redemption (and vengeance) in his self-inflicted death under the falling house of the Philistines. But given the number of correspondences to Empedocles, especially the metaphors of fruit and of chariot racing, Rilke could just as easily have had Hölderlin's tragic hero in mind. Nevertheless, I am not suggesting that Hölderlin's drama directly influenced Rilke's poem. There is no material evidence that Rilke ever read *The Death of Empedocles,* though he did express his admiration for *Hyperion* as well as the later hymns (see *Br* 471). The commonalities between Hölderlin and Rilke are too numerous to detail here.[25] However, it is worth mentioning that Rilke honed his elegy-writing skills on his predecessor's own classical emulations of the genre. Moreover, there can be no doubt that Rilke consciously sought to carry on Hölderlin's legacy as a leading poet-prophet of the German language. Whether or not Empedocles provided Rilke with a prototype for the hero that "plunges ahead"—as I will argue in the case of Heidegger's Empedoclean conception of forward-running Dasein—remains open to debate, but one cannot fail to notice a number of affinities between both literary attestations of a heroic downfall.

In addition to heroes, Rilke praises the holistic existence of other representative beings. These include the "great lovers" and the "early-departed." Both groups rise above the limited and self-conscious state in which most of humanity finds itself. Great lovers like Gaspara Stampa live in unbounded emotion, free from the need of one-to-one reciprocation; and children who die young are never forced to experience the divided consciousness of the adult world. But the ultimate representative of totality are the angels, who, true to their symbolic function, appear as a unifying motif throughout the *Elegies*. Some disagreement exists as to the precise meaning of these allegorical figures and even Rilke's oft-cited explanation in a letter to his Polish translator Hulewicz (see *Br* 899–900/*SL* 395–96) has not succeeded in settling the debate. Given my particular focus, I only wish to draw attention to the role of these angels with respect to the issue of death. In one of the most lucid passages of the *Elegies,* Rilke writes:

> Aber Lebendige machen
> alle den Fehler, daß sie zu stark unterscheiden.
> Engel (sagt man) wüßten oft nicht, ob sie unter
> Lebenden gehn oder Toten.
>
> [Yes, but all of the living
> make the mistake of drawing too sharp distinctions.
> Angels, (they say) are often unable to tell
> whether they move among living or dead.]   (*DE* 24/25)

Based on this excerpt it seems clear that angels are nonmetaphysical (and decidedly non-Christian) beings that do not separate life from death.

Whereas humans dwell in a world full of "sharp distinctions," whether between interiority and exteriority, immanence and transcendence, or being and nonbeing, angels inhabit if not embody the space of *Weltinnenraum*. Like Orpheus, they are home on either side of the metaphysical boundary that humans have erected over the course of their history to keep the negative at bay: "Ist er ein Hiesiger? Nein, aus beiden / Reichen erwuchs seine weite Natur" ("Does he belong here? No, out of both / realms his wide nature grew") (*SO* 26/27). This angelic and Orphic space goes by various names in the *Elegies* and *Sonnets,* but basically corresponds to the notions of *(Welt)Innenraum*. These designations include: *das Offene* (the open), *der reine Raum* (the pure space), *der reine Bezug* (the pure relation), and *der klarste Bezug* (the clearest relation). Although all of these expressions are more or less synonymous, *das Offene* is arguably the most important due to its philosophical provenance and literary application in the "Eighth Elegy."

Rilke borrowed the concept of *das Offene* from Alfred Schuler, a mystically inclined philosopher-historian who advanced his own theory about the totality of life and death. In 1915 Rilke attended the last of three lectures that Schuler gave in Munich and recorded his impressions a few days letter in a letter to Princess Marie. Here he gives a brief synopsis of Schuler's ideas: "he attempted to give an explanation of the world that represented the dead as the actual beings, the realm of the dead as a singular unheard-of existence, our minimal lease on life as a kind of exception to the rule" (*Br* 484). Schuler, who employs the terms "*das offene Leben*" (the open life) and "*das geöffnete Leben*" (the opened life) in his lectures,[26] drew on the example of ancient Rome to demonstrate his point, claiming that the dead of the imperial city exerted their influence from a domain that was not completely separated from life. He further characterizes this state of openness as a "feeling of fulfillment, satiation, teletae, passivity, lingering in the moment [*Augenblick*], perpetuation of the moment, suspension of time, feeling of absolute being. . . . everything becomes interior life [*Innenleben*], everything symbolizes interior life."[27] While Rilke admits that he does not understand Schuler's entire argument (the lectures contain many arcane references to Roman culture and lore), he is obviously fascinated by the presenter's eccentric personality and unique point of view. The half-historical, half-numinous explanation of death as a reality that interjoins and even holds sway over life only reaffirmed Rilke's own holistic outlook. Upon Schuler's death in 1923, Rilke acknowledged his debt to a man who had furnished him with yet another poetic term for the holism of death and who had now definitively entered that open realm of totalistic being.[28]

If the *Duino Elegies* and *Sonnets to Orpheus* can be said to have a plot, Rilke states that it is "[t]he increasingly growing resolve in our hearts [*Gemüt*] to keep life open toward death [*das Leben gegen den Tod hin offen zu halten*]" (*Br* 852). In the "Eighth Elegy," Rilke relies on Schuler's notion of the "open life" to designate the space in which being and nonbeing form a whole.[29] We humans, he claims, are shut out from this dominion, since our consciousness erects spatial barriers between us as perceiving subjects and our environment as a perceived object. The elegy begins as follows:

> Mit allen Augen sieht die Kreatur
> das Offene. Nur unsre Augen sind
> wie umgekehrt und ganz um sie gestellt
> als Fallen, rings um ihren freien Ausgang.

> [With all its eyes the creature-world beholds
> the open. But our eyes, as though reversed,
> encircle it on every side, like traps
> set round its unobstructed path to freedom.]   (*DE* 66/67)

We thus try to dispose over this nonlocatable space of being as if it conformed to the laws of logic and to the coordinates of scientific spatiality. As Rilke says later in the poem, we stand "opposite . . . always opposite" (*DE* 69) and thus fail to apprehend death because we find ourselves too close to, and enclosed by, its presence. Death acts as a kind of metaphysical wall that prevents us from seeing the open vista of being. Due to their more transparent forms of consciousness, animals are better attuned to the world in which they exist. A child also has access to the open, but we "turn it round and force it to look backwards / at conformation [*Gestaltung*]" (*DE* 67), which is to say that we teach the child how to see the structures and definitions of the world according to a subject-based perception. Rilke's assertion in the ninth and tenth lines of the poem that animals are "free from death" (frei von Tod) while "we alone see it" (as the more accurate rendition of "*Ihn* sehen wir allein" should read) carries the following implication: because animals have a sense of the open, they lead a more care-free existence, not worrying about the eventuality of their end the way that humans do. The animal, in other words, is a more harmonious being, one that is not affected by the constraints of time and space:

> Doch sein Sein ist ihm
> unendlich, ungefaßt und ohne Blick
> auf seinen Zustand, rein, so wie sein Ausblick.
> Und wo wir Zukunft sehn, dort sieht es Alles
> und sich in Allem und geheilt für immer.

> [But its own being for it
> is infinite, inapprehensible,
> unintrospective, pure, like its outward gaze.
> Where we see Future, it sees Everything,
> itself in Everything, for ever healed.]   (*DE* 68/69)

The limitations of human existence are precisely what give rise to Rilke's *Elegies* or "poems of lament." Given the fact that we persist in such a woeful state of individuation and alienation, one wonders how we are ever to attain the openness in which life and death form an ever-present totality. The first eight elegies oscillate between optimism and pessimism, though the latter mood seems to outweigh the former. However, in the final two poems Rilke moves toward a more positive avowal of existence.

In the "Ninth Elegy," Rilke encourages us to embrace our mortality and rejoice in our immediate state of being. Throughout the poem he develops a kind of dialectics according to which we are advised to interact with our world and transform the visible into the invisible, the finite into the infinite. This task of transformation may not seem easy in view of our undeniable condition of finitude, emphasized in the following lines:

> Aber weil Hiersein viel ist, und weil uns scheinbar
> alles das Hiesige braucht, dieses Schwindende, das
> seltsam uns angeht. Uns die Schwindendsten. *Ein* Mal
> jedes, nur *ein* Mal. *Ein* Mal und nichtmehr. Und wir auch
> *ein* Mal. Nie wieder. Aber dieses
> *ein* Mal gewesen zu sein, wenn auch nur *ein* Mal:
> *irdisch* gewesen zu sein, scheint nicht widerrufbar.

[But because being here amounts to so much, because all
this Here and Now, so fleeting, seems to require us and strangely
concerns us. Us the most fleeting of all. Just once,
everything, only for once. Once and no more. And we, too,
once. And never again. But this
having been once, though only once,
having been once on earth—can it ever be cancelled?]   (*DE* 72/73)

Rilke's highlights in the standard German edition (see *SW* 1:717,
where the word "einmal" is written "*ein* Mal") make his point all the
more obvious: we are purely immanent beings, with only *one* shot at
life. The reader finds absolutely no hint of metaphysical transcendence
in these verses or elsewhere in the poem. Rilke remains adamant that
the existence of every living thing is a singular occurrence and he formulates his conviction in a manner that even those not accustomed to
the finer nuances of poetry will readily understand. For Rilke, there
is only the "Here and Now," and humans are consequently defined not
by their relation to a transcendent Being, but by their fundamental condition of *Hiersein*. This limitation is not a cause for lament; Rilke, rather,
praises the transitoriness of our terrestrial existence. He thus aligns
himself with Nietzsche, who declares through his mouthpiece
Zarathustra: "*remain faithful to the earth,* and do not believe those who
speak to you of otherwordly hopes!" (*KSA* 4:15/*Z* 125).

   The death of God, as proclaimed by Zarathustra and insinuated by
Rilke, marks the decline of metaphysics and paves the way for values that are predicated on life rather than on an unknowable beyond.
The *Übermensch* can be considered Nietzsche's postmetaphysical
ideal of a human being whose only transcendence lies in its immanence; that is, in its continual act of *self*-overcoming. Rilke also advocates transformation in the "Ninth Elegy," specifically of the visible
into the invisible through the faculty of human speech. Of course as
a poet, Rilke is able to articulate the world far better than the average
person, but he stresses that we can all do our part in this mission. In
fact, he tells us to focus on the simple objects of our immediate surroundings rather than try to impress the angels with lofty concepts that
have nothing to do with our everyday experiences. A certain degree
of reciprocity obtains to this relation between human existence and
the world: objects need us to speak for them in order to gain

permanence; we in turn can enrich our finite being by internalizing these objects and making them relevant to our lives. Our intimacy with the earth also gives us a firmer grasp of our own "intimate/friendly death" (*der vertrauliche Tod*) (*DE* 76/77). The acceptance of death as a precondition of life leads to a more complete apprehension of existence, whereby the past and future blend into an eternal present. In the final verses of the elegy, Rilke alludes to a state of wholeness that essentially corresponds to the Brahe mode of being: "Weder Kindheit noch Zukunft / werden weniger. . . . Überzähliges Dasein / entspringt mir im Herzen" ("Neither childhood nor future / are growing less. . . . Supernumerous existence / wells up in my heart") (*DE* 76/77). "Supernumerous existence" implies a qualitative rather than a quantitative state of sheer abundance. One finds here yet another affinity to Nietzsche, whose idea of eternal recurrence also seeks "to achieve the mode of transcendence within the consciousness of pure immanence."[30] In the section of *Thus Spoke Zarathustra* entitled "On the Vision and the Riddle," Nietzsche describes the point at which individual existence and eternal recurrence intersect as an *Augenblick* or "moment" (see *KSA* 4:200/Z 270). Although it may seem paradoxical to equate eternity with a mere instant, Nietzsche envisions an everlasting rather than a fleeting moment, an increment of time that endlessly repeats itself and that contains infinite possibilities. Like Rilke's notion of a continuous present, the metaphor of eternal recurrence urges us to enjoy life to the fullest, as if each of its moments were to recur without end. Both Rilke and Nietzsche thus impart the same basic message: given the absence of a transcendent reality, we must learn to convert our finitude into plenitude. As Rilke formulates this problem in his early diaries: "We need eternity; for only eternity can provide space for our gestures. Yet we know that we live in narrow finiteness. Thus it is our task to create infinity within these boundaries, for we no longer believe in the unbounded."[31]

The "Ninth Elegy" concludes Rilke's pursuit of a holistic existence. As quoted earlier from his letter to Hulewicz, to affirm life means simultaneously to affirm death. It simply cannot be any other way given Rilke's lack of faith in all categories of metaphysical transcendence. Rilke has succeeded in showing that death forms a constant presence in our lives rather than a distant gateway to the beyond. Those who still fail to grasp his point can benefit from a reading of the "Tenth Elegy," an epilogue of sorts, in which Rilke metaphorically takes his readers by the hand and leads them into the open space where life and death dialectically coexist.

In the "Tenth Elegy" Rilke paints an allegorical landscape of the human condition. From a structural standpoint, this final elegy of the cycle resembles the story of the prodigal son in *Malte*. In both cases, Rilke adopts a more detached narrative perspective in order to provide a conclusion that both sums up the content and reflects on the meaning of the work in question.[32] The City of Pain is a homogenous center of activity full of mindless diversions and empty pleasures. The carnival-like atmosphere only reinforces the triviality of existence in this symbolic metropolis, which is as reminiscent of Paris as of the city that Zarathustra condemns in his speech "On Passing By" (see *KSA* 4:222–25/Z 287–90). Through a host of metaphors, most of which draw on the imagery of amusement parks (game booths, shooting galleries, and even peep-shows), Rilke gives an extended list of the vices that prevail in modern urban settings. The most important image with respect to the theme of death is found on the placards that have been posted at the edge of the city. These advertise a product called "Deathless" (*Todlos* in the original), which is a "bitter beer that tastes quite sweet to its drinkers / so long as they chew with it plenty of fresh distractions" (*DE* 81). Here Rilke sardonically hints at the modern tendency to "sweeten" and thereby cheapen the experience of death. In his earlier poem "Der Tod," he compared this bitter reality to an undrinkable residue in a broken cup; now he suggests that we have become savvy enough to conceal if not outright falsify a crucial aspect of our being. The fact that a church sits squarely in the "market of comfort" (*DE* 79) further hints at the empty metaphysics of death that typifies this microcosm of modern existence. But just beyond these city billboards lies a "real" (*DE* 81) realm where the familiar representatives of a more natural and total existence dwell: children, lovers, and dogs. Even further out into the open is the Land of Pain. Here the dead are guided by Laments through a topography that Rilke obviously based both on his recollections of Egypt, the traditional land of the dead in Western civilization, and on his impressions of the Swiss countryside that surrounded him at Muzot. Rilke has us follow a Lament who leads a recently expired youth past the various features of this deathscape to the so-called Mountains of Primal Pain. At this point the equilibrium of life and death becomes expressed in highly metaphorical language. Two images appear at the conclusion of the elegy: the hanging catkins of a hazel and the falling rain of early spring. Rilke suggests that this downward trajectory has an upward side to it; the descent of both natural phenomena brings about future growth. The highlighted juxtaposition of the verbs *steigen* (to climb) and *fallen* (to fall) in the final stanza points to a reversal of death's common negative meaning:

> Und wir, die an *steigendes* Glück
> denken, empfänden die Rührung,
> die uns beinah bestürzt,
> wenn ein Glückliches *fällt*.
>
> [And we, who have always thought
> of happiness climbing, would feel
> the emotion that almost startles
> when happiness falls.]   (*DE* 84/85)

Much like his previous combination of *Aufgang* and *Untergang,* this dialectic of rising and falling illustrates that the ostensibly destructive force of death actually heightens our overall sense of being. Moreover, Rilke aptly closes his poetic cycle with yet another variation on the organic metaphors that have accompanied his reflections on human finitude since the third *Book of Hours* from some 20 years before.

After the completion of the *Duino Elegies* and the *Sonnets to Orpheus* in 1922, Rilke's health began to decline. In November 1926 he was diagnosed with a rare form of leukemia; a month later, on December 29, he was dead. On his deathbed he composed one final poem in which he gave voice to his intense sufferings through a new metaphorical image, indeed a decidedly Empedoclean one. Here he describes a state of fiery consumption that could just as well apply to the dissolution of Empedocles in the flames of Etna. The beginning of the poem reads:

> Komm du, du letzter, den ich anerkenne,
> heilloser Schmerz im leiblichen Geweb:
> wie ich im Geiste brannte, sieh, ich brenne

in dir; das Holz hat lange widerstrebt,
der Flamme, die du loderst, zuzustimmen,
nun aber nähr ich dich und brenn in dir. . . .
O Leben, Leben: Draußensein.
Und ich in Lohe. Niemand der mich kennt.   (*SW* 2:511)

[Come, you last thing, which I acknowledge,
unholy agony in the fleshly weave;
just as I burned in spirit, look, I burn
in you; the wood has long held back,
long recoiled from those flames you blaze,
but now I feed you and burn in you. . . .
O life, life: externality.
And I in flame. No one knowing me.][33]

    Despite his burning torment, Rilke rejected painkillers and refused to be told the nature of his fatal disease. He thus lived out his long-held belief that death is a deeply existential experience rather than an extraneous event that bears some arbitrary medico-scientific name. As he is reported to have said during these final days: "I don't want the death of doctors—I want to have my freedom."[34] To my knowledge, this is the only instance that Rilke uses this precise term—a term that plays such a critical role in Hegel, Hölderlin, and especially Nietzsche—in connection with death. Nevertheless, his views on human finitude display numerous affinities to the ideas of his predecessors, and if Rilke tends to downplay the notion of freedom, he places all the more weight on the issue of holism. Life and death, for Rilke, comprise the unity of existence, "the real, whole, and full sphere and globe of *being*" (*Br* 807). Heidegger, who quotes these very words in his only publication devoted to Rilke, will take this existential ideal of wholeness to a new level by examining the structural totality of Dasein from the standpoint of fundamental ontology.

5

Heidegger
The Ontology and Onticity of Death

[D]eath [is] the highest and utmost testimony of being.
—Heidegger, *Contributions to Philosophy*

Heidegger's analytic of death in *Being and Time* forms the culmination of the literary and philosophical thanatology that I have discussed in the foregoing chapters of this study. His understanding of human finitude as a supreme possibility of existence that both intimates freedom and reveals selfhood has obvious precedents in the works of Hegel, Hölderlin, Nietzsche, and Rilke. Numerous parallels with respect to main ideas, specific terms, and even minor motifs exist between Heidegger's views and those of his predecessors. Whether this means that Heidegger was directly influenced by their writings remains difficult to say or at least to prove conclusively. As I will demonstrate below, while it is clear that he was reading these authors throughout his early academic career, his tendency to obscure the deeper sources of his thought makes it impossible to stake any definite claims in the realm of intellectual property. Furthermore, Heidegger's own belief that thinking ultimately stems from being rather than from individual beings effectively immunizes him from all ontic-positivistic inquests into his reading background—to say nothing of his political past.

But overall I am concerned less with the question of influence than with the factual implications of Heidegger's analyses. For Heidegger, ontology must in the end be grounded in onticity and his formal existential sketches similarly require existentiell attestation if they are to be more than just arbitrary constructs. I hold that such factical testimony can be further concretized in examples from literature and nonabstract philosophies such as Nietzsche's and the early Hegel's. I am therefore interested in determining whether such works as the *Phenomenology of Spirit, The Death of Empedocles, Thus Spoke Zarathustra, The Notebooks of Malte Laurids Brigge,* and the *Duino Elegies* can provide "pre-ontological evidence" (*BT* 405) of an authentic and inauthentic being-toward-death. Heidegger himself finds prior corroboration of Dasein's basic care-structure in the ancient *cura* fable, which Herder and Goethe have taken up in the poem "Das Kind der Sorge" (The Child of Care) and *Faust II* respectively (see *BT* 184–85; 405). In calling attention to this mythological-anthropological text and its literary transformations, Heidegger suggests that at various points in its history Dasein has in fact been able to understand itself according to the existential classifications—the so-called *Existenzialien*—of fundamental ontology. Other allusions to literature occur in his exposition of death and similarly serve to substantiate his ontological models. He cites, for instance, Johannes von Saaz's *The Bohemian Ploughman* as an exemplification of being-toward-the-end (see *BT* 228; 408) and later refers to Tolstoy's *The Death of Ivan Ilyich* in the context of an inauthentic being-toward-death (see *BT* 235; 409). Robert Bernasconi has examined the function of Tolstoy's tale as a "literary attestation" of Dasein's relation toward its end. Bernasconi correctly observes that the story not only illustrates Dasein's everyday attitude toward death but, as Heidegger's footnote clearly states, "the shattering and the collapse" of this inauthentic outlook.[1]

It is my contention that Heidegger could just as easily have mentioned works by Hölderlin, Nietzsche, Rilke, and even the more theoretical Hegel as documentary proof of the formal structures of existence outlined in *Being and Time*. Indeed, these sources inform his ontology of death far more than do the writings of Tolstoy and Johannes von Saaz. Throughout my discussion of *Being and Time* I will point out various connections to the texts dealt with thus far. For reasons of space, I cannot scrutinize all the parallels aligning Heidegger with his forerunners but must leave some to the power of suggestion based on my comments in the previous chapters, where I anticipated several of these links in a gradual effort to bolster the ever-widening thematic web that extends from dialectical to existential conceptions of death. In the end, I believe that my approach lends support to Herman Philipse's theory about the underlying patchwork structure of *Being and Time*. According to Philipse, "Heidegger's philosophy is a patchwork made out of many different materials that Heidegger borrowed from others and transformed to suit his purposes, materials that do not fit together very well."[2] Philipse pursues a number of themes that Heidegger picked up from his eclectic reading habits and integrated rather incongruously into *Being and Time,* a book that was rushed in its composition (for reasons of academic promotion) but whose main ideas were formed over several years of lecturing at the University of Marburg. In the course of his study, Philipse reveals the influence of such diverse figures as Aristotle, Luther, Pascal, and Husserl. To these I will add a handful of additional authors that Heidegger, the "master patchworker,"[3] specifically utilized for the philosophical elaboration of his death analytic.

I begin this chapter by considering the general place that Hegel, Hölderlin, Nietzsche, and Rilke occupy in Heidegger's thinking, independent of the narrower thanatological focus of my study. This excursus fulfills two useful purposes: (1) it provides a broader Heideggerian context in which to situate his philosophical and literary antecedents; and (2) it further serves as an introduction into his own thinking, especially into the problem of being and its long history of concealment through metaphysics. I then give a close reading of the existential-ontological analysis of death in *Being and Time,* with special emphasis on the concept of *Vorlaufen* or "running ahead." Here I also address the intricate problem of ontology versus onticity, which proves crucial for the later determination of Dasein's attested authenticity. The third and final section of this chapter explores precisely this factical ideal of authentic Dasein as forward-running resoluteness. After elucidating the difficult notions of conscience, guilt, and resoluteness,

I conclude with a reassessment of *The Death of Empedocles* based on the existential and implicit existentiell postulations of *Being and Time*.

My principal focus thus lies on the early Heidegger and his potential reception of authors whom one tends to associate with certain philosophical and poetological currents of his later thought. Yet long before he publicly engaged with such figures as Hölderlin, Nietzsche, and Rilke, the still "hidden king"[4] of philosophy had been quietly grappling with their views on death, all the while piecing together his totalistic conception of human existence within the broader scope hemeneutical phenomenology.

THE AUTHENTICITY OF THINKING AND THANKING

Heidegger's analytic of death in the second division of *Being and Time* is as famous as it is notorious. It had a profound effect on both major camps of twentieth century continental philosophy, existentialism and neo-Marxism, paving the way for a long-standing debate on such issues as the ontology, ideology, and authenticity of death. A diverse assemblage of figures ranging from Jean-Paul Sartre to Theodor Adorno, from Paul Tillich to Herbert Marcuse, and from Alexandre Kojève to Bertolt Brecht have all responded in their own way to Heidegger's interpretation of human finitude as a radically individualizing and authenticating possibility of existence. Be it as an object of criticism, a hailed anthropological ideal, or a measuring stick of neutral comparison, his analysis has significantly shaped the development of modern thanatological discourse.

In the end, Heidegger's views are hardly as unprecedented as they may seem at first sight. Granted, he credits various predecessors for their own life-related positions on death; but at the same time, he points out the unprofitable limitations of such ontically rooted theories for his own ontological endeavor. In one of the most detailed footnotes of *Being and Time,* a number of authors—including Wilhelm Dilthey, Georg Simmel, and Karl Jaspers—receive mention for their insights into the most basic problem of human existence: that we all must die (see *BT* 408). Here Heidegger also remarks that the Christian theological tradition from Paul to Calvin tends to interpret death in connection with life. Subsequent notes refer to *The Death of Ivan Ilyich, The Bohemian Ploughman,* and a less literary study from 1924 by Eugen Korschelt entitled *Lebensdauer, Altern und Tod* (*Lifespan, Aging, and Death*) (see *BT* 408–09). All of these references are, as befits the nature of a footnote, both cursory and marginally relevant to the analysis at hand. In the bulk of his inquiry Heidegger appears to divorce himself entirely from tradition, as though he were pioneering previously uncovered ground. However, the case proves to be quite the opposite and it may come as no surprise that Hölderlin and Nietzsche, the two most consistent guiding stimuli in Heidegger's later thinking, are among those who have anticipated several aspects of his reflections on death. The influence of Hegel and Rilke, both of whom Heidegger also dealt with more closely after the publication of *Being and Time* in 1927, seems no less apparent. Since I have dealt with each of these four figures rather closely myself in the foregoing chapters, their general place in Heidegger's thought deserves at least brief mention. In the following, I will proceed in the relative order of importance for Heidegger, who has devised his own list of key players in the history of being.

While Heidegger devoted more lectures and writings to Nietzsche than to Hölderlin, it is the latter that becomes his chief collaborator in the quest for being. Together as poet and thinker, Hölderlin and Heidegger find themselves engaged in a dialogue about our relation to this forgotten ground of existence. Yet the exact nature and precise content of their dialogue ultimately remain unclear, as Heidegger is never able to tell us in plain language what poet and thinker actually do in this process of saying/naming/bestowing being. As he for example states in the postscript to "What is Metaphysics?": "We may know much about the relation between philosophy and poetry. Yet we know nothing of the dialogue between poets and thinkers, who 'dwell near one another on mountains most separate'" (*GA* 9:312/*PM* 237). One thing that seems certain, however, is that through language the poet creates an opening or clearing (*Lichtung*) for the emergence of being in the work of art. Language is to be understood not as an instrument or faculty by means of which the poet communicates his ideas, but as "the clearing-concealing advent of being itself" (*GA* 9:326/*PM* 249) or more metaphorically as "the house of being" (*GA* 9:333/*PM* 254). Poetry thus issues from a higher source than the individual lyricist. Disclosure, truth (both conveyed by the Greek *alêtheia*), clearing, and language all function as corresponding events of being, which has the tendency to withdraw in concealment as well as to reveal itself in certain moments of its history. But not every aesthetic creation shares an equal status in this revelatory event or *Ereignis*. Poetry enjoys a special standing and it is symptomatic of this prejudice that Heidegger's publications on aesthetics revolve almost entirely around this language-based genre. Even the broader consideration found in "The Origin of the Work of Art," which addresses graphic media such as painting (van Gogh's depiction of peasant shoes) and architecture (an ancient Greek temple), affirms the preeminence of poetry. This becomes most evident in the concluding pages, throughout which Heidegger proceeds to qualify his categorical statement: "Nonetheless, the linguistic work, poetry in the narrower sense, has a privileged position among the arts as a whole" (*GA* 5:61/*OBT* 45). Evidently, there is little if any room for the dramatist and novelist in Heidegger's house of being. Although in the course of his lectures on Hölderlin he occasionally refers to *Hyperion, The Death of Empedocles,* and even some of the theoretical writings, he does so more as an aside to his ongoing discussion of the poems but neglects to deal with these nonlyric works on their own terms. Nevertheless, given the principal themes of death and guilt in *Empedocles,* it seems highly probable that the drama furnished Heidegger, if not with an ideal case of disclosure in the work of art, then at least with concrete material for a phenomenological analysis of death and resoluteness.

Heidegger's preoccupation with Hölderlin reached its peak during the mid-1930s and early 1940s, but like many young Germans immediately before World War I he was deeply affected by Hölderlin's poems, especially the Pindar translations and later hymns edited by Norbert von Hellingrath.[5] Nevertheless, scholarship seems to focus exclusively on the role of Hölderlin in Heidegger's later thought, thereby ignoring the poet's relevance for the philosophical ideas that gestated throughout the teens and twenties, and eventually saw print with the release of *Being and Time*. But the fact is, in contrast to his years as an established university professor, Heidegger never openly manifested his interest in Hölderlin during the early stages of his career. And after he had finally achieved national recognition based on the success of his first book, the entire direction of his thinking soon shifted. The so-called *Kehre* or "turn" occasioned a new approach in tackling the question of being. As a result of this reorientation, Heidegger abandoned his phenomenological analyses of Da*sein* as the premier access to *Sein* and instead attempted to pursue being through its various other manifestations or at least intimations. As mentioned above, poetry is one such aperture through which being can momentarily appear in the world. Hölderlin's poems are a prime example of an event in which being is founded in the word and bestowed to humans. Thinking, thanking and poeticizing (*denken, danken,* and *dichten*) are thus all intimately related: poets and thinkers give thanks to that which is placed in their care. By thinking and poeticizing being, they at the same time celebrate it. Their respective acts should therefore not be construed as creative, original, or however else we tend to describe intellectual feats that are carried out by an active subject. The poet does not produce a poem out of inspiration or a desire to depict reality, nor does the thinker originate his thoughts for the transmission of a worldview. Both, rather, remain in the employ of being and hence express, each in his own way, their self-effacing and grateful acknowledgement of that which on occasion reveals itself but all too quickly retreats into obscurity. We will soon see that this passive if not quietistic outlook points to a number of problems regarding Heidegger's reluctance to acknowledge the main sources of his early thinking, particularly the potential impulses he received from Hegel, Nietzsche, Rilke, and of course his fellow bestower of being, Hölderlin.

Heidegger's preoccupation with Nietzsche was also at its most intense from the mid-1930s to early 1940s. He later revised his university lectures along with other manuscripts from the period and published them in his colossal two-volume *Nietzsche,* which appeared in 1961. Here Heidegger explicates, reconciles, and generally rethinks five fundamental principles that govern Nietzsche's philosophy: the will to power, eternal recurrence of the same, the *Übermensch,* nihilism, and the transvaluation of all values. Heidegger interprets these "basic thoughts" (*Grundgedanken*) as the culmination of Western metaphysics within the larger context of the history of being. Nietzsche thus becomes the last great metaphysician in a long line beginning with Plato, whose transcendent world of ideal truth Nietzsche claimed to have reversed. Yet according to Heidegger, Nietzsche's revaluation of Platonism is but an overturning from within the metaphysical tradition and hence remains trapped inside the same speculative confines that it professes to surmount. Nietzsche, that is, fails to recognize the ontological difference between being and particular beings; he is therefore not truly revolutionary despite his widespread reputation as the definitive destroyer of metaphysical transcendence and the leading promoter of new, life-affirming values. For Heidegger, the Platonic forms and the Nietzschean will to power are both ideas rooted in metaphysics, which he generally defines as a philosophical perspective that confuses being with its various instantiations. Heidegger's notion of metaphysics is thus not a conventional one, which is why such a staunch opponent of transcendent ideals like Nietzsche can become an unwitting accessory of Plato, whose nihilistic paradigm he spared no effort to overcome, especially in its most pervasive and pernicious form as Christianity—or, as he alternatively dubbed it, "Platonism for 'the people'" (*KSA* 5:12/*BGE* 193).

This understanding of Nietzsche as an unsuspecting yet deeply entrenched metaphysician is rooted in the long-term project that Heidegger announced in the introduction to *Being and Time:* a destruction of the history of ontology as a concealment of being. Parallel to his pursuit of what he calls *die Seinsfrage* or the "question of being" Heidegger carries out this project of destruction by reinterpreting the entire Western philosophical tradition. His critical evaluation (in its own way a kind of Nietzschean transvaluation) of such figures as Plato, Aristotle, Descartes, Kant, and Nietzsche is not a self-serving attempt to prove his predecessors wrong in terms of their systematized views. Heidegger seeks, rather, to uncover the hidden presence of being that these and other philosophers have buried beneath centuries if not millennia of metaphysical thinking, a thinking that falsely passes for ontology. In contrast to Heidegger's revisionist notion of

Fundamentalontologie, which pursues Sein through the localization of Dasein, the traditional branch of inquiry that calls itself ontology has "forgotten" being and at best poses questions about beings in their entirety (*das Seiende im Ganzen*). Heidegger's radical task of destroying this errant history does not entail an act of destruction in the narrow sense of the word but literally seeks to get at the roots of the problem. His intention is both a positive and productive one. He deliberately employs the Latinate *Destruktion* rather than, say, the Germanic *Zerstörung,* thereby capitalizing on the etymological implication (*de-struere*) that this metaphysical tradition is to be stripped of the many layers that have settled upon its originally sound ontological foundations over the last 2,000-plus years. The history of Western philosophy thus resembles an intellectual stratification in which being becomes increasingly covered up and forgotten.

Such is the role that Nietzsche tends to play in Heidegger's thought, and the greater part of both German and Anglo-American scholarship consequently focuses on this connection between the last metaphysician and the self-proclaimed thinker of being. Yet remarkably little attention has been paid to the role of Nietzsche in Heidegger's earlier philosophy, specifically in *Being and Time,* the work in which he first declared his intention to destroy the history of ontology.[6] Given the dramatic surge in readership of Nietzsche, and for that matter Hölderlin, in the early part of the twentieth century, it seems highly unlikely that Heidegger remained immune from their near epidemic popularity. Nearly every major German intellectual of the era became in some way affected—in certain cases infected—by Hölderlin and Nietzsche, or at least by one of the two. Dilthey, Rilke, Hermann Hesse, Robert Musil, and the George circle all drew inspiration from the life and work of both figures, while writers and philosophers such as Thomas Mann, Gottfried Benn, Karl Jaspers, Ludwig Klages, Georg Simmel, and Oswald Spengler were less moved by Hölderlin but all the more so by Nietzsche. This modishness may in part explain Heidegger's reticence in matters concerning their potential impact at this point in his career. David Ferrell Krell for instance speculates that, after some initial contact with Nietzsche in his student and early professorial years, Heidegger "apparently wished to distance himself from the Nietzsche adopted by *Lebensphilosophie* and by the philosophies of culture, worldview, and value."[7] Heidegger most likely considered these fashionable movements of the early twentieth century insignificant in light of the philosophical tradition that he was carefully exploring in his lectures on Plato, Aristotle, Kant, Husserl, and others. Perhaps he already counted Nietzsche among this tradition but had yet to study the latter's writings to the extent that he had those of other philosophers. All such claims must ultimately remain within the realm of conjecture. What can be said for certain is that cursory references to Nietzsche occur sporadically in Heidegger's early writings and lectures, including *Being and Time*. Hölderlin, on the other hand, is mentioned only marginally in a lecture course from 1919 entitled *Die Idee der Philosophie und das Weltanschauungsproblem (The Idea of Philosophy and the Problem of Worldviews)* (see *GA* 56–57, 74). Here Heidegger relies on a passage from *Antigone,* quoting the original Greek as well as Hölderlin's German translation. It is worth pointing out that the standard Hölderlin edition to which Heidegger refers contains both the Sophocles translations and the *Empedocles* fragments in the same volume.[8] Moreover, according to his own testimony Heidegger avidly read both Hölderlin and Nietzsche in his youth (see *GA* 1:56). Other authors that he mentions reading in his formative years include Rilke and Hegel.[9]

In 1946 Heidegger's gave a lecture entitled "Why Poets?" to commemorate the twentieth anniversary of Rilke's death. The title of this piece, which appeared four years later in *Holzwege,* actually stems from a verse by Hölderlin, not Rilke: "und wozu Dichter in dürftiger Zeit" or, "and why poets in a desolate time?" Using Hölderlin to foreground his discussion, Heidegger gives a close but typically idiosyncratic reading of some improvised verses by Rilke. It soon becomes clear that "Rilke's poetry, in its course within the history of being, remains behind Hölderlin in rank and position" (*GA* 5: 276/*OBT* 206). This is but another way of saying that Rilke does not enjoy the same proximity to being as Hölderlin. Like Nietzsche, he instead persists in a metaphysical way of thinking that restricts its focus to the being of beings as a worldly presence. Rilke thus becomes an analogue of

Nietzsche: each represents the final phase of metaphysics in his own particular domain, poetry and philosophy. It is indicative of this status that their respective models of holism, Zarathustra and the angel of the *Elegies,* remain *"metaphysically the same,* with all their differences in content" (*GA* 5:312/*OBT* 234). In other words, these two prototypes of existence embody beings in their entirety rather than being as envisioned by Heidegger, which eludes all forms of objectification, including the inherently representing acts of poetic depiction and philosophical conceptualization. This tendency to turn being into an objective presence through representation is precisely what defines Rilke's poetry as metaphysical. Like Nietzsche, Rilke has his own basic concepts that would seem to rise above metaphysics. *Weltinnenraum, das Offene,* and *der reine Bezug* all designate a holistic realm that exists independently of the everyday reality determined by time and space. But much like Heidegger cleverly turned Nietzsche against himself, transforming him into the most consummate of Platonists despite such anti-idealistic doctrines as the will to power, he effects a similar reversal with Rilke, insisting that the poet's totalistic notions never get past expressing the world, nature, and human existence. Rilke, in sum, remains entangled in metaphysics whether he realizes it or not. From Heidegger's privileged and unassailable perspective, Rilke's poetry stops short of *being,* for his holism merely reflects the totality of *beings.*[10]

Heidegger's philosophical dialogue with Hegel is much more tentative and open-ended than his discourses with Hölderlin, Nietzsche, and Rilke. Only a handful of writings attest to his preoccupation with Hegel and even these make no sweeping statements about his place in the history of metaphysics. For the most part, Heidegger gives close and sensitive readings of Hegelian texts, especially the first four chapters of the *Phenomenology* and its introduction (see *GA* 32 and *GA* 5:115–208, respectively),[11] but refrains from injecting too much of his own agenda into his line of argument. Heidegger's critique generally revolves around the question of time, which he alleges Hegel objectifies according to the laws of nature. Heidegger in fact argues that Hegel took his concept of time right out of Aristotle's *Physics,* which only underlines his point about scientifistic objectification (see *BT* 416–17). Heidegger insists that Hegelian Spirit moves forward *in* time, which of course implies physical motion and furthermore spatiality (see *BT* 395–96). Dasein, in contrast, exists *as* time, which is to say that it *is* its time. Similarly, Heidegger maintains that being is also fundamentally temporal, although he never successfully demonstrated this in *Being and Time,* which remained a not even half-completed philosophical torso. Nevertheless, the very title of his book spells out the two main problems that he grappled with throughout his life. Hegel's philosophy is also characterized by these very themes, and Heidegger insists that the basic difference between their respective ways of thinking can be reduced to the theses: time is the essence of being (Heidegger) and being is the essence of time (Hegel) (see *GA* 32:211).[12] In Hegel this being is infinite, but it is still predicated on a metaphysics of presence, specifically on the perception of time as a chronological and consequently calculable flow—whether in the case of the dialectically synthesized nows of sense-certainty or the grand-scale history of Spirit. It is therefore no surprise that Hegel becomes yet another unwitting, and probably unwilling, metaphysician in Heidegger's rewritten history of being.

Heidegger's silence regarding any kinship with some of his most obvious forebears has elicited a variety of reactions among scholars, ranging from puzzlement to irritation, and in some cases trenchant criticism. The explanation of his reticence suggested above, namely that he was wary of literary and philosophical fashions, is a rather charitable one. Some are less inclined to give him the benefit of the doubt when it comes to the question of properly acknowledging his sources. In fairness to Heidegger, it needs to be mentioned that he had his own particular notion of what constitutes influence. According to his view, philosophers do not depend on one another in the sense that they take over and pass on ideas, thereby creating a chain of intellectual causes and effects. This is the perspective adopted by the positive sciences, which reduce phenomena to convenient, present-at-hand objects of study and can therefore better posit ontic details and correlations. Not the "influence" (*Einfluß*) of individuals but the "influx" (*Ein-fluß*) of being remains the true force linking the movers and shakers of history.

According to this corrective definition, Hegel, Hölderlin, Nietzsche, and Rilke cannot be said to have inspired Heidegger in the manner commonly posited in source studies. That they are, from a chronological standpoint, precursors is an ontic-positivistic claim that has no bearing on their status within the history of being. Nevertheless, this sovereign (ontological) attitude does not alter the fact that Heidegger is utterly arbitrary in showing his (ontic) indebtedness to people he had obviously read and profited from. The many footnotes in *Being and Time* conceal far more than they reveal. Some representative voices of scholarly reservations about Heidegger's negligence therefore deserve mention, especially since they raise important questions concerning his own metaphysical tendency to cover up and forget the true foundations of his thought in a kind of personal reenactment of *Seinsvergessenheit* or the forgetting of being.

In his voluminous and detailed study, *The Young Heidegger: Rumor of the Hidden King,* John van Buren discusses this problem of acknowledgment in light of Heidegger's celebrated statement that thinking is at bottom a form of thanking. As van Buren suggests, Heidegger the thinker does not live up to this etymological equation in terms of his profitable reading background:

> Though maintaining that "thinking" is really "thanking," the later Heidegger was, as has been well documented, often puzzlingly reluctant to acknowledge his profound indebtedness to those philosophical traditions that originally helped to put him on the way of the being-question in his early Freiburg period, such as the young Luther, Kierkegaard, Jaspers, Aristotle's practical writings, Husserl's Sixth Investigation, and Dilthey.[13]

Heidegger's casualness about crediting those that inspired him most seems especially striking in the case of *Being and Time,* a work that evolved over several years from university lectures on such diverse topics as phenomenology, ontology, theology, and temporality. In his exhaustive study, *The Genesis of Heidegger's Being and Time,* Theodore Kisiel delineates three distinct drafts of the book based on lecture transcripts, noting that only in the final published version does Heidegger display the tendency to snub the philosophical tradition upon which much of his thinking draws. Like van Buren, Kisiel also remains puzzled by this fact: "For whatever reasons, some perhaps unconscious or simply inadvertent, Heidegger in his final draft, contrary to the previous draft, is subtly downplaying, disguising, or otherwise distorting some of the deepest roots of his thought."[14] Another scholar, Jacques Taminiaux, points to a number of covert contributors that helped lay the ground for *Being and Time.* These include Hegel and Nietzsche. In essays collected in the volume *Heidegger and the Project of Fundamental Ontology,* Taminiaux justifies his attempt to unearth such hidden sources by citing Heidegger's motto from a 1924–25 lecture course on the Platonic dialogue *Sophistes:* "It is in any case a dubious thing to rely on what an author himself has brought to the forefront. The important thing is rather to give attention to those things he left shrouded in silence."[15] Taminiaux reflects on this matter of silence as follows:

> Indeed, it very quickly appeared to me that while he made abundant references to his readings, Heidegger continued to maintain, or only partly discarded, the original reticence of *Sein und Zeit,* especially when discussing the most burning issues, such as the question of his methodology and the articulation of fundamental ontology. As for the reason for this reticence . . ., I have no answer. Is it the pride of the pathfinder? Is it the fear of being misunderstood or lumped and leveled with all-too-common theses? Perhaps both.
>
> I realized also—and this remark is in keeping with the above assessment—that the thinkers he mentioned least often in his publications and in his lecture courses, Nietzsche in particular, may well have been those he had most in mind.[16]

Karl Jaspers has deeper reservations about Heidegger's silence. According to Jaspers, Heidegger is remiss in citing the critical forerunners of his thought and instead makes a habit of recognizing minor figures, in *Being and Time* mainly professors.[17] Jaspers also notes the unacknowledged theological provenance of Heidegger's ideas, particularly the work of Kierkegaard, Schelling, Luther, and Augustine.[18] Despite his annoyance at this practice of obfuscation, Jaspers still tends to marvel at the overall originality of Heidegger's thinking. The same cannot be said of Walter Kaufmann, who remains one of the most vehement critics of Heidegger. In his series *Discovering the Mind,* Kaufmann finds few if any original ideas in Heidegger's entire oeuvre and charges him with obscurantism, dogmatism, and even authoritarianism.[19] He furthermore holds that Heidegger appropriated many of his ideas from Christian theology and passed them off as his own. The sixth and final thesis of his critique in fact reads: "Heidegger secularized Christian preaching about guilt, dread, and death but claimed to break with two thousand years of Western thought."[20]

Here Kaufmann points to an important facet of Heidegger, one that has received a great deal of attention in recent years thanks to the publication of his early university lectures. These reveal the theological wellsprings out of which he fashioned the conceptual and terminological apparatus of *Being and Time*. His early Freiburg lecture courses on Paul, Augustine, and mysticism from 1918–21, not to mention the religious training he received during the years 1909–11 in preparation for the priesthood, gave him a solid foundation on which to construct a philosophy oriented toward human existence and a more encompassing notion of being. While I do not mean to imply that being serves Heidegger as some kind of post-Nietzschean surrogate for a "dead" God, there can be no disputing the claim that, as Kaufmann points out above and others have since demonstrated in far greater detail, *Being and Time* is saturated with primal Christian notions such as anxiety, conscience, care, the moment, even the dualism of authenticity and inauthenticity.[21] Then of course there is the matter of death, which has been interpreted as a fundamental aspect of existence by the likes of Paul, Luther, Pascal, and Kierkegaard. As Heidegger observes in a 1925 lecture that prefigures his analyses of *Being and Time:* "It was through Christian theology that the problem of death first appeared in connection with the question of the sense [*Sinn*] of life."[22]

Heidegger himself would readily admit that he is not a philosopher in the traditional sense of the word—hence his later preference for the epithet "thinker." Like Nietzsche, he comes from a completely different background: whereas the latter was schooled in classical philology, the former was weaned on theology at least as much as philosophy. As Herman Philipse puts it: "Arguably [Heidegger] was the most creative religious writer of the twentieth century, who outwitted both official theologians and many philosophers by going underground and by concealing his religious message in secular philosophical garments."[23]

It therefore comes as no surprise that Heidegger's views on death do not chiefly derive from the time-honored tradition of philosophy and that he furthermore does not operate according to the principles of modal logic. As a number of critics have shown, his interpretation of death is riddled with logical fallacies but is all the more replete with verbal flourish.[24] Based on the conventions of rigorous philosophical reasoning, much of what he says—and the manner in which he says it—is simply unsound. One could of course endlessly debate this question, but here is not the place to do so. My purpose is merely to expose some of the probable and previously uncovered sources of his analytic of death. Since my concentration lies on the German tradition, I will not enter into a discussion of the deep and tangled theological roots underlying his investigation. But as I mentioned earlier, more important than the question of authorial influence is the issue of factical attestation, which provides the necessary existence-based fundament for all ontological inquiry. And it is with this existentiell testimony in mind that my discussion of Heidegger's existential-ontological analysis of death begins.

THE EXISTENTIAL-ONTOLOGICAL ANALYTIC OF DEATH IN *BEING AND TIME*

Heidegger's interpretation of death in the second division of *Being and Time* carries out what his preparatory fundamental analysis of human existence in the first division failed to achieve: the examination of Dasein in its complete and authentic state. As it soon becomes apparent, this task—that of experiencing the entirety of Dasein's existence—poses inherent difficulties: "As long as Dasein *is* as a being, it has never attained its 'wholeness.' But if it does, this gain becomes the absolute loss of being-in-the-world. It is then never again to be experienced *as a being*" (*BT* 220).[25] This paradoxical situation, in which the effort to experience a complete existence is inevitably thwarted by the very termination thereof, arises from the traditional view of death as an external event occurring at the end of life. Terminally tacked on to existence as though it were a separate and often higher form of reality, death remains an existentially empty category with no relation to Dasein and its being-in-the-world. Heidegger further states that the common metaphysical notion of death as a fixed and final point only reduces it to the status of an object. Death is indeed an end, but not in a chronological sense. Different modes of being are characterized by different kinds of finitude, and as often throughout his analysis Heidegger distinguishes between entities that are ready-at-hand, present-at-hand, and imbued with the existence of Dasein. He draws on a number of examples to illustrate the notion of wholeness (*Ganzheit*), some of which we have previously encountered as key metaphors in the writings of Hölderlin, Nietzsche, and Rilke.

A Preliminary Sketch of Being-toward-Death

The idea of death as "something outstanding" (*ein Ausstand*) is one approach in interpreting the incompleteness of Dasein. The problem with defining death as a missing piece of a greater whole or as a not-yet lies in an implicit metaphysics of presence that makes a disposable object of the entity in question. Although the lack may gradually be filled and totality eventually attained, such a process remains more a "cumulative placing together" (*BT* 225) than a fluid and self-motivated development. Taking the example of an owed debt, Heidegger points out that the outstanding (*ausstehend-*) amount is but the missing sum of the whole settlement. The sum thus becomes the total of its parts, an aggregation of composite units that can be used as ready-at-hand instruments of accounting. If abstracted and speculated on as in mathematics, the parts take on the qualities of present-at-hand objects. Dasein, however, falls under neither of these varieties of being, but is characterized by existence, which defies all modes of objectification.

In his next example of an outstanding lack, Heidegger modifies an image of totality that Rilke once elaborated in a letter from January 6, 1923: "like the moon, life surely has a side continually turned away from us, which is *not* its opposite, but rather its complement toward perfection, toward completeness, toward the real, whole, and full sphere and globe of *being*" (*Br* 806–07). Since Rilke's letters were not published until the 1930s, Heidegger could not have directly borrowed this particular metaphor, although he does later quote precisely this passage in "Why Poets?" (see *GA* 5:302/*OBT* 226). Nevertheless, the example that they both independently rely on seems basic enough. However, Heidegger problematizes the qualities of complementarity and perfection that Rilke takes for granted. Departing from the ordinary observation that "the last quarter of the moon is outstanding until it is full" (*BT* 226)—a locution that is somewhat more felicitous in the original German: "am Mond steht das letzte Viertel noch aus, bis er voll ist" (*SZ* 243)—Heidegger maintains that this lack or not-yet in the fullness of the moon has nothing to do with its actual state, but merely with our perception of it from earth. The moon is full at all times; in fact even when we see what is supposedly a full moon, we observe only one half of its bulk, as the so-called dark side remains forever obscured from our planet. Rilke for his part capitalizes on this phenomenological aspect of the moon in his statement: "Death is the *side of life* that is turned away from, and unillumined by, us" (*Br* 896/*SL* 393), which Heidegger also cites in his lecture (see *GA* 5:302/*OBT* 227). But as he points out in the present context of his existential analytic, human existence is not complete from the start, regardless of one's perspective. Instead Dasein must *become* its not-yet, and so Heidegger takes up an example that demonstrates a more internal process of becoming.

A fruit reaches ripeness or completion through its own growth. In contrast to the above examples, this process of maturation cannot be equated with an aggregate state in which missing parts become added until a whole is eventually obtained. Nor can it be said that the fruit is always already ripe but only fails to appear so to an outside perceiver. Its prolonged condition of not yet being what it is and of being what it not yet is—in short, of being its ontological not-yet—distinguishes it from static objects of presence. Here a far more dynamic action is at work: in its course of ripening, the fruit finds itself in a constant state of immaturity but at the same time undergoes progressive stages of maturation. Put plainly, albeit tautologically: "ripening, it *is* the unripeness" (*BT* 226). Despite the potentially useful implications of this organic construct for determining the nature of human death as an end, there remains a crucial difference between the two ontological structures of consummation. Whereas a fruit becomes complete in the sense of fulfillment or perfection (*Vollendung*), Dasein does not necessarily attain such a state with death. Unlike the apple, which is perfect/finished (cf. the Latin *perficere*) only when ripe, human existence can—and in fact often does—end prematurely. Just because Dasein has completed its development by dying does not guarantee that it has thereby fulfilled itself. Heidegger thus undermines the function of this traditionally important symbol in conceptions of death that extend from antiquity to his immediate twentieth century predecessor Rilke. The organic growth of the fruit remains a phenomenologically unsound model for his investigation into the wholeness of an entity that is distinguished by the being of Dasein.

These deliberations on totality are fraught with the inherent difficulty of determining the precise nature of Dasein's finitude. Since Dasein is neither subject nor object, but an unbounded project (*Entwurf*), all attempts to limit its trajectory by positing an end are doomed to failure. Dasein does not attain completion on a chronological or otherwise calculable scale. Nor should its specific manner of ending be confused with modes of termination that principally modify objects. The notion of stopping (*Aufhören*), for instance, inadequately describes Dasein's coming to an end, as only objectively present things can be said to stop. These have the character of being-at-an-end (*zu-Ende-sein*), which implies that they cease to be at a determinate point in time. Much like Hegel effected a reversal of consciousness through dialectics in order to get at the inner dynamic of reality, Heidegger takes a similar inverted approach in his efforts to elucidate the finitude of Dasein. As he states in his own terms: "The end *toward* which Dasein *is,* as existing, remains inappropriately defined by being-at-an-end. At the same time, however, our reflections should make it clear that their course must be reversed " (*BT* 228). This turnaround leads him to designate Dasein's finite existence as a "being-toward-the-end" (*Sein zum Ende*) rather than a "being-at-an-end" (*Zu-Ende-sein*).

Through this key terminological inversion, Dasein's life-long relation to its death is contrasted with the sudden, one-time occurrence that befalls and extinguishes human existence. Heidegger, who consistently asserts the primacy of *existentia* over *essentia* for Daseins's being-in-the-world, adheres to precisely the same practice with regard to Dasein's termination. The existential potential implicit in the statement

"*The 'essence' of Dasein lies in its existence*" (*BT* 40) still holds for the process of death: "First of all, we must characterize being-toward-death as a being *toward a possibility*, toward an eminent possibility of Dasein itself" (*BT* 241). Heidegger cites in this context *The Bohemian Ploughman*, a work that I have referred to earlier for its organic imagery and contrasting attitudes of death: "'As soon as a human being is born, he is old enough to die right away'" (*BT* 228). Because the prospect of dying remains continually present throughout the course of human existence, including from the very moment of birth, the line commonly drawn between life and its preemption inevitably becomes blurred. Having been thrown into the world, Dasein is at the same time delivered into the facticity of its death, which implies that it exists in a constant state of dying. Dasein's existence is not defined by the epistemological self-certainty of the Cartesian *cogito sum,* but by the more ontological awareness of *moribundus sum:* "*moribundus* not as someone gravely ill or wounded, but insofar as I am, I am *moribundus. The* MORIBUNDUS *first gives the* SUM *its sense*" (*GA* 20:437–38).[26] With this statement from his 1925 lecture course *History of the Concept of Time,* Heidegger uses Descartes as a foil to overturn the metaphysical paradigm of death. *Sum moribundus* is a more provocative formulation of *Sein zum Tode,* the term that Heidegger definitively employs to describe Dasein's existential relation toward its end. In these preliminary pages of his analytic Heidegger has striven to eliminate the traditional dividing line between human existence and the nonbeing of death. In words that seem especially reminiscent of Rilke, he can thus make the claim: "In the broadest sense, death is a phenomenon of life" (*BT* 229).

By viewing death as a phenomenon of, rather than subsequent to, life, Heidegger integrates a traditionally separate realm into the very core of human existence. The ontological structure of this interiorized death will soon be explored further, but first a problem in the above statement must be addressed, a problem that resides in a word that would normally seem self-evident, namely life. The statement that "death is a phenomenon of life" carries certain restrictions for Heidegger, who does not consider himself a proponent of *Lebensphilosophie* (which was much in vogue at the time) but as the first philosopher since at least Aristotle to seriously pose the question of being. Since Heidegger is not primarily concerned with life on an ontic level, he forgoes any kind of biological or physiological explanation of death. His reawakening of the question of being instead calls for an ontological analysis, one that examines the basic structures of human existence as they relate to our still vague understanding of what it means to be. As only one of the ways in which Dasein exists in the world, life cannot be the main object of investigation. Heidegger therefore insists on a fundamental ontological approach in the face of such established disciplines as biology, psychology, and theology, all of which have their own methods of interpreting life and death. Given the dominant claim that such fields of inquiry have come to hold on these two basic phenomena, he emphasizes the need for an ontology that is free of scientific and indeed metaphysical prejudice. Since Dasein is characterized by existence and potentiality, it cannot be disposed over as an object of theoretical investigation. Even the otherwise broad concept of life amounts to a limitation of possibility and inadequately describes the full extent of Dasein's being-in-the-world. Life in the biological sense remains only one facet of existence, and just as there are diverse regions of being, so too there are distinct typologies of dying. Whereas perishing (*Verenden*) refers to the decline of animal life, demise (*Ableben*) denotes the purely biological aspect of Dasein's death. Dying (*Sterben*), in contrast, designates Dasein's existential relation toward finitude, that is "the *way of being* in which Dasein *is toward* its death" (*BT* 229). We have seen that Hegel makes an analogous distinction between the decay (*Verwesen*) of plants and the dying (*Sterben*) of human beings (see *W* 1:246–47/*ETW* 305–06). Heidegger, however, develops a more rigorous and consistent terminology with respect to categories of death and their application to the different entities that inhabit the world.[27] The term dying pertains only to Dasein, whose manner of being does not conform to that of other living organisms such as plants and animals. As Heidegger's highlighted words above illustrate, Dasein *is toward* its death; that is, it continually relates to its end and is always aware that this limitation of being forms its horizon of existence. Dasein's specific brand of finitude can thus best be formulated as a "being-toward-death" (*Sein zum Tode*), which is the expression that Heidegger finally settles on and adds to his list of existentialia.

Once he establishes human existence as a fundamental being-toward-death, Heidegger attempts to determine the ontological structure of finitude. It will be necessary to bear in mind that throughout his analysis he operates within a strictly existential-ontological framework and does not seek to address the practical implications of his findings on an existentiell-ontic level. Ultimately, his investigation aims at elucidating the existence of Dasein in relation to being. Dasein can perhaps best be understood as a kind of key to unlocking the mystery of being. (*Entschlossenheit* in its original sense of *ent-schließen* will later become an important notion.) Lexically, this key function of Dasein is borne out by the separable prefix *da* and the verb stem *sein:* being manifests itself, however obscurely, in this locus or *Da*. Dasein, then, supplies the access for being to appear or literally "be there" in the world and thus become an issue at all. Put most pointedly in German, not however in so many words by Heidegger: "Dasein ist das Da des Seins." Only by equating Dasein with concrete human existence, which is perhaps only natural given the everyday meaning of the word in German, can one expect from *Being and Time* a commentary on practical life. As already mentioned, Dasein loosely corresponds to our common conception of human reality, but does not exhaust itself therein. Much like Hegelian Geist was anthropomorphized by twentieth century French philosophy, Dasein suffered a similar anthropological reduction through Sartre and Kojève, who both translated—indeed transformed—the ontologically privileged Dasein into a metaphysical *realité humaine*. But as Heidegger never ceases to emphasize, the dynamic potentiality of Dasein places it beyond the realm of any positivistic categorization. This is precisely what makes talking about Dasein so difficult, for it cannot be de-fined in the proper limiting sense of the word (*de-finis*); it tends to elude our theorizing attempts because of its projectional character and continual being-ahead-of-itself.

Like Hegel, Heidegger has dissolved the fixed limits of life and death. As a result he has succeeded in erasing long-established divisions between these two traditionally separate states of being and nonbeing.

Death may well figure as a horizon of possibility against which we structure our existence, but this limiting horizon does not separate so much as contain. That is, in contrast to the traditional view of a border as a line of disjunction segregating two realms yet belonging to neither, Heidegger's "boundary situation" (in deference to Karl Jaspers he employs the term *Grenzsituation* at various points) of death forms part of that which it limits. What is more, it becomes functionally integrated into the enclosed whole. This process of interiorization runs counter to the more common act of demarcation, which creates such dichotomies as *Diesseits* and *Jenseits*. Heidegger, who seeks to avoid metaphysical and theological dualisms of this sort, states in this regard:

> The ontological analysis of being-toward-the-end . . . does not anticipate any existentiell stance toward death. If death is defined as the "end" of Dasein, that is, of being-in-the-world, no ontic decision has been made as to whether "after death" another being is still possible, either higher or lower, whether Dasein "lives on" or even, "outliving itself," is "immortal." Nor is anything decided ontically about the "otherwordly" [*Jenseits*] and its possibility any more than about the "this-worldly" [*Diesseits*]. (BT 230)

The numerous quotation marks in this passage attest to Heidegger's reservations about commonly held ontic opinions regarding death. It is not that he holds them in low esteem or views them as a lesser regionality of being. He is simply forced to reject them for the purposes of his ontological enterprise. As he points out often enough, death is an ontically well-explored phenomenon in such realms as biology, psychology, theology, and philosophical anthropology. But he must distance himself from these approaches if he is to have any success in clarifying the meaning of death (or what it means to die) from the perspective of being (or what it means to be). Nevertheless, he cannot always avoid the deeply entrenched metaphysical concepts that have dominated philosophy for over 2,000 years. He thus admits, in a mixture of fundamental ontology and traditional metaphysics, that his "analysis of death remains purely 'this-worldly' in that it interprets the phenomenon solely with respect to the question of how it *enters into* actual Dasein as its possibility-of-being" (*BT* 230). His investigation in other words remains thoroughly grounded in existence and has no pretensions of looking beyond Dasein's being-in-the-world. As he alternatively puts it in a lecture from 1925, shortly before the composition of *Being and Time:* "Our aim here is not to offer a metaphysics of death but to understand the ontological structures of death within life."[28]

For the most part, Heidegger shows an acute awareness of the difficulty involved in divorcing the ontic from the ontological and in making existential claims that should not be construed as existentiell ideals. He is even willing to concede that a certain degree of overlap can occur between these two provinces of being, but insists that this must be kept to a minimum in the ensuing examination of death:

> The fact that existentiell possibilities of being toward death have their resonance in an existential analysis of death, is implied by the essence of any ontological inquiry. All the more explicitly, then, must an existentiell neutrality go together with the existential conceptual definition, especially with regard to death, where the character of possibility of Dasein can be revealed most clearly of all. The existential problematic aims solely at developing the ontological structure of the being-*toward*-the-end of Dasein. (BT 231)

Heidegger's philosophy can thus be said to rest on two kinds of underpinnings. As fundamental ontology, his inquiry into the structures of being seeks to restore the proper ground to philosophy, which has all too long failed to discern the ontological difference between being and particular beings. On the other hand, he is well aware that ontology requires an "ontical foundation" (*GA* 24:26)[29] if it is to have any relevance to human existence.[30] We will see that his existential analytic of being-toward-death serves as a necessary springboard to arrive at the existentielly attested ideal of forward-running resoluteness. Heidegger's interpretation of death thus gradually progresses from the ontological to the ontic, but within the greater hermeneutic circularity of his thinking he oscillates between these two spheres, just as he constantly moves back and forth from part to whole, from Dasein to being.

An initial sketch of the ontological structure of Dasein's being-toward-the-end reveals the following characteristics: "Thus *death* reveals itself as the *ownmost nonrelational possibility not to be bypassed"* (*BT* 232). These three aspects can be elucidated as follows. Death as "ownmost" (*eigenst-*) possibility underscores the extreme individual nature of finitude. Death is to be seen as the most personal and inalienable claim one has on existence, for it cannot be experienced by anyone else. Granted, one can die in another's place through an act of sacrifice, but no one can die another's death. In *com*prehending its end as ownmost possibility, Dasein at the same time *ap*prehends itself, laying hold of its being. This double act of grasping constitutes the first step toward an authentic mode of existence. The German root *eigen* further implies the notion of personal property: authentic (*eigentlich-*) Dasein is aware of its own (*eigen-*) existence whereas its inauthentic counterpart does not have this understanding and is therefore not in full ownership of itself. Heidegger has in effect radicalized Rilke's concept of *eigener Tod,* turning it into a grammatical and conceptual superlative. Dasein's sense of self-possession reaches an extreme in the face of its extinction. The nonreferentiality (*Unbezüglichkeit*) of death equally suggests Dasein's pronounced singularity. As a supreme individualizing experience, death isolates Dasein from all relations with its environment so that it remains completely on its own, without the aid or presence of its fellow kind. Dasein thus dies alone existentially and not merely sociologically.

The fact that death cannot be outstripped or bypassed (*überholt*) is crucial for its potentiating function. Heidegger's notorious statement "Death is the possibility of the absolute impossibility of Dasein" (*BT* 232) may appear to be but one of his many rhetorically strategic tautologies. But again, one must adopt an inverted perspective to make sense of death as an existential phenomenon. The prospect of death offers Dasein possibility precisely because it looms as a final horizon that cannot be transcended. Dasein, in a fashion, constantly projects itself toward, and at the same time rebounds from, the unsurpassable frontier set by finitude. In view of this Sartrean "wall," death becomes *"an eminent* imminence" (*Bevorstand*) (*BT* 232) as opposed to an outstanding lack (*Ausstand*) awaiting gradual fulfillment. This perpetual impendency of death is *supreme* for the simple reason that it is an *extreme*. As previously mentioned, Heidegger cannot, from an ontological standpoint, posit any form of reality beyond the limit of death. Existence thus becomes all the more charged with possibility, even if this results in an inevitable impossibility of Dasein.

These three existential-ontological aspects of death are, in a privative or otherwise qualifying sense, just as applicable to the far more frequent inauthentic mode of everyday Dasein or *das Man*. Heidegger's concept of *das Man* ("the they" or "the one"), which was introduced in section 27, remains a crucial component of his deliberations on Dasein's finitude. Like Hölderlin, Nietzsche, and Rilke, Heidegger conceives of two polar attitudes toward death. This tension between authenticity and inauthenticity runs through most of his analysis and indeed through a significant portion of his book. Dasein's relation to death, however, is what ultimately determines whether it chooses a self-apprehended style of existence or elects to remain entangled in the they. As Heidegger makes perfectly clear, there is no a priori when it comes to authenticity and inauthenticity; the degree of separation between these two modalities of being is in constant flux and only through a confrontation with death does the difference plainly emerge. Hence it is somewhat misleading to speak of authentic versus inauthentic Dasein at this early stage of the analysis. Heidegger's basic tactic is to depart from our everyday average existence and, based on these findings, tease out more authentic possibilities. Nevertheless, he does not always follow this practice, as his initial sketch of being-toward-death demonstrates. Due to constraints of space and for the sake of argumentative convenience, I will simplify matters and anticipate the contrasts between these two genres of being, employing the terms authentic and inauthentic perhaps a bit prematurely. I will, however, qualify this approach by saying that (1) Heidegger repeatedly invokes this polarization long before his analytic of death; and (2) that I tend to view the opposition between authenticity and inauthenticity more as a fluid dialectic than a rigid schematic. In other words, I believe that we continually oscillate between both possibilities of being and that much of Heidegger's argument is a rhetorical strategy meant to extract us from our comfortable *Man*-like existence and point us toward a more holistic way of life.

The self of everyday existence is not you or I, but *das Man*. This impersonal pronoun (literally "the one") designates "the others," however not definite others, nor the sum of all others taken together. *Das Man* stands for, rather, the anonymous rule of public opinion that operates on all levels of society and exerts control over every aspect of life. Whether we realize it or not, we in fact belong to "them" and unknowingly consolidate "their" power. In the process, all sense of selfhood is lost and identities become interchangeable. Unlike Hölderlin and Nietzsche, who have their main characters unleash condemning words to the multitude, Heidegger does not see himself in the role of a moralist and thus has no intention of criticizing this predominant modality of existence. Ontic value judgments have no place in his ontological investigation. In the tradition of his mentor Husserl, he considers his observations to be purely phenomenological; that is, an unprejudiced analysis of the manifold phenomena that make up our life-world. As mentioned earlier, the English "inauthenticity" can easily be misconstrued in this context. By *Eigentlichkeit* Heidegger does not mean a qualitatively higher or more genuine form of existence, as is often implied even in standard German. Again, *eigentlich* refers to that which is one's own or *eigen*. For Heidegger, selfhood resembles a personal possession (*Eigentum*) that has for the most part been co-opted by the public sphere of *das Man*.

Death as "the *ownmost nonrelational possibility not to be bypassed*" is converted into a public affair by the they. Instead of viewing death as possibility, *das Man* deals with the phenomenon as a "constantly occurring event, as a 'case of death'" (*BT* 234). It is aware merely of instances in which death strikes others, but it fails to see in these isolated cases any kind of personal relevance. *Das Man* knows well enough that people die, but this is as far as it will allow its perception to go. The notion that it is always an anonymous other that dies while one himself remains unscathed, is summed up by the formulation *man stirbt*. According to this everyday mentality, the ownmost and non-referential qualities of death are shrugged off onto an impersonal collective. The they fails to acknowledge the singular nature of its finitude and is consequently unable to sever its ties to the world and act on strictly individual terms. It thereby forfeits any chance for self-determination. Everyday Dasein furthermore attempts to counter the inevitability of death by bringing its dying fellows back into the world of its daily affairs through either emotional or spiritual consolation. This appeasement in the face of finitude is not only directed toward the dying person, but also serves to mitigate the fears of the consoler.

Of course death can only be postponed, never ultimately avoided, and when it does finally occur it is viewed as an embarrassing breach of propriety. Here Heidegger refers to Tolstoy's *The Death of Ivan Ilyich* and even assumes from the text such expressions as "social inconvenience" (*Unannehmlichkeit*) and "tactlessness" (*Taktlosigkeit*) in his description of *das Man*'s discomfort in the presence of death (see *BT* 235). As we have seen, Rilke also profited from Tolstoy's moral tale and he describes this very same phenomenon of alienation in *The Book of Poverty and Death* and *The Notebooks of Malte Laurids Brigge*. In the latter work, he even utilizes the identical phrase *man stirbt* to characterize the anonymous death that lurks behind hospitals walls. Malte, whom Rilke once referred to in remarkably Heideggerian terms as a *Daseinsentwurf*,[31] finds himself immersed in a veritable they-like milieu. He continually fears becoming one of the countless and in some cases literally "faceless" (*SW* 6:712/*MLB* 7) outcasts that surround him on the streets of Paris and threaten to engulf his identity. Like Dasein, he is moreover caught between the modern brand of depersonalized death and the more existentially fulfilling *eigener Tod* that prevailed in earlier times. Of course Malte is free to choose a third option, namely the holistic outlook cultivated by the maternal side of his family. No such additional alternative exists in Heidegger's world, but we will soon see that his fully developed model of authentic being-toward-death results in a comprehensive apprehension of existence. By the end of his analysis, he will show that Dasein not only attains existentiell authenticity but also ontological totality.

Malte and Dasein have yet another thing in common: they both experience anxiety and fear in the face of death. Rilke does not differentiate between these two affects; he uses them interchangeably to describe the existential anguish that invades Malte at various points in the narrative. Following a line of thought that extends from Augustine to Kierkegaard, Heidegger on the other hand strictly separates *Angst* from *Furcht*.[32] Whereas we *fear* something definite, whether tangible or intangible, *anxiety* stems from no particular source. When overcome with this latter mood, we feel a temporary sense of nothingness: we are anxious about no-thing. In the earlier examination of attunement, this nonentity was Dasein's being-in-the-world. As Heidegger demonstrated in this segment (section 40), anxiety isolates Dasein and produces an "existential 'solipsism'" (*BT* 176) that discloses Dasein's existentiality, potentiality of being, and freedom for choosing itself. In other words, anxiety reveals to Dasein that it does not have the constitution of a present-at-hand object. It now becomes apparent that this primordial mood further intimates the ultimate state of no-thingness: death. Anxiety frees Dasein up for an unveiled confrontation with its finality and hence functions as a critical ingredient for determining an authentic comportment toward death. The they, in contrast, refuses to acknowledge the importance of anxiety, instead preaching the virtue of indifference in view of its eventual extinction. As a result, everyday Dasein becomes estranged from its death and will evade the issue of mortality at all costs, including at its own existential expense of self-autonomy.

Two further authenticating characteristics of finitude are introduced in section 52: certainty (*Gewißheit*) and indefiniteness (*Unbestimmtheit*). The certainty of death must be understood apodictically and not empirically. That is, Dasein's certainty arises from its ontologically privileged status as a locus in which being manifests itself in the world. As Heidegger already explained in section 44, Dasein possesses a basic relation to truth, which is defined as disclosure (from the Greek *alêtheia*) rather than traditionally as correspondence (*adaequatio*). Yet Dasein equally has a tendency toward concealment or untruth. As the alpha-privative in *a-lêtheia* indicates, the notion of obscurity is prior to that of clarity. Dasein's potential to be in the light of disclosure carries the reciprocal implication that it can just as easily find itself in the dark, for only that which is concealed can be uncovered. Everyday Dasein does indeed find itself shut out from truth; its state of *Verfallen* or ensnarement in mundane affairs obscures its ontological transparency. Its only form of truth is empirical certitude. As a mere witness to external cases of death, *das Man* perceives these as affecting solely others and hence ignores their existential import. Death remains an "undeniable 'fact of experience'" (*BT* 237), but an experience based on aloof observation rather than on a primordial relation to being. The they thus staidly goes about its existence, devoting itself to everyday concerns and avoiding any direct confrontation with death. Disclosure, on the other hand, leads authentic Dasein to apply the consequences of an inescapable end to its own potentiality. Dasein lives with the knowledge of death as an underlying truth of existence and structures its projects based on this continual awareness. Carried one step further, certainty involves an indefiniteness as to the precise moment of death's occurrence. Heidegger's notion of indefinite certainty recalls the age-old adage *mors certa, hora incerta* and simply means that death is sure to come about, only its when remains indeterminate. In an authentic being-toward-death, Dasein becomes aware that its end is always impending and projects itself accordingly. In its contrasting empirical certitude, *das Man* denies the perpetual imminence of its extinction, comforting itself with the thought: "death certainly comes, but not right away" (*BT* 238).

With the five concepts discussed above, Heidegger has succeeded in outlining the existential-ontological structure of death. As he summarizes: *"As the end of Dasein, death is the ownmost nonrelational, certain, and, as such, indefinite and not to be bypassed possibility of Dasein"* (*BT* 239). This conception of death, however, remains a formal sketch and is thus far from complete. Heidegger even expresses his doubts about the present stage of his enterprise: "Is not the project of the existential possibility of such a questionable existentiell potentiality-of-being a fantastical undertaking? What is needed for such a project to get beyond a merely poetizing, arbitrary construction?" (*BT* 240). In other words, Heidegger's exposition of death is still in a preliminary phase; it lacks a stable foundation and like any outline needs to be fleshed out in greater detail. He must now directly pursue the question of possibility, which all of the above characteristics only modify but do not adequately illuminate. This endeavor will lead him to the important conceptions of running forward into death (*Vorlaufen in den Tod*) and freedom toward death (*Freiheit zum Tode*), and it is here that the presence of Hölderlin and Nietzsche manifests itself most clearly.

Running Forward into Death

Everyday Dasein's comportment toward death has become apparent. In their everyday inauthentic mode, the above five characteristics have only concealed the extreme possibility of death. Clinging to life at all costs, *das Man* will put off the eventuality of its end any way it can. By refusing to lay claim to its most personal belonging and instead passing it off onto others, inauthentic Dasein becomes alienated from its ownmost possibility of being. Its constant flight from death results in a forfeiture of an authentic existence, and so it persists in a state of ontological concealment, where it inconspicuously loses itself in everyday affairs. How does this behavior compare with an authentic being-toward-death? Heidegger explores a number of attitudes under the guiding words: "First of all, we must characterize being-toward-death as a being *toward a possibility,* toward an eminent possibility of Dasein itself" (*BT* 241).

One can relate to something possible by "being out" (*Aussein*) for it in the sense of being intent on it and therefore seeking its actualization. Possibilities, after all, are there to be realized; they present themselves as attainable goals. However, as soon as they become actualized they are no longer possibilities but are made real and final. Similarly, being out for death would only bring about just such a definitive reality and thus annihilate the very possibility that an authentic existence was supposed to hold. One might call this situation an existential impasse: Dasein undermines its own potentiality by attempting to capitalize on it. Yet this problem is not limited to the futile result; the entire process of *Aussein* remains functional and pragmatic, characterized by an "in-order-to." Possibility here serves some greater end for the benefit of Dasein and thereby reveals itself as a ready-at-hand object that can be utilized for a specific purpose. Even a less active comportment toward death such as contemplation is problematical. In brooding over my approaching end, I do not directly seek its actualization as though bent upon it, but nonetheless think about this possibility, desiring to know when and how death might come about. Essentially, this is a form of calculation through which I dispose over finitude, albeit in thought rather than deed. Yet acts of thought are still just that—acts. They are in Husserl's sense intentional: directed at a particular object. Brooding over death only succeeds in diminishing the extreme character of possibility, which cannot be infringed on in any way:

> As something possible, death is supposed to show as little as possible of its possibility. On the contrary, if being-toward-death has to disclose understandingly the possibility which we have characterized as *such*, then in such being-toward-death this possibility must not be weakened, it must be understood as possibility, cultivated [*ausgebildet*] *as possibility*, and *endured [ausgehalten] as possibility*. (*BT* 241)

What Heidegger in other words seeks is some form of pure spontaneity in the face of finitude. He is trying to find a conduct that, like the life of Hegelian Spirit, does not "shrink" from death but rather "endures [*erträgt*] it and maintains itself [*sich erhält*] in it" (*W* 3:36/*PhS* 19).[33] Or as he has described this problem more effectively in another work: "To stand before a possibility means to grasp it *as* a possibility. To *endure* [*aushalten*] the possibility of death means to have it there for oneself in such a way that it stands before one purely as what it is—indefinite regarding its 'when' and certain regarding its 'that.'"[34] In view of this delicate balance between actuality and possibility, Heidegger rejects all attitudes that might objectify death. A third proposal, "expectation" (*Erwartung*), would at first appear to be a satisfactory relation to possibility, since it remains at bottom a passive attitude that does not impinge on its object. In expecting something possible, I let it come to me and thus do not diminish or take away from its likelihood of occurring. But I do not fully endure it as possibility, for in the end I am waiting for some sort of actualization despite my inactive stance. I have, so to speak, one foot in the thick of possibility yet one still firmly planted in reality, which of course results in more than just a physical split: my being-toward-death itself becomes torn between the perpetual imminence of the possible and a sudden irruption of the actual.

Heidegger finally settles on the notion of *Vorlaufen* or "running ahead," which has been problematically rendered in English as "anticipation."[35] A number of objections can be raised concerning this translation, which tends to distort the fundamental concept that Heidegger has just painstakingly worked out. First of all, anticipation does not appear to differ significantly from expectation, the attitude that was just rejected due to its curtailment of possibility. Granted, when I anticipate something, I reckon with its likelihood less than when I expect it, but I am still anticipating some*thing* to occur—however indefinable this event may be or however nonintentionally I may relate to it. Furthermore, anticipation remains a strictly mental and temporal notion, whereas running ahead has obvious physical and spatial overtones. Finally, *Vorlaufen* is a metaphor, indeed a highly animated and refreshing one in view of the predominantly austere prose of *Being and Time*.[36] As such, it carries all kinds of implications that the commonplace "anticipation" cannot but lack. It is worth noting that Kierkegaard employs this Latinate word rather than, say, a Germanic variant in his discussion of death from *Concluding Unscientific Postscript:* "Then I would have to ask whether it is at all possible to have an idea of death, whether death can be anticipated [*anticiperes*] and *anticipando* be experienced in an idea, or whether it is only when it actually is."[37] Heidegger, whose early thinking is permeated by Kierkegaardian ideas and terminology, thus deviates from his philosophical-theological precursor in a crucial aspect of his analytic. Such a divergence only underlines the importance of his choice expression *Vorlaufen*. In the following, I will probe the semantic and syntactic multivalencies of this key term in an effort to arrive at a more complete picture of what it means, existentially, to "run forward into death."

Vorlaufen is a form of understanding and thus harks back to the discussion of *Verstehen* in section 31. This earlier examination of understanding showed it to be a projecting act (*Entwerfen*) that reveals to Dasein its possibilities. Dasein understands itself through its projects, and this futural tendency is reflected in its anticipatory fore-structure.

Vorlaufen is at bottom an awareness of one's possibilities in view of their very preemption through death. *Vorlaufen* too has a projectional, indeed propulsive, character, one that seems to build in momentum and push the limits of possibility. As such, it causes the boundary toward which it moves, namely death, to increase in magnitude, much like a mountain seems to grow in size the closer one approaches: "In running ahead to this possibility, it becomes 'greater and greater,' that is, it reveals itself as something which knows no measure at all, no more or less, but means the possibility of the measureless impossibility of existence" (*BT* 242). *Vorlaufen* thus has an infinite aggrandizing effect, but it does not completely encroach on its objective nor does it reach any particular point (death is of course not a definite moment in time) at which Dasein's utmost possibility becomes actualized. As often the case in Heidegger, common conceptions of spatiality do not apply here. Not exactly an easy concept to describe in concrete terms, *Vorlaufen* would seem to be a sheer dynamic and endlessly potentiating process that does not pursue readily attainable goals. Moreover, it is an idea deeply grounded in metaphor. With the full formulation of his concept as *Vorlaufen in den Tod,* Heidegger does not intend to suggest that Dasein literally "runs forward into death." Similarly, his description of *das Man*'s opposite conduct of flight (*Flucht*) does not mean that one literally "flees" in panic when confronted with the issue of mortality. Both attitudes, authentic running forward and inauthentic flight, are based on physical movement yet they remain in essence tropes.[38] Nevertheless, it would seem that Heidegger desires a term that is not overly conceptual or abstract but that retains some degree of literalness.

Heidegger's problem with this issue of overconceptualization is reflected in some posthumously published notes on Hegelian negativity, where he expresses reservations about the implicit harmlessness of death as it functions within the dialectic of Spirit:

> Negativity as strife [*Zerrissenheit*] and separation is "death"—*the absolute lord* and "*life* of absolute Spirit" means nothing less than to endure [ertragen] and to bear [*austragen*] death. (But this "death" can never be serious; no katastrophê possible, no fall [*Sturz*] and upheaval [*Umsturz*] possible; everything is absorbed and equalized. Everything is *already unconditionally* safeguarded and accommodated.) (*GA* 68:24)

Heidegger thus seeks at least some element of danger that is not automatically neutralized by a higher teleological force. His choice of words "fall," "upheaval," and "catastrophe" suggests a kind of tragic action—not unlike the climactic plunge of Empedocles. His phrase *Vorlaufen in den Tod* therefore seems to have deliberate connotations of movement and dynamism. The preposition *in* plus the accusative further accentuates the image of a headlong charge *into* death. The alternative expression that Heidegger employs, *Vorlaufen zum Tode,* involves a lesser degree of motion, since the preposition *zu* not only translates as "to" but can equally indicate a relation "unto" or "toward," as in the phrase *Sein zum Tode.* As for the verb *vorlaufen,* it covers a wide range of meaning and needs to be explored in greater detail, particularly as Heidegger makes use of it and its components (*vor/laufen*) in variant forms and various contexts.

It first ought to be noted that Heidegger displays a rather strange penchant for the prefix *vor* throughout *Being and Time.* Words like *vorhanden, vorläufig, vorontologisch, Vorgabe,* and *Vorrang* permeate its pages to such a degree that the key component *vor* becomes a kind of leitmotif. One might ask, as Heidegger does: "How are we to conceive the character of this 'fore'?" (*BT* 141). This question, which is posed in the context of understanding's interpretive practices (*Vorhabe, Vorsicht,* and *Vorgriff*), equally pertains to the structure of *Vorlaufen.* As both a prefix and preposition, *vor* can imply either spatiality or temporality, just like the English "before." *Vorlaufen* as a literal running forward is naturally a spatial notion, whereas the *vor* contained in the nearly identical *vorläufig* (temporary) has obvious connotations of time. Heidegger even seems to play on the contrary meaning of these two words when speaking of similarly contrasting attitudes toward death. *Das Man*'s source of solace that "death certainly comes, but not right away" (der Tod kommt gewiß, aber vorläufig noch nicht) (*BT* 238/*SZ* 258), is the precise opposite of authentic Dasein's conduct of *Vorlaufen.*

The upshot of all this is that *Vorlaufen in den Tod* remains at root a highly problematical concept that cannot be interpreted too narrowly. In all likelihood, it derives from the Latin *cursus ad mortem,* which can be found both in Augustine's *City of God* (book 13, chapter 10) and Luther's exegesis of Genesis 2:17. In the former case, Augustine writes that "the whole of our lifetime is nothing but a race towards death [*cursus ad mortem*], in which no one is allowed the slightest pause or any slackening of pace."[39] Luther, for his part, comments on Paul's statement that "daily we die" as follows: "[Life] is nothing else than a perpetual running ahead toward death."[40] As I mentioned earlier, the importance of primal Christians like Augustine and Luther for Heidegger's development has been the subject of much scholarship in recent years. Given these connections, it only seems logical that *Vorlaufen* has its origins in theological discourse, although it should be noted that the phrase *currere ad mortem* (to run toward death) appears in a number of classical authors, including Seneca and Pliny.[41] But a more political reading of *Vorlaufen in den Tod* is equally plausible. As Johannes Fritsche has argued, Heidegger's concept purposely evokes the bravery (or recklessness) of countless German soldiers who were mowed down by artillery fire as they rushed toward the enemy trenches during World War I. The fact that these "heroes of Langemarck and Verdun resolutely ran forward into death," as was often proclaimed in the nationalistic discourse of the 1920s and 1930s, only reinforces this less charitable interpretation not to mention the controversy surrounding the political dimension of Heidegger's philosophy and its specialized vocabulary.[42] In public speeches that Heidegger held in 1933 commemorating the Battle of Langemarck and the death of the nationalist hero Albert Leo Schlageter, he even cloaks the political virtues of military resolve and sacrifice in the philosophical language of his existential analytic from 1927.[43] But whether Heidegger is carrying on the tradition of Luther or capitalizing on ideological trends between the wars, his idea of *Vorlaufen in den Tod* has greater ramifications than can be fully accounted for by either of these theories.

As previously suggested, *Vorlaufen* can be interpreted in both temporal and spatial terms. Its prefix *vor* allows it to acquire the meanings of "running ahead in time" and "running forward in space." The former signification ties in with Dasein's character of being-ahead-of-itself. True to its forward tendency, Dasein is always one step ahead of real time, not unlike a fast-running clock. As Heidegger later demonstrates in his discussion of temporality, authentic Dasein's essential orientation toward the future is crystalized in the very expression *Vorlaufen*. Given that Dasein's finitude forms the basis of its temporality, its *Vorlaufen in den Tod* is thus bound to take on connotations of time. Authentic Dasein continually becomes its future, which it does not regard as a moment that has not yet arrived but as the *Zu-kunft* in which it comes toward itself and better grasps its possibilities. In this sense, the temporal idea of running ahead seems logical enough, as it conforms to Heidegger's existential understanding of the future. Dasein runs ahead even as it comes toward itself, which is but another way of saying that it perdures in possibility.

But Heidegger's text is also full of spatial concepts such as de-distancing, directionality, and situation. As a pro-ject, Dasein literally finds itself "thrown forward" (*pro-jacere*) into space. This notion of projection is conveyed in Dasein's factical condition of *Geworfenheit*, its self-understanding as *Entwerfen*, and its existential constitution as *Entwurf*—all of which are rooted in the verb *werfen*, "to throw." *Vorlaufen*, however, would better seem to suggest the forward direction of this trajectory. Much as *das Man*'s conduct toward death is characterized by a metaphorical *Flucht* (flight) or what one might in this context call a *Weglaufen* (running away), authentic Dasein chooses to rush in the opposite direction: forward into possibility. Heidegger generally tends to think in such projectional terms with regard to Dasein. Earlier in a discussion of concern or solicitude (*Fürsorge*), he differentiates between the inauthentic mode of "leaping in" (*einspringen*) and "dominating" (*beherrschen*) and the authentic variation of "leaping ahead" (*vor[aus]springen*) and "liberating" (*befreien*). Here the underlying image may be one of leaping rather than running or throwing, but the implications of forward motion remain no less graphic. His second major work, *Contributions to Philosophy*, concretely links the notion of springing ahead with that of projection: "The leap is the enopening *self*-throwing [das eröffnende *Sich*werfen] 'into' Dasein. This is grounded in the leap" (*GA* 65:303).[44] The concept of *Sprung* in fact takes on weight for the entire work, one of whose chapters bears this very heading. It is perhaps telling that Heidegger recapitulates his analysis of death from *Being and Time* in precisely this section entitled "Der Sprung," although the term becomes so figurative that it hardly seems to designate any one thing. Rather, many such forward "bounds" are required in the pursuit of being, from the original leap (*Ur-sprung*) of even raising the basic question "What does it mean to be?" to a grounding of the *Seinsfrage* through a plunge into (*Einsprung in*) the ontological disclosure of Dasein. Heidegger however gets nebulous here as he abandons his phenomenological method of *Being and Time*.[45] It suffices to note that his conception of *Vorlaufen,* however difficult it may be to imagine or comprehend in all its consequences, definitely suggests some kind of propelled motion, whether a literal running forward or an analogous action such as casting or springing. These vivid overtones will soon prove to be important in connection with Empedocles and his projected, but never realized, plunge into the seething crater of Mount Etna.

Whatever images *Vorlaufen* may evoke, there can be no doubt about its crucial function in Heidegger's analysis. As a form of understanding, *Vorlaufen* reveals to authentic Dasein the supreme possibility of death, and it does so by disclosing to Dasein its immersion in *das Man*. The five characteristics of finitude that Heidegger introduced in his preliminary sketch from section 50 become grounded in *Vorlaufen* and reinforced as contrasting modes of conduct to an inauthentic being-toward-death. As such they take on even greater significance in their respective functions as preliminary indicators of authenticity. Death as ownmost possibility, for instance, makes it "evident to Dasein that in the eminent possibility of itself it is torn away from the they, that is, anticipation [*vorlaufend*] can always already have torn itself away from the they" (*BT* 243). The nonreferentiality that becomes unveiled in *Vorlaufen* further underscores authentic Dasein's separation from its inauthentic counterpart. Here the anticipation of death completely isolates Dasein and forces it to act on its own potentiality rather than be swayed by others. There seem to be no new realizations or major reformulations with regard to the notions of certainty and indefiniteness. For the most part Heidegger repeats what he has already said, emphasizing the fact—and thereby satisfying his previous demand that death should show as little as possible of its possibility—that a certain but indefinite end compels Dasein to cultivate and endure the eminent and imminent possibility that death holds: "In anticipating

[*Im Vorlaufen zum*] the indefinite certainty of death, Dasein opens itself to a constant *threat* arising from its own there. Being-toward-the-end must hold itself in this very threat, and can so little phase it out that it rather has to cultivate the indefiniteness of the certainty" (*BT* 245).

The final characteristic of death, its nonsurpassablity, leads to several new insights. In an authentic being-toward-death, Dasein understands that its end cannot be avoided, and instead of sidestepping the perpetual threat to its existence as *das Man* habitually does, it frees itself for the impossibility of circumventing its fate. This self-liberating action is described as: "Becoming free *for* one's own death in anticipation" (*BT* 243). In the original, this key phrase reads: "Das vorlaufende Freiwerden *für* den eigenen Tod" (*SZ* 264). In letting itself become free for an unsurpassable death as its utmost possibility, Dasein is released from its lostness in the chance possibilities of the they. Such a process enables Dasein to understand and choose the possibilities that lead up to its extreme and definitive end. Thus, Dasein not only gains an understanding of its continual prospects throughout the course of its existence; it further gains a perspective on its being as a whole by projecting itself against the ultimate horizon of death. By reckoning with its end at any conceivable moment, it is able to "anticipate" the entirety of its existence. Here Heidegger employs the verb *vorwegnehmen* for the first and only time, which would seem to necessitate an alternative translation of *Vorlaufen* as "anticipation." Compare the use of the two terms in this context: "Because anticipation [*das Vorlaufen*] of the possibility not-to-be-bypassed also disclosed all the possibilities lying before it, this anticipation includes the possibility of taking the *whole* of Dasein in advance in an existentiell way [eines existenziellen Vorwegnehmens des *ganzen* Daseins], that is, the possibility of existing as a *whole potentiality-of-being*" (*BT* 244). More important than the question of an adequate English translation is the fact that Heidegger has found a solution to the initial dilemma of his inquest. Dasein's inability to experience itself as a whole was due to the erroneous view that its existence becomes terminated from an outside source, specifically, from its perception of death as a one-time event. This impasse has now been overcome: through an internal and anticipatory comprehension of death, Dasein is able to grasp the totality of its existence. Heidegger's basic point here has been well articulated by Foucault, who describes the function of the Stoic *meletê thanatou* as follows: "What accounts for the particular value of the death meditation is not just the fact that it anticipates what is generally held to be the greatest misfortune; it is not just that it enables one to convince oneself that death is not an evil; it offers the possibility of looking back, in advance as it were, on one's life."[46]

Even more radically, *Vorlaufen* reveals to Dasein that its utmost possibility lies in its potential for a final act of self-surrender: "Anticipation [*Vorlaufen*] discloses to existence that its extreme inmost possibility lies in giving itself up and thus shatters all one's clinging to whatever existence one has reached" (*BT* 244). This perspective does not necessarily imply suicide or self-sacrifice. As we have seen with the Stoics, the idea of suicide is as much a philosophical and rhetorical idea about attaining the good life as it is a physical act motivated by any number of outside circumstances. Although Heidegger never broaches this question of a self-inflicted death in *Being and Time,* he does comment on it, however briefly, in other writings of the period. In *History of the Concept of Time* (see *GA* 20:439) and "Wilhelm Dilthey's Research and the Struggle for a Historical Worldview," for instance, he outright rejects any form of suicidal conduct, contending that such an attitude only coverts possibility into actuality.[47] He thereby suggests that the deliberation of suicide belongs to the same kind of representing mindset as being out for something, brooding, and expectation. Dasein should not actively seek to bring about its annihilation, for this would only turn it into an inert object. Dasein, rather, continually projects itself forward, even in the face of death, which it does not allow to impair its potentiality-of-being. Contrary to *das Man*'s stubborn refusal to relinquish its prolonged and stagnant existence, authentic being-toward-death cultivates a free relation to finitude so as to keep from lapsing into stasis. It is in the context of this "shattering" of a static existence that Heidegger obliquely alludes to Nietzsche's *Thus Spoke Zarathustra:* "In anticipation [*vorlaufend*], Dasein guards itself against falling back behind itself, or behind the potentiality-for-being that it has understood. It guards against 'becoming too old for its victories' (Nietzsche)" (*BT* 244). Heidegger's reference is both parenthetical and paraphrastic. He loosely quotes the following line from Zarathustra's speech "On Free Death": "Some become too old even for their truths and victories" (*KSA* 4:94/*Z* 184). This casual citation hints at a deeper connection between Heidegger and Nietzsche with respect to their views on death.

Soon after this allusion Heidegger introduces the concept of "freedom toward death" (*Freiheit zum Tode*), which not only recalls the Zarathustrian ideal of free death (*freier Tod*) but corresponds word to word to a formulation that Nietzsche recorded in his notebooks during the initial stages of his *Zarathustra* project: "Sickness, conduct toward it, freedom toward death" (*KSA* 10:21). With this remark, Nietzsche is presumably referring to the general state of infirmity that tormented his existence from the late 1870s onward. I have already discussed the intersections between his biographical afflictions and his philosophical ideas about mortality. In both cases, the prospect of dying at any moment gave him a kind of foretaste of existential freedom, though in the end he failed to capitalize on this supreme possibility and instead wasted away in a state of dementia. Nevertheless, his notion of free death as expressed in *Thus Spoke Zarathustra* clearly prefigures Heidegger's ontological analytic, the conclusion of which reads as follows:

> Anticipation reveals to Dasein its lostness in the they-self, and brings it face to face with the possibility to be itself, primarily unsupported by concern taking care of things, but to be itself in passionate anxious *freedom toward death* which is free of the illusions of the they, factical, and certain of itself. (*BT* 245)[48]

The implication here is that Dasein freely determines its time to die and does not fail to act upon this moment of radical possibility. Freedom toward death characterizes authentic Dasein as an open project and at the same time accentuates the privation of autonomy that underlies *das Man*'s dogged resistance toward dying. The charter of Dasein's being is such that it constantly projects itself forward, never once falling behind itself so as not to acquire the fixity of an object. This forward trajectory continues even with respect to death: Dasein runs toward its perpetually imminent end as the supreme possibility of a self-determined existence. For Heidegger, the right time for Dasein to give up its existence occurs at that moment when it finds itself unable to move onward and shatter its already attained states of being. Nietzsche for his part proposes a "yes-saying" not only to life, but also to death, which he idealizes as one's crowning achievement. Such an affirmation is, strictly speaking, a negation, for it leads to the demise of the individual. Hence the paradox that the yea-sayer inevitably becomes a nay-sayer (see *KSA* 4:95/*Z* 185), a paradox reminiscent of Heidegger's attempt to convert the negativity of death into the ultimate possibility of existence. Both Heidegger and Nietzsche furthermore discriminate between two opposing comportments toward death. As Zarathustra's speech makes polemically clear, there are those (the "all too-many" and "superfluous") who languish long past their prime and those select few that depart at the height of their powers. Heidegger's distinction is less impassioned but just as firm: generally we live and die according to the habits of everyday Dasein, but he goes to great lengths to point us toward a more authentic style of existence, which of course presupposes an authentic comprehension of death.

THE ATTESTATION OF AN AUTHENTIC BEING-TOWARD-DEATH: FORWARD-RUNNING RESOLUTENESS IN HEIDEGGER AND HÖLDERLIN

Heidegger's project of an authentic being-toward-death is a strictly existential-ontological undertaking, and as such a kind of philosophical blueprint. As he himself realizes, it lacks ontic-existentiell concretization: "And yet this existentially 'possible' being-toward-death remains, after all, existentielly a fantastical demand. The ontological possibility of an authentic potentiality-for-being-a-whole of Dasein means nothing as long as the corresponding ontic potentiality-of-being has not been shown in terms of Dasein itself" (*BT* 246). Heidegger thus attempts to find an existentiell fundament for Dasein's authenticity. Through an investigation of conscience and guilt, he arrives at the concept of resoluteness (*Entschlossenheit*), which, when fused with the attitude of *Vorlaufen,* culminates in the authentic attested existence of Dasein as forward-running resoluteness. This existentiell testimony will prove of central importance for determining the deeper connections to Hölderlin's Empedocles, who, in his own authentic way, resolutely runs forward into the freedom of death.

Conscience, Guilt, and Resoluteness

The first thing to be established about conscience is that it intimates something to Dasein and hence has a disclosing function. It therefore ranks among the existential phenomena that constitute the *Da* of Dasein. These include attunement, understanding, and discourse. Fallenness (*Verfallen*) also plays an important role in this context. As Heidegger has already demonstrated in the first division and now summarizes in preparation for his analysis of conscience, Dasein's factical condition of thrownness is revealed through its attunement, principally through the mood of *Angst*. Understanding remains inextricably caught up with attunement, for it allows Dasein to project itself beyond its facticity and upon its future possibilities, which can authentically be its own or stem from the they. In the latter case, Dasein becomes addicted or falls prey to *das Man,* which is the true sense of *Verfallen.* Dasein's entanglement in everydayness is not to be construed as an onto-theological fall from grace, but as a form of existential addiction best borne out by the German: *Dasein verfällt dem Man.* (My example, not Heidegger's.) Due to its lostness in the inauthentic discourse of idle talk (*Gerede*), Dasein literally fails to hear its own self. By listening (*hören*) to others, Dasein cannot help but belong (*gehören*) to them and consequently surrender its authentic potentiality-of-being. If Dasein is to extricate itself from the quagmire of inauthenticity, it must cease listening to others by instigating some form of interruption, one however that will be heard above the din of everyday discourse. This signal comes from conscience.

Conscience is fundamentally characterized as a call. The act of calling necessarily entails four dimensions: the caller, the person being called, the issue of the call, and the task to which one is called. All four of these dimensions ultimately involve the self, albeit in its diverse functions: it is the self that calls, it is the self that is called, the self is at stake in the call, and the self is called to apprehend itself. Heidegger's point becomes clearer when one considers that German has an assortment of verbs modifying the basic act of calling: *rufen, anrufen,* and *aufrufen.* The caller (*der Rufer*) is Dasein in its anxiety. When struck by this mood, Dasein loses the comfortable and complacent feeling of togetherness with the they. The self that is called (*der Angerufene*) is, on the other hand, Dasein in its inauthentic being. Hence, the summoner and the summoned are one and the same, only in different modalities. The self that calls seeks to disentangle the self that is called from its enmeshment in *das Man.* Thus, the call of conscience concerns the self insofar as it draws attention to the particular mode of existence in which Dasein happens to be. Whether addresser or addressee, authentic or inauthentic, Dasein realizes what is at stake: selfhood. The question then remains: "*What* does conscience call to the one summoned?" Heidegger glibly answers: "Strictly speaking—nothing" (*BT* 252). Conscience has nothing definite or practical to say, nor does it attempt to initiate a conversation through its summons. The self, rather, "is *summoned* to itself, that is, to its ownmost potentiality-of-being" (*BT* 252). This summons "calls Dasein forth (ahead-of-itself) to its most unique possibilities" (*BT* 252). In the original German, this *Vor-(nach-'vorne'-)Rufen* recalls both the lexical form and the general function of *Vorlaufen.* Both conscience and *Vorlaufen* are types of understanding that intimate existential possibilities, thereby giving Dasein a better apprehension of itself. In this process of self-understanding, Dasein takes hold of its existence, thereby becoming ever more authentic.

Conscience, for Heidegger, is a form of self-knowledge. Its call comes as an inner voice of sorts, but does not correspond to the traditional notion of a moral reproach. Like the authentic mode of discourse known as *Verschwiegenheit* or "reticence," the call of conscience is, rather, a silent appeal. This silence contrasts with the loudness of *das Man* who fails to hear itself (that is, its self) above the clamor of its incessant chatter. Furthermore, this call does not impart any specific message but summons Dasein *from* its inauthentic entanglement in the they and *forward into* an authentic understanding of its possibilities. A further departure from the common view of a good or bad conscience concerns the aspect of guilt upon which one's pangs are based. One typically feels guilty because of a committed transgression, and the internal voice unremittingly reminds one of this wrong. For Heidegger, however, the roots of such guiltiness run deeper and the consequences extend much further.

Guilt is at bottom an ontological problem. Just as truth and knowledge arise through a primordial awareness of being rather than through cognition, guilt likewise remains attached to the predicate of "I am." Dasein *is* guilty in its being. Moreover, this ontological notion of guiltiness implies an equally originary deficit or lack. Dasein is guilty because of a constant shortfall, a *not,* in its existential constitution. Heidegger thus defines guilt as "being-the-ground of a nullity" (*Grundsein einer Nichtigkeit*). What he means by this requires one to recall the being of Dasein as care, whose structure consists of facticity, existence, and fallenness. Dasein's facticity lies in its thrownness; that is to say, Dasein has been thrown into this world—literally into its Da—and there can be no undoing this brute fact. Thrust into the world through no accord of its own, Dasein can never "get back behind" its thrown condition but must settle for the fact "'that-it-is-and-has-to-be'" (*BT* 262). This thrownness does not lie behind Dasein as a one-time occurrence that has since become separate and remote. Thrownness is a "factical" (*faktisch-*) rather than a "factual" (*tatsächlich-*) phenomenon, which means that it belongs to Dasein as an ever-present constituent of its being. As care, Dasein is its perpetual "that," which is but another way of saying that Dasein is the ground of its potentiality-of-being. But it has not laid the ground itself, since it cannot possibly bring about its own existence. Dasein's facticity does not allow it to gain control over its ground, so it must instead exist *from* that ground and *as* that ground, and it does so by projecting itself (*sich entwerfen*) upon the possibilities with which it is faced in its factical condition of thrownness. Put in more ontic terms, we are not responsible for the irreversible fact that we have been born into this world, but must nevertheless take responsibility for our lives. In its projection Dasein does not so much overcome its existential ground as take it over. It thus continually confronts the not of its thrownness: Dasein has *not* laid the ground for itself, it can *not* fall behind or undo this ground, and it is *not* able to gain power over this ground. Dasein can only seek to capitalize upon its facticity by existing, that is by understanding itself in terms of possibilities. What Heidegger means here is the following:

for every possibility that Dasein chooses, it excludes others, thereby annulling the role these could potentially play in existence. Choosing necessarily involves *not* choosing, but even these nonchosen possibilities belong to the structure of Dasein's being. Dasein is thus a constant ground of a nullity and as such is always guilty. This guilt does not arise from a specific action that Dasein has taken; on the contrary, it is incurred through Dasein's very freedom *not* to choose certain courses of action or modes of existence. Dasein is guilty for the very reason that by being in such a way it is the ground for not being in another way. Its guilt lies in its never-ending might-have-been.

Only because Dasein is fundamentally, that is ontologically, guilty does conscience have existential meaning. The call of conscience points Dasein in two directions: forward into possibility and backward into thrownness. That is, conscience gives Dasein to understand that it exists as both a projected (*geworfen-*) and projecting (*entwerfend-*) being whose null ground furnishes the necessary basis for choosing possibilities. Dasein is free to choose itself, yet rarely does so in its everydayness. As previously discussed, the call of conscience has the purpose of summoning Dasein from its addiction to the they. Dasein, however, must be ready to follow the call's command, which means that it must first understand its primal guilty condition as a potentiality-of-being. Guilt thus takes on the function not of an emotional burden but of an existential directive. *Das Man* has no such awareness of its guilt and hence never bothers listening to the summons of its conscience, which it would fail to hear anyway above the tumult of its everyday affairs. Authentic understanding, on the other hand, displays a readiness to be addressed and thereby becomes free for the call. By recognizing that its guilt constitutes the existential ground of nullity upon which all particular existentiell decisions are based, Dasein is able to choose itself in its ownmost possibility of existence. Heidegger equates understanding the call with a "wanting to have a conscience" (*Gewissen-haben-wollen*). That is to say, the desire for a conscience implies both the willingness for being summoned and the acceptance of guilt. As a kind of self-understanding, wanting to have a conscience is a mode of disclosure that reveals to Dasein its potentiality-of-being. Indeed, *Gewissen-haben-wollen* is a preeminent form of disclosedness, one which Heidegger calls "resoluteness"—a correlation that is better borne out by the near isomorphism of *Erschlossenheit* and *Entschlossenheit.*

This latter term can be misleading in the original German and all the more so in its English translation as "resoluteness." Heidegger emphasizes the difference between his use of the word and its common meanings of "determination" and "resolve." From an etymological standpoint, his intention seems reasonable enough: just as *erschließen* is linguistically based on *schließen* and semantically follows from it ("to *dis*close" is the opposite in meaning of "to close"), *entschließen* should likewise signify "to open" or "to unlock." Like *Erschlossenheit,* Dasein's *Entschlossenheit* is a transparent mode of self-apprehension, only grounded in guilt, conscience, and a freely chosen selfhood. While *erschlossenes* Dasein becomes aware of itself in the truth of (self-)disclosure, *entschlossenes* Dasein puts this ontological truth into practice so as to lead a self-aware and self-determined existence. Here one senses a connection to the ordinary meaning of *Entschlossenheit* as "resoluteness": the fact that Dasein has chosen itself based on its call of conscience and primordial guilt implies decision-making, determination, resolve. Dasein's unlocking of itself translates into an act of self-disclosure that allows for a firm seizure of existence. Much like an authentic being-toward-death, *Entschlossenheit* enables Dasein to grasp itself in its transparency and ownmost potentiality-of-being and thus firmly, that is, resolutely, go about its business.

As an existential form of disclosure, resoluteness still has an existentiell indefiniteness about it. Being resolute necessarily involves particular decisions; that is, Dasein must resolve itself upon definite courses of action in its daily existence. This determination of one realizable possibility over another is a "resolution" or *Entschluß.* Heidegger's claim that "[r]esoluteness is certain of itself only in a resolution" (*BT* 275) suggests that the former notion designates the general condition in which Dasein opens itself up for choices whereas the latter refers to the actual decisions that Dasein makes in its factical existence. Here the call of conscience summons resolute Dasein forth into a "situation," where it settles on particular resolutions concerning its being. Dasein thus always acts in a specific context, thereby concretizing its existential projection in a determinate type of behavior. This seizure of distinct possibilities in a situation is what grounds Dasein's selfhood on an ontic-existentiell level. Through his analyses of conscience, guilt, and resoluteness, Heidegger proves that authenticity is "neither an empty term nor a fabricated idea" (*BT* 277) but an attested potentiality-of-being. Such an attestation comes about through resolute choice. What has yet to be achieved, however, is a similar testimony with regard to an authentic being-a-whole. The pursuit of this goal leads to an amalgam of the still existential and as such unreasonable demand of *Vorlaufen* with the existentiell possibilities that arise out of *Entschlossenheit*. Dasein projects itself from its ground of nullity for as long as it exists—that is, unto its end. As an authentic understanding of guilt, resoluteness thus simultaneously becomes a "*being-toward-the-end-that-understands*" (*BT* 282), which is precisely the definition of *Vorlaufen:* an anticipatory understanding of the constant threat to one's existence. Both resoluteness and anticipation are thus prime ways in which Dasein authentically comprehends itself. Their connection is therefore anything but arbitrary. Indeed, they arise from the equiprimordial phenomena of guilt and death upon which Dasein's entire being is predicated. With this organic fusion of *Vorlaufen* and *Entschlossenheit,* Heidegger has finally managed to interpret Dasein in its existentiell authenticity and existential totality.

Forward-running resoluteness can perhaps best be described as an acute awareness and anticipation of death resulting from the choices one has made throughout existence. Dasein's relation to its end stems from resolutions made in concrete situations and hence can no longer be considered "some kind of unattached behavior" (*BT* 285) lacking a stable foundation for practical existence. What was originally a formal ontological sketch of death has now found ontic corroboration. Heidegger refuses to explore the existentiell possibilities of resolute Dasein in further detail, as this would lead far beyond the scope of his book. Nevertheless, he claims to have uncovered an ideal mode of conduct through his lengthy and painstaking analyses: "But does not a definite ontic interpretation of authentic existence, a factical ideal of Dasein, underlie our ontological interpretation of the existence of

Dasein? Indeed" (*BT* 286). This factical ideal of forward-running resoluteness points to Hölderlin's Empedocles and thus concludes my
detailed discussion of death and guilt in *Being and Time*. It is in
Hölderlin's drama that the search must continue for further testimony
of Heidegger's ideas—and potential ideals. To take a cue from David
Farrell Krell: "No reading of *Being and Time* ever finishes the book.
For that matter, no writing ever finished it. By rights we ought to follow Heidegger's search for ontic attestation of the ontological possibility that constitutes existence, namely, its running ahead into death."[49]

Empedocles the Forerunner

In general, the manner in which Hölderlin's Empedocles conducts himself toward his end can be viewed as a literary attestation of Heidegger's
philosophical exemplar of forward-running resolute Dasein. Indeed
the drama's main themes of death and guilt reflect the key function of
these very same phenomena for an authentically apprehended existence. In the following, I will round off this chapter by recapitulating
some of the points I made earlier about Hölderlin's drama and con-
textualizing them within Heidegger's analyses. In the process, I intend
to show that *The Death of Empedocles* can be read as preontological
evidence of an authentic being-toward-death. While I do not consider
there to be enough material proof for making definitive claims about
an influence of the poet/dramatist upon the self-proclaimed thinker, I
do believe that a Heideggerian reading of the play can add yet another
thread to the patchwork of ideas that comprise the fabric of *Being and
Time*.[50]

The notion of *Vorlaufen*, which carries all kinds of conceptual as
well as metaphorical implications, is the most obvious correspondence
to Heidegger's existential analyses. Whether interpreted literally as
an act of running forward or more figuratively as a deportment of anticipation, *Vorlaufen* perfectly describes Empedocles's confrontation
with death. Not only does he anticipate his end throughout the fragments, but his self-sacrifice in the crater of Etna also carries the physical connotations of running or, more precisely, leaping. True to the
literal and graphic meaning of *Vorlaufen in den Tod*, Empedocles

rushes forward into the possibility of death. Due to the fragmentary nature of the drafts, he never reaches this climactic point, but the fact remains that he is *projected* to die in such a manner—and not just insofar as Hölderlin intends for him to perish within the overall context of the dramatic project. Empedocles, rather, also finds himself caught up in a Heideggerian "projection" toward death. He speaks of this trajectory a number of times and in a variety of ways. Some of the images involving forward movement include that of "wandering along on a path of death" (see *SWB* 2:300) and "racing on a chariot" (see *SWB* 2:316, 385/*PF* 317). With respect to the latter metaphor, Hölderlin stresses that this death-bound vehicle only increases in momentum the closer it comes to its goal: "The pain makes faster / His flight, and like the charioteer / When wheels begin to smoke on the track, / All the more swiftly / He, the endangered, rushes towards its garland" (*SWB* 2:385/*PF* 317). Similarly, Heidegger claims that *Vorlaufen* allows the possibility of death to become "'greater and greater'" and indeed grow beyond measure (see *BT* 242). And while he discounts conventional notions of spatiality and does not believe that forward-running Dasein ever reaches any kind of finish-line, a sense of sheer intensity and endless possibility nevertheless unites his view with Hölderlin's. Empedocles's propulsion into death, whether as conveyed in the imagery of leaping or racing, thus seems a vivid realization of the existential conduct outlined in Heidegger's analytic. In fact, due to the incompleteness of all three drafts Empedocles is never able to actualize his death, which only aligns him all the more with forward-running Dasein. His death therefore remains as charged with possibility as Dasein's own perpetually imminent end. Of course this open-ended nature of Empedocles's death is reinforced through external circumstances, namely Hölderlin's inability to finish his drama. But even internally, within the confines of his own character, Empedocles embraces death as both freedom and existential fulfillment. He furthermore makes it clear that his fate has been determined from the very moment of his birth—through both divine decree and his own prophecy (see *SWB* 2:333, 347). His life is thus primordially grounded in a kind of being-toward-death and he constructs his existence accordingly. This acknowledgment of his mortal condition is what separates him from his adversaries, the high priests and their subservient followers. While Hölderlin does not capitalize on the linguistic potential of such terms as *eigentlich* and *uneigentlich,* he nonetheless distinguishes between Empedocles's unwavering acceptance of death and the evasive attitude that prevails among the masses.

Empedocles's death is motivated by guilt. While the specific nature of his guiltiness varies from draft to draft, it nevertheless remains the driving force behind his determination to die in each version of the play. Moreover, Hölderlin underscores the magnitude of his tragic hero's guilty condition by associating it with the hubris of Greek mythology and the Original Sin of Christianity. Although these forms of transgressions may not qualify as ontological in Heidegger's special sense of the word (cf. his disassociation of Dasein's guilt from Original Sin in *BT* 410–11), they are as originary as can be in an existentiell testimony. As Schopenhauer has for instance remarked: "The true sense of tragedy is the deeper insight that what the hero atones for is not his own particular sins, but original sin, in other words, the guilt of existence itself."[51] More importantly, Empedocles's guilt forms the very ground of his existence; he *is* fundamentally guilty and only his expiatory death can undo this basic fact. This quandary accounts for his single-minded sense of purpose. Empedocles has his sights trained on the summit of Mount Etna and no one is able to sway him from his resolve to die in its flames. His very name accentuates the commitment to his cause: *empedos* translates as "firm-set," "steadfast," or literally "in the ground."[52] But of course the more appropriate word remains "resolute," the ordinary meaning of which perfectly captures the nature of Empedocles's conduct toward death. The fact that it denotes something completely different in Heidegger's ontologically purified language does not automatically preclude it from comparative consideration. Heidegger generally tends to base his philosophical vocabulary on everyday words, either redefining them in the name of radical etymology (in which ostensible roots are often twisted to the extreme) or modifying them slightly to create vaguely familiar neologisms. *Dasein, Gerede,* and *Angst* are examples of the former practice; *Befindlichkeit, eigenst-,* and *das Man* of the latter. But in many of his attempts to recapture original significations, a certain ontic residue remains attached to his linguistic upgrades. This especially seems the case with an expression like *Entschlossenheit*. Although this precise term does not appear in any of the *Empedocles* drafts, the variant "resolution" or *Entschluß* is mentioned three times in the brief "Frankfurt Plan," thereby giving some minor literary attestation of Heideggerian terminology.[53] Heidegger could thus easily have been prompted by Hölderlin for his own elaboration of *Entschluß* and its related concept of *Entschlossenheit*. At he very least, he might have had Empedocles in the back of his mind when putting together his formula of *vorlaufende Entschlossenheit* and applying it to his philosophical protagonist Dasein. Whatever the case, it cannot be ignored that several of his most important ideas regarding an authentic being-toward-death also make their appearance in Hölderlin's drama.

In view of the above correlations, Empedocles can be said to function as a literary embodiment of anticipatory resoluteness. His guilt-driven, forward-running course toward death fulfills Heidegger's search for existentiell testimony of an authentic existential mode of conduct: "Does Dasein ever project itself factically into such a being-toward-death? Does it even *demand,* on the basis of its ownmost being, an authentic potentiality of being which is determined by anticipation [*Vorlaufen*]?" (*BT* 246). While there is some undeniable evidence to suggest that Heidegger's notion of *Vorlaufen in den Tod* has both theological and ideological roots, whether as a direct translation of Luther's *cursus ad mortem* or a coded slogan referring to World War I, it would seem that Hölderlin's Empedocles is a more fleshed-out *Vorläufer* in the dual sense of the word. He is both a literal forward-runner who factically attests to Heidegger's existential paradigm and a temporal forerunner who prefigures and perhaps even helped shape some of the ideas articulated in *Being and Time.*

Epilogue
The Dignity of Death and the Right to Die

For death is what I seek. It is my right.
—Hölderlin, *The Death of Empedocles*

The more we are making advances in science, the more we seem
to fear and deny the reality of death.
—Elisabeth Kübler-Ross, *On Death and Dying*

Death, as conceived in a line of thought stretching from the late
eighteenth to early twentieth century, is far more than a narrow philosophical concern or isolated literary theme. As I have tried to illustrate in the foregoing chapters, it is intimately connected with a host
of other underlying issues that feed into a comprehensive worldview.
Each of the authors that I have examined, whether dialectician, existentialist, or whatever other label one wishes to append, seeks a greater
wholeness of existence amidst the compartmentalization of modern
humanity. For Hegel and Hölderlin, dialectical unification philosophy
offers a conciliatory solution to the discordant tenor of their time. Far
more than a mere method or heuristic device, dialectics serves as an
ontological model that encompasses the entire flux of reality. Even
Nietzsche, at least in the initial stages of his career, asserts the primacy
of being over becoming. In both theory (*The Birth of Tragedy*) and
practice (literary ambitions to dramatize the death of Empedocles), he
strives for cosmic unity through the experience of the tragic, which

he views not as a requisite component of drama but as an underlying problem of human existence. With respect to Rilke, this yearning for holism reaches its extreme in a quasimystical poetics of being whereby the boundaries between subjectivity and objectivity yield to a heightened sensation of oneness with the world. And of course it is in Heidegger that this totalistic (some would say potentially totalitarian) conception of being reaches its extreme: Dasein is complete, both ontically and ontologically, only in view of its end. The ontological grounding of death that begins with the Hegelian dialectic, specifically with the inward turn of consciousness, thus culminates in the Heideggerian dynamic of ontology and onticity. In the course of this development from dialectical to existential explanations of human finitude, death increasingly acquires an individualizing function. Whereas dialectics negates categories of individuality and raises them to a more universal level, existentialist thought remains focused on the individual and his unique possibilities. For Hegel, death ultimately carries no personal meaning but furthers the life of Spirit. Heidegger, on the other hand, converts death into the determining factor of selfhood, into the prerequisite for an authentic and holistic existence.

These qualities of holism and individuality also play an essential role in the medical humanization of death that arose during the 1950s and still stimulates public discourse today. The "dignity of death" and the "right to die" have evolved into everyday catchwords and the news regularly brings examples of final acts committed in the cause of personal freedom. Karen Ann Quinlan, Nancy Cruzan, and Jack Kevorkian are household names in the ongoing debate about the ethics of dying. Whereas the former two life-support victims have become landmark cases in the moral and legal quagmire of euthanasia, the latter has gained notoriety for carrying out the wishes of terminally ill patients that were still able to make decisions about their fate. The year 2005 was particularly notable from a thanatological standpoint: the controversy surrounding Terri Schiavo threatened to cause a political rift on a national scale, and two films dealing with the issue of assisted suicide received Academy Awards for best picture: *Million Dollar Baby* and, in the foreign language category, *Mar Adentro (The Sea Inside)*.[1] This popularized focus on the human dimension of dying can be interpreted as a positive signal that we are ready for an alternative to the medical or high-tech death of recent decades. Of course a host of poets and philosophers ranging from Hölderlin to Heidegger have warned us about our estrangement from death all along. By way of conclusion, I would like to comment on more recent scientific research in an effort to show the contemporary resonance of the ideas pursued throughout this study.

It is a well-known fact among sociologists and psychologists that death has been repressed in the age of modernity. Whereas sexuality is widely regarded as the major taboo of the nineteenth century, death holds this distinction in the twentieth. In an influential essay from 1955 entitled "The Pornography of Death," the British sociologist Geoffrey Gorer points to a new form of prudery that has its own pernicious effect on human relations, specifically on the social custom of grieving. According to Gorer: "The natural processes of corruption and decay have become disgusting, as disgusting as the natural processes of birth and copulation were a century ago; preoccupation about such processes is (or was) morbid and unhealthy, to be discouraged in all and punished in the young."[2] Psychologists such as Otto Rank, C. W. Wahl, and Ernest Becker have taken this perspective a step further, arguing contra Freud that the fear of death is more primal than any kind of sexual anxiety.[3] Freud has in a sense corroborated this thesis in spite of himself: the fact that his only two fainting spells occurred when he was confronted with the issue of death hint at a deeper source of repression than the one he spent his whole life investigating.[4] As I have already suggested in the introduction to this book, the twentieth century denial of death manifests itself throughout our society, most visibly—or according to Ariès, "invisibly"—in the institutions that were established to handle this ever more distasteful reality. Hospitals and funeral homes can be considered a social reflection of our inner discomfort with the *factum brutum* of human mortality. Both create a space that, on a par with our own psychological buffers, shields us from our anguish about death. Behind their institutional walls death is either covered up through the cosmetic mask of embalming and casketing or tucked away behind the facades of bureaucracy and architectural design. In sum, the vast system of twentieth century death management has divested us of arguably the most crucial experience that defines us as human beings.

In 1969 the trained psychiatrist Elisabeth Kübler-Ross published *On Death and Dying,* an eventual bestseller that would help pave the way for a reversal of our modern alienation from death. As she states in the preface, her book "is simply an account of a new and challenging opportunity to refocus on the patient as a human being."[5] Her resolve to overturn the status of medicine as a "depersonalized science in the service of prolonging life rather than diminishing human suffering"[6] can perhaps best be understood by a consideration of her background. Raised in rural Switzerland, where technology had yet to make a significant impact on everyday life, Kübler-Ross evokes a formative incident from her youth. A local farmer, who had fallen from a tree, lay on his deathbed. Summoning not only his wife and daughters but a number of villagers as well (including the Kübler siblings), he said his good-byes, put his affairs in order, and died tranquilly in the home that he had built. At his funeral there was no embalming or other aesthetic techniques that only conceal a perfectly natural human event. This scene recalls of course the "good" or "tame" death that, in the historical scheme of Ariès, remained the dominant trend throughout the course of premodern Europe: one died at home in bed, surrounded by family and friends. Kübler-Ross's later travels through war-devastated Europe, which included contact with concentration camp survivors, only fueled her ambition to study medicine and, more importantly, to treat her patients as individual human beings rather than anonymous objects of science. But as Kübler-Ross was to discover during her clinical work in the United States, the quintessential land of modernity, death was not such a familiar and accepted part of life. As she states in this regard: "Instead the days are gone when a man was allowed to die in peace and dignity in his own home."[7]

As for the specific methodology of her book, she and her students conducted interviews with terminally ill patients, who talked with surprising candor about their condition. As a result of this approach, based on the intimacy of human communication as opposed to the standard of professional distance, we are able to learn valuable lessons from the dying: they instruct how to die more peacefully and live more fully.

Through her research Kübler-Ross famously posited five stages of dying: (1) denial/isolation, (2) anger, (3) bargaining, (4) depression, and (5) acceptance. Interestingly, these phases have been shown to conform to the emotional and psychological journey of Ivan Ilyich in Tolstoy's classic tale.[8] But the relevance of her project to the ontological views of death from Hegel to Heidegger transcends any such reductionist schematic. Kübler-Ross is simply searching for a sense of both wholeness and individuality in our modernized mode of existence, and this basic ambition unites her with a chain of German authors who have similarly endeavored to humanize death in a world that grows ever more scientistic and, to borrow a term from Foucault, subjectivistic.

Nevertheless, preserving one's dignity in the face of death is not always an easy task given the constantly changing menace of fatal diseases. The so-called epidemiologic transition from a quick death by infection to a prolonged demise by chronic illness has an ongoing effect on our relation toward mortality. As science continues to eliminate or at least retard particular threats to our existence, it influences our way of living as much as our manner of dying. Tuberculosis and pneumonia are, for instance, no longer the killers that they were for past generations. Even cancer and AIDS, once practical synonyms for death, have now become managed or at least degenerative conditions. Throughout human history, people have tended to die young and within a relatively short period of time. Even in 1900 the average life expectancy in a modernized country like the United States was 50, and for the most part one's sufferings were brief. Today we are projected to live well into our seventies and are largely guaranteed a pain-free death thanks to modern technology and medicine. But these advances can act as a double-edged sword. As numerous thanatologists have pointed out, the most prevalent form of death in our contemporary age is "medicide."[9] That is, we are medicated to death through the very scientific progress that supposedly betters life by extending it to the maximum. It is now estimated that 80 percent of deaths occur in institutions, whether hospitals, nursing homes, or other chronic-care facilities. And yet studies have shown that the number of people who prefer to die at home is as high as four to one.[10] Clearly, there is a fundamental incongruity between our human needs and the societal structures that have been designed to meet them.

In response to this discrepancy, various efforts have been undertaken to restore a semblance of dignity to the widespread technologization of death. The hospice movement is one such option that aims to "put dying back into the realm of the human."[11] Founded in 1967 by the British doctor Cicely Saunders and launched in the United States in 1974, the hospice closely attends to both the physical and emotional needs of its patients. This comprehensive approach includes home care and communal gatherings at the bedside. The terminally ill are hence enabled to die as in days of old, in accordance with the principles of the "tame death." As described by the National Hospice Organization: "Hospice provides support and care for persons in the last phases of incurable disease so that they may live as fully and as comfortably as possible. Hospice recognizes dying as part of the normal process of living and focuses on maintaining the quality of remaining life. Hospice affirms life and neither hastens nor postpones death."[12] The hospice, often defined as a philosophy rather than a method, is thus based on a totalized vision of health; it embraces a whole range of factors— bodily, psychological, and spiritual—that help shape our existence. It is as holistic in its practice as the ideas of Heidegger and others are in theory. In both cases, the human being (or its philosophical analogue known as Dasein) is perceived in terms of its overall completion, and the experience of death forms the capstone to this totality. Death consequently functions not as the brutal negation of life, but as its promise and summation.

While the hospice philosophy "neither hastens nor postpones death," other humanistic alternatives to the trend of medicalization openly advocate what they call "rational" suicide. We have seen that Nietzsche already used this term as an equivalent for "voluntary" or "free" death, and that it further harks back to the Stoic tradition of perfecting one's existence through an opportune exit. Over the last several decades, numerous right-to-die movements have been formed, including one whose name alludes to the most famous self-inflicted death in antiquity. The Hemlock Society, which bears the motto "Good life, good death," was initiated in 1980 by the English journalist Derek Humphry in response to the devastating experience of participating in the suicide of his cancer-stricken wife. Humphry later published a book that would rival the success of Kübler-Ross's *On Death and Dying*. His *Final Exit: The Practicalities of Self-Deliverance and Assisted Suicide for the Dying*[13] is a practical guide detailing procedures by which terminally ill patients can put an end to their plight. Whether or not readers actually opt for one of Humphry's panaceas, which include lethal drug dosages, inert gases, and even asphyxiation by plastic bag, his book has obviously resonated with a broad segment of the American populace. It spent 18 weeks on the *New York Times* bestseller list and has now entered a third edition since debuting in self-published form in 1991. Even the medical profession, which remains hamstrung by the illegality of assisted suicide (except in the Netherlands and Oregon), seems to sympathize with the message of Humphry's book. A 1988 Hemlock Society poll of doctors in California reveals the following statistics: 57 percent had been asked by their dying patients to aid them in "self-deliverance," 76 percent considered this option morally acceptable, and 23 percent admitted they had at least once enabled someone to die while in their care. Moreover, 51 percent stated they would practice euthanasia if it were legalized.[14] These figures, which stem no less from the very authorities that were long responsible for obscuring the relationship between life and its cessation, attest to yet another shift in attitudes about the place of death within the greater arc of human existence.

As for the arc of this study, which stretches from literature and philosophy to medicine and psychology, it is best closed with a key image that underscores the notion of death as both individual fulfillment and existential completion. As previously discussed, Rilke illustrates the holism of life and death through a metaphor that ties in with his concept of *Weltinnenraum:* "O shooting star / seen from a bridge once, a penetrating ray: / Never to forget you. Stay" (*SW* 2:104).[15] Elisabeth Kübler-Ross, although a psychiatrist rather than poet by training, employs the same literary technique and speaks with comparable eloquence in the context of her work with the terminally ill:

Watching a peaceful death of a human being reminds us of a falling star; one of the million lights in a vast sky that flares up for a brief moment only to disappear into the endless night forever. To be a therapist to a dying patient makes us aware of the uniqueness of each individual in this vast sea of humanity. It makes us aware of our finiteness, our limited lifespan. Few of us live beyond our three score and ten years and yet in that brief time most of us create and live a unique biography and weave ourselves into the fabric of human history.[16]

Notes

NOTES TO INTRODUCTION

1. In my ensuing discussion of death as a biological and cultural phenomenon I have profited from a number of secondary studies in addition to the original works mentioned. These former include: Choron, *Death and Western Thought;* Dollimore, *Death, Desire, and Loss;* Karl Löwith, "Die Freiheit zum Tode"; and Schulz, "Zum Problem des Todes."

2. Plato, *Phaedo, Complete Works,* 55 (sec. 64a).

3. Demske, *Being, Man, and Death,* 1.

4. Tolstoy, *The Death of Ivan Ilyich,* 137.

5. Demske, *Being, Man, and Death,* 2.

6. Hume, "Of Suicide," 595.

7. Ibid., 586, 587.

8. Hegel, *Philosophy of Right,* 43, 237.

9. Marcuse, "The Ideology of Death," 67.

10. Ibid., 70.

11. Ibid., 69–71.

12. Baudrillard, *Symbolic Exchange and Death,* 126.

13. Ibid., 147.

14. Ibid., 147.

15. Elias, *The Loneliness of the Dying,* 60.

16. See ibid., 12–16.

17. Lerner, "When, Why, and Where People Die," 21, 24.

18. Benoliel and Degner, "Institutional Dying," 123.

19. I am aware that in giving these particular perspectives their due, I am necessarily excluding others. Two important models that I will not consider here are Freud's theory of the death drive and the Marxist ideal of dying for the collective. With respect to the former, I fail to see any revealing connection to the dialectical and existential views that extend from Hegel to Heidegger. In this sense I concur with Baudrillard, who similarly regards Freud as an anomaly in Western thanatological thinking. (See Baudrillard, *Symbolic Exchange and Death,* 148–54.) The Marxist tradition in twentieth century Germany, on the other hand, is more directly involved with figures like

Heidegger, whose views on death have been soundly criticized by Adorno, Marcuse, Bertolt Brecht, and others. I have to some extent already explored this debate between Marxism and existentialism by focusing on Brecht's effort to assert the social(ist) over the individualized function of death. See Ireton, "Brechts 'Zertrümmerung' von Heidegger." Further examination of this issue in the present context would, however, only lead too far astray.

20. Two representative voices, one German and one Anglo-American, in this regard are: Henrich, "Hegel und Hölderlin"; and Solomon, *In the Spirit of Hegel,* 136–40.

21. Solomon, *In the Spirit of Hegel,* 59.

Notes to Chapter 1, "Hegel"

1. Hoffmeister, *Briefe von und an Hegel,* 1:18.

2. Although there is a complete lack of biographical testimony as to the precise nature of this intellectual exchange, one can get some idea of its intensity from a scene described by Hölderlin's stepbrother, Karl Gok, during a visit to Frankfurt in the spring of 1797. Hölderlin immediately introduced Gok to Hegel, who received him warmly. But the newcomer's presence was soon forgotten amidst a passionate philosophical dispute between the two ex-seminarians. See Hölderlin, *Sämtliche Werke* 7, 82.

3. Hoffmeister, *Briefe von und an Hegel,* 1:42. See also Hölderlin, *SWB* 3, 243.

4. This is also the thesis of Christoph Jamme, who more specifically maintains that Hölderlin's words to Hegel function as a maxim for their common philosophical campaign against rationalistic, Enlightment thinking. Jamme's study, an in-depth account of the interaction between the two reunited colleagues, even draws its title from Hölderlin's programmatic phrase. See Jamme, *"Ein ungelehrtes Buch,"* 139.

5. Due to his unhappiness with the demands of his job (the official reason given in letters) but probably more because of an escalating affair with his employer's wife, Susette Gontard, Hölderlin left Frankfurt in September of 1798, taking up residence in nearby Homburg von der Höhe. This move did not, however, greatly affect his contact with Hegel. Hölderlin traveled to Frankfurt once a month in order to exchange love letters with Susette, while Hegel, for his part, often visited his friend in Homburg.

6. See for example Lukács, *The Young Hegel,* 64; and Kaufmann, "The Young Hegel and Religion," 62–63.

7. I am dispensing with a discussion of Hegel's "Life of Jesus" essay, which is not included in his *Werke* since it contains many of the same ideas as his other early religious fragments. The interested reader can find this text in *Three Essays,* 104–65.

8. Jamme, *"Ein ungelehrtes Buch,"* 140.

9. The text is often included in editions of Hölderlin's and Schelling's works. For an overview of its reception and an analysis of its content, see Jamme and Schneider, *Mythologie der Vernunft;* and Hansen, *Das älteste Systemprogramm.* For more on the theory of Hegel's authorship, see Pöggeler, "Hegel, der Verfasser."

10. Hegel, *Selections,* 86–87.

11. Cassirer, "Hölderlin und der deutsche Idealismus," 120. Although Cassirer speaks here of Hölderlin rather than Hegel, his words easily apply to both, as is later

implied in his essay. This will also become clear in my coming observations on Hegel's unification philosophy.

12. Lukács, *The Young Hegel*, 100.

13. For an English version, see "The Frankfurt Sketch on Faith and Being," trans. H. S. Harris, *Miscellaneous Writings of G. W. F. Hegel*, 137.

14. Hegel, *Miscellaneous Writings of G. W. F. Hegel*, 134.

15. For an exhaustive account of the rise of dialectics in Hegel as well as Hölderlin and Schelling, see Kondylis, *Die Entstehung der Dialektik*. For a much briefer discussion of unification philosophy in the eighteenth century (e.g. Shaftsbury, Hemsterhuis, Herder, Schiller) and its impact on Hegel and Hölderlin, see Henrich, "Hegel und Hölderlin."

16. Hegel, *Science of Logic*, 82.

17. For a critique of this widespread misunderstanding of Hegel's dialectic, see Kaufmann, *Hegel: A Reinterpretation*, 153–62.

18. Dilthey, *Die Jugendgeschichte Hegels*, 68.

19. Ibid., 138–57.

20. Lukács, *The Young Hegel*, 209.

21. Hegel, *The Encyclopaedia Logic*, 128.

22. Hegel, *Jenaer Realphilosophie*, 166.

23. Some examples that offer an orientation include: Forster, *Hegel's Idea of a Phenomenology of Spirit*, 248–55, 316–22; Kelly, "Notes on Hegel's 'Lordship and Bondage,'" 189–217; and Solomon, *In the Spirit of Hegel*, 425–55. Beyond their lucid and nuanced analyses, all three authors discuss much of the previous literature on the topic.

24. Solomon, who generally maintains that the master-slave dialectic is ahistorical or in his words "*pre*-social" (*In the Spirit of Hegel*, 427), nevertheless remarks, "The imagery here is . . . that of a feudal lord, growing fat and lazy on the sweat of his servant" (ibid., 451). In the more recent study by Forster, which aims to correct previous scholarship, *Herrschaft* and *Knechtschaft* are shown to have definite historical referents. Forster argues that Hegel drew on J. F. Reitemeier's study from 1789, *Geschichte und Zustand der Sklaverei und Leibeigenschaft in Griechenland* (*The History and Condition of Slavery and Bondage in Greece*), which examines the dramatic growth of slavery in fifth century Athens as a result of the Persian Wars. The conflict between master and slave should thus be read as an historical commentary on political oppression and freedom in the ancient world. Despite Forster's convincing arguments (see *Hegel's Idea of a Phenomenology of Spirit*, esp. 316–22), the actual language that Hegel employs throughout his parable of *Herr* and *Knecht* has a broad range in connotation and is by no means historically restrictive.

25. Solomon, *In the Spirit of Hegel*, 450.

26. See the first chapter of Taylor, *Hegel*, 3–50.

27. Ibid., 28.

28. Solomon, *In the Spirit of Hegel*, 395.

29. Findlay, *Hegel: A Re-Examination*, 116.

30. Solomon, *In the Spirit of Hegel*, 549.

31. Taylor, *Hegel*, 121.

32. Also to be found in Heidegger, *The Phenomenology of Religious Life,* esp. 67–74.

33. Baugh, *French Hegel.* "The Anthropological Turn" is the title of the first chapter and also the general theme of chapter 2.

34. For a discussion of some early twentieth century French Hegelians who anticipate Wahl but whose impact on the greater philosophical scene in France was fairly minor, see Baugh, *French Hegel,* 10–17.

35. See Koyré, "Hegel à Iéna," 135–73.

36. Hyppolite, *Genesis and Structure,* 301.

37. Ibid., 150.

38. Ibid., 301.

39. Ibid., 49. Jean Wahl had already emphasized this point. Compare for instance the following remark, which no doubt inspired Hyppolite: "Thus, generally speaking, what Hegel examines in the *Phenomenology* are not philosophic doctrines, but ways of life; or better put, the two are inseparable" Jean Wahl, *Le malheur de la conscience dans la philosophie de Hegel,* 7; my translation.

40. Hyppolite, *Genesis and Structure,* 496.

41. Ibid., 18.

42. See ibid., 341–44, 567–70.

43. Ibid., 343.

44. See Hyppolite, "The Concept of Existence."

45. Ibid., 24.

46. See ibid., 26, 29.

47. Ibid., 28–29. The last sentence of this passage has been omitted in the English translation, but I include it here due to its importance as a summation of the existentialist attitude. The original French reads: "Son *exister* est cet acte même." See Hyppolite, "L'existence dans la *Phénoménologie* de Hegel," 100.

48. Hyppolite, "The Concept of Existence," 30; "L'existence dans la *Phénoménologie* de Hegel," 101.

49. See Merleau-Ponty, "Hegel's Existentialism," 63–70.

50. Ibid., 65.

51. Ibid., 67.

52. Baugh argues that this reputation is undeserved, for interpreters such as Jean Wahl and Koyré anticipated and indeed directly influenced many of Kojève's ideas. See Baugh, *French Hegel,* 1, 27.

53. Aimé Patri, "Dialectique du maître et de l'esclave," *Le contrat social* 5, no. 4 (July–August 1961): 234. Cited in *IRH* vii.

54. Kojève's lectures have traditionally been regarded as a major influence on Sartre's *Being and Nothingness,* but recent scholarship tends to be skeptical of these claims. See for instance Baugh, *French Hegel,* 98–100.

55. Albert Camus and Maurice Blanchot deal more thoroughly with Kirilov's death and the question of freedom. See Camus, "Absurd Creation," 77–83; and Blanchot, *The Space of Literature,* 96–100.

56. Kojève points to an earlier statement by Hegel that does in fact support the suicidal nature of the fight for recognition. As he quotes from Hegel's lectures at the University of Jena: "It appears to each consciousness that it seeks the death of another;

but it seeks its own, [it is] suicide insofar as it exposes itself to *danger*." Hegel, *Jenaer Realphilosophie*, 211. See also *IRH* 248n. I have slightly modified Kojève's translation from the German.

57. Jean Wahl, *Le malheur de la conscience dans la philosophie de Hegel*, 72. My translation. Karl Rosenkranz's classic biography of Hegel from 1844 provided Wahl with this anecdote.

NOTES TO CHAPTER 2, "HÖLDERLIN"

1. As modern linguistics has shown, the *Ur-* in *Urteil* does not actually derive from the common prefix *ur-*, which can be added to nouns and adjectives to denote an originary or arch- dimension. *Urteil* stems rather from the Old High German *urteil*, whose *ur-* prefix corresponds to the Modern High German *er-*, as in *erteilen*. In fairness to Hölderlin, it should however be noted that he adopted this false etymology from Fichte's lectures at Jena. Hegel, incidentally, draws a similar connection in his *Spirit of Christianity* essay, suggesting that through judgment (*Urteil*) one divides (*teilt*) the greater whole into more manageable parts. This ultimately remains an act of positivistic subjugation (see *W* 1:335/*ETW* 222–23).

2. See for example his letters to Hegel from January 26, 1795 and to Schiller from September 4, 1795. The former has been translated in *ELT* 124–26 (see also *SWB* 3:175–77). For the latter, see *SWB* 3:203–04.

3. For an exhaustive study of Hölderlin's intellectual development during this crucial period, see Henrich, *Der Grund im Bewußtsein*. Henrich devotes special attention to the fragment "Judgment and Being" and to Hölderlin's reception of such philosophical forebears as Fichte.

4. Both Hölderlin and Hegel also tend to associate Geist with *Gest* (yeast) and *Gischt* (foam), two terms that are related to the verb *gären:* "to ferment." The idea here is that Geist has an effervescent quality that inspires and stirs us to action. This connection between spirit and inner fermentation/agitation is evident throughout *The Death of Empedocles* and occasionally in *Hyperion*, whose hero is for instance called *der gärende Mensch*, translated as the "turbulent man" (*SWB* 2:99/*H* 72). The relation between the two notions is, however, not supported by etymology. For further discussion, see Zuberbühler, *Hölderlins Erneuerung*, 51–52.

5. Scholarly theories about the "eccentric path" and its function tend to vary widely, which is no doubt due to the fact that Hölderlin himself does not elaborate on it, thus leaving it wide open for interpretation. For some representative examples of this disagreement, compare the following studies: Schadewaldt, "Das Bild der exzentrischen Bahn bei Hölderlin"; Ryan, *Hölderlins "Hyperion"; and the review of Ryan's book by Gaier, Review of *Hölderlins "Hyperion."*

6. See *The Symposium*, 187a, where the phrase in question appears in the middle voice, as it does in the original fragment by Heraclitus: "*hen . . . diapheromenon . . . heautô.*" Plato, *Complete Works*, 471.

7. See for instance Diels and Kranz, *Die Fragmente der Vorsokratiker,* fragment 22B51. Since there are several editions of the pre-Socratic fragments available in both English and German, I will as a general practice give the fragment number based on

the standard numeration found in Hermann Diels and Walther Kranz, *Die Fragmente der Vorsokratiker,* 6th ed. (Berlin: Weidmann, 1951). I will also refer to the more recent and highly useful study by Richard McKirahan, *Philosophy before Socrates: An Introduction with Texts and Commentary* (Indianapolis: Hackett, 1994). Here the full fragment by Heraclitus is translated and elaborated as follows: "They do not understand how, though at variance with itself, it agrees with itself [or, how by being at variance with itself it agrees with itself; more literally, how being (or by being) brought apart it is brought together]. It is a backwards-turning [or, backwards-stretching] attunement like that of the bow and lyre." McKirahan, *Philosophy before Socrates,* 120–21.

8. Various critics have pointed to the connections between the *Phenomenology* and the uniquely German genre of the *Bildungsroman.* In his classic study *Natural Supernaturalism,* M. H. Abrams for instance discusses Hegel's philosophical narrative in juxtaposition with *Hyperion, Faust,* and works by Novalis. See Abrams, *Natural Supernaturalism,* 225–52. My own discussion of *Hyperion's* structure partly draws on Abrams's insights but has also benefited from Ryan, *Hölderlins "Hyperion,"* esp. 223–30; and Santner, *Friedrich Hölderlin,* esp. 45–55.

9. Walter Silz draws attention to many of the unrealistic and implausible details of the exchange between Hyperion and Bellarmin. Although his points of critique are for the most part well taken, they do not alter the fact that Hölderlin exploits the genre of the epistolary novel in order to create a metalevel of reflection from which the narrator reconstructs his experiences through previously written letters. See Silz, *Hölderlin's "Hyperion,"* esp. 17–23.

10. This passage from Coleridge's letters is quoted by Abrams, *Natural Supernaturalism,* 271.

11. Santner, *Friedrich Hölderlin,* 54.

12. Abrams, *Natural Supernaturalism,* 184. For a complete discussion of the Romantic spiral, see 183–87.

13. Hegel, *The Encyclopaedia Logic,* 39.

14. Among the few scholars that have recognized the importance of death in *Hyperion* are Ryan, *Hölderlins "Hyperion,"* esp. 183–205; and Bertaux, *Friedrich Hölderlin,* esp. 617–25.

15. See Bertaux, *Friedrich Hölderlin,* 619.

16. For some interesting conjectures on why the work was never finished, see Bertaux, *Friedrich Hölderlin,* 308–09; and Ulrich Gaier, *Hölderlin: Eine Einführung,* 318–19.

17. For an overview of the editorial practices throughout the nineteenth and twentieth centuries, see Beißner, "Hölderlins Trauerspiel."

18. See Schmidt's commentary "Zur Textkonstitution" in *SWB* 2:1113–18. See also the more detailed article by Katharina Grätz, Schmidt's editorial assistant: "Der 'Empedocles.'"

19. See *SW* 1:557. Stefan Zweig and Johannes Hoffmeister have more directly compared the fragmentary form of *Empedocles* with a Greek torso. See Zweig, *Der Kampf mit dem Dämon,* 110; and Hoffmeister, *Hölderlins Empedokles,* 5–6.

20. Gadamer, *Truth and Method,* 99.

21. For a thorough study of the pre-Socratic Empedocles and his modern reincarnations in the work of Herder, Goethe, Schiller, Hölderlin, and others, see Kranz, *Empedokles*.

22. Diogenes Laertius, *Lives of Eminent Philosophers* 2:385–89 (book 8, sec. 71–74).

23. As already indicated, Horace speaks, however sarcastically, of Empedocles's cold-blooded leap into Etna's flames. Another central work of antiquity that Hölderlin undoubtedly studied at Maulbronn and Tübingen, Lucretius's *De rerum natura* (*On the Nature of Things*), does not directly mention Empedocles's death, but nonetheless links the philosopher with the volcano. See Lucretius, *De rerum natura,* 53 (book 1, vv. 716–33).

24. Opinions vary with regard to this question. For a sampling of scholarly literature that deals more thoroughly with the role of Empedocles's cosmogony in Hölderlin's drama, see for instance Hölscher, *Empedokles und Hölderlin;* and Harrison, *Holderlin and Greek Literature,* 121–59.

25. Readers interested in these philological matters are referred to: Osborne, "Empedocles Recycled."

26. Fragment 117; McKirahan, *Philosophy before Socrates,* 253. The reader should be aware that although McKirahan gives the standard Diels-Kranz number, he does not always follow their order, arranging the fragments, rather, according to topics. Hence, for the following translations I will cite both DK fragment number and the page on which they appear in *Philosophy before Socrates*.

27. Fragment 126; McKirahan, *Philosophy before Socrates,* 253.

28. Fragment 136; McKirahan, *Philosophy before Socrates,* 254.

29. Here and for all following definitions of Greek words, I draw on the standard Liddell and Scott, *Greek-English Lexicon,* 7th ed.

30. Fragment 115; McKirahan, *Philosophy before Socrates,* 235.

31. See Fragment 146; McKirahan, *Philosophy before Socrates,* 253.

32. Fragment 112; McKirahan, *Philosophy before Socrates,* 232.

33. For the most comprehensive study of the genesis of Hölderlin's *Empedocles* project, see Birkenhauer, *Legende und Dichtung.*

34. See Goethe, *West-Östlicher Divan, Werke,* 2:18–19.

35. It is worth recalling that the second volume of *Hyperion* (which did not see print until 1799) and much of *Empedocles* overlap in their genesis. The simultaneity of these two projects is illustrated in the fact that his pupil Henry Gontard's notebook, into which Hölderlin sometimes copied his literary plans, contains not only the "Frankfurt Plan" but also a number of sketches to *Hyperion.*

36. See in chronological order: Schadewaldt, "Die Empedokles-Tragödie Hölderlins"; Staiger, "Der Opfertod von Hölderlins Empedokles"; Hoffmeister, *Hölderlins Empedokles,* 49; Söring, *Die Dialektik der Rechtfertigung;* and Kocziszky, "Die Empedokles-Fragmente als Übersetzung."

37. Hölderlin here seems to be mixing testimonia in Diogenes, confusing Empedocles with his grandfather of the same name, who rode to victory in the 71st Olympiad. Cf. Diogenes Laertius, *Lives of Eminent Philosophers,* 369 (book 8, sec. 52). There is, however, no evidence in Diogenes that Empedocles the younger

participated in chariot racing let alone in Olympic competition. His only attested adventure with a chariot in fact led to anything but a sublime death: "But afterwards, as he was going in a carriage to Messene to attend some festival, he fell and broke his thigh; this brought an illness which caused his death at the age of seventy-seven" (Diogenes Laertius, *Lives of Eminent Philosophers,* 387–89; book 8, sec. 73).

38. Cf. the chorus in Sophocles's *Oedipus at Colonus,* vv. 1224–25.

39. See Staiger, *Der Geist der Liebe und das Schicksal,* 94–95; and Allemann, *Hölderlin und Heidegger,* 18n. These views of Staiger and Allemann are to some extent a reaction against early interpretations that emphasize the themes of guilt and atonement in the drama as well as in Hölderlin's general thinking. See for instance Böhm, *Hölderlin,* 1:362–68; and Böckmann, *Hölderlin und seine Götter,* 260–67, 278–82. For a more general assessment of this problem of *Wortschuld* in the drama and the difficulties it has posed for scholars, see Haberer, *Sprechen, Schweigen, Schauen,* 58–63.

40. There is hardly a major study of Hölderlin's drama that does not to some extent address the parallels between Empedocles and Christ. Among the scholars that have pointed to the "genetically vivid" representation of guilt in the drama are Beda Allemann and Johannes Hoffmeister. See Allemann, *Hölderlin und Heidegger,* 18; Hoffmeister, *Hölderlins Empedokles,* 89–90.

41. See Hoffmeister, *Hölderlins Empedokles,* 89–90.

42. See Lessing, "Wie die Alten den Tod gebildet," 181.

43. The most recent edition of Hölderlin's works dubs the essay "Über das Tragische" (Concerning the Tragic) and reserves the title "Grund zum Empedokles" for only one major section of the text. See *SWB* 2:425–39; 1187–91.

44. See for example Meetz, "Zu Hölderlins Quellen für den 'Empedocles,'" 392; and Hölscher, "Empedokles von Akragas," 39.

45. See Beißner, "Hölderlins Trauerspiel," 71.

46. For a more detailed treatment of these parallels, see Jamme, *"Ein ungelehrtes Buch,"* 296–316. See also Peters and Schäfer, "Selbstopfer and Repräsentation," esp. 296–302.

NOTES TO CHAPTER 3, "NIETZSCHE"

1. I borrow this expression from both the thesis and title of David Farrell Krell's *Postponements: Woman, Sensuality, and Death in Nietzsche.* Here Krell discusses Nietzsche's *Empedocles* plans from 1870 to 1871 and their "postponement" to the *Zarathustra* project of the 1880s. He also does not ignore the influence of Hölderlin's drama. For my own discussion of this important link between Hölderlin and Nietzsche, I cannot but defer to Krell, though most of my ideas were formed independently and do not always overlap with his. Rather than continually footnote Krell's observations, I refer the reader in advance to especially the second and third chapters of *Postponements,* 33–69. Krell has also published a book whose first part offers a sometimes deviant— or deliberately "lunatic"—analysis of Hölderlin's *Empedocles.* See Krell, *Lunar Voices,* esp. 3–51. I have, however, profited little from this rather rhapsodic study. For a more informative, philological article dealing with the genesis of Nietzsche's

Empedocles project, see: Söring, "Nietzsches Empedokles-Plan"; and for a broader exploration of this complex, see Fóti, "Empedocles and Tragic Thought." Despite the promising title of this last essay, one finds only a limited analysis of the actual affinities between Hölderlin, Nietzsche, and Heidegger with respect to the tragedy of Empedocles.

2. Nietzsche, *Werke in drei Bänden,* 3:98.

3. Ibid., 3:96.

4. Ibid., 3:96–97.

5. Cited in Janz, *Friedrich Nietzsche,* 1:80.

6. See Nietzsche, *Kritische Gesamtausgabe,* 2.1:75–167. This collection of Nietzsche's philological writings from 1867 to 1873 also contains two other articles on Diogenes published in *Rheinisches Museum:* "Analecta Laertiana" and "Beiträge zur Quellenkunde und Kritik des Laertius Diogenes." See 169–90. and 191–245.

7. See Janz, *Friedrich Nietzsche,* 1:191.

8. See Pindar, *Pythia* 2, v. 72. In most of the extant manuscripts, this phrase contains a key participle, *mathôn,* which tends to alter if not undercut the urgency and pithiness of the imperative. The original text reads *"genoi hoios essi mathôn,"* which can be translated along the following lines: "Become such a person as you have learned to be." For further details concerning Nietzsche's appropriation of Pindar, see Collins, "On the Aesthetics of the Deceiving Self." According to Collins, Nietzsche applies Pindar's verse to his own notion of self-construction and self-aestheticization. Karl Jaspers and Alexander Nehemas stress the more general notion of freedom that Nietzsche seeks to express through his frequent invocation of this Pindarian phrase. See Jaspers, *Nietzsche,* 155–59; and Nehemas, *Nietzsche: Life as Literature,* 170–99.

9. Jochen Schmidt does not include these verses of Pausanias in his edition of the play, but previous editors do. See for instance the *Stuttgarter Ausgabe* by Friedrich Beißner: Hölderlin, *Der Tod des Empedokles, Sämtliche Werke,* 4:127.

10. *Einai,* the verb "to be," exists only in the present and future. For all other tenses, pasts and perfects, *gignesthai* (to become) is used.

11. In his editorial variants, Friedrich Beißner shows that Hölderlin changed the imperative *Seie* to *Werde,* an act that only underscores the peculiar relation between these two verbs. See Hölderlin, *Übersetzungen, Sämtliche Werke,* 5:390.

12. Cited in Janz, *Friedrich Nietzsche,* 1:227.

13. He announced this course for the winter semester of 1869–70, his second term at the University. Whether he actually held the lecture during this period cannot be determined. It is known, however, that he did so in the summer semester of 1872, the winter of 1875–76, and again in the summer of 1876. See Nietzsche, *Vorlesungsaufzeichnungen (WS 1871/72–WS 1874/75), Kritische Gesamtausgabe,* vol. 2.4.

14. For his explanation of this unorthodox grouping, see Nietzsche, *Kritische Gesamtausgabe,* 2.4:214.

15. Ibid., 2.4:318.

16. Ibid., 2.4:321.

17. Ibid., 2.4:321.

18. A brief note from 1875 draws a connection between Faust, Hölderlin, and Empedocles, yet only further obscures the problem of tragedy that Nietzsche is

wrestling with: "Passage about Faust / Hölderlin / Conclusion Empedocles" (*KSA* 8:9). One possible interpretation of this memo would be that Nietzsche was working on the final stages of an *Empedocles* drama and sought to integrate a quote from *Faust* as well as aspects from Hölderlin's work.

19. Heidegger has written an essay on Anaximander's fragment, a near word-for-word analysis of the Greek, in which he presents his own—typically idiosyncratic—suggestions for translation against both Nietzsche's and the standard one by Diels. See "Anaximander's Saying," in *OBT* 242–81. It should be noted that the Greek text upon which Nietzsche based his translation does not contain the key word *allêlois* but that an earlier version discovered by Diels does. The reflexive function of this dative radically alters the implication of the fragment. Compare for instance the translation by Diels, who renders *allêlois* as *einander* or "each other": "But where things derive their coming into being, there their passing away also occurs according to necessity; for they pay *each other* (my emphasis) punishment and penalty for their dastardliness according to firmly established time" (Cited in *OBT* 242.) With this single, seemingly minor, textual amendment the cosmic necessity of Nietzsche's point is undermined. Still, interpreting the pre-Socratics is by no means an exact science and often gives better insight into the preconceptions of the modern interpreter than into the original thoughts of the ancient author.

20. In some instances I will indicate the aphorism or notebook number that corresponds to quotations from Nietzsche, *KSA*. This information will follow the usual volume and page citation.

21. Overtones of *Oedipus Rex* (e.g., the plague and Empedocles's role as king) cannot be ignored, and Nietzsche no doubt also had this tragedy in mind, which Aristotle of course praised as a model of the genre.

22. *Poetics, The Basic Works of Aristotle,* 1460 (49b).

23. Janz, *Friedrich Nietzsche,* 1:389.

24. Krell, *Lunar Voices,* 5.

25. See Janz, *Friedrich Nietzsche,* 1:390.

26. See the published lecture by Heidegger from 1953 "Wer ist Nietzsches Zarathustra?" in *GA* 7:99–124. See also the article that bears the title of Heidegger's guiding question: Wohlfart, "Wer ist Nietzsches Zarathustra?" Of course there exists a plethora of further interpretations dealing with the figure and function of Zarathustra, but this is hardly the place to give them their due. Only select studies relevant to the topic of death will be considered here.

27. Wohlfart, "Wer ist Nietzsches Zarathustra?" 324.

28. See Janz, *Friedrich Nietzsche,* 2:223.

29. See Wohlfart, "Wer ist Nietzsches Zarathustra?" 319. Wohlfart probes further into the possibility that Zarathustra is Nietzsche's "portrait" of Heraclitus. This connection has long been recognized in Nietzsche scholarship and readers will find useful references in Wohlfart's article.

30. A number of parallels between *The Death of Empedocles* and *Thus Spoke Zarathustra* are discussed by Vivarelli, "Empedokles und Zarathustra." Readers in search of parallel motifs, especially with regard to language and imagery, are referred to this article, which is largely a mechanical compilation of quotes drawn from both

texts and juxtaposed for the sake of comparison. Here in my analysis, I will address aspects that Vivarelli either overlooks or underemphasizes. This includes the theme of death, which she explores thoroughly enough given the scope of her article, but which I will flesh out even more through a discussion of Nietzsche's larger *Zarathustra* project and a consideration of his other writings.

31. Compare the following excerpt from Hyperion's critique: "It is a hard saying, and yet I speak it because it is the truth: I can think of no people more at odds with themselves than the Germans. You see artisans, but no men, thinkers, but no men, priests, but no men, masters and servants, but no men, minors and adults, but no men— is this not like a battlefield on which hacked-off hands and arms and every other member are scattered about, while the lifeblood flows from them to vanish in the sand?" (*SWB* 2:168/*H* 128).

32. In part 2 of the published version there is still mention of a nameless "fire-spewing mountain" which, like Etna, lies on an island. Zarathustra in fact enters the caverns of this volcano, but death does not await him there. See the chapter "On Great Events" in *KSA* 4:167–71/*Z* 241–45.

33. Von Saaz, *Death and The Ploughman,* 19.

34. Von Saaz, *Death and The Ploughman,* 11.

35. Quoted in Minois, *History of Suicide,* 92.

36. In his correspondence, Nietzsche sometimes refers to his own body, which was perpetually wracked by ill health, as a malfunctioning "machine." See *KSB* 5:64, 413; *KSB* 8:269, 347.

37. See Jaspers, *Nietzsche,* 324–25.

38. Kaufmann, *Nietzsche: Philosopher, Psychologist, Antichrist,* 402. Kaufmann maintains that Zarathustra's speech contrasts Socrates's free death with that of Jesus, who died not at the right time but "too early."

39. See Hirzel, "Der Selbstmord," 244. In my discussion of suicide in antiquity I rely on this lengthy three-part article as well as the following other sources: Benz, *Das Todesproblem in der Stoischen Philosophie;* Rist, *Stoic Philosophy,* 233–55; Grisé, *Le suicide dans la Rome antique;* and Minois, *History of Suicide,* 42–56.

40. Minois, *History of Suicide,* 43.

41. Michel Foucault, "The Ethics of the Concern for Self as a Practice of Freedom," *Ethics: Subjectivity and Truth,* ed. Paul Rabinow, vol. 1 of *Essential Works of Foucault 1954–1984* (New York: The New Press, 1997), 286.

42. See Foucault, "On the Genealogy of Ethics," *Ethics: Subjectivity and Truth,* 262.

43. Foucault, "The Hermeneutic of the Subject," *Ethics: Subjectivity and Truth,* 104.

44. Seneca, *Ad Lucilium epistulae morales,* 1:191 (letter 26, sec. 10).

45. Ibid., 2:55 (letter 69, sec. 6).

46. Ibid., 2:65 (letter 70, sec. 14).

47. Ibid., 2:59 (letter 70, sec. 4).

48. Ibid., 2:171 (letter 77, sec. 4).

49. Ibid., 2:181 (letter 77, sec. 20).

50. See Solomon, *In the Spirit of Hegel,* 20.

51. For a discussion of suicide within the context of English literature and culture, see Minois, *History of Suicide,* 179–209.

52. See for instance the classic study by Bonhoffer, *Die Ethik des Stoikers Epictet,* 26–39.

53. Elsewhere I have attempted to interpret free death as a rhetorical device in connection with Zarathustra's more famous doctrine of eternal recurrence. See Ireton, "Heidegger's Ontological Analysis of Death," esp. 416–18.

54. Blanchot, *The Space of Literature,* 97.

55. For a detailed and graphic account of Nietzsche's routine physical ordeals, see Zweig, "Friedrich Nietzsche," in *Der Kampf mit dem Dämon,* a partial English translation of which can be found in Walter Kaufmann's commentary to *Thus Spoke Zarathustra* (*Z* 116–17).

56. To some extent, David Ferrell Krell discusses these postponements of Zarathustra's death, though more in light of the two other themes, woman and sensuality, that distinguish his book. See especially the chapter "Pana" in Krell, *Postponements,* 53–69.

NOTES TO CHAPTER 4, "RILKE"

1. For these differences between Jacobsen and Rilke, I am indebted to Buddeberg, *Rilke: Eine innere Biographie,* 150–51.

2. Brodsky, *Russia in the Works of Rilke,* 153.

3. For an illuminating analysis of Malte's identity in light of these three realms, see Sokel, "Zwischen Existenz und Weltinnenraum." For an English version of this essay, see Sokel, "The Devolution of the Self." Sokel also devotes a great deal of attention to the theme of death. Other revealing discussions of this major theme include: Blanchot, *The Space of Literature,* 120–59; Brodsky, *Russia in the Works of Rilke,* 153–76; and Ziolkowski, *Dimensions of the Modern Novel,* 225–35. For the most extensive study of death in Rilke, but one that has little to say about this theme in *Malte,* see Rehm, *Orpheus, der Dichter und die Toten,* 379–669.

4. For a discussion of Tolstoy's impact on *The Notebooks of Malte Laurids Brigge,* see Brodsky, *Russia in the Works of Rilke,* 159–76. Rilke originally intended to round off his *Malte* novel with a meditation on Tolstoy, "that great fearer of death" (*SW* 6:967). This so-called *Tolstoi-Schluß* (Tolstoy conclusion) exists in two versions and can be found in *SW* 6:967–78.

5. Tolstoy, *The Death of Ivan Ilyich,* 127.

6. Blanchot, *The Space of Literature,* 128.

7. Mann, *Buddenbrooks,* 492.

8. It has also been suggested that Rilke based Brigge's death scene on accounts that he found in Danish sources such as the historical *Posthumous Papers from the Reventlow Family Circle* and Jens Peter Jacobsen's novel *Marie Grubbe.* See Schoolfield, "*Die Aufzeichnungen des Malte Laurids Brigge,*" 160.

9. The Swabian poet Christian Daniel Schubart, with whom Hölderlin was personally acquainted, was buried alive in 1791. According to Felix Bertaux, this death had a profound impact on Hölderlin, but it remains unclear whether he learned of all the grisly details, as for instance described in one report: "Alerted by loud noises from

underground, the gravedigger dug up and opened the casket on the evening after the burial . . . and in the opened casket he found Schubart lying face down, with his nails all bloody and scratched, but lifeless." Quoted in Bertaux, *Friedrich Hölderlin,* 609–10.

10. For a revealing discussion of the novel's structure, including some of the implausibilities concerning Malte's Parisian journals and the external reality they record, see Hoffmann, "Zum dichterischen Verfahren in Rilkes *Aufzeichnungen des Malte Laurids Brigge.*" Numerous other studies examine the structural and narrative dimensions of the novel. See for instance: Ziolkowski, *Dimensions of the Modern Novel,* 3–36; Fülleborn, "Form und Sinn der *Aufzeichnungen des Malte Laurids Brigge,*" 175–98; and Stephens, *Rilkes Malte Laurids Brigge.*

11. Andreas Huyssen has probed the modernist dimensions of the novel based in part on this issue of fragmentation. See Huyssen "Paris/Childhood." Huyssen contends that Malte's experiences of disjuncture derive from his fear of death and points out that they go back as far as his childhood. While this is certainly true on a semantic level (Malte even uses the word "fragment" in the context of his memories of Urnekloster), my more structural analysis will show that the novel becomes less splintered as Malte moves progressively backwards and, so to speak, picks up the pieces of his past.

12. He read the Brigge death scene on November 8, 1907 at a Viennese bookshop where the audience included Hugo von Hofmannsthal. A few days earlier, on November 3, he recited the Christine Brahe story at a literary club in Prague. See Schoolfield, "*Die Aufzeichnungen des Malte Laurids Brigge,*" 160, 162.

13. Rilke claimed to have had contact with a number of spirits that haunted the various castles in which he took up residence, including Duino and Muzot. He even published a series of poems supposedly dictated to him by Count C. W., a deceased inhabitant of Schloß Irchel in Switzerland. See "Aus dem Nachlaß des Grafen C. W.," *SW* 2:112–29.

14. Blanchot, *The Space of Literature,* 135.

15. Ibid., 135.

16. The English translation of this lengthy letter omits one relatively brief section of the original text. For the missing lines, see *Br* 513–14.

17. Gass, *Reading Rilke,* 167–68.

18. For this quote and the account of Rilke's two visions, see Princess Marie von Thurn und Taxis-Hohenlohe, *Erinnerungen an Rainer Maria Rilke,* 80–81.

19. In a letter Rilke refers to the cup's complete motto "Faith, Hope, Charity," thereby underscoring his critique of Christian values (see *Br* 516; *SL* 267).

20. Some of the studies from which I have profited for a better understanding of Rilke's complex *Elegies* include: Guardini, *Rilkes Deutung des Daseins;* Steiner, *Rilkes Duineser Elegien;* and Komar, *Transcending Angels.*

21. This statement cannot be completely corroborated but is invoked by Angelloz, *Rilke: L'évolution spirituelle du poète,* 322. Angelloz, who translated the *Elegies* into French and edited various other works by Rilke, does not reveal his source for this ostensible and perhaps ultimately apocryphal quote.

22. The play *Madame La Mort* by Rachilde (pseudonym of Marguerite Eymery Vallette) probably provided Rilke with the name for his figure. In this piece, written

in 1891, the eponymous main character also has an allegorical function, but is not a hatmaker. For more on this connection, see Judith Ryan, *Rilke, Modernism, and Poetic Tradition,* 192–93.

23. According to the philosopher Rudolf Kassner, a close friend of Rilke's and one to whom he dedicated the "Eighth Elegy," the second line of the sixth originally lacked the key qualifier *beinah* (almost), as Rilke was of the opinion that the fig tree did not blossom at all before producing its fruit. Kassner, however, set this misconception straight and Rilke inserted the necessary adverb. This anecdote serves to show the extreme rate of acceleration that Rilke envisioned for his metaphor. See Kassner, *Rilke: Gesammelte Erinnerungen,* 33. For further botanical observations on the fig tree and the later image of the hazel bush in the "Tenth Elegy," see Loose, "Notes on Rilke's *Duineser Elegien,*" 430–34.

24. Komar, *Transcending Angels,* 109–110. See also Komar, "Rilke's Sixth Duino Elegy."

25. For the most comprehensive study of Rilke's relation to Hölderlin, see Singer, *Rilke und Hölderlin.* Singer mentions three motifs from Hölderlin's poetry that play a role in the "Sixth Elegy": enthusiasm (*Begeisterung*), destiny (*Schicksal*), and constellations (*Sternbilder*). However, he discounts any relation with respect to the motif of the hero, which he attributes more to the influence of Rudolf Kassner. Furthermore, he completely ignores the theme of death.

26. See Schuler, "Vom Wesen der ewigen Stadt," *Fragmente und Vorträge aus dem Nachlaß,* 157. Also found in *Kosmogonische Augen: Gesammelte Schriften,* 219.

27. Schuler, *Fragmente und Vorträge aus dem Nachlaß,* 273.

28. See Freeman, *Life of a Poet: Rilke,* 510. Freeman cites from unpublished sources belonging to Rilke's literary estate.

29. Rilke's usage of the term "the open" in his first "Erlebnis" sketch from 1913, two years before he met Schuler, seems to be more idiomatic than conceptual: "In general, he was able to observe how all objects yielded themselves to him more distantly and, at the same time, somehow more truly; this was no doubt due to his vision, which was no longer directed forwards, and which out there, *in the open* [my emphasis], thinned away" (*SW* 6:1039/*DE* 125).

30. Heller, "Rilke and Nietzsche," 164.

31. Rilke, *Tagebücher aus der Frühzeit,* 71. Quoted and translated by Heller, "Rilke and Nietzsche," 162.

32. For an insightful discussion of the metafunction of the "Tenth Elegy," see Komar, *Transcending Angels,* 169–97. Komar notes that Rilke seeks to fuse "subject and object, consciousness and world" (171) in this final elegy, which underscores not only the parallel to *Malte* but to *Hyperion* as well.

33. Rilke, *Uncollected Poems,* 251.

34. As communicated by Nanny Wunderly-Volkart to Gudi Nölke in: Rilke, *Die Briefe an Frau Gudi Nölke,* 135. Also quoted in Leppmann, *Rilke: A Life,* 386.

NOTES TO CHAPTER 5, "HEIDEGGER"

1. See Bernasconi, *Heidegger in Question*, 76–97. A more limited consideration of the connections between Tolstoy's tale and *Being and Time* can be found in Spanos, "Leo Tolstoy's 'The Death of Ivan Ilych,'" 1–64, esp. 2–6. Walter Kaufmann's comparison is even more concise but all the more cutting in its thesis: "Heidegger on death is for the most part an unacknowledged commentary on *The Death of Ivan Ilyitch*." See Kaufmann, "Existentialism and Death," *Existentialism, Religion, and Death: Thirteen Essays*, 198–99. We will see that Kaufmann's statement is a gross simplification and that Heidegger's analysis draws on far more than a single text or author.

2. Philipse, *Heidegger's Philosophy of Being*, 71.

3. Ibid., 74.

4. Heidegger's reputation as the "hidden king" of German philosophy derives from Hannah Arendt and has inspired the title of John van Buren's detailed study *The Young Heidegger: Rumor of the Hidden King*.

5. Rilke, who was personally acquainted with Hellingrath, was no less moved by this newly edited poetry and even dedicated verses of his own to Hölderlin's memory (see *SW* 2:93–94).

6. One of the first lengthy studies of *Being and Time* to appear in print, Adolf Sternberger's *Der verstandene Tod: Eine Untersuchung zu Martin Heideggers Existenzial-Ontologie*, examines Nietzsche's possible influence, specifically: the relation between "running forward into death" and *amor fati;* and between authentic Dasein and the so-called *Herrenmensch* (see 110–28). (A facsimile edition was issued in 1979 by Garland Publishing in New York. For a reprinted version, see Sternberger, *Über den Tod*, 69–264, esp. 195–210.) However, this initial tendency to posit a connection between Nietzsche and the early Heidegger did not catch on, perhaps due to the intellectual hiatus brought about by Nazism and World War II. The first major study of Heidegger after the War, Otto Pöggeler's *Der Denkweg Martin Heideggers*, comments only briefly on the young Heidegger's Nietzsche reception and has perhaps set a precedent in this regard. Pöggeler's opinion that Heidegger essentially remained free of any Nietzschean influence until after the appearance of *Being and Time* has remained the common view among scholars over the years. The most notable exception to this trend is David Ferrell Krell, who claims: "However rarely cited in *Being and Time*, Nietzsche may well be the regnant genius of that work." Krell, *Intimations of Mortality*, 128. This statement seems, on the other hand, somewhat of an exaggeration—or perhaps more of a deliberate Nietzschean hyperbole. For two studies that take a middle ground between Krell and scholars such as Pöggeler, see: Taminiaux, "The Presence of Nietzsche in *Sein und Zeit*"; and Ireton, "Heidegger's Ontological Analysis of Death."

7. Krell, *Intimations of Mortality*, 127.

8. See Hölderlin, *Sämtliche Werke und Briefe*, vol. 3, ed. Franz Zinkernagel.

9. He further lists Kierkegaard, Dostoyevsky, Schelling, Dilthey, Georg Trakl, and Adalbert Stifter (see *GA* 1:56). Heidegger's passion for literature spurred him to organize an extracurricular reading circle with fellow *Gymnasium* students. In the words of one of his religion teachers, "at times [Heidegger] pursued German literature—in which he is very well read—a bit too much, to the detriment of other disciplines."

Quoted in van Buren, *Young Heidegger,* 62. The influence of Trakl seems particularly pronounced with respect to the question of death. In his youth, Heidegger even wrote some dark and melancholy verses reminiscent of Trakl's poems on dying and decay (see *GA* 13:5–7). On a biographical level, Heidegger's short-lived military service during World War I may have profoundly shaped his views on human mortality, which only reinforces the parallel to Trakl, whose experiences as a medic on the eastern front resulted in some of his most powerful poetry on death—as well as in his actual suicide on November 4, 1914. The fact that Heidegger's only public dealings with Trakl revolve around poetological matters recalls his (misleading) reception of Hölderlin and Rilke. See *GA* 12:31–78; or "Language in the Poem: A Discussion on Georg Trakl's Poetic Work," *On the Way to Language,* 159–98. Once again, he may well be obscuring the deeper sources of his early thinking about death.

10. Else Buddeberg submits Heidegger's reading of Rilke to an incisive critique, convincingly arguing that the latter's poetic vision closely corresponds to the Heideggerian notion of being after all. Generally, she finds fault with Heidegger's practice of forcing his predecessors "back" into a history of being rather than summoning them "forward" into a meeting ground where a more fruitful dialogue could take place. See Buddeberg, "Heideggers Rilkedeutung." For another solid discussion of the dialogue between Heidegger and Rilke, one that additionally addresses some parallels in their respective views on death, see Storck, "Rilke und Heidegger."

11. Heidegger, "Hegel's Concept of Experience," *OBT* 86–156; and *Hegel's Phenomenology of Spirit.*

12. Heidegger, *Hegel's Phenomenology of Spirit,* 145.

13. Van Buren, *Young Heidegger,* 12.

14. Kisiel, *Genesis of Heidegger's Being and Time,* 422. Kisiel distinguishes and names the three drafts as follows: "The Dilthey Draft" from 1924–25; "The Ontoeroteric Draft" from 1925–26; and "The Final Draft" published in 1927. For a detailed discussion of all three, see 309–444.

15. Taminiaux, *Heidegger and the Project of Fundamental Ontology,* i.

16. Ibid., xvii–xviii.

17. Jaspers, *Notizen zu Martin Heidegger,* 66.

18. Ibid., 164.

19. See Kaufmann, *Discovering the Mind,* 167–238. See also his related critique in "Heidegger's Castle," 339–69.

20. Kaufmann, *Discovering the Mind,* 209.

21. See for instance van Buren, *Young Heidegger,* 157–202; and Kisiel, *Genesis of Heidegger's Being and Time,* 69–115, 149–219. See also: van Buren, "Martin Heidegger, Martin Luther"; and Kisiel, "Heidegger on Becoming a Christian."

22. Heidegger, "Wilhelm Dilthey's Historical Worldview," 167. A similar note in *Being and Time* that I alluded to earlier slightly downplays the primacy of this Christian tradition. Here Heidegger remarks: "The anthropology developed in Christian theology—from Paul to Calvin's *meditatio futurae vitae*—has always already viewed death together with its interpretation of 'life'" (see *BT* 408).

23. Philipse, *Heidegger's Philosophy of Being,* 374.

24. See for instance: Edwards, *Heidegger's Confusions;* and Philipse, *Heidegger's Philosophy of Being,* 352–74.

25. Joan Stambaugh's excellent translation of *Sein und Zeit* hyphenates the key term Dasein into Da-sein. While this recourse goes against the original practice of *Being and Time,* Heidegger himself tends to do precisely the same in his later writings, especially *Contributions to Philosophy,* which many regard as his second major work. I prefer, however, to keep Dasein unhyphenated as it originally appeared and has since become the standard. My reasons are philosophical, pragmatic, and aesthetic: hyphenation/separation undermines the organic totality that Heidegger seeks for this analogue of human existence; there is really no good reason for breaking down this ordinary German word in the first place; and it simply looks ungainly. I will therefore adhere to this policy of nonhyphenation even when quoting from Stambaugh's translation.

26. Heidegger, *History of the Concept of Time,* 317.

27. David Ferrell Krell raises, however, the following question: "Is it possible that the existential-ontological interpretation derives its most powerful idea, the idea of being toward and unto death, *Sein zum Tode,* precisely from the biology and the life-philosophy that it claims to abjure?" Krell, *Daimon Life,* 85. Krell specifically suggests that the ontic-biological treatises on death by Georg Simmel (*Lebensanschauung: Vier metaphysische Kapitel*) and Eugen Korschelt (*Lebensdauer, Altern und Tod*) may have more in common with fundamental ontology than Heidegger, the master ontologist, is willing to admit. Both of these studies describe the coexistence of life and death within all advanced living organisms, which recalls the anatomo-pathological perspective outlined by Foucault in *The Birth of the Clinic.* See Krell, *Daimon Life,* esp. 84–98.

28. Heidegger, "Wilhelm Dilthey's Historical Worldview," 166.

29. Heidegger, *Basic Problems of Phenomenology,* 19.

30. For an excellent discussion of Heidegger's "ontic ontology," see Kisiel, *Genesis of Heidegger's Being and Time,* 424–39. Robert Bernasconi also grapples with this problem of ontology versus onticity and even explores the notion of "metontology" which Heidegger briefly entertained in his 1928 lecture course *The Metaphysical Foundations of Logic.* See Bernasconi, *Heidegger in Question,* 25–39.

31. Letter from April 11, 1910. See Rilke, *Briefe aus den Jahren 1907–1914,* 99. It is an attested fact that Heidegger read Rilke's novel. He gives a lengthy quote from it in a lecture course from the summer semester of 1927, just as *Being and Time* was appearing in print. See *GA* 24:244–46; *Basic Problems of Phenomenology,* 172–73. Moreover, Walter Kaufmann further reports: "In 1975 I learned from Hans-Georg Gadamer that he had introduced Heidegger to *Malte Laurids Brigge* in 1923, long before the publication of *Sein und Zeit.*" Cited in Kaufmann, "The Reception of Existentialism in the United States," *Existentialism, Religion, and Death,* 107n.

32. Given the fact that Rilke studied Kierkegaard intensely around the turn of the century, even learning Danish in order to read the latter's works in the original, it seems surprising that he did not pick up on the key distinction between *frygt* (fear/*Furcht*) and *angest* (anxiety/*Angst*) as elaborated for instance in *The Concept of Anxiety.*

Nevertheless, it is important to remember that Rilke is a poet and not a philosopher. Hence, while he is certainly attentive to the nuances of language, he is not necessarily concerned with developing a strict conceptual vocabulary.

33. Several years later, in a lecture course on Hölderlin's hymn "Germanien," Heidegger would cite in its entirety Hegel's key passage on death from the preface of the *Phenomenology*. See *GA* 39:131.

34. Heidegger, "Wilhelm Dilthey's Historical Worldview," 168. For the original German version, see Heidegger, "Wilhelm Diltheys Forschungsarbeit und der Kampf um eine historische Weltanschauung," 168.

35. The first English translation of *Being and Time* from 1962 contains the following explanatory note with regard to this term: "While we have used 'anticipate' to translate 'vorgreifen,' which occurs rather seldom, we shall also use it—less literally—to translate 'vorlaufen,' which appears very often in the following pages, and which has the special connotation of 'running ahead.' But as Heidegger's remarks have indicated, the kind of 'anticipation' which is involved in Being-towards-death, does not consist in 'waiting for' death or 'dwelling upon it' or 'actualizing' it before it normally comes; nor does 'running ahead into it' in this sense mean that we 'rush headlong into it.'" Heidegger, *Being and Time,* trans. Macquarrie and Robinson, 306n. Joan Stambaugh's more recent translation, which has the advantage of being corrective after some 30 years of Anglo-American Heidegger scholarship and translational efforts, also adheres to "anticipation" despite her (faulty) observation in the preface that Macquarrie and Robinson render *Vorlaufen* as "running forward in thought." Notwithstanding the awkwardness of the latter formulation, she admits that "it may be the better choice." See Stambaugh, "Translator's Preface," *BT* xv. As I will demonstrate in the course of this study, especially later in my discussion of Hölderlin, Heidegger's concept of *Vorlaufen* needs to be not only retranslated but fundamentally rethought based both on its provenance and multivalent connotations.

36. Heidegger probably first used the term *Vorlaufen* in his posthumously published work from 1924 *Der Begriff der Zeit,* which exists both as a treatise and condensed talk. See *GA* 64. and/or *Concept of Time*. (The English translation is of the shortened talk only.) Many such writings and lectures from the mid-1920s can be considered prototypes of *Being and Time,* which Heidegger after all composed based on his ongoing attempts to elaborate the general philosophical questions of being and time.

37. Kierkegaard, *Concluding Unscientific Postscript,* 168. For the original Danish version, see Kierkegaard, *Afsluttende uvidenskabelig efterskrift, Samlede værker,* vol. 9–10, 9:140.

38. The physical and metaphorical implications of *Vorlaufen* have been criticized by Dolf Sternberger and Herman Philipse, who both insist that existential possibility cannot be conceived in spatial terms. Philipse moreover discusses the numerous logical and argumentative fallacies that underlie Heidegger's concept of *Vorlaufen,* claiming that it is "a confused and misleading metaphor." See Sternberger, *Der verstandene Tod,* 91–92, or *Über den Tod,* 175–76 (reprinted version); and Philipse, *Heidegger's Philosophy of Being,* 365–70.

39. Augustine, *Concerning the City of God,* 518. For this reference I am indebted to Parkes, "Rising Sun over Black Forest," 85.

40. Luther, *Werke,* 42:146. For this quote and its translation I am indebted to van Buren, *Young Heidegger,* 175. Also to be found in: van Buren, "Martin Heidegger, Martin Luther," 171.

41. See for example Seneca, *Ad Lucilium epistulae morales,* 1:178 (letter 24, sec. 22); and *Naturales Quaestiones,* 1:244 (3.18.6); and Pliny, *Letters and Panegyricus,* 1:70 (*Epistulae,* 1.22.10). Here Pliny even uses the verb *procurrere,* which in its morphology more closely corresponds to *vorlaufen.* For these examples from the Latin, I am grateful to Raymond Marks of the University of Missouri-Columbia.

42. See Fritsche, *Historical Destiny,* 3–6. Fritsche further points out that Heidegger could have employed any number of alternate phrases less charged with the rhetoric of Weimar conservatism. For example: "sich konfrontieren mit dem Tod" (to confront death), "sich dem Tode aussetzen" (to expose oneself to death), or "dem Tode ins Angesicht schauen" (to look death in the face). See 233–34.

43. See Schneeberger, *Nachlese Heideggers,* 47–49, 155–60. Also discussed in Bambach, *Heidegger's Roots,* 57–68.

44. Heidegger, *Contributions to Philosophy,* 214.

45. Although he fails to shed any new light on the conception of *Vorlaufen* in this work (the only novelty is that he hyphenates it into "Vor-laufen" as he similarly does with "Da-sein"), he dissociates his analytic from its widespread interpretation as a "philosophy of death." This leads him to lash out in uncharacteristic fashion at scholars, journalists, and philistines who misconstrued his point the first time around. See *GA* 65:282–86; Heidegger, *Contributions to Philosophy,* 198–201.

46. Foucault, *Ethics, Subjectivity, and Truth, Essential Works,* 105.

47. See Heidegger, *History of the Concept of Time,* 317; and "Wilhelm Dilthey's Historical Worldview," 168.

48. It is interesting, indeed puzzling, that passion should suddenly enter the equation. In contrast to the case of anxiety, which is a primordial mood of Dasein, there has been no previous indication that passion plays any role in fundamental ontology. Indeed, this human emotion seems strikingly out of place in Heidegger's otherwise sober diagnosis of existence. The phrase "passionate anxious freedom" contains, rather, a string of notions that could have been lifted right out of Kierkegaard, which only reinforces the patchwork nature of Heidegger's theory of death. Heidegger later speaks of another emotion that results from an authentic confrontation with death: "unshakable joy" or *"gerüstete Freude"* (*BT* 286/*SZ* 310).

49. Krell, *Daimon Life,* 98.

50. To my knowledge, the only scholar to have discerned a link between *The Death of Empedocles* and *Being and Time* is Beda Allemann, whose *Hölderlin and Heidegger* from 1954 remains the first book-length study of the relationship between poet and thinker. But Allemann only briefly hints at the common theme of running forward into death and then rejects its validity altogether, since he perceives a fundamental difference between Hölderlin's and Heidegger's respective notions of temporality. See Allemann, *Hölderlin und Heidegger,* 91–92. Apart from Allemann, the only other

interpreter who comes close to suggesting a connection between *The Death of Empedocles* and *Being and Time* is Jürgen Söring, whose *Die Dialektik der Rechtfertigung: Überlegungen zu Hölderlin's Empedokles-Projekt* is so replete with Heideggerian jargon that one would expect it to at least hint at some parallisms. Strangely, this is not the case. See Söring, *Die Dialektik der Rechtfertigung,* esp. 266.

51. Schopenhauer, *World As Will and Representation,* 1:254.

52. In the context of time, *empedos* takes on the meaning of "lasting" or "continual." The historical Empedocles himself seems to play on this latter signification of his name in Fragment 17, v. 11 of *On Nature:* "in that way they [mortal things] come to be and their life is not lasting" (*tê men gignontai te kai ou sphisin **empedos** aiôn*). Translation in McKirahan, *Philosophy before Socrates,* 236.

53. Andrzej Warminski goes so far as to claim that "already in *Being and Time* Heidegger's language is saturated by Hölderlin's," a statement that I find only mildly exaggerated. See Warminksi, *Readings in Interpretation,* 46.

NOTES TO EPILOGUE

1. These films were actually released at the end of 2004 but attracted most of their attention the following year, especially after the awards ceremony in February 2005.

2. Gorer, "The Pornography of Death," 196.

3. See for instance: Rank, *Will Therapy;* C. W. Wahl, "Fear of Death"; and Becker, *Denial of Death.* For a more comprehensive discussion of death anxiety across the disciplines, including literature, philosophy, biology, and psychology, see Choron, *Death and Modern Man.*

4. See Jung, *Memories, Dreams, Reflections,* 156–57.

5. Kübler-Ross, *On Death and Dying,* xi.

6. Ibid., 11.

7. Ibid., 7.

8. See Dayananda, *"The Death of Ivan Ilych,"* 423–35.

9. My observations on death and dying in modern-day society are in part informed by Wass and Neimeyer, *Dying: Facing the Facts;* Moller, *Confronting Death;* and Webb, *Good Death.*

10. See Moller, *Confronting Death,* 43.

11. Webb, *Good Death,* 406.

12. *Standards of a Hospice Program,* iii.

13. See Humphry, *Final Exit.*

14. See Webb, *Good Death,* 383–84.

15. Translated in Gass, *Reading Rilke,* 168.

16. Kübler-Ross, *On Death and Dying,* 276.

Bibliography

Abrams, M. H. *Natural Supernaturalism: Tradition and Revolution in Romantic Literature.* New York: W. W. Norton, 1971.

Allemann, Beda. *Hölderlin und Heidegger.* 2nd ed. Zurich: Atlantis, 1956.

Angelloz, Joseph-François. *L'évolution spirituelle du poète.* Paris: Mercure, 1936.

Ariès, Philippe. *The Hour of Our Death.* Translated by Helen Weaver. New York: Vintage, 1982.

Aristotle. *The Basic Works of Aristotle.* Edited by Richard McKeon. New York: Random House, 1941.

Augustine. *Concerning the City of God against the Pagans.* Translated by Henry Bettenson. London: Penguin, 1972.

Bambach, Charles. *Heidegger's Roots: Nietzsche, National Socialism, and the Greeks.* Ithaca, N.Y.: Cornell University Press, 2003.

Baugh, Bruce. *French Hegel: From Surrealism to Postmodernism.* New York: Routledge, 2003.

Baudrillard, Jean. *Symbolic Exchange and Death.* Translated by Iain Hamilton Grant. London: Sage, 1993.

Becker, Ernest. *The Denial of Death.* New York: The Free Press, 1973.

Beißner, Friedrich. "Hölderlins Trauerspiel *Der Tod des Empedokles* in seinen drei Fassungen." In *Hölderlin: Reden und Aufsätze,* 67–91. Weimar: Hermann Bühlhaus, 1961. Originally published in *Neophilologus* 42 (1958): 186–212.

Benoliel, Jeanne Quint, and Lesley F. Degner. "Institutional Dying: A Convergence of Cultural Values, Technology, and Social Organization." In *Dying: Facing the Facts,* edited by Hannelore Wass and Robert A. Neimeyer, 3rd ed., 117–41. Washington, D.C.: Taylor & Francis, 1995.

Benz, Ernst. *Das Todesproblem in der Stoischen Philosophie. Tübinger Beiträge zur Altertumswissenschaft.* Stuttgart: Kohlhammer, 1929.

Bertaux, Pierre. *Friedrich Hölderlin.* Frankfurt am Main: Suhrkamp, 1978.

Bernasconi, Robert. *Heidegger in Question: The Art of Existing.* Atlantic Highlands, N.J.: Humanities Press, 1993.

Birkenhauer, Theresia. *Legende und Dichtung: Der Tod des Philosophen und Hölderlins Empedokles.* Berlin: Vorwerk 8, 1996.

Blanchot, Maurice. *The Space of Literature.* Translated by Ann Smock. Lincoln: University of Nebraska Press, 1989.

Böckmann, Paul. *Hölderlin und seine Götter.* Munich: C. H. Beck'sche Verlagsbuchhandlung, 1935.

Böhm, Wilhelm. *Hölderlin.* 2 vols. Halle: Niemeyer, 1928.

Bonhoffer, Adolf. *Die Ethik des Stoikers Epictet. Anhang: Exkurse über einige wichtige Punkte der Stoischen Ethik.* Stuttgart: Ferdinand Enke, 1894.

Brodsky, Patricia Pollock. *Russia in the Works of Rainer Maria Rilke.* Detroit: Wayne State University Press, 1984.

Buddeberg, Else. "Heideggers Rilkedeutung." *Deutsche Vierteljahresschrift für Literaturwissenschaft and Geistesgeschichte* 27 (1953): 387–412.

———. *Rainer Maria Rilke: Eine innere Biographie.* Stuttgart: J. B. Metzlersche, 1955.

Camus, Albert. "Absurd Creation." In *The Myth of Sisyphus and Other Essays.* Translated by Justin O'Brien. New York: Vintage, 1955.

Cassirer, Ernst. "Hölderlin und der deutsche Idealismus." In *Idee und Gestalt: Goethe, Schiller, Hölderlin, Kleist,* 113–55. Berlin: Bruno Cassirer, 1924.

Choron, Jacques. *Death and Modern Man.* New York: Collier, 1964.

———. *Death and Western Thought.* New York: Collier, 1963.

Collins, Derek. "On the Aesthetics of the Deceiving Self in Nietzsche, Pindar, and Theognis." *Nietzsche-Studien* 26 (1997): 276–99.

Dayananda, Y. J. *"The Death of Ivan Ilych:* A Psychological Study *On Death and Dying." Literature and Psychology* 22 (1972): 191–98.

Demske, James M. *Being, Man, and Death: A Key to Heidegger.* Lexington: The University Press of Kentucky, 1970.

Diels, Hermann, and Walther Kranz. *Die Fragmente der Vorsokratiker.* 6th ed. Berlin: Weidmann, 1951.

Dilthey, Wilhelm. *Die Jugendgeschichte Hegels.* In *Gesammelte Schriften,* 3rd ed., 4:1–187. Stuttgart: B. G. Teubner, 1959.

Diogenes Laertius. *Lives of Eminent Philosophers.* Translated by R. D. Hicks. 2 vols. Loeb Classical Library. London: Heinemann, 1925.

Dollimore, Jonathan. *Death, Desire, and Loss in Western Culture.* New York: Routledge, 1998.

Ebeling, Hans, ed. *Der Tod in der Moderne.* Königstein: Hain, 1979.

Edwards, Paul. *Heidegger's Confusions.* Amherst, N.Y.: Prometheus Books, 2004.

Elias, Nobert. *The Loneliness of the Dying.* Translated by Edmund Jephcott. Oxford: Blackwell, 1985.

Findlay, J. N. *Hegel: A Re-Examination.* New York: Collier, 1962.

Forster, Michael N. *Hegel's Idea of a Phenomenology of Spirit.* Chicago: University of Chicago Press, 1998.

Fóti, Véronique M. "Empedocles and Tragic Thought: Heidegger, Hölderlin, and Nietzsche." In *The Presocratics after Heidegger,* edited by David C. Jacobs, 277–94. Albany: State University of New York Press, 1999.

Foucault, Michel. *The Birth of the Clinic: An Archeology of Medical Perception.* Translated by A. M. Sheridan Smith. New York: Vintage, 1994.

———. *Essential Works of Foucault 1954–1984.* 3 vols. New York: The New Press, 1997–2000.

Freeman, Ralph. *Life of a Poet: Rainer Maria Rilke.* New York: Farrar, Strauss and Giroux, 1996.

Fritsche, Johannes. *Historical Destiny and National Socialism in Heidegger's Being and Time.* Berkeley and Los Angeles: University of California Press, 1999.

Fülleborn, Ulrich. "'Form und Sinn der *Aufzeichnungen des Malte Laurids Brigge:* Rilkes Prosabuch und der moderne Roman." In *Materialien zu Rainer Maria Rilke, "Die Aufzeichnungen des Malte Laurids Brigge,"* edited by Hartmut Engelhardt, 175–98. Frankfurt am Main: Suhrkamp, 1974.

Gadamer, Hans-Georg. *Truth and Method.* 2nd ed. Translated by Joel Weinsheimer and Donald G. Marshall. New York: Continuum, 1994.

Gaier, Ulrich. *Hölderlin: Eine Einführung.* Tübingen: Francke, 1993.

———. Review of *Hölderlins "Hyperion": Exzentrische Bahn und Dichterberuf,* by Lawrence Ryan. *The German Quarterly* 39 (1966): 244–49.

Gass, William H. *Reading Rilke: Reflections on the Problems of Translation.* New York: Knopf, 1999.

Goethe, Johann Wolfgang. *West-Östlicher Divan.* In *Werke: Hamburger Ausgabe,* edited by Erich Trunz, 15th ed., 2:7–125. Munich: C. H. Beck, 1986.

Gorer, Geoffrey. "The Pornography of Death." In *Death, Grief, and Mourning.* Garden City, N.Y.: Doubleday & Co., 1965.

Grätz, Katharina. "Der 'Empedocles'-Text der Großen Stuttgarter Ausgabe und der Frankfurter Ausgabe. Editionskritik und Folgerungen für die Neu-Edition im Deutschen Klassiker Verlag." *Hölderlin-Jahrbuch* 28 (1992–93): 264–99.

Grisé, Yolande. *Le suicide dans la Rome antique.* Paris: Belles Lettres, 1982; Montreal: Bellarmin, 1983.

Guardini, Romano. *Rainer Maria Rilkes Deutung des Daseins: Eine Interpretation der Duineser Elegien.* Munich: Kösel, 1953.

Haberer, Brigitte. *Sprechen, Schweigen, Schauen: Rede und Blick in Hölderlins "Der Tod des Empedokles" und "Hyperion."* Bonn: Bouvier, 1991.

Hansen, Frank P. *Das älteste Systemprogramm des deutschen Idealismus: Rezeptionsgeschichte und Interpretation.* Berlin: de Gruyter, 1989.

Harrison, Robin B. *Hölderlin and Greek Literature.* London: Clarendon, 1975.

Hegel, G. W. F. *Early Theological Writings.* Translated by T. M. Knox. Chicago: University of Chicago Press, 1948.

———. *The Encyclopaedia Logic.* Translated by T. F. Geraets et al. Indianapolis: Hackett, 1991.

——. *Jenaer Realphilosophie: Vorlesungsmanuskripte zur Philosophie der Natur und des Geistes von 1805–1806*. Edited by Johannes Hoffmeister. Hamburg: Meiner, 1969.

——. *Miscellaneous Writings of G. W. F. Hegel*. Edited by Jon Stewart. Evanston: Northwestern University Press, 2002.

——. *Phenomenology of Spirit*. Translated by A. V. Miller. Oxford: Oxford University Press, 1977.

——. *Philosophy of Right*. Translated by T. M. Knox. London: Oxford University Press, 1973.

——. *Science of Logic*. Translated by A. V. Miller. Atlantic Highlands, N.J.: Humanities Press, 1989.

——. *Selections*. Edited by M. J. Inwood. New York: Macmillan, 1989.

——. *Three Essays, 1793–1795: The Tübingen Essay, Berne Fragments, The Life of Jesus*. Edited and translated by Peter Fuss and John Dobbins. Notre Dame, Ind.: University of Notre Dame Press, 1984.

——. *Werke*. Edited by Eva Moldenhauer and Karl Markus Michel. 4th ed. 20 vols. Frankfurt am Main: Suhrkamp, 1986.

Heidegger, Martin. *The Basic Problems of Phenomenology*. Translated by Albert Hofstadter. Bloomington: Indiana University Press, 1982.

——. *Being and Time*. Translated by John Macquarrie and Edward Robinson. New York: Harper & Row, 1962.

——. *Being and Time: A Translation of Sein und Zeit*. Translated by Joan Stambaugh. Albany: State University of New York Press, 1996.

——. *The Concept of Time*. Translated by William McNeill. Oxford: Blackwell, 1992.

——. *Contributions to Philosophy (On Enowning)*. Translated by Parvis Emad and Kenneth Maly. Bloomington: Indiana University Press, 1999.

——. *Gesamtausgabe: Ausgabe letzter Hand*. Frankfurt am Main: Vittorio Klostermann, 1975–.

——. *Hegel's Phenomenology of Spirit*. Translated by Parvis Emad and Kenneth Maly. Bloomington: Indiana University Press, 1988.

——. *History of the Concept of Time: Prolegomena*. Translated by Theodore Kisiel. Bloomington: Indiana University Press, 1985.

——. *The Phenomenology of Religious Life*. Translated by Matthias Fritsch and Jennifer Anna Gosetti-Ferencei. Bloomington: Indiana University Press, 2004.

——. *Off the Beaten Track*. Edited and translated by Julian Young and Kenneth Haynes. Cambridge: Cambridge University Press, 2002.

——. *On the Way to Language*. Translated by Peter D. Hertz. New York: Harper & Row, 1982.

——. *Pathmarks*. Edited by William McNeill. Cambridge: Cambridge University Press, 1998.

——. *Sein und Zeit*. 18th ed. Tübingen: Niemeyer, 2001.

——. "Wilhelm Diltheys Forschungsarbeit und der Kampf um eine historische Weltanschauung." *Dilthey-Jahrbuch* 8 (1992): 143–80.

———. "Wilhelm Dilthey's Research and the Struggle for a Historical Worldview." In *Supplements: From the Earliest Essays to Being and Time and Beyond,* edited by John van Buren, 147–76. Albany: State University of New York Press, 2002.

Heller, Erich. "Rilke and Nietzsche, With a Discourse on Thought, Belief, and Poetry." In *The Disinherited Mind: Essays in Modern German Literature and Thought,* 123–77. New York: Harcourt Brace Jovanovich, 1975.

Henrich, Dieter. *Der Grund im Bewußtsein: Untersuchungen zu Hölderlins Denken (1794–1795).* Stuttgart: Klett-Cotta, 1992.

———. "Hegel und Hölderlin." In *Hegel im Kontext,* 9–40. Frankfurt am Main: Suhrkamp, 1971.

Hirzel, Rudolf. "Der Selbstmord," *Archiv für Religionswissenschaft* 11 (1908): 75–104, 243–84, 417–76.

Hoffmann, Ernst Fedor. "Zum dichterischen Verfahren in Rilkes *Aufzeichnungen des Malte Laurids Brigge.*" In *Materialien zu Rainer Maria Rilke, "Die Aufzeichnungen des Malte Laurids Brigge,"* edited by Hartmut Engelhardt, 214–44. Frankfurt am Main: Suhrkamp, 1974.

Hoffmeister, Johannes, ed. *Briefe von und an Hegel.* 2 vols. Hamburg: Meiner, 1952.

———. *Hölderlins Empedokles.* Bonn: Bouvier, 1963.

Hölderlin, Friedrich. *Essays and Letters on Theory.* Translated and edited by Thomas Pfau. Albany: State University of New York Press, 1988.

———. *Hyperion and Selected Poems.* Edited by Eric L. Santner. The German Library 22. New York: Continuum, 1990.

———. *Poems and Fragments.* Translated by Michael Hamburger. Cambridge: Cambridge University Press, 1980.

———. *Sämtliche Werke: Große Stuttgarter Ausgabe,* edited by Friedrich Beißner et al. 8 vols. Stuttgart: J. G. Cottasche/W. Kohlhammer, 1943–85.

———. *Sämtliche Werke.* Edited by Norbert von Hellingrath et al. 4 vols. Berlin: Propyläen, 1913–23.

———. *Sämtliche Werke und Briefe.* Edited by Franz Zinkernagel. 5 vols. Leipzig: Insel, 1914–26.

———. *Sämtliche Werke und Briefe.* Edited by Jochen Schmidt. 3 vols. Frankfurt am Main: Deutsche Klassiker Verlag, 1992–94.

Hölscher, Uvo. *Empedokles und Hölderlin.* Frankfurt am Main: Insel, 1965.

———. "Empedokles von Akragas: Erkenntnis und Reinigung." *Hölderlin-Jahrbuch* 13 (1963–64): 21–43.

Hume, David. "Of Suicide." In *Essays: Moral, Political, and Literary,* 585–96. London: Henry Frowde, 1904.

Humphry, Derek. *Final Exit: The Practicalities of Self-Deliverance and Assisted Suicide for the Dying.* Eugene, Oreg.: Hemlock Society; Secaucus, N.J.: Carol Publishing, 1991.

Huyssen, Andreas. "Paris/Childhood: The Fragmented Body in Rilke's *Notebooks of Malte Laurids Brigge.*" In *Modernity and the Text: Revisions of German Modernism,* edited by Andreas Huyssen and David Bathrick, 113–41. New York: Columbia University Press, 1989.

Hyppolite, Jean. "The Concept of Existence in the Hegelian Phenomenology." In *Studies on Marx and Hegel,* translated by John O'Neill, 22–32. New York: Basic Books, 1969.

———. "L'existence dans la *Phénoménologie* de Hegel." In *Figures de la pensée philosophique,* vol. 1, 92–103. Paris: Presses Universitaires de France, 1971.

———. *Genesis and Structure of Hegel's Phenomenology of Spirit.* Translated by Samuel Cherniak and John Heckman. Evanston, Ill.: Northwestern University Press, 1974.

Ireton, Sean. "Brechts 'Zertrümmerung' von Heidegger: *Das Badener Lehrstück vom Einverständnis* als mögliche Kritik an *Sein und Zeit,*" *Das Brecht-Jahrbuch* 24 (1999): 292–309.

———. "Heidegger's Ontological Analysis of Death and Its Prefiguration in Nietzsche." *Nietzsche-Studien* 26 (1997): 405–20.

Jamme, Christoph. *"Ein ungelehrtes Buch": Die philosophische Gemeinschaft zwischen Hölderlin und Hegel in Frankfurt 1797–1800. Hegel-Studien,* Beiheft 23. Bonn: Bouvier, 1983.

Jamme, Christoph, and Helmut Schneider, eds. *Mythologie der Vernunft: Hegels "ältestes Systemprogramm des deutschen Idealismus."* Frankfurt am Main: Suhrkamp, 1984.

Janz, Curt Paul. *Friedrich Nietzsche: Biographie.* 3 vols. Munich: Hanser, 1978.

Jaspers, Karl. *Nietzsche: An Introduction to the Understanding of His Philosophical Activity.* Translated by Charles F. Wallraff and Frederick J. Schmitz. Baltimore: The Johns Hopkins University Press, 1997.

———. *Notizen zu Martin Heidegger.* Edited by Hans Saner. Munich: Piper, 1989.

Jung, Carl Gustav. *Memories, Dreams, Reflections.* New York: Pantheon, 1961.

Kassner, Rudolf. *Rilke: Gesammelte Erinnerungen 1926–1956.* Edited by Klaus E. Bohnenkamp. Pfullingen: Neske, 1976.

Kaufmann, Walter. *Discovering the Mind, Volume Two: Nietzsche, Heidegger, and Buber.* New York: McGraw-Hill, 1980.

———. *Existentialism, Religion, and Death: Thirteen Essays.* New York: Meridian, 1976.

———. *Hegel: A Reinterpretation.* Garden City, N.Y.: Anchor, 1966.

———. "Heidegger's Castle." In *From Shakespeare to Existentialism,* 339–69. Princeton, N.J.: Princeton University Press, 1980.

———. *Nietzsche: Philosopher, Psychologist, Antichrist.* 4th ed. Princeton, N.J.: Princeton University Press, 1974.

———. "The Young Hegel and Religion." In *Hegel: A Collection of Critical Essays,* edited by Alasdair MacIntyre, 61–99. Garden City, N.Y.: Anchor, 1972.

Kelly, George Armstrong. "Notes on Hegel's 'Lordship and Bondage.'" In *Hegel: A Collection of Critical Essays,* edited by Alasdair MacIntyre, 189–217. Garden City, N.Y.: Anchor, 1972.

Kierkegaard, Søren. *Afsluttende uvidenskabelig efterskrift.* In *Samlede værker,* vol. 9–10. Copenhagen: Gyldendal, 1994.

—. *Concluding Unscientific Postscript to Philosophical Fragments*. Edited and translated by Howard V. Hong and Edna H. Hong. Princeton, N.J.: Princeton University Press, 1992.

Kisiel, Theodore. *The Genesis of Heidegger's Being and Time*. Berkeley and Los Angeles: University of California Press, 1993.

—. "Heidegger (1920–21) on Becoming a Christian: A Conceptual Picture Show." In *Reading Heidegger from the Start: Essays in His Earliest Thought*, edited by Theodore Kisiel and John van Buren, 172–92. Albany: State University of New York Press, 1994.

Kocziszky, Éva. "Die Empedokles-Fragmente als Übersetzung." *Hölderlin-Jahrbuch* 26 (1988–89): 134–61.

Kojève, Alexandre. "The Idea of Death in the Philosophy of Hegel." Translated by Joseph J. Carpino. *Interpretation* 3 (1973): 114–56.

—. *Introduction to the Reading of Hegel*. Assembled by Raymond Queneau. Edited by Allan Bloom. Translated by James H. Nichols. Ithaca, N.Y.: Cornell University Press, 1980.

Komar, Kathleen L. "Rilke's Sixth Duino Elegy or The Hero as Feige(n)baum." *Monatshefte für deutschen Unterricht, deutsche Sprache und Literatur* 77 (1985): 26–37.

—. *Transcending Angels: Rainer Maria Rilke's Duino Elegies*. Lincoln: University of Nebraska Press, 1987.

Kondylis, Panajotis. *Die Entstehung der Dialektik: Eine Analyse der geistigen Entwicklung von Hölderlin, Schelling und Hegel bis 1802*. Stuttgart: Klett-Cotta, 1979.

Koyré, Alexandre. "Hegel à Iéna." In *Études d'histoire de la pensée philosophique*, 135–73. Paris: Librairie Armand Colin, 1961.

Kranz, Walther. *Empedokles: Antike Gestalt und romantische Neuschöpfung*. Zurich: Artemis, 1949.

Krell, David Farrell. *Daimon Life: Heidegger and Life-Philosophy*. Bloomington: Indiana University Press, 1992.

—. *Intimations of Mortality: Time, Truth, and Finitude in Heidegger's Thinking of Being*. University Park: Pennsylvania State University Press, 1986.

—. *Lunar Voices: Of Tragedy, Poetry, Fiction, and Thought*. Chicago: University of Chicago Press, 1995.

—. *Postponements: Woman, Sensuality, and Death in Nietzsche*. Bloomington: Indiana University Press, 1986.

Kübler-Ross, Elisabeth. *On Death and Dying*. New York: Macmillan, 1969.

Leppmann, Wolfgang. *Rilke: A Life.* Translated by Russell M. Stockman. New York: Fromm, 1984.

Lerner, Monroe. "When, Why, and Where People Die." In *The Dying Patient*, edited by Orville Brim Jr. et al., 5–29. New York: Russell Sage Foundation, 1970.

Lessing, Gotthold Ephraim. "Wie die Alten den Tod gebildet." In *Werke,* 3: 172–223. Frankfurt am Main: Insel, 1967.

Liddell, H. G., et al. *Greek-English Lexicon.* 7th ed. London: Oxford University Press, 1964.

Loose, Gerhard. "Two Notes on Rainer Maria Rilke's *Duineser Elegien." Modern Language Notes* 78 (1963): 430–34.

Löwith, Karl. "Die Freiheit zum Tode." In *Der Tod in der Moderne,* edited by Hans Ebeling, 132–45. Königstein: Hain, 1979.

Lucretius. *De rerum natura (On the Nature of Things).* Translated by W. H. D. Rouse. Loeb Classical Library. London: Heineman, 1924.

Lukács, Georg. *The Young Hegel: Studies in the Relations between Dialectics and Economics.* Translated by Rodney Livingstone. Cambridge, Mass.: MIT Press, 1976.

Luther, Martin. *Werke: Kritische Gesamtausgabe.* Vol. 42. Weimar: Hermann Böhlhaus Nachfolger, 1911.

Mann, Thomas. *Buddenbrooks: The Decline of a Family.* Translated by John E. Woods. New York: Knopf, 1993.

Marcuse, Herbert. "The Ideology of Death." *The Meaning of Death,* edited by Herman Feifel, 64–76. New York: McGraw-Hill, 1959.

McKirahan, Richard. *Philosophy before Socrates: An Introduction with Texts and Commentary.* Indianapolis: Hackett, 1994.

Meetz, Anni. "Zu Hölderlins Quellen für den 'Empedokles': Empedokles—Porphyrios—Muhammed asch-Schahrastani—Hölderlin," *Euphorion* 50 (1956): 388–404.

Merleau-Ponty, Maurice. "Hegel's Existentialism." In *Sense and Non-Sense,* translated by Hubert L. Dreyfus and Patricia Allen Dreyfus, 63–70. Evanston: Northwestern University Press, 1964.

Minois, Georges. *History of Suicide: Voluntary Death in Western Culture.* Translated by Lydia G. Cochrane. Baltimore: Johns Hopkins University Press, 1999.

Moller, David Wendell. *Confronting Death: Values, Institutions, and Human Mortality.* New York: Oxford University Press, 1996.

Nehemas, Alexander. *Nietzsche: Life as Literature.* Cambridge, Mass.: Harvard University Press, 1985.

Nietzsche, Friedrich. *Basic Writings of Nietzsche.* Edited and translated by Walter Kaufmann. New York: Modern Library, 2000.

———. *The Gay Science.* Translated by Walter Kaufmann. New York: Vintage, 1974.

———. *Philosophy in the Tragic Age of the Greeks.* Translated by Marianne Cowan. Chicago: Henry Regnery, 1962.

———. *The Portable Nietzsche.* Edited and translated by Walter Kaufmann. New York: Viking Penguin, 1982.

———. *Sämtliche Briefe: Kritische Studienausgabe.* Edited by Giorgio Colli and Mazzino Montinari. 2nd ed. 8 vols. Berlin: de Gruyter, 2003.

———. *Sämtliche Werke: Kritische Studienausgabe.* Edited by Giorgio Colli and Mazzino Montinari. 2nd ed. 15 vols. Berlin: de Gruyter, 1988.

———. *Werke in drei Bänden.* Edited by Karl Schlechta. 3 vols. Munich: Hanser, 1954–56.

———. *Werke: Kritische Gesamtausgabe.* Edited by Giorgio Colli and Mazzino Montinari. 40 vols. Berlin: de Gruyter, 1968–.

Oates, Whitney J., ed. *The Stoic and Epicurean Philosophers: The Complete Extant Writings of Epicurus, Epictetus, Lucretius, Marcus Aurelius.* New York: Modern Library, 1940.

Osborne, C. "Empedocles Recycled." *Classical Quarterly* 37 (1987): 24–31.

Parkes, Graham. "Rising Sun over Black Forest: Heidegger's Japanese Connections." In *Heidegger's Hidden Sources: East Asian Influences on His Work,* by Reinhard May, translated by Graham Parkes, 79–117. London: Routledge, 1996.

Peters, Sibylle, and Martin J. Schäfer. "Selbstopfer and Repräsentation: *Der Tod des Empedokles* und der Tod des Empedokles." *Hölderlin-Jahrbuch* 30 (1996–97): 282–307.

Philipse, Herman. *Heidegger's Philosophy of Being: A Critical Evaluation.* Princeton, N.J.: Princeton University Press, 1998.

Pindar. *Olympian Odes, Pythian Odes.* Edited and translated by William H. Race. Loeb Classical Library. Cambridge, Mass.: Harvard University Press, 1997.

Plato. *Complete Works.* Edited by John M. Cooper. Indianapolis: Hackett, 1997.

Pliny. *Letters and Panegyricus.* Translated by Betty Radice. Loeb Classical Library. Cambridge, Mass.: Harvard University Press, 1969.

Pöggeler, Otto. *Der Denkweg Martin Heideggers.* Pfullingen: Neske, 1963.

———. "Hegel, der Verfasser des ältesten Systemprogramms des deutschen Idealismus." In *Hegel-Tage Urbino 1965,* edited by Hans-Georg Gadamer, Hegel-Studien 4, 17–32. Bonn: Bouvier, 1968.

Rank, Otto. *Will Therapy and Truth and Reality.* Translated by Jessie Taft. New York: Knopf, 1945.

Rehm, Walther. *Orpheus, der Dichter und die Toten: Selbstdeutung und Totenkult bei Novalis, Hölderlin, Rilke.* Düsseldorf: L. Schwann, 1950.

Rilke, Rainer Maria. *Briefe.* Edited by the Rilke-Archiv. Wiesbaden: Insel, 1950.

———. *Die Briefe an Frau Gudi Nölke.* Edited by Paul Obermüller. Wiesbaden: Insel, 1953.

———. *Briefe aus den Jahren 1907–1914.* Edited by Ruth Sieber-Rilke and Carl Sieber. Leipzig: Insel, 1939.

———. *Duino Elegies.* Translated by J. B. Leishman and Stephen Spender. New York: W. W. Norton, 1939.

———. *The Notebooks of Malte Laurids Brigge.* Translated by Stephen Mitchell. New York: Vintage, 1990.

———. *Selected Letters of Rainer Maria Rilke, 1902–1926.* Translated by R. F. C. Hull. London: Macmillan & Co., 1946.

———. *Sonnets to Orpheus*. Translated by M. D. Herter Norton. New York: W. W. Norton, 1942.

———. *Sämtliche Werke*. Edited by Ruth Sieber-Rilke and Ernst Zinn. Frankfurt: Insel, 1987.

———. *Tagebücher aus der Frühzeit*. Edited by Ruth Sieber-Rilke and Carl Sieber. Leipzig: Insel, 1942.

———. *Uncollected Poems*. Translated by Edward Snow. New York: North Point Press, 1996.

Rist, J. M. *Stoic Philosophy*. Cambridge: Cambridge University Press, 1969.

Ryan, Judith. *Rilke, Modernism, and Poetic Tradition*. Cambridge: Cambridge University Press, 1999.

Ryan, Lawrence. *Hölderlins "Hyperion": Exzentrische Bahn und Dichterberuf*. Stuttgart: J. B. Metzlersche, 1965.

Saaz, Johannes von. *Death and The Ploughman* or *The Bohemian Ploughman*. Translated by Ernest N. Kirrmann. Chapel Hill: University of North Carolina Press, 1958.

Santner, Eric L. *Friedrich Hölderlin: Narrative Vigilance and the Poetic Imagination*. New Brunswick, N.J.: Rutgers University Press: 1986.

Sartre, Jean-Paul. *Being and Nothingness*. Translated by Hazel E. Barnes. New York: Washington Square Press, 1992.

Schadewaldt, Wolfgang. "Das Bild der exzentrischen Bahn bei Hölderlin." *Hölderlin-Jahrbuch* 6 (1953): 1–16.

———. "Die Empedokles-Tragödie Hölderlins." *Hölderlin-Jahrbuch* 11 (1958–60): 40–54.

Schneeberger, Guido, ed. *Nachlese Heideggers: Dokumente zu seinem Leben und Denken*. Bern: Buchdruckerei AG, 1962.

Schoolfield, George C. "*Die Aufzeichnungen des Malte Laurids Brigge*," In *A Companion to the Works of Rainer Maria Rilke,* edited by Erika A. Metzger and Michael M. Metzger, 154–87. Rochester, N.Y.: Camden House, 2001.

Schopenhauer, Arthur. *The World As Will and Representation*. Translated by E. F. J. Payne. 2 vols. New York: Dover, 1969.

Schuler, Alfred. *Fragmente und Vorträge aus dem Nachlaß*. Edited by Ludwig Klages. Leipzig: Verlag Johann Ambrosius Barth, 1940.

———. *Kosmogonische Augen: Gesammelte Schriften*. Edited by Baal Müller. Paderborn: Igel Verlag, 1997.

Schulz, Werner. "Zum Problem des Todes." In *Der Tod in der Moderne,* edited by Hans Ebeling, 166–83. Königstein: Hain, 1979.

Seneca. *Ad Lucilium epistulae morales* (*Moral Letters to Lucilius*). Translated by Richard Gummere. Loeb Classical Library. Cambridge, Mass.: Harvard University Press, 1970.

———. *Naturales Quaestiones*. Translated by Thomas H. Corcoran. Loeb Classical Library. Cambridge, Mass.: Harvard University Press, 1971.

Silz, Walter. *Hölderlin's Hyperion: A Critical Reading*. Philadelphia: University of Pennsylvania Press, 1969.

Singer, Herbert. *Rilke und Hölderlin*. Cologne: Böhlau, 1957.

Sokel, Walter H. "The Devolution of the Self in *The Notebooks of Malte Laurids Brigge*." In *Rilke: The Alchemy of Alienation,* edited by Frank Baron et al., 171–90. Lawrence: Regents Press of the University of Kansas, 1986.

———. "Zwischen Existenz und Weltinnenraum: Zum Prozeß der Ent-Ichung im Malte Laurids Brigge." In *Rilke heute: Beziehungen und Wirkungen,* edited by Ingeborg H. Solbrig and Joachim W. Storck, 105–29. Frankfurt am Main: Suhrkamp, 1975.

Solomon, Robert. *In the Spirit of Hegel: A Study of G. W. F. Hegel's Phenomenology of Spirit*. New York: Oxford University Press, 1983.

Söring, Jürgen. *Die Dialektik der Rechtfertigung: Überlegungen zu Hölderlins Empedokles-Projekt*. Frankfurt am Main: Athenäum, 1973.

———. "Nietzsches Empedokles-Plan." *Nietzsche-Studien* 19 (1990): 176–211.

Spanos, William V. "Leo Tolstoy's 'The Death of Ivan Ilych': A Temporal Interpretation." In *De-Structuring the Novel: Essays in Applied Postmodern Hermeneutics,* edited by Leonard Orr, 1–64. Troy, N.Y.: Whitston, 1982.

Staiger, Emil. *Der Geist der Liebe und das Schicksal: Schelling, Hegel und Hölderlin*. Frauenfeld: Huber, 1935.

———. "Der Opfertod von Hölderlins Empedokles." *Hölderlin-Jahrbuch* 12 (1963–64): 1–20.

Standards of a Hospice Program of Care. Arlington, Va.: The National Hospice Organization, 1993.

Steiner, Jakob. *Rilkes Duineser Elegien*. Bern: Francke, 1962.

Stephens, Anthony R. *Rilkes Malte Laurids Brigge: Strukturanalyse des erzählerischen Bewußtseins*. Bern: Peter Lang, 1974.

Sternberger, Adolf. *Der verstandene Tod: Eine Untersuchung zu Martin Heideggers Existenzial-Ontologie*. Leipzig: S. Hirzel, 1934. Facsimile edition. New York: Garland, 1979. Reprinted in *Über den Tod,* 69–264. Frankfurt am Main: Suhrkamp, 1981.

Storck, Joachim W. "Rilke und Heidegger: Über eine 'Zwiesprache' von Dichten und Denken." *Blätter der Rilke-Gesellschaft* 4 (1976): 35–71.

Taminiaux, Jacques. "The Presence of Nietzsche in *Sein und Zeit*." In *Heidegger and the Project of Fundamental Ontology,* translated by Michael Gendre, 175–89. Albany: State University of New York Press, 1991.

Taylor, Charles. *Hegel*. Cambridge: Cambridge University Press, 1975.

Thurn und Taxis-Hohenlohe, Princess Marie von. *Erinnerungen an Rainer Maria Rilke*. Munich: R. Oldenbourg, 1932.

Tolstoy, Leo. *The Death of Ivan Ilyich.* Translated by Rosemary Edmonds. London: Penguin, 1960.

———. *La mort.* Translated by M. E. Halpérine. Paris: Perrin et cie, 1886.

van Buren, John. "Martin Heidegger, Martin Luther." In *Reading Heidegger from the Start: Essays in His Earliest Thought,* edited by Theodore Kisiel and John van Buren, 159–74. Albany: State University of New York Press, 1994.

———. *The Young Heidegger: Rumor of the Hidden King.* Bloomington: Indiana University Press, 1994.

Vivarelli, Vivetta . "Empedokles und Zarathustra: Verschwendeter Reichtum und Wollust am Untergang." *Nietzsche-Studien* 18 (1989): 509–36.

Wahl, C. W. "The Fear of Death." *Bulletin of the Menninger Clinic* 22 (1958): 214–23.

Wahl, Jean. *Le malheur de la conscience dans la philosophie de Hegel.* Paris: Rieder, 1929.

Warminksi, Andrzej. *Readings in Interpretation; Hölderlin, Hegel, Heidegger.* Minneapolis: University of Minnesota Press, 1987.

Wass, Hannelore, and Robert A. Neimeyer, eds. *Dying: Facing the Facts.* 3rd ed. Washington, D.C.: Taylor & Francis, 1995.

Webb, Marilyn. *The Good Death: The New American Search to Reshape the End of Life.* New York: Bantam Books, 1997.

Wohlfart, Günter. "Wer ist Nietzsches Zarathustra?" *Nietzsche-Studien* 26 (1997): 319–30.

Ziolkowski, Theodore. *Dimensions of the Modern Novel: German Texts and European Contexts.* Princeton, N.J.: Princeton University Press, 1969.

Zuberbühler, Rolf. *Hölderlins Erneuerung der Sprache aus ihren etymologischen Ursprüngen.* Berlin: Erich Schmidt, 1969.

Zweig, Stefan. *Der Kampf mit dem Dämon: Hölderlin, Kleist, Nietzsche.* Leipzig: Insel, 1929.

Index